"Cutler Dawson was able to transfer seamlessly a lifetime of lessons learned in six commands at sea to the highest levels of civilian leadership in the financial sector. Along the way, he created a legion of followers through his dedicated mentorship of the generation of naval officers coming along behind him. I count myself personally lucky to have relied on his mentorship, advice, and counsel throughout my naval career and beyond. He sails true north every day, and the results show it."

—**Adm. James Stavridis, USN (Ret.),**
Operating Executive of The Carlyle Group and
former Supreme Allied Commander at NATO

"True to form, Cutler Dawson delivers the same valuable insight on leadership that I have experienced firsthand through my interactions with him as a mentor, friend, and business partner. This book allows the reader to experience that same refreshing and unvarnished approach to leadership through Cutler's words."

—**Wes McMullan,** President and Chief Executive
Officer, Federal Home Loan Bank of Atlanta

"Sportsman, athlete, decorated naval officer, and Fortune 100 CEO! What a trajectory. A CEO who gives responsibility to those who deserve it, can handle it, and thirst for more. Vice Admiral Dawson listens to people first and finds a way to get to 'yes.' Reading this book won't make you a leader, but understanding the examples will put you on the right path."

—**Richard L. Armitage,**
former Deputy Secretary of State

"Cutler Dawson is a master of leading in context, and here he shares the wisdom accumulated from his many remarkable experiences in both the military and corporate worlds. This highly conversational and practical book is like having a private chat with Cutler—one that is sure to inspire and develop leaders at all levels!"

—**John R. Ryan,** President and Chief Executive
Officer, Center for Creative Leadership

"An ocean-class Navy admiral and a world-class chief executive, Cutler Dawson describes empowering sailors and employees on the one hand, and better supporting customers on the other. From a young Navy officer to a respected admiral and then Navy Federal CEO, his lessons and results in *From the Sea to the C-Suite* speak volumes."

—**Adm. Robert J. Natter, USN (Ret.),**
President, R.J. Natter & Associates, LLC

"Cutler eloquently articulates by his experiences that the art of management is by 'doing.' Articulating visions, embodying values, and creating the right environment are necessary. A passion to excel, teamwork, and commitment to people are aspects that are well highlighted through the narrative. A must-read for all aspiring leaders."

—**S. Ramadorai**, former Vice Chairman,
Tata Consultancy Services

"Cutler Dawson's unparalleled experience as a naval leader and successful CEO of the world's largest credit union has given him an incredible prism of knowledge into what works and what doesn't. The robust leadership lessons in his book have a common theme: people. You will learn how to communicate, motivate, and inspire the people around you."

—**B. Dan Berger**, President and
Chief Executive Officer, National Association of
Federally-Insured Credit Unions

"Having known and collaborated with Vice Adm. Cutler Dawson for 50+ years, I'm delighted he's sharing leadership lessons, often humbly learned, over a lifetime of service and accomplishment. From all walks of life, aspiring leaders will learn from this fast-paced, must-read book."

—**Joe R. Reeder**, former U.S. Army Undersecretary
and Chairman of the Panama Canal Commission
(1993–97)

"Vice Adm. Cutler Dawson's *From the Sea to the C-Suite* is a unique and vitally needed book that addresses two critical areas that are not typically blended—leadership and financial EQ. Leveraging his U.S. Navy and Navy Federal Credit Union leadership roles, he helps the reader understand how putting people first is always a winning strategy."

—**Capt. George Galdorisi, USN (Ret.)**,
Director of Strategic Assessments and Technical
Futures at Naval Information Warfare Center Pacific,
and *New York Times* bestselling author

From the

SEA
to the C★SUITE

LESSONS LEARNED *from the*
BRIDGE *to the* CORNER OFFICE

CUTLER DAWSON
WITH TAYLOR BALDWIN KILAND

Foreword by
Vice Adm. John A. Lockard, USN (Ret.)
Chairman of the Board, Navy Federal Credit Union

NAVAL INSTITUTE PRESS | ANNAPOLIS, MARYLAND

Naval Institute Press
291 Wood Road
Annapolis, MD 21402

Library of Congress Cataloging-in-Publication Data
Names: Dawson, Cutler, author. | Kiland, Taylor Baldwin, 1966– author.
Title: From the sea to the C-suite : lessons learned from the bridge to the
  corner office / Cutler Dawson, with Taylor Baldwin Kiland ; foreword by
  Vice Adm. John A. Lockhard, USN (Ret.).
Description: Annapolis, Maryland : Naval Institute Press, [2019]
Identifiers: LCCN 2019029386 | ISBN 9781682474730 (hardcover)
Subjects: LCSH: Dawson, Cutler. | Navy Federal Credit Union—Management. |
  Bankers—United States—Biography. | United States.
  Navy—Officers—Biography. | Leadership. | Success.
Classification: LCC HG2463.D39 A3 2019 | DDC 658.4/092—dc23
LC record available at https://lccn.loc.gov/2019029386

♾ Print editions meet the requirements of ANSI/NISO z39.48–1992
(Permanence of Paper).
Printed in the United States of America.

27 26 25 24 23 22 21 20 19   9 8 7 6 5 4 3 2

*This book is dedicated to all Navy Federal Credit Union
employees, past and present. I'm proud of you.*

CONTENTS

FOREWORD

The year was 2009, and the "Great Recession," as it soon was called, was hitting the United States at flank speed. The financial services industry was trying to determine how to deal with the housing bust, mortgage defaults, liquidity concerns, and workforce layoffs. This was a time for active engagement for influential leaders at every level, from the president to frontline supervisors in just about every corner of our country. They were trying to find solutions to a series of unprecedented issues in our national economy. It wasn't another 1929-style Great Depression, but it could have been—and it had elements that were much different. Things were unraveling very fast, and time for action was immediate. This was a crisis on a national scale, but in the end it was going to be felt at the individual level. It was going to impact everyone, including you and me.

Financial institutions were dealing with major structural issues throughout the industry that required sector consolidation, driven by institutional foreclosures and bankruptcies. There were many defaults on home mortgages that demanded restructuring of major debt. The Federal Reserve purchased much of the banking system's mortgage debt to preserve the safety and soundness of our national economy and to minimize the impact on institutions and individuals. Everyone involved with the financial sector—from the Federal Reserve to your local credit union—was at General Quarters.

The C-Suite (where senior executives have their offices) at Navy Federal Credit Union was no exception. Thankfully, we had a leader—Cutler Dawson—who was prepared, and a workforce that was ready to deal with the uncertainty of the moment. I had led the selection committee in 2004 that recommended Cutler to the board of directors as the preferred candidate to be the next president and CEO of Navy Federal Credit Union. I had first met Cutler in the Navy and was familiar with his reputation as a strong leader, but I had never worked closely with him or had been given an opportunity to observe his leadership skills firsthand. His résumé was accompanied by some great references, but I decided to do some of my own research on him. I talked to individuals who had worked for him and with him. What I heard time and again was that he put people in the forefront of accomplishing the mission. This people-first attitude was exactly what we were looking for in our CEO selection. He was the right person for the job, and the board was unanimous in his selection.

Cutler's leadership philosophy served Navy Federal well in 2009. This financial crisis had many similarities that you would find in battle—the fog of war, with uncertain information and no clear path to the finish line, and an extreme and urgent need for rapid decision-making. But, above all, it required a laser focus on the impact on the individual member. That is what this book is all about—managing risk while engaging with people to find and implement solutions to real problems that each of us might face in our own lives.

Cutler led Navy Federal through this difficult time by steering his team to solutions that focused on our members' well-being. It was not happenstance. It was the result of immersed leaders at every level and Cutler's individual engagement focused on doing the right thing for them collectively and individually. Each of Cutler's leadership attributes discussed in this book was in play. The result was truly impressive.

The financial challenges of the Great Recession were significant. Credit losses began to rise, but Navy Federal's commitment to each member and each employee created an environment that fostered a balanced approach. In addition, Cutler had the wisdom to recognize that the long-term success of Navy Federal was based on the loyalty of its members, which led the organization to take actions that both helped individual members and were sound financial decisions for the long-term future of the credit union.

With a long history of helping members experiencing financial difficulty, we continued this practice through the recession. Thousands of members received relief each month. Cutler continued to remind the entire team that we owed the members a consistent experience in these difficult times. This philosophy paid off as Navy Federal's mortgage and loan default rates remained a tiny fraction of industry averages. Simply put, our members recognized our loyalty and commitment to them and reciprocated that loyalty in spades.

Navy Federal emerged from the Great Recession without dipping into our reserve funding and with an even greater focus on our member engagement. Sure, we had a few bruises, but ours were minor. Despite the economic pressures, we refused to lay off anyone from our global workforce, and we learned ways to make our member service even better. More important, we were able to insulate our members and our brand from any major negative impact. Our belief that "members are our mission"—and Cutler Dawson's focus on people—were critical to our accomplishment.

In this book, Cutler does a great job of discussing the value of focusing on the individual, interacting with people to understand their personal financial issues, and bringing them and the organization together to find the "right thing to do." He takes the philosophy of "management by walking around" to a whole new level as he "puts employees first." He truly believes that if you make your people your priority, they will rise to a level of performance that takes customer satisfaction to the top. Cutler has given employee empowerment a whole new definition. He shares his leadership "secret sauce" that has empowered the Navy Federal team to achieve world-class results. The credit union quadrupled in size during his fourteen years at the helm, while setting an all-time high for customer satisfaction. Enjoy the read—and don't miss the "foot stompers" at the end of each chapter.

—JOHN LOCKARD, May 2019

ACKNOWLEDGMENTS

Everyone at Navy Federal Credit Union has contributed to our success story, and they are the reason that we wrote this book. In addition, a handful of people were willing to provide their own personal stories and give some extra hours to help bring this book to fruition. Mary McDuffie and Pam Piligian were the architects and contractors, but the list of employee contributors and supporters of this project is long. Thanks to the many who provided great stories, anecdotes, and statistics, such as Aaron Aggerwal, Julie Auel, Sun Bayless, Debbie Beatty, Josh Bell, Bob Berger, Carey Boyd, Lou Brenner, Susan Brooks, Darleen Brumley, Della Butler, Debbie Calder, Kara Cardona, Janelle Cash, Jaspreet Chawla, Mike Christian, Maria Collins, Tom Connelly, Noel Cottrell, Kimberly Cox, Brian Creagh, Tim Day, Nancy DeDona, Endira DeGefa, Jennifer Felts, Dave Fitzgerald and the men and women at Fitzco, Randy Hopper, Nel Ignacio, Sylvia Jackson, Jessica Jewell, Stacy Keller, Ishmael Lamptey, Casey Pelfrey, Vince Lascara, Meredith Lawrence, Lauren Lloyd, John Lockard, Katie Miller, Sana Mirza, Kanessa Moyer, Michelle Patterson, John Peden, Casey Pelfrey, Vince Pennisi, Carlos Perez, Lauren Rhodes, Bev Rodriguez, Steve Romano, Bobbie Ruce, Kate Schulz, Annie Sebastian, Robbie Sullivan,

Sheraye Thomas, Joe Ulsh, Andrea Watson, Tishona Watson, Dara Wicken, Erin Wilcox, Gail Williams, Justin Williams, Leslie Williams, Cindy Williamson, and Dave Willis.

I would not have made it to Navy Federal without the mentoring, support, and contributions of some very fine naval officers with whom I served during my Navy career, and who were willing to offer stories and assistance for this book—among them Mike Barclift, Kevin Campbell, Marty Chanik, Dick Couch, George Galdorisi, Pete Hedley, Ted Hontz, Sai Manning, Mike Mullen, and Bob Natter. They all influenced me and helped me, in both my time in the Navy and my work at Navy Federal.

Thank you to Taylor Kiland for helping me write this book. You are lovely, brilliant, and totally professional. It simply could not have been done without you.

Finally, central to my success has been the unconditional love of my family—my parents, Jim and Betty Dawson; my brother, Craig Dawson; and my children, Daryl, Devon, and Cutler Dawson. And to my wife, Debbie, you are the captain of *our* ship. This book would not have been created without your inspiration and persistence. As usual, you made it all work!

PROLOGUE

U nlike in past generations, when many people worked for the same organization for their entire professional lives, it is now not uncommon for employees to make up to a dozen job changes during their careers. This means that many workers are repeatedly in transition. Taking what you learn from each experience and applying it to your next job can be a challenge, but it is a critical one if you want to advance your career. This is most important for those in leadership positions or those aspiring to be in leadership positions. When you switch jobs frequently, how do you grow professionally and become a better leader?

For those of us who serve in the armed forces—either for four years or thirty—making the transition from the military to the civilian world can be even more daunting. For us, everything in the civilian workplace seems different. How do you avoid the trap of feeling as though you are starting over?

When I decided to retire from the Navy in 2004 after thirty-four years of serving in uniform, I told my family that I was going to do a bit of exploration to figure out where I wanted to spend the next chapter of my life. I knew that I wanted to work for an organization that made me proud. In the Navy, we are always laser-focused on our mission—maintaining, training, and equipping combat-ready naval forces capable of winning wars, deterring aggression, and maintaining freedom of the seas. I knew that I wanted to work for an organization with an equally strong mission.

I found it at Navy Federal Credit Union, where our goal is to make life better for our members. Members are our mission. When I got the opportunity to lead Navy Federal, I told my wife, Debbie, who is my most trusted adviser and best friend, "This is it." I had been a member of Navy Federal since 1977, and was one of its volunteer officials and board members. I have always felt that it was committed to its core members—the sailors and Marines who serve around the world and their families. Then and now, I believe that that is the strength of Navy Federal. I have always felt that the people there were looking out for my personal best interests.

The challenge for me was, how would I take the lessons that I learned on the front lines and in many leadership positions in the U.S. Navy—the most lethal and capable in the world—and successfully apply them to my role at the helm of Navy Federal, the largest credit union in the world and the twenty-ninth largest financial institution in the United States?

I discovered that it was a much easier task than I had thought. The lessons I learned in the Navy were directly transferable to the business world. I hope the following chapters will bring a smile to your face as you are thinking, "That makes sense to me!"

From the

SEA

to the C★SUITE

Introduction

UNLESS OTHERWISE DIRECTED

*Take command often. The more you do it, the better
you will get at it.*

—Capt. Pete Hedley, USN (Ret.)

Camp Lemonnier, located near the Djibouti-Ambouli International Airport in Africa, is a dusty and hot place, even in October. It is the only permanent U.S. military base on that continent. Navy sailors and Marines who are deployed there spend months at a time performing highly dangerous missions all over the Horn of Africa. In 2004, I was a Navy vice admiral, the deputy Chief of Naval Operations for resources, requirements, and assessments—what I like to call the last stop for the money in the Navy's $100 billion budget. I worked out of the Pentagon, but I wanted to talk to the service members who were stationed and see for myself whether they had what they needed to get their jobs done. I toured the facilities and walked around, meeting with lots of sailors and Marines of all ranks who were stationed there for six months or more. I wanted to learn what these service members had—and what they wished they had—in order to perform their mission more efficiently.

While I was there I was surprised to receive a call from John Lockard, chairman of Navy Federal Credit Union's board of directors. He congratulated me and told me that I had been selected to become the new president of Navy Federal, the company's fourth in the past forty years. I beamed at hearing the news, and thanked him for the call.

As I hung up the phone, I looked out over the harsh desert terrain. Reflecting on my career in the Navy, I thought about all the times that I had been forward-deployed, just like all the sailors and Marines whom I was meeting in Djibouti. In all, I had made fourteen overseas deployments. And now, after thirty-four years of serving in the Navy, I would soon be taking off the uniform and trading it in for a suit. My visit to Djibouti most likely would be my last trip overseas as a naval officer.

I grew a bit nostalgic. I started to reminisce about the beginning of my naval career, when, at the ripe old age of twenty-seven, I was given command of USS *Molala*, an oceangoing tug named for the indigenous people of Oregon. *Molala* was a small and tested old ship, built during World War II and combat-seasoned with multiple tours in the Pacific, including the Battle of Saipan, the Battle of Luzon, and the invasions of Iwo Jima and Okinawa. She also had been deployed to Korea and Vietnam, providing towing and salvage support. She earned five battle stars in World War II and four campaign stars in the Vietnam War.

When I took command of this thirty-two-year-old ship and her eighty-five-man crew in 1975, I was the youngest seagoing commanding officer in a Navy of more than 550 ships. I was fortunate that my previous commanding officer, Pete Hedley, also had enjoyed a command tour early in his career. I wanted to follow a piece of advice that he had given me early on: "Take command often. The more you do it, the better you will get at it." I thought I was ready to try my hand at the helm, and he agreed. His support of my request for this assignment was a critical moment in my career. I also expected that I would learn a lot on the job from my crew. What I learned most about was "UNODIR," pronounced "you-no-deer."

A ship and her crew often are isolated out in the middle of the ocean. It might be days or weeks before you reach another port or see another ship. It could take a long time before you could get more supplies, or a tool you might need, or advanced medical treatment, or a helping hand from another ship's crew. Many times, you have to improvise and innovate to get the job done. Out there you are your own boss with little supervision. The Internet has changed this dynamic somewhat, of course. But the culture of being a commanding officer at sea has remained a solitary and independent one, where the CO's actions and the crew's performance make or break the ship's success. "Unless otherwise directed"—or UNODIR—is a grant of power that is almost unique to the U.S. Navy. It means that in some cases you—and only you—may have to call the shots. You are responsible for and accountable for those decisions. You are given a broad objective, but very few specifics. You are not told how to do your job. UNODIR means that you don't need to ask your boss back at the base, hundreds (or thousands) of miles away, for permission for each move you make—although you might need to ask for forgiveness later if something goes wrong. This experience breeds a certain kind of bravery mixed with some humility. You have to be unafraid, bold, and competitive, but you also need to be grounded in what is realistic.

During the Cold War era, we frequently found ourselves playing a cat-and-mouse game with Soviet submarines, fighters, surveillance aircraft, and ships—sometimes at close range. In 1976, *Molala* was assigned the task of shadowing a Soviet AGI, a Russian intelligence-gathering ship that was spying on us in international waters off the West Coast between Los Angeles and San Diego. The

Soviet ship was larger than *Molala*, but she had a much smaller and civilian crew, with a complement of thirty to thirty-five mariners. The Soviet crew members knew that *Molala* was trailing her, and that we knew that they were collecting any kind of intelligence they could. Most likely they were intercepting voice or electronics transmissions or tracking the movements of U.S. Navy ships in and out of port.

We followed her, always maintaining a safe distance. We didn't want a collision, but we got close enough to see each other from our bridges. It was a delicate dance. We both were very careful to follow the rules of the road at sea, and there was no hostile action by either one of us. We, too, were tasked with collecting any type of intelligence we could, but we were not told how to do this. After several days, I decided to shake things up a bit.

Using the ship's flashing signal lamp, I sent the civilian "master" of the ship a message: "Would you like to come over to *Molala* for lunch?" Why would I do this? What was my rationale? *Molala* was a World War II–era ship. There was no technology on board my ship that would yield any valuable intelligence for the Soviet captain. However, a conversation with him, in person, might yield some interesting data for me that could never be collected at arm's length. Keep in mind that I was twenty-seven years old, with only about five years of Navy experience under my belt. Some of my peers might have called me somewhat foolish. But, I knew I could learn more from the Soviet master than he could learn from me. That is the nature of spying—right?

My invitation initially was met with silence. The master most likely was taken aback and, as it turns out, he also probably had to make a call back to Moscow. After what seemed like a long interval, I received a polite regret from the master, indicating that he was not given permission to come aboard. That told me a lot. He didn't have the same latitude and trust that I had been given by my boss back in San Diego. In hindsight, I often have wondered what the Pentagon's reaction would have been if the lunch *had* taken place, and how my report on the meeting would have been received. It could have been one for the history books. We'll never know. But what I did know was that the culture of Unodir had given me the confidence to take this bold initiative to achieve my mission.

I took that ingrained Unodir attitude to my next five tours as a commanding officer. Having leadership positions early and often in my Navy career gave me a degree of fearlessness. The more I practiced being a leader, the better I got at it. Now that I was at the end of my Navy career, I planned to bring that fearlessness with me to Navy Federal. I believed in the mission of the organization, but what I didn't fully understand was how passionate Navy Federal members are about Navy Federal. After my visit to Camp Lemonnier, I traveled on to Fallujah, Iraq, to do the same thing: check on the sailors and Marines deployed there and see what they needed. I had dinner in the officers' mess the first night I arrived. I shared the news that I had just received about my new job. And that's all they wanted to talk about—Navy Federal. They wanted to share their personal experiences and proudly tell me how long they had been members of the credit union. It was an eye-opener that day in Fallujah how much Navy and Marine Corps men and women in combat depended upon Navy Federal for their financial well-being. It hit me hard that I had an important new responsibility.

At the time I took over, Navy Federal was a seventy-one-year-old organization, founded in 1933 by seven Department of the Navy civilian employees working in Washington, D.C. It was established as a type of early cooperative whose membership was open to Navy civilian employees. It was originally run by a tiny group of volunteers—seven persons, with $450 in assets. They treated each other like family, which was not unusual among credit unions at the time.

Credit unions have an interesting history in this country. Adopting a European model that was founded in the late nineteenth century, cooperative credit unions started springing up in the United States in the early twentieth century during an era when many banks were underserving the professional and middle classes, as well as the poor. After the Great Depression, when the U.S. economy was in shambles, the idea of a group of people with a common bond—such as geography or employment—pooling their savings and using the money to provide loans to each other had tremendous appeal. The credit-union model enabled these small groups to recycle their money to members. At the time, commercial banks were not willing to offer consumer credit, so the credit unions filled a growing need.

One year after it was formed, the Navy Department Employees' Credit Union of the District of Columbia, as it was called, had more than quadrupled in size and assets. Three years later, the organization paid its first dividend. It continued to be managed by volunteers, and had no dedicated office until 1941. It was rechartered as a federal credit union in 1947, renamed the Navy Federal Credit Union in 1954, and became the largest credit union in the country in 1962—dwarfing the rest of the industry.

When I retired from active duty and started my second career at Navy Federal Credit Union in December 2004, the organization had 2.5 million members and $22.8 billion in assets, having grown slowly and steadily, and it had never experienced a layoff. It was, and still is, governed by an unpaid board of directors who are elected by fellow members. It still has the spirit—and many of the practices—of a cooperative. In many ways, Navy Federal is still a family business, albeit a very large one. We pride ourselves on treating our members like family, and we consider that to be one of our core values. Of course, all of our members—and many of our employees—have something in common. We all share the bond of service to our nation. Despite Navy Federal's considerable size, we have tried to retain this value as a bedrock principle.

Before becoming the president, I had volunteered for Navy Federal at several points in my career. In the early 1990s, while I was on active duty at the Pentagon, I wanted to get a different look at business outside the Navy. Since I had a master's degree in financial management, my friend Gary Hall suggested that I become a volunteer official at Navy Federal. I worked on a supervisory committee for a few years and then was appointed to serve on the board of directors in 1996. Back then, I had no intention of being an employee of a credit union. Like most career officers, I soon was sent off on another sea tour, and I had to resign my board position. I enjoyed the experience, however, and rejoined the board again upon my return to the Pentagon in 1999.

Serving on the organization's board of directors had given me some knowledge of its history, its finances, and its leadership. But I knew relatively little about its detailed operations, nor did I know what the average employee's experience was working on the front lines. I planned to spend a lot of time my first year finding out.

I believed that I could bring some of my leadership experience from the Navy to bear. I had followed Captain Hedley's advice to take command often. After six commands at sea, extensive experience leading people, and several tours working with the Navy's budget, I had some ideas on how I wanted to run a large financial institution. I arrived with a passion for the mission to "serve those who serve" and a great deal of respect for the organization's accomplishments. I was eager to see what I could do to make this great organization even better.

At my first leadership off-site meeting, I suggested that we explore the idea of expanding our field of membership—offering our products and services to the Army, the Air Force, and the Coast Guard. Why couldn't we offer membership to them? After all, they are part of the big military "family." My suggestion was met with silence and everyone at the meeting just looked down at the table. Immediately, I thought to myself, "Hmmm. There's a problem here." And then, John Peden, my chief operating officer, who had been at Navy Federal for more than thirty years, spoke up: "Cutler, it's hard for the leadership here to think about expanding our membership when we are not serving our current members very well."

It was an epiphany of sorts. We could not serve new customers until we satisfied our existing ones. With the enthusiastic support of the entire management team at Navy Federal, we set out on a course to invest heavily in people, products, processes, infrastructure, and technology that would vastly improve our member service.

And that has resulted in tremendous growth. Over the past 14 years, we have grown from $23 billion in assets to more than $100 billion; from 2.5 million members to more than 8 million; from 4,200 employees to more than 19,000; from 103 branches to 335; from 290 automatic teller machines (ATMs) to 671; from $14 billion in loans to more than $76 billion; from $17 billion in savings to more than $77 billion; and we launched robust digital services that have grown exponentially—with more than 1 billion mobile sign-ins and more than 4.4 million individual users in 2018. And we took steps to open up our membership to many, many more service members, veterans, and their families. Today, we are the largest credit union in the world and the twenty-ninth largest financial institution in the United States. In spite of this dizzying growth rate, getting bigger did not reduce the quality of our service to our members.

I did not arrive with an objective of exponentially expanding Navy Federal, but I did come with the goal of making it a better place for my Navy Federal team and doing more to improve the lives of our members. Here's how we did it.

Chapter 1
GO TO THE DECKPLATES

As a leader you need to intimately understand your organization—its people, its products, its processes, its customers. To do so, you have to "go to the deckplates."

In the summer of 1967, after I finished my first year at the Naval Academy, I packed my sea bag—the Navy's term for a duffel bag—and headed down to the quay on the Severn River in Annapolis, Maryland. There, along with fifty of my classmates, I was greeted by the sight of a World War II–era cruiser, the USS *Newport News*. The ship made a big impression on us teenagers. She was 717 feet long with nine 8-inch guns, twelve 5-inch guns, and twelve .50-caliber guns—all staring us down as we stepped aboard. It was my first time at sea, and I was a little nervous. Although both my parents had served in the Navy during World War II, I grew up in Richmond, Virginia, where the largest nearby body of water was the James River. Getting underway on this big ship and going to sea in the Atlantic Ocean was an entirely new experience. The two-month summer training cruise aboard *Newport News* was an apprenticeship of sorts. The Naval Academy sends midshipmen, as its students are known, to sea every summer. This first time underway was intended to "show us the ropes"—that is, to teach us about the fundamentals of the Navy through the eyes of the enlisted crew. The Academy wanted the Navy's future leaders, its officer corps, to understand what its most junior crew members do and how their tasks contribute to the larger mission. They wanted us to "go to the deckplates."

That summer, I lived with, ate with, showered with, and worked with the most junior sailors on *Newport News*. My first assignment was to help clean the heads—nautical terminology for the ship's bathrooms. The young seaman who was working with me started by putting a sign on the door: "Head closed 0800–1000." Then we shut the door behind us and went to work scrubbing the toilets, the sinks, and the decks. Apparently we were efficient; we finished the job in thirty minutes. "What do we do next?" I asked him. "Nothing," he said. "We take a nap until 1000." So we curled up on the floor, under the urinals, and took a siesta. The sailor's supervisor clearly did not know how long it actually took to clean a head, and the sailor wasn't motivated to tell him. It was an easy first lesson for my future career.

I also was sent to "holystone" the ancient teak weather decks on the ship—that is, to clean them. The process involved an age-old procedure. Each midshipman was given a sandstone brick attached to a broom handle, and told to use it to scour the deck with a mixture of water and bleach, moving our bricks back and forth. Holystoning is gone from today's Navy, but it still is the best way to keep teak decks in sparkling condition, especially when the wood is exposed to large amounts of salt water. Our supervisor, an especially cheerful petty officer, even choreographed our movements, and got us to sing while we did it so that we could sweep in unison to the beat of the song. (Either he loved his work or he liked being a conductor.) The holystoning both cleaned and whitened the teak planks. We were able to see the fruits of our labor instantly—and appreciate the importance of teamwork in accomplishing the task. What a difference this sailor made in our work and our day!

I never forgot those experiences. They instilled in me a lifelong habit of "going to the deckplates" in every job I have. In order to understand any leadership challenge, you need to learn about your business and your people from the ground up. You have to get up from your desk, get out of your office, and spend a lot of time walking around, listening and learning. Since then, I have made it my practice as a commanding officer and later as chief executive officer (CEO) at Navy Federal to show my crew that I care for them, their families, their professional development, and their well-being—both personally and professionally. You do this by going to the deckplates regularly—not just when you are new to the job. If you can demonstrate to your crew members that you care about them and truly understand the difficulty of their tasks, they will do remarkable things for you; by contrast, if they think you are there just to further your own career, they will do no more than the minimum. The crew members and civilian staffers alike know whether someone is merely *managing* from the C-Suite or actually is *leading* them.

When I arrived at Navy Federal, my first order of business was to let the employees know that they were my highest priority. Some leaders put customers first; I put employees first. It's simple: take good care of your employees, and they will take good care of your customers (or members—as we call customers at Navy Federal). I was excited about leading this well-established organization, and I really had no concrete plans about how I was going to do it, but I knew that I wouldn't find out by sitting in my office. My plan was to get out, walk around, listen, and learn from my employees—just as I had done as a third-class midshipman (a sophomore at the Naval Academy). I set out to do some exploring.

In my first year at Navy Federal I walked the halls, listened to member service calls, visited our offices and branches all over the world, and hosted large town-hall-style employee meetings and small groups of cross sections of the company's workers. I would always ask: What can I do to help? Why do we do it this way? What should we start? What should we stop? What should we continue? I wanted to identify the "pain-points," or the "rocks in the road" that were keeping employees from doing their jobs more efficiently and more effectively. I wanted to help them serve our members better so that we could serve *more* members. To do this, I demanded honesty and transparency from my employees. I didn't realize how unusual this was.

One of the first branches that I went to visit outside the Washington, D.C., area was our largest—located in Virginia Beach, Virginia, where we conducted more than a million transactions per year. It was run by a longtime Navy Federal employee named Della Butler. I soon gave her the nickname "Queen of Tidewater" because she, along with Cindy Williamson and Bev Rodriguez, oversaw all of our operations in the Hampton Roads area of Virginia. They were three tremendously capable leaders. Hampton Roads is the home to the largest concentration of military installations in the country. We have a lot of members and employees in the region. Della said that over the years the management had schooled our employees on a strict rule to follow when leadership made visits to the branches. "Don't create any snowflakes." What that meant was, when leaders from Washington came to town for a field visit we should show them nothing but smiles and tell them only the good news. The branch managers and regional managers did not want employees to complain directly to the CEO, lest it produce a "snowstorm" of repercussions—and extra work for middle management.

When I started asking pointed questions and requesting hard facts from tellers, loan processors, and member service representatives, it made some managers nervous and I got lots of "deer-in-the-headlights" stares from their employees. The frontline staff just was not used to receiving direct inquiries from its CEO. Many were not accustomed to having the CEO sit down at their desks and ask for honest opinions and feedback. After town hall meetings at two branches in San Diego early in my tenure at Navy Federal, I noticed that I was getting the same questions at each location. It was obvious to me that the questions had been scripted. Later I asked the regional manager if the attendees had been fed questions, and he admitted that they had. "Well," I said, with a smile on my face, "never do that again." He apologized and promised it wouldn't happen a second time. It didn't, and that manager is still working with us. I also promised him that there would never be adverse consequences for employees who ask tough questions and that I would always provide them with honest answers. I have always made it a habit to tell employees everything I know. I want them to be confident that I will not keep secrets from them—and in return I expect them to be candid with me.

When I first visited our branches in Virginia Beach, I saw lines out the door. I had photos taken of me standing in the teller line at different times and at different locations. I showed these images to the headquarters staff and our board of directors with the caption: "Where's Waldo?"—a reference to a popular children's book whose main character, Waldo, travels all over the world, leaving readers to find him in illustrations of his adventures. The long lines in Virginia Beach reminded me of the same long lines of sailors and Marines that I had seen outside the Bahrain branch during the little free time they had on deployment—their precious lunch hours. The lines at all our branches were a big problem. When I asked Della Butler what she would need to reduce the teller lines in Virginia Beach, she said she could use more staff and more automation. "How about more branches?" I asked. It was obvious to me that we needed more of them. She agreed.

In our call center at the time, we had a digital scoreboard that marks how many members are calling us and how long their wait time is. In my walkabouts around headquarters, I saw that our average on-call wait time was as long as forty-five minutes on military paydays. In addition, we only had the capacity to answer about 70 percent of incoming calls. Before I arrived, we also had had a three-month waiting list for home mortgages. Our members were loyal, but with these kind of wait times, I knew they wouldn't be loyal for long. I asked some of our call center supervisors what they needed to improve these statistics. In the past, we had hired a few new member service employees every year, but not nearly enough to overcome the shortage. One employee told me, "If I wanted to hire three more employees, I asked for five." The senior management had considered the call centers an "expense"—a necessary budget item, but one that had to be balanced against other needs.

To me, if we were missing 30 percent of our incoming calls, we were missing at least 30 percent of our potential revenue. When we asked the call center supervisor how many employees she *actually* needed, her answer was 50.

I authorized those new hires immediately, and we saw instant results. Our membership grew significantly in the first year, and the increased demand continued. Over the next eighteen months, we actually hired one thousand new member service representatives, reducing our average on-call wait times from forty-five minutes to forty-seven seconds. Further, the member service representatives reported that they could now afford to spend quality time on the phone with members, getting to know them, probing them to better understand their needs, and patiently answering all their questions and solving their problems. They didn't feel rushed anymore to get off the phone. What a novel concept: you open the door and answer the phone, and people will do business with you. It sounds like a simple solution, but I never would have uncovered the problem if I had stayed in my headquarters office.

Foot Stomper

Going to the deckplates gives you the perspective that no corner office can offer. Make it your habit as a leader to go to the deckplates regularly. It should be a continual effort—not a "one-and-done." It can be time consuming, but it will be one of the most important *investments* of time that you make.

Note: In the military, the term "foot stomper" is used to emphasize what is important. Navy instructors will often stomp their feet during their lectures as a signal that what they are about to say will be on the test.

Chapter 2

TAKE A LESSON FROM JOHN PAUL JONES

★

As the famous Revolutionary War naval officer said,
"He who does not risk cannot win."

All incoming midshipmen at the Naval Academy are
required to memorize the contents of a small volume called *Reef Points*—the official handbook of
the brigade of midshipmen, as the student body is called.
The book teaches Naval Academy history and Navy traditions. One quotation stood out to me: "He who does
not risk cannot win." It is attributed to Commodore John
Paul Jones, a Revolutionary War figure who is known as
the Father of the American Navy.

Jones was quite the risk-taker—most famous for
the battle between his ship, the American naval vessel *Bonhomme Richard*, and the British warship HMS
Serapis. At the time, the Americans and their allies had
decided to raise the stakes in the war and take the fight
directly to the enemy. Commodore Jones was at the pointy
end of the spear, just off the coast of Scotland, in an aging
warship that had been built as a merchant vessel. He was
facing down a larger ship from the best naval force in the
world—the Royal Navy. But Jones believed that capturing
a British convoy escort right off the enemy coast would win
the Americans a much-needed supply booty and a boost to
their morale. He also had a good crew. So he fired a daring
first shot at *Serapis*, and a fierce, close-range battle ensued.
The two ships were only twenty-five yards from each other.

Bonhomme Richard was no match for the newer and faster *Serapis*. The two vessels dodged and circled each other like fighters in a boxing ring until the *Bonhomme Richard* collided with the stern of the enemy's ship, leaving Jones and his crew defenseless against the guns mounted on the stern of the *Serapis*. The commander of the *Serapis*, Capt. Richard Pearson, shouted to Jones: "Has your ship struck?" (When a ship "strikes" her colors, she takes down her flag, signaling that her captain is surrendering.) Jones famously replied, "I have not yet begun to fight!"

The battle continued for three more hours. *Bonhomme Richard* was able to free herself from the stern of the *Serapis* and maneuver to strike the *Serapis* at a right angle, hooking the two vessels together again. Fires were breaking out on both ships, and the *Bonhomme Richard* appeared to be sinking. Defeat seemed inevitable until a massive explosion rocked the deck of the *Serapis*, killing dozens of sailors and wounding many more. What was the cause? One of Jones' young sailors had lobbed a hand grenade onto the *Serapis*, and it set off a series of devastating explosions. Captain Pearson and his crew could not recover from the blow, and he surrendered.

The story of Jones' bravery and unwillingness to give up in this famous battle are legendary. His victory against the British was historic, and it earned the American Navy newfound respect around the world. What I learned about Jones when I was a midshipman stuck with me. I have never forgotten it.

Although I haven't faced any sea battles like John Paul Jones did, I know that no one lives in a world of zero risk. During my career in the Navy risk took many forms; some risks involved the health and welfare of my crew, and some were just political. Early in my Navy career, I served in the destroyer USS *Albert David* as a weapons officer, responsible for a department that comprised some seventy-five sailors. Unfortunately, the CO was a man with a short temper and a sour view of the world, and was obsessed with how others viewed him. He thought that everyone was out to get him, and he doled out unwarranted and harsh discipline that only served to alienate him from the crew. I have always said that ships' crews often take on the personality of their COs, especially when the commanding officer is a really good one. With a good CO, the ship has mojo—a spirit that is infectious and permeates the ship and her crew. Similarly, if a ship has a bad CO, the ship will have no spirit. Under the leadership of the *Albert David*'s CO, the crew's spirit and morale could not have gotten any lower.

One day, we were conducting helicopter operations, and the helos were using our small flight deck for taking off and landing—training that ensured that we were able to get helos safely onboard to deliver personnel or supplies where and when we needed it. On that afternoon, one of my sailors, a boatswain's mate second class (BM2), waved off a helicopter for safety reasons—in other words, he did not allow it to land. The CO flew off the handle. "Get that BM2 up here and I'm going to get him to captain's mast!" he said. Captain's mast is the lowest court in the Navy's judicial system, and it gives commanding officers wide latitude in disciplining sailors for infractions. The CO was incensed that the helicopter was not permitted to land. He ignored the reasons for the BM2's decision—he was just worried that the wave-off would embarrass him in the eyes of his peers on other ships.

I knew that that was not the right thing to do. The BM2 had done nothing wrong. In fact, the sailor had averted a potentially dangerous scenario. There was some debris on the flight deck that could have been caught up in the helicopter's rotors if the pilot had tried to land. It could have damaged the helicopter or, even worse, it could have injured the crew.

So I said, "No, Captain, we're not going to bring him to the bridge. It's not the right thing to do." The captain was furious, and he turned his anger on me. He sent me to my stateroom, ordering me to remain "in hack" for a few days. Essentially, I was under house arrest, not allowed to leave my stateroom until he told me I could. After two days in hack, I went to the executive officer, the number-two officer on the ship, and I emphatically told him, "I'm taking *myself* out of 'hack.' I gotta get back to work." And I did. Tellingly, the captain never addressed the issue again—with me or the BM2. The CO was a bully. Someone just had to stand up to him. Once I did he backed down, and the BM2's career was saved.

My defiance of the CO's edict was risky. I could have ended up facing my own captain's mast, and my insubordination could have resulted in even more disciplinary measures taken against both me and the BM2. But I knew that I was right: the BM2 had done *nothing* wrong, and I wanted to go to bat for him. He deserved the support and he deserved my taking a risk for him.

Knowing your crew members' strengths and abilities—as well as their weaknesses—can help you evaluate risk better. Every time I assumed command, I would spend a considerable amount of time reviewing the service records of every crew member on the ship. I would look at where he grew up, whether he had one parent or two, what jobs he had held before he joined the Navy, what level of education he had achieved, and how he had advanced in his Navy career. I wanted to gain some insights into their personalities and values as well as their performance history. I also made an effort to spend time with them—one on one. My old boss, Capt. Pete Hedley, had taught me the value of doing this. He used to go sit on the capstans at the stern of the ship and just share a cup of coffee or a soda with any sailor he could find. Captain Hedley would sit there and ask the sailor about his family, where he was from, what motivated him to join the Navy, and what his aspirations were. It would make the chief petty officers, the sailors' direct supervisors, really nervous. They wondered what was *really* being shared in those conversations. But the impression it left on that sailor and his shipmates was that the CO *really* cared about them. I vowed that I would do the same thing for my crew.

The knowledge that I had spent the time to acquire also helped me evaluate how to deal with my sailors when they got in trouble. And, when they did, I did not hesitate to call their parents. In some cases, that's all it took to get a young sailor to shape up. Sometimes it took more severe actions. When I was the CO of the frigate USS *Bronstein*, I had a sailor who had decided that he truly hated the Navy. He talked back to every supervisor and sometimes refused to do his job. I could have kicked him out of the Navy for insubordination and he told me that he wanted "out." But I also knew that he was a good young man, just immature. His service record told me that he had good grades in high school and was from a small town in rural Iowa. I thought the sailor just might be a bit homesick. And I knew that years later he would regret it if he succeeded at getting kicked out of the Navy and had a less-than-honorable discharge on his service record that could haunt him for the rest of his life. I wanted to take a chance on him and give him a wake-up call. It was a risk to the morale of the crew to hang onto a poor performer. I took a chance and told him, "When you start quitting this early in life, it's a slippery slope to be on. You need to fulfill your obligation to the Navy."

I sentenced him to three days in the brig—the Navy's term for a jail. There, he was allowed only bread and water—although all that he could eat. It sounds harsh, and it is. The punishment could have backfired; he could have hated me and the Navy even more. The crew could have resented me. But I had enough information about his background and skills and talents to know that he knew *how* to be a good sailor. He just needed some motivation. The next week I was walking around the ship and I overheard him on the mess decks talking to one of his buddies. "Man," he said, "I never want to go back to the brig. They treat you like a prisoner over there." The light bulb went on: he didn't want to be a prisoner in his life. He was an outstanding sailor from then on. He just needed for someone *not* to give up on him.

Now, some risk is purely political, and I've taken my fair share of it, but there was always some calculation to it. Once again, Captain Hedley showed me that political risks are important to take when the well-being of your crew is involved. When Captain Hedley assumed command of the *Albert David* from the sour CO he noticed that the atmosphere on the ship was heavy and somber. No one smiled, and the entire crew seemed very unhappy. Hedley wanted to do something to boost the morale and have a little fun. At the time, we were at Apra Harbor in Guam, a tropical, warm-water setting, and we were itching for a swim. So Captain Hedley decided that we should enjoy a little recreational activity in Apra Harbor. We spent the day in his gig (a small motorboat stored on board our ship), swimming and waterskiing.

The next morning, he was called ashore to a meeting at the admiral's office, where the senior officer's chief of staff, a notoriously humorless and crusty old submariner, told Captain Hedley that he was in big trouble. There was a gasoline shortage around the country, and publicity about the waterskiing episode—in which the Navy would be portrayed as having wasted precious fuel—was going to damage the Navy's reputation, the chief of staff asserted. Hedley walked out with his tail between his legs and into a meeting with the admiral, George Morrison, the father of Jim Morrison (yes, the front man for the rock band The Doors). "Sit down, son," Rear Admiral Morrison said. "I hear you have been waterskiing with your crew and a few nurses and dental technicians in Apra Harbor? Why?" Captain Hedley was forthright. "Well, sir," he said, "we are out here defending the shipping lanes, and morale on my ship has been in the toilet. I just wanted to pump them up a bit."

Morrison was impressed. After a long silence, he told the captain, "You keep it up! And the next time you want to do it, you can use my barge—but you have to take Mrs. Morrison with you." And we did. Indeed, we took the entire dental and medical clinic staff with us. The secret was that Captain Hedley had known that Rear Admiral Morrison was a naval aviator. Aviators are known for having a different leadership style from that of their ship-driving and submarine-driving peers. They tend to push the envelope, and they can be somewhat irreverent. Captain Hedley was banking on the promise that Rear Admiral Morrison would see the benefit of our little excursions. He took a calculated risk and it paid off—for all of us.

Years later, when I was the CO of the frigate USS *Bronstein*, we frequently participated in large-scale training exercises off San Diego. One Friday afternoon, at the end of a particularly tiring, weeklong exercise, my crew and I were champing at the bit to pull into port and enjoy some liberty (Navy jargon for time off). But the admiral's staff had ordered that we should return to port in order of seniority, and I was the most junior among the COs of the twenty ships that had taken part in this training, which meant that I was supposed to be last in line to moor and go home. It could have been a very long afternoon, and it would probably mean that my crew would not get home until very late on Friday night. But I also knew that the port services team, the unit in charge of providing the pier support for each ship, had twenty ships to service that day and they didn't care who came in first, as long as they assisted all twenty. I asked my engineer to crank up the engine to full speed and get to San Diego harbor first. "Let's go," I said. "Giddy-up!"

As we overtook the first ship in line, I looked back and could see with my binoculars that the admiral, now on the ship behind us, was looking at me with *his* binoculars—a grin on his face! I smiled, waved, and kept going . . . *fast*. We arrived in port first and, sure enough, port services was ready, and took care of us first. My crew members went on liberty and got to see their families—five hours before the rest of the ships. And we didn't cause a delay in service to any of the other ships that required port services that day.

I never had a discussion with the admiral or his staff about it, but I heard through the rumor mill later that he shrugged and said something to the effect of, "Well, we weren't ready. They were." This might not seem like a big risk to someone who is not familiar with the military, but it is important to understand the importance placed on the chain of command in the Navy. You are not supposed to sidestep it; the political risks for you and your career are high. I knew I was living on the edge. I had loosely interpreted an order from the admiral and perhaps had been a tad brazen, but it was worth the reward for my crew. The fact that I knew that the admiral had once been a very young CO himself also helped.

I'm not a reckless risk-taker, but I am a big risk-*evaluator*. I look closely at the risk versus the rewards. If the rewards outweigh the risk—even ever so slightly—I grab them. And I have always erred on the side of taking risks *if it benefits other people*. A leader's job is to make decisions. At Navy Federal, my consideration always was, "What does it mean for the members?" If the rewards for the members outweighed the risk for the organization, then I took the risk every time.

One of the first big chances that I took was to move the company into risk-based lending. Historically, Navy Federal offered the same loan rate to anyone who applied. This was a common practice in the credit union industry at the time. It didn't matter what your track record was, what your credit score was, what your history was. It was part of the credit union philosophy that every customer was a member and all of them should be treated equally, without regard to rank. We felt strongly that a Navy admiral should get the same loan rate as a Navy seaman recruit. In the early 2000s, however, Navy Federal started to re-evaluate that philosophy and had begun discussing moving to a risk-based lending model. Why? Members with the best credit profiles—regardless of their income—could get better rates elsewhere. We were missing a lot of business.

When I arrived at Navy Federal, my predecessor said that he was going to leave this decision up to me. The very first briefing that I received after I took over was provided by my one of my key executives, Mary McDuffie. She and her team had conducted a thorough analysis on the issue. They made a very convincing case that we should move to a risk-based lending model, one that gives consumers loan rates based on their credit history (and other factors). Credit is a discriminator, but it is behavioral. You can control your credit history and improve your loan rate with better credit scores.

I agreed with Mary, and I decided to take it to the board of directors for a vote. In the board meeting, two people voted against it—the previous CEO and the chairman of the board. But eight other members of the board and I voted for it. The fact that the previous CEO and the chairman disagreed with me gave me pause, given their deep knowledge of the organization and their experience. But I had been given all the facts, a sound analysis, and a strong recommendation from my entire Navy Federal team—the group on the front lines of this issue. I said with confidence to the team, "We are going to treat all our members fairly, but not necessarily equally. We will move forward and we're going to show them that this will work."

Initially, the decision was not well-received by all our employees, especially those who had been working at Navy Federal for a long time. They didn't think that risk-based lending was the "credit-union way." They felt strongly that, in our culture, "whether you're a seaman or an admiral, you should get the same rate." My branch managers told me that their staffs were very vocal about this. They just didn't think it was fair.

I went to the deckplates. I visited many branches and talked to their staffs. I held town hall meetings in our customer care centers in Pensacola, Florida, and Winchester,

Virginia, and at our headquarters in Vienna, Virginia. I met weekly with small groups of new and seasoned employees. We needed to have the buy-in from *everyone* or the new model would not be successful. I told them that the lending team was strongly in favor of this move and had conducted a thorough analysis of the industry. I also had to admit to them that most companies in the financial services industry were already doing this. I also told them that I was concerned that Navy Federal might begin to become a subprime lender, but with prime pricing, if we continued our one-size-fits-all lending policy. Finally, I told them that with risk-based lending we would be able to say "yes" to a loan request much more often. Indeed, I talked repeatedly about how refreshing it would be to say "yes" to many more members because we could offer different rates.

Within a year, our loan portfolio exploded, giving us even *more* revenue to provide even *more* loans. And three years later, when the nation went into the Great Recession of 2008–09, our lending model helped us ride out that financial storm. Unlike some other financial institutions, we never resorted to subprime lending.

While risk-based lending was a bold move for our organization, we *were* actually lagging the rest of the financial services industry. There were statistics and case studies to back up the proposed change in policy. But when we began to consider another big and risky decision, there was *no* model to follow. At no time in my tenure at Navy Federal did the financial risks for a decision seem so big as they did in April 2011.

That month, President Obama and Congress were at loggerheads over the budget and there was a serious threat of a government shutdown. Congress had made this threat before, but this time it really seemed imminent.

The prospect of an impending shutdown and its impact on our members loomed large at our Navy Federal board meetings. For the first time, military personnel were being included in the list of federal employees who wouldn't be paid if the shutdown took effect. At the time, about 16 percent of our members were serving on active duty, and were likely to be affected, and we wanted to do something to help them. We decided to consider enabling them to make up for the loss of their salaries by providing them with no-interest loans equal to the amount of their pay that the government would be holding back. I asked our CFO how much that might cost, and the answer was daunting: it could mean an outlay of hundreds of millions of dollars, and there was no way to guarantee the return. We had that amount of money in reserve, but we didn't know how long the shutdown would last. It was a very big gamble, but it was hard to put a price tag on the peace of mind that it could give our members serving on active duty around the world—and their families. In my opinion, that reward trumped any financial risk, and the board of directors agreed unanimously. Why should our hardworking military service members be the ones to pay the price for a political showdown between the White House and Congress?

At the encouragement of Mary McDuffie, we decided that we would make this announcement in advance of the government's decision—to further ease our members' concerns further. We wanted our members to be able to focus on their jobs—not on politics. We issued a press release the night before the impending shutdown, announcing that we would provide a "payday advance" to all our affected members who had direct deposit arrangements with Navy Federal. The response was immediate and overwhelming. We had only recently launched our company Facebook page, and all the posts were thankful and quite emotional. A few days later, my wife and I were visiting a branch in Yuma, Arizona, and a young Navy hospital corpsman (a medic) came up to me and introduced herself. She was a single mom, and had no financial safety net outside of her salary. She said that the potential shutdown was terrifying to her, since she had no idea how she was going to pay her rent or her childcare, much less eat. She started to cry and thanked me. She felt as though Navy Federal had lifted the weight of the world off her shoulders and that we really cared. I remember asking her to stop crying. I told her with a chuckle that if she continued to cry, then I would start crying as well, and how would that look for the CEO of Navy Federal?

When we made the decision to cover the pay of active-duty members who had direct deposit agreements with us, we had no idea the overwhelming amount of goodwill that it would produce from our members. In turn, our entire team at Navy Federal felt the so-called halo effect of that goodwill. Since then, we have continued to provide paycheck relief to our members during three additional government shutdowns. We believe that public service is a defining characteristic of our membership, and we don't want our customers to be penalized for the government's failures.

Over the past fourteen years we have evaluated several major initiatives, such as risk-based lending, that we felt would better serve our members' needs. Our decision to increase the number of our branches significantly is another example of risk-taking designed to meet their needs.

At a time when many banks were closing branches and pushing their customers to do business online, we made a calculated decision to open more branches—lots of them. We felt strongly that we needed to be accessible to our members in many different ways: on the phone, online, *and* in person. Despite our increasing use of the Internet to do business, many people still like to bank in person. When I was visiting a branch near an Air Force base, a young airman in motorcycle gear was standing in the teller line. I asked him what brought him into the branch that day. He said he was depositing a check. I said, "Well, you know, you can use your phone to deposit a check," and I offered to show him how. "I know," he said, "but I'm single and I like to see the people working in the branch." My senior branch manager in the Tidewater area, Della Butler, told me that a very old widower, a Navy World War II vet, came into her branch once a week and she always greeted him with a big hug. Some weeks, he had banking business to do; some weeks, he didn't. Mainly, he told Della, he came into the branch for the hug. Clearly, the personal element of our business is still important and a computer can't achieve that. It was clear to me that Navy Federal, which had only 104 branches in 2004, was far from being what I call "over-branched."

To me, the rewards in such cases far outweighed the risks of building lots more brick-and-mortar branches, which were significant. These were capital investments— and expensive ones. If you choose a bad location for a branch, it may not be successful, and you could lose money. We opened thirty-four new branches in 2006, another twenty-three branches in 2008, and another thirty-three in 2010—almost one every two weeks. By contrast, before I arrived, we were opening only one to three new branches per year. With every new branch opening, we immediately noticed an uptick in business around the zip codes where we opened them. We now have 335 branches and we are committed to opening twenty a year for the foreseeable future.

This decision was validated for me recently when I made an unannounced visit to a branch in Virginia Beach. We were one of the few banks or credit unions open over the July 4th holiday weekend. I introduced myself to a young couple talking to one of our mortgage experts about getting a home mortgage loan. The husband had a full beard, but had a military regulation haircut. I had a hunch that he was a Navy Seal (a member of the Sea Air Land special forces team). I said to him, "I think I know what you do. When did you get back?" He nodded and gave me a big smile. "Yesterday," he said. He had been gone for six months and he and his wife were trying to buy their first home. The first thing they did was to walk into Navy Federal. They wanted to talk to someone face-to-face—not on the phone. It was that important to them. If it is important to the member, it should be important to our employees. And so, we helped them get a mortage that day.

Foot Stomper

Taking on the Royal Navy in the 1700s was risky business. At the time, England had the most capable Navy in the world. I'm sure that John Paul Jones' legendary large ego drove some of his battle decisions, but he also probably knew that the British did not expect the Americans to take the fight all the way across the Atlantic. The gamble probably was a calculated one, but the rewards outweighed the risk. A leader's job is to make decisions and to be accountable for them. Sometimes these are fraught with risk—big and small. It's good to remember: "He who does not risk cannot win."

Chapter 3

FOCUS ON THE TARGETS THAT COUNT

*To be a successful leader of your organization,
you have to discover the targets of opportunity that
really make a difference and home in on them.*

During the Vietnam War, when American tacticians were deciding where to mount an offensive, they would look for a what they called a "target-rich" environment—a location that contained a large number of high-value assets and also was poorly defended. That combination offered greater odds that U.S. forces would be able to accomplish their mission with minimal risk—especially if they were able to retain the element of surprise. In such situations, the prospect of success was really tilted in our favor.

Standing on the bridge of the aircraft carrier USS *Enterprise* in the middle of the Persian Gulf in December 1998, I was looking for my own rich targets—at the request of President Bill Clinton. I could see my breath in the frigid air as I looked out over the horizon to a winter seascape of choppy waters and an occasional seagull. My battle group was about to change that peaceful scene. It was ten days before Christmas, and we were poised to launch a massive bombing campaign against Iraqi President Saddam Hussein—the largest since Operation Desert Storm seven years before. Our objective was to reduce Iraq's ability to produce weapons of mass destruction. I was the battle group commander, in charge of an aircraft carrier, four to six destroyers, one cruiser, seventy-five aircraft, and 7,500 sailors and Marines. We were leading Operation Desert Fox, designed to punish Iraq for its failure to comply with United Nations Security Council resolutions and its interference with U.N. inspectors. Over the next four days, we were going to fill the skies above Iraq with bombs and missiles. Our targets were Iraq's air-defense systems, weapons research-and-development facilities, and the headquarters of Saddam's elite military forces, known as the Republican Guard.

The battle group that we had replaced in the Persian Gulf just a few days before had been ready to make history and launch the first strike, but the operation was called off. The group left for home without having fired a shot. We took its place in the Gulf and waited anxiously for orders.

Then, on the night of December 16, we received word that the operation had been revived. From the bridge, I watched as an Aegis cruiser launched the first salvo. Seeing the flash of a Tomahawk missile light up the dark sky in the distance, looking like a space rocket launch, made it real. The game was on.

Over the next seventy hours we executed 297 combat bombing missions, with some seventy aircraft, dropping more than 690,000 pounds of ordnance. Iraq's ground forces fired surface-to-air missiles (SAMs) at us, but we saw no opposition from any Iraqi aircraft. Thankfully, we did not lose any pilots. It was indeed a target-rich environment, because Saddam's air defense batteries were no match for our offense. The bomb-damage intelligence that we collected suggested that we had set back Saddam Hussein's missile program by at least a year.

In business, we look for a different kind of "*opportunity-rich environment*"—a situation in which you realize that you have a chance to offer a valuable product or service that previously has been overlooked, either by you or your competitors. At Navy Federal, there is an in-house marketing research group that helps identify these targets of opportunity. By having a research arm in house, Navy Federal is able to customize an analysis. And the art form is tailoring this research to what the targets are. Early on in my tenure as CEO, this group analyzed our membership base and discovered that only 16 percent of our members had taken out car loans from us, even though we offered very competitive rates. Clearly, this was an opportunity to offer a good product to existing members. Why weren't the other 84 percent of our car-buying members securing their financing from us? Our car-loan marketing promotions were not bringing in more loans. With our membership growing, it should have been simple for us to increase our car loan business. As it turned out, however, we were making the loan-approval process much harder than it had to be.

As I often did over a long holiday weekend, I wandered into our headquarters on a Saturday to listen in on the calls that some of our member service folks were taking. One employee was talking to a young sailor who wanted a car loan. I heard her tell him that he would have to wait until Tuesday to get a decision from the Navy Federal lending committee about his loan application. At the time, the lending committee was not available on the weekends to approve loans. A light bulb went on. This sailor was not going to wait until Tuesday. He was probably calling from the dealership and wanted to purchase a car that afternoon. We needed to be able to approve loans on the weekend. It reinforced my philosophy to always concentrate on targets that count—by making service improvements that enable us to help more of our members and increase revenue.

A few years later, we went one step further and instituted the "Ten-Minute Car Loan," and, later, an online algorithm that approved loans automatically. I was visiting a branch in Hawaii a few years ago and struck up a conversation with a young Navy submariner. He had a car loan from another bank with an 18 percent interest rate and, not surprisingly, wanted to refinance. I knew something was up: either he had bad credit or he was getting fleeced. I asked the branch employee who was reviewing his loan application to let me know the answer. Eight minutes later, I received an e-mail message from her informing me that he was approved for a new loan with us at 3.26 percent. Think about the difference we made in his life and how fast we were able to make it. Think about the bank that was giving him an 18 percent car loan. It wasn't treating him very well. But that doesn't matter now. That sailor is home with us.

One evening, when I was walking around one of our call centers, I overheard one of the member service staffers lamenting the fact that she couldn't help a soldier who was on deployment in Baghdad. She was frustrated. I asked her what was wrong. She said she had just been on the phone with a Marine there, helping him fix a technical problem with his direct deposit. The leatherneck thanked her and then said to her, "You know, I just got off patrol with Sergeant Jones, who is sitting next to me here. He wants to join Navy Federal, but he's in the Army and he's not eligible. Why not?" Well, the member service representative at headquarters didn't have a good answer for the Marine. Neither did I.

In the latter part of my Navy career, the Department of Defense had placed a higher emphasis of working in a "joint" environment—one in which members of the Navy, Marine Corps, Army, and Air Force all work together seamlessly (at least in theory). When I arrived at Navy Federal, I wanted to explore how we could make the organization more "joint." What that meant to us was opening up our membership to personnel from the Air Force and Army. We knew how to serve active-duty sailors and Marines; we understood those constituencies and their needs. We were confident that we also could provide great products and service to the rest of the military. The story of Sergeant Jones only reinforced in my mind the value of doing this.

In 2008, we applied to the National Credit Union Administration, which regulates the credit union industry, to expand our customer base to include members of the Army and the Air Force and Department of Defense civilian employees. In 2013, we applied again, to expand our membership to the Coast Guard as well. The NCUA approved our request both times. Now, Sergeant Jones could join, and so could Airman Jones and Coast Guardsman Jones.

In 2017, NCUA decided to permit *all* veterans—including those who have served but are no longer on active duty—to join military-oriented credit unions, increasing our field of membership (and that of other, smaller credit unions) even more. With more than 20 million veterans and their families in the United States, our potential marketplace all but exploded.

By expanding our field of membership to all veterans, we are now able to offer our products and services to everyone who serves or has served *and* their families.

We suspected that the demand from these newly eligible veterans would be high. The expanded pool helped us add some 400,000 new members in the first year. It was a target of opportunity that really made a difference.

When we decided to increase the number of branches that we operate around the country and around the world, we knew we had to pick our locations carefully. We knew that our branches on and just outside military bases were successful. But were we missing out on an opportunity to reach members (and potential members) who didn't live near a military base? Again, our in-house marketing team did some research and discovered areas with a significant number of members who were not using us as their primary financial institution. They might have a credit card with us or even a Navy Federal home mortgage, but they didn't have a checking account with us. Our educated guess was that they had a checking or savings account with another bank because that other bank had a branch near their homes or offices and we did not. For instance, we discovered that we had 30,000 members in Atlanta, but not a single branch to serve them. And there were pockets of members like this concentrated in cities all over the country where we had no retail presence. Talk about some missed opportunities!

We opened four new branches in Atlanta on the same day. We continued this branch expansion strategy in cities all over the country, including Dallas, Phoenix, Raleigh, and Houston. We also experimented with some stand-alone, branded ATMs in some locations; we even put a few branches inside Walmarts because our research told us that our members buy a lot there. Moreover, we found that every time we opened a branch in these targeted locations, we immediately saw an increase in our business from longer-time members in those areas. Indeed, 46 percent of our new members join by walking into a branch. This clearly was a target that counted.

Although our branch surge certainly helped us reach more members who want to bank in person, we all knew that we could never have enough branches to serve all our members with brick-and-mortar buildings. Many of our active-duty members and their families served and lived all over the world—especially those between the ages of eighteen and thirty-four, who were on the move frequently. Often they could not take advantage of a bank near their homes; sometimes they were in very remote places where they don't even have access to a computer. Banking by mail or by calling our contact center may have satisfied these members thirty years ago, or even twenty years ago, but not anymore. As we looked at the rapid changes in technology, we knew that we needed a better way for them to bank with us—in real time.

When Apple launched the iPhone in 2007 and opened its "App Store" in 2008, my son, Cutler, was serving as a naval officer on a ship. He bought one of these phones as soon as they were available. One day he told me, "Dad, you guys need an app." A what, I asked?

We started offering some rudimentary "text-banking" in early 2010, where members could enroll to receive text messages with banking updates—i.e., balance updates, deposits received, etc. From January to May of that year, 62,000 members enrolled. Then, we built a mobile-friendly website—to enable members to visit our website from their phones. But these offerings were not enough. Our digital banking team was reading the technology trade press and watching the rapid adoption of the iPhone and, to a lesser degree, the Android phone. At the same time, we were all recognizing how much time *we* were spending on our phones and the increasing number of transactions that *we* were making with them. If *we* were doing so, what about our members?

In May of 2010, we launched our first mobile app for the iPhone, but did not provide any of the care and feeding that is required to keep up with the rapidly evolving mobile landscape. Despite that, 364,000 members enrolled and they signed in 8 million times from their phones that year. Clearly, we had discovered a big demand among our members.

As a result, we created a dedicated mobile team in 2011, led by a dynamic and energetic IT (information technology) professional, Tim Day. He brought an innate understanding of the millennial generation and he recruited equally talented technology gurus to build on, improve, and innovate our mobile product and service. In 2012 we began offering mobile deposits on our app, which in turn propelled the growth in usage of our mobile app, which surpassed our online usage in 2014. That same year, Visa went to bat for us and convinced Apple to include us as one of the initial partners for the launching of their Apple Pay electronic credit-card system. It was exciting for our digital team to be on the cutting edge of financial technology. In 2018, eight years after launching our first mobile app, we witnessed more than 1 billion mobile sessions and more than 4.4 million unique users.

Developing a way for our highly dispersed membership to conduct transactions and bank in real time was an obvious outgrowth of our longtime slogan, "We serve where you serve." Mobile banking indeed had been an opportunity-rich target.

But the most important target on which any CEO must focus is the company's employees. Some companies and CEOs put their customers first; I have always made my employees my number-one priority. My philosophy at Navy Federal was simple: take good care of your employees and they will take good care of our members. My greatest satisfaction came from providing a great place for a lot of people to work. Demonstrating to members of your work team that you care about them and proving that you have their best interests at heart is a constant that withstands the test of time. Caring cannot be hyped, faked, or spun. It needs to be proven in leadership's everyday actions. Take care of your people, ensure they are proud of the work that they are doing, and you will have a great place to work.

Near the end of my term as Navy Federal's president, we had a disturbing incident inside one of our branches. Out of the blue, a member pulled out a large knife and stabbed one of our member service representatives in the neck. Several employees rushed to her defense, and they called 911. Our member service representative was transported to a nearby hospital. (The assailant fled the scene but was caught and arrested by police a few miles away.) I received word shortly after the incident from Steve Romano, the Navy Federal executive who ran our branches at the time. He was able to relay to me that, fortunately, our member service representative's injuries were not life-threatening, although she was understandably shaken. I told Steve, "Get someone from Navy Federal to the hospital immediately. I don't want her to be alone." Steve dispatched Regional Manager Tishona Watson, who rushed to her side and held her hand until her family could get there. Tishona told her, "Your main responsibility is to get better. You're strong. You're amazing." The member service representative was surprised and touched by the personal visit from Navy Federal leadership. We dispatched additional executives and resources to the branch over the next few days to provide counseling, food, and our presence. I wanted to reassure the MSR that the entire Navy Federal leadership was behind her. She told Tishona that she did not want to let the incident define her. She was a young lady who had only recently been hired by Navy Federal. We were all impressed with her resilience. The incident shocked me, and I was pleased when she returned to work about a week later. We offered to send her to a drive-through branch, where she could work with a bit of distance between her and our members. But, no, she said wanted to go back to the branch where the incident occurred, because "that branch is my family." We hired additional security at the branch. Whatever they needed. We continue to provide support with phone calls, e-mails, visits. Tishona said that the way we responded to this incident "renewed my love for Navy Federal."

In truth, some in our company leadership might have been thinking about liability or damage to the company's reputation, but I was worried about our employee's physical and emotional well-being. That's my job and my highest priority. It comes before everything else at Navy Federal. Indeed, we won't hesitate to close a branch that is unsafe for our employees, even if it is a profitable, with good foot traffic. We recently closed one near Joint Base Andrews in Maryland, even though the branch was serving the large and busy military installation, after numerous employees expressed some fear about walking to their cars at night and local statistics demonstrated that the area was becoming crime-ridden.

I used the symbol of a triangle when I talked to my employees about how I managed our organization. It is a pretty simple symbol, but it helped me explain what Navy Federal is all about. One side represents our employees, the second side our members, and the third side our infrastructure—the products and services that we offer. You have to work all three sides to make it work. And when you are successful, all three sides have to benefit. In other words, when you bring in more revenue, you're more successful and you have more money to invest. You build more branches and you incorporate more new technology—such as a website and mobile applications—in order to keep pace with your membership's demands and become more accessible for them. At the same time, you try to get your products down to the very lowest price that you can sustain in order to move forward. On the member side, you try to keep their satisfaction levels and value up, so that they benefit from your being more successful. But, at the base of the triangle—at its foundation—are the employees. Without them, you have nothing.

Taking care of your employees by providing great benefits is one way to do this. In 2011, I started the President's Challenge, an opportunity for employees to pledge to do something to improve their health. I had instituted something like it when I was the battle group commander on the aircraft carrier USS *Enterprise*. There, I challenged the crew to stop smoking and promised to everyone who did a souvenir admiral's coin. It might not sound like a big incentive, but time alone with the admiral on a ship with five thousand persons was valued. I told each and every sailor who successfully stopped smoking that I was proud of him or her. One master chief contacted me ten years later and told me that he still has the coin on his desk as a reminder of his accomplishment.

I wanted to motivate my employees at Navy Federal with a similar challenge. The goal might be a promise to take the stairs instead of the elevator, drink fewer sodas, quit smoking, get eight hours of sleep a night, practice yoga, or run in a 5K race. Every year, employees register their individual "challenge" in July and log their progress through the end of the calendar year. The biggest winners receive a cash prize and get a thank-you card and gift to give the person who supported them the most in meeting their goals. I personally delivered the prizes to the biggest winners. When we started the program, about 20 percent of our employees participated. In 2018, 51 percent of our employees participated—and the stories I have heard have moved me to tears. The winners told me over and over that losing weight or quitting smoking didn't just improve their health—it changed their lives. One woman told me that she set a goal to stop watching television and eating fast food, in hopes that it would also motivate her mother to quit her thirty-seven-year smoking habit. She sold her TV and stuffed her refrigerator with healthy food. Looking for a way to fill the time that she normally spent watching TV, she and her husband started taking long walks with their dogs. Motivated by how good she felt, she bought a treadmill and committed herself to walking fifteen miles every week. She lost a few pounds and reconnected with her husband. And she started a chain reaction in her family: her mom, her two sisters, and her brother-in-law all quit smoking as well. As she said, "I am excited for next year's President's Challenge, for new goals and new beginnings. Thank you for making a commitment to your employees to live healthier and for bringing a balance between the work and home life. We appreciate it!"

While other companies had stopped matching their employees' 401(k) contributions, we increased ours—to 7 percent. We offer every single employee an annual bonus, predicated on individual performance goals and the company's overall performance (member growth, financial performance, and member satisfaction). Every employee is eligible. Every employee and contractor also receives a

Christmas gift of cash—including our partner companies that provide security, janitorial, and cafeteria services, as well as the staff at our fitness centers. In my opinion, they are all part of our team. We offer great career paths with continued growth opportunities and upward mobility. It is one of the reasons that we have so many employees who have worked for the company ten, twenty, even thirty years. In fact, about 20 percent of our employees have been with us for more than ten years and almost one thousand employees have called Navy Federal home for more than twenty years. I used to meet with small groups of employees who are celebrating these anniversaries, and I heard time and time again from them that they have stayed with Navy Federal because they believe in the mission, they enjoy great benefits, and they have great opportunities to grow with us.

I knew that our business didn't take place in my office. Our business took place where our employees interact with members—in our branches, on the phone, and online. By keeping my focus on the well-being of our employees, I was able to provide them with the incentive to take care of our members and increase our business. Expanding our business was not merely a focus; it was an outcome—an outcome of our focus on our employees, our members, and our infrastructure.

Foot Stomper

Just as in the military, there will be lots of targets of opportunity to pursue in building and expanding a great business. Too many people get wrapped up in the numbers and forget about what really matters in an organization. The key is to pursue the targets of opportunity that *really* make a difference in the lives of your employees and in the service that you can provide to your customers. Employees and members are the targets that count the most for me. Processes are simply a means to the desired end result of supporting them. Pick the targets that count.

Chapter 4

Look Past the Lifelines

Leaders are responsible for setting the course and direction of an organization. To do so effectively, you need to look up and out—way past your lifelines—and get the view from the bridge.

As I mentioned before, early on in my Navy career, I had a bad boss—a *really* bad boss. He made my life miserable. In fact, he made the whole crew miserable. It was no surprise that the morale on our ship was terrible. We all walked on eggshells in his presence, always afraid of incurring his unpredictable wrath over perceived offenses. It felt as though there was a dark veil covering the ship—as if we were in a perpetual state of gloom. To make matters worse, the CO's boss, the squadron commander, knew about the situation and did nothing about it; the CO's abusive behavior was left unchecked. The whole experience was starting to sour me on a long-term career in the Navy and on a life in ships. Did I really want to stay in a Navy that allowed this kind of leader to make it to the top? At the time, the U.S. economy was starting to improve, and many of my peers who had recently chosen to get out of the Navy were doing interesting jobs—and making more money than I was. I began to think about changing my career.

Then Pete Hedley arrived to relieve the morale-souring CO. The change-of-command on the frigate USS *Albert David* took place at sea. The first thing Captain Hedley did was get on the ship's intercom system, known as the 1MC, and tell us all how happy he was to be serving *with* us, that he knew we were an experienced group of *professionals*, and that he *trusted* us. Wow—what a difference! Furthermore, he immediately started delegating many routine tasks to us, his wardroom of junior officers, and he eliminated much of the laborious back-up paperwork that the previous CO had required us to submit to justify our actions. He showed us that he really *did* trust us. He also smiled and laughed with us. Within a few weeks, the veil had been lifted and the boost in our spirits was evident throughout the ship.

When it came time for me to talk about my next assignment, Captain Hedley called me into his office for a one-on-one counseling session. He asked me what I wanted to do next. I told him that I was thinking about getting out, that this assignment had been my toughest yet, and that the previous CO had really quashed my enthusiasm for the Navy. He noticed that I was looking down at the deck, and he wondered if I was a bit embarrassed even to *tell* the CO that I was thinking about getting out of his beloved Navy. He told me a story about his early days in the service. His father had had a career in private industry and had fully expected his son to do the same. After Pete had served a few years in the Navy, his dad arranged an interview for him at the Bethlehem Steel Corporation, a revered company whose management valued military service and was willing to offer Pete an engineering position with a promising career path. But when the Bethlehem interviewer heard about Pete's experience in the Navy and how much responsibility Pete had at such a young age, the interviewer looked him in the eye and said, "Pete, I can offer you a really good job today that will quadruple your pay and give you interesting work until you retire. But I can tell you that you will not have the same level of responsibility you have today in the Navy for another ten years at Bethlehem Steel." Pete stayed in the Navy because, for him, serving in command at sea was a calling, not just a job. He was in charge of a large group of sailors supporting an important national mission. Over his Navy career he served as the officer-in-charge of a small boat and commanded three ships and two squadrons, racking up thirteen overseas deployments in defense of his country. He loved every minute of it.

I looked up at Captain Hedley and suddenly realized that I, too, felt that calling, and that he had recognized that. He told me that, with my permission, he was going to call Washington and recommend that I be given command of a ship—as a *lieutenant*. This was unusually early for a first-time command at sea. I was only twenty-seven years old, but he believed that I was ready. He also said that I should not let the bad experience of working for his predecessor taint my whole perception of the Navy. I needed to get some perspective, he advised. I went topside and looked way out over the horizon.

Captain Hedley was right. It was a big ocean out there and I was part of a big Navy. I loved the Navy and I loved serving at sea. I needed someone like Pete Hedley to grab my chin and help me look up and out. I needed to look past the lifelines on the ship—those lines that run around the perimeter of the vessel and help keep you from falling overboard. I needed to see the big picture of my career and not get bogged down by one boss and his bad leadership. Pete Hedley's advice has stayed with me and helped me make many good decisions during my career—both in the Navy and at Navy Federal.

Like the Navy, Navy Federal has a strong tie to tradition and a history of being very conservative in its decision-making. Management was deliberate and measured, which had served the organization well for many years. Sometimes, however, this can lead to big missed opportunities and a lack of perspective. When I arrived at Navy Federal, the organization was considering expanding its operations in Pensacola. With several military bases in Escambia County, in the panhandle region of Florida, and a low cost of living (compared to that of the Washington, D.C., area where our headquarters are located), Pensacola was a natural place for us to set up a field operation. We had opened a small call center there in 2003. The local workforce, including many military spouses, was attracted to our mission, and we had a reputation as a good place to work. Indeed, when the first sixty positions were advertised, we received 1,500 applications in five days. By 2005, we were contemplating an expansion. I had already seen at other Navy Federal locations how a modest increase in the number of member service personnel that year had resulted in improved employee satisfaction, a reduction in employee turnover, and an immediate increase in revenue.

As I stood on the top floor of one of our buildings and looked out over the sixty-three acres of land that we owned, I turned to one of my associates and said, "What do you think about adding another building down here?" He thought about it and responded, "Oh, we're going to have to study that for a couple of years before we can make a good decision on that." His opinion reflected the military culture from which he came—measured, conservative, and thoughtful. This conservative approach to risk had been prevalent at Navy Federal, but I knew that we needed to be more aggressive on this issue. I looked him in the eye and said, "No, we're going to start now." I put the project in motion, and as soon as we put the new building in operations we ran out of space and needed more. As I explained to him, if we had waited two years, we would have missed the train. As a leader, you will never get 100-percent certainty on any decision. You have to make reasoned judgment calls with imperfect information.

In 2018, we employed 7,300 people in Pensacola and are on track to reach our goal of employing 10,000 by 2026. Indeed, Navy Federal may reach that number by the end of 2022. We are about to complete construction of our eighth building there. We pride ourselves on being a high-quality employer of entry-level personnel, providing them with training, excellent benefits, and a good career path. When we conducted employee forums, we often found that half the people in the room had been promoted three, four, even five times over the past five years.

While the Navy's large presence in Pensacola made our choice to build offices there an obvious one, there were few other regional employers that had a more positive impact on the local economy and quality of life in Pensacola. In addition to our capital investment—which will top $1 billion by 2026—we offer an average starting salary of more than $44,000 for a member-service representative, well above the Florida average. We found that the workforce in Escambia County is highly competent and has a very strong work ethic. Clay Ingram, president and CEO of the Pensacola Chamber of Commerce, called our investment in the region a "generational game-changer."

I later heard a story that drove home the impact of our investment. My wife, Debbie, was chatting with some member service representatives on our last visit to Pensacola and met a woman who drove fifty miles from Alabama every day to work at Navy Federal. Why did she cross the state line to work so far away? Well, the best job she could find in her little town only paid $10 an hour, and it offered no benefits. Her oldest child was twenty, and for the first time they were able to go on a vacation, thanks to the salary and vacation time that she was earning at Navy Federal.

My point in telling this story is that if I had worried only about the cost of that one new building, we would have missed a huge opportunity. I wanted to be well-positioned to hire more people fast. We were already on a growth curve and, looking past the lifelines, I could envision a steep one. All we needed was to have the infrastructure in place.

We also were planning to generate significant demand for our products and services—to increase our marketing outreach nationwide. Our company traditionally had been very conservative in its advertising. In fact, it was only in the late 1990s that we began to call the function "marketing." Before then, it was known as "education and information," and this department was responsible for producing member newsletters, bank statement inserts, and branch posters. Indeed, we had a strongly held view that credit unions didn't "market" or "sell" their products and services. Instead, we told ourselves that we "educated" our members about them. We ran some advertisements in print media, and Mary McDuffie, our marketing executive, told me that it always had generated an immediate increase in customer inquiries. But our directors had been wary about its high cost. Now, we were about to discover that an investment in marketing and advertising could pay big dividends.

Standing on the bridge and looking past the lifelines at Navy Federal, I could see that we needed to change the organization's comfort level with risk. We needed to manage risk carefully, not avoid it completely. Advertising was a place where we could take some incremental risks. If a small amount of advertising produced a small increase in business, what would a *lot* more advertising produce? I believed that if more people knew we existed, more people would do business with us. In 2009, we set out to recruit a national advertising agency that could give us greater reach and exposure for our brand. We wanted a partner, not a vendor. We looked for a company that understood our mission and our culture as much it understood our products and services. We were especially concerned about active-duty members, whom we considered to be at the core of our mission. After much research, we hired the Fitzgerald & Company advertising agency in Atlanta.

The people at Fitzgerald (now known as Fitzco) worked hard to learn who we were. They spent a few days at sea on an aircraft carrier, observing flight operations; they visited branches; and they listened in on member-service calls. Seeing our members performing their professional duties crystallized for Fitzgerald how important our mission is and how dedicated our employees are to that mission. The partnership between Navy Federal and Fitzgerald has become trusted and valued.

One of the things that both Fitzgerald and Mary McDuffie recommended was that we advertise on national network television, which was an expensive proposition and a radical departure from the way that Navy Federal had always thought about marketing and advertising. We ran the risk of paying to reach a lot of people who were ineligible for membership. The Procter & Gamble Company can easily justify national advertising because almost everyone uses shampoo. But not everyone who watches network television is eligible to become a member of Navy Federal. We could be wasting a lot of money in the short term.

But when I looked past the lifelines I could visualize our future—one with exponentially more members. In 2009,

Navy Federal had 3.4 million members, mostly Navy and Marine Corps active duty and retirees. But we had just expanded our field of membership to all Department of Defense employees. With 2 million newly eligible people there, we still had a huge growth opportunity—and these potential members lived all over the country. They also had immediate family members living all over the country who were eligible for membership as well. I recalled that when we began opening new branches in areas outside our core market, we experienced an instant increase in business in those zip codes. We also heard feedback from employees and anecdotal stories about members express-ing pride in our brand when they saw the advertising. This more than offset the few letters of complaints we received from some members who thought we were spending too much money on marketing and advertising. Worrying about the upfront cost of advertising would have been very shortsighted.

As soon as we started advertising on network television—specifically on "Monday Night Football"—our member service representatives started reporting a curious trend. On the day after the New England Patriots were playing we received an unprecedented number of membership inquiries from Boston, a nontraditional mar-ket for us. The following Tuesday we received an unusu-ally high number of calls from San Francisco. Who had been playing football the night before? The San Francisco 49ers.

Foot Stomper

Sometimes you can get mired in the daily details and minutiae that challenge your ship. You can worry too much about where you want to be at the end of the day or the end of the year. As a leader, you need to have a much longer view than that. You have to get up to the bridge and look way past the lifelines to get the right perspective.

My parents, Betty and Jim Dawson, both
of whom served in the Navy in World
War II, married in Pensacola, Florida, during their wartime service. *Author family
collection*

My fourth-grade school photo in 1958,
when I was ten years old. *Author family
collection*

My parents and my younger brother, Craig, visited me during plebe summer at the Naval Academy in August 1966. New midshipmen spend the summer before their freshman (plebe) year getting indoctrinated into military life. Craig followed in my footsteps three years later. *Author family collection*

My midshipman first class (senior year) portrait for the 1970 Naval Academy yearbook. *United States Naval Academy*

This was my official photo when I took command of the ocean-going tug USS *Molala*. I was twenty-seven years old, at that time the youngest commanding officer of a U.S. Navy ship. *U.S. Navy*

As a lieutenant in charge of the weapons department, I spent a lot of time topside on the ship. Here, I am monitoring a gun shoot on board the frigate USS *Albert David* in 1974 somewhere off the coast of southern California. *Author family collection*

Conducting training while in command of the USS *Princeton*, circa 1992. *Author family collection*

My wife, Debbie, posed on the pier in Long Beach, California, with our three children, (*left to right*) Cutler III, Devon, and Daryl, in 1993 at my change-of-command ceremony, when I was relieved as the commanding officer of the cruiser USS *Princeton*. *Author family collection*

This photo was taken on board the aircraft carrier USS *Enterprise* in 1998, when I was deployed to the Persian Gulf as battle group commander in support of Operation Desert Fox. *U.S. Navy*

As commander, Striking Fleet Atlantic, I monitored activities from the joint operations center on board my flagship, USS *Mount Whitney*, in 2002. The ship and Striking Fleet Atlantic staff were participating in the largest NATO military exercise in the Baltics in history. *U.S. Navy*

When serving as commander of the Second Fleet, I frequently interacted with the media. Here, I answered questions concerning the joint military experiment "Millennium Challenge 02" (MC-02) during a press conference held at the Point Loma Naval Submarine Base in 2002. I served as the Joint Force Maritime Component Commander for Fleet Battle Experiment Juliet, the Navy's contribution to MC-02. MC-02 is this nation's premier joint integrating event, bringing together both live field exercises and computer simulation. *U.S. Navy photo by PM2 Michael R. McCormick*

Former Chief of Naval Operations Adm. Vernon Clark presided at my Navy retirement ceremony in Memorial Hall at the U.S. Naval Academy in November 2004. *U.S. Navy*

I always had fun interacting with employees and taking selfies with them. Here, I'm with Navy Federal employees at our operations center in Winchester, Virginia. *Navy Federal Credit Union*

Navy Federal Credit Union employees pose with me for a photo to encourage participation in Navy Federal's annual President's Challenge, a program that encourages employees to commit themselves to a personal wellness goal and to track their progress. *Navy Federal Credit Union*

Former Florida governor Rick Scott presented me with Florida's Business Ambassador Medal during a news conference on April 3, 2013. Navy Federal and the state government had just announced an expansion of the credit union's Greater Pensacola operations, involving two new buildings and 1,500 new jobs. *Navy Federal Credit Union*

Our family ski trip to Sun Valley, Idaho, in 2013. *Left to right*: Devon, Cutler, Cutler III, Debbie, Daryl. *Author family collection*

This is a still photo from one of Navy Federal's popular television advertisements. I'm proud of our partnership with advertising agency Fitzgerald & Company. Our highly successful, multimillion-dollar advertising and branding campaign is built around telling stories of service from Navy Federal members' perspectives. Initiated in 2009, the campaign has tripled the organization's brand awareness and preference. *Fitzgerald & Company*

I always enjoyed spending time with students from Thoreau Middle School in Vienna, Virginia. Navy Federal has partnered with the school since 1989, helping to provide the students with mentors, pen pals, and even school supplies and gifts to children in need. *Navy Federal Credit Union*

Here, I'm observing one of our member service representatives at a Navy Federal call center. I frequently listened in on member service calls to learn what kinds of questions the MSRs received and what problems they were asked to solve. *Navy Federal Credit Union*

I joined the new Fredericksburg, Virginia, branch team with a ribbon-cutting ceremony to celebrate the opening of the branch in 2018. I visited dozens of branches every year during my tenure as CEO. *Navy Federal Credit Union*

My former boss, Capt. Pete Hedley, USN, always said, "If you want to know what is going on, go get a haircut." At Navy Federal, if I wanted to gauge the morale of our staff, I would spend time in the cafeteria, chatting with employees. *Navy Federal Credit Union*

For the past twenty-six years, Navy Federal has sponsored a 5K run/walk in Vienna, Virginia, as a way to support the community surrounding our headquarters. I always liked to warm up and run with all my fellow employees. *Navy Federal Credit Union*

I taught some Naval Academy midshipmen the "collector's pose" following the school's Distinguished Graduate Award ceremony in 2017. That year, I was honored with this award for a "lifetime commitment to service, personal character, and distinguished contributions to our nation." The collector's pose signifies "we mean business." *Naval Academy Alumni Association*

Official photo inside the headquarters branch at Navy Federal. *Navy Federal Credit Union*

Chapter 5
REMEMBER THE USS *CONSTITUTION*

The size of Constitution's *armament during her last fight in the War of 1812 was far outmatched by that of her enemy, but the range of her guns far surpassed those of the British. By changing the dynamics of the battle, the* Constitution *fundamentally altered the outcome of the battle.*

The first time I saw the wooden-hulled frigate USS *Constitution* in Boston harbor, I was struck by her vulnerability. The world's oldest commissioned naval vessel still afloat, the *Constitution* was launched in 1797 and still is in active naval service. She has a wooden hull and three masts. In a battle of her day, she would depend upon the wind to help her maneuver, and she had only a wooden hull to protect her and her crew. I thought about the sophisticated defenses that our Navy ships have today—steel hulls, four gas-turbine engines, Global Positioning System–based navigation systems, and an arsenal of weapons. I shook my head thinking about how hard life had been for sailors during the Revolutionary War. Today, *Constitution* is treasured by the Navy, and is lovingly maintained, mostly for tourists and history buffs. But for old salts like me, the ship is a touchstone of sorts— an important relic of our Navy's past.

In February 1815, during the waning days of the War of 1812, *Constitution* was engaged in a battle with two British vessels, the HMS *Cyane* and HMS *Levant*, off the western coast of Africa. Both Royal Navy warships launched a series of broadsides against the U.S. vessel, which was commanded by Capt. Charles Stewart. Although the combined broadsides that the two Royal Navy ships possessed—an accepted measure of weapon power—far outnumbered and outweighed that of their American enemy, *Constitution*'s 24-pound long guns proved to be decisive: her cannonballs had a far superior range. She could hurl her projectiles 1,200 yards, while the *Cyane*'s and the *Levant*'s fusillades could reach only 400 yards. In effect, *Constitution* could inflict significant damage on *Levant* and *Cyane* long before the Royal Navy could fire a shot.

Although the Royal Navy ships had more guns, *Constitution* fired hers at a longer range and outmaneuvered the Royal Navy vessels, serving up a decisive victory for the Americans: both *Cyane* and *Levant* surrendered to *Constitution*.

Captain Stewart and his crew achieved this by positioning their ship so that they would be able to fire the first volley long before their adversaries could—and exploit the advantage that the longer range of their guns afforded them. When the two British ships finally were able to strike back, it was from a much weaker position. In effect, Americans had changed the *dynamics* of the battle in order to ensure a different *outcome*—without having to alter the fundamental structure of the vessel. That historic example has stuck with me. When I look to make changes—in a ship, an organization, a process, or a cultural tradition—I always look for ways to change the dynamics without changing the culture.

When I assumed command of the cruiser USS *Princeton* in 1991, the ship was recovering from significant battle damage. Just a few months before, she had struck two Iraqi mines in the northern Arabian Gulf while deployed in support of Operation Desert Storm. The first mine exploded on the port side, near the stern of the ship, sending shock waves radiating along the ship's keel. It caused a whiplash effect from stern to bow and tossed crew members around for several seconds, throwing the aft lookout into the water and the forward lookout about 10 feet into the air. The quarterdeck of the ship was pushed upward, snapping beams and deckplating above it. The reverberations that rippled through the sea from the first explosion triggered a second mine about 350 yards off the ship's starboard side. It caused a violent cradle-rock—side to side—that almost split the ship in half and flung the crew members around again.

The explosions and concussions ruptured internal fuel tanks and a water main, causing flooding and fires, which the crew was able to contain within about two hours. Three crew members suffered severe injuries and had to be evacuated for treatment. They later received Purple Hearts.

It was amazing that the ship didn't sink. The actions of her commanding officer, Capt. Ted Hontz, and his crew saved USS *Princeton* that day. She returned home to Long Beach, where I assumed command from Captain Hontz. We then entered the Long Beach Naval Shipyard for extensive repairs. But the crew members were damaged as well. They were reeling from the shock of the explosion. You could say they were suffering from post-traumatic stress disorder, or PTSD.

No ship's crew likes being in the shipyard, because it is like working in a house that's under construction—dusty, dirty, and loud. Ships and their crews are supposed to be at sea. Morale can easily suffer during the time that ships undergo repairs and upgrades in the shipyard, but this was different. The *Princeton* was in very bad shape, and so were some of the sailors. In addition, we had to work with a lot of strangers—the shipyard workers—who were in our spaces all day and night all over the ship. For some reason, there always seems to be a somewhat adversarial relationship between the shipyard workers and the ship's crew—not unlike contractors and their clients, I suppose.

I had my work cut out for me to get the ship and the crew back into fighting shape. Imagine if you took over a company or an organization that had just been bombed and employees injured. Your job would be to oversee the reconstruction of the building *and* the rehabilitation of the employees. In 1991, the *Princeton* was just like that. It was a turnaround challenge.

I wanted to change the dynamics of the working relationship between the ship and the shipyard fundamentally, and I had to improve the morale of my men radically.

I focused on getting things fixed. I went to the deck-plates and got to know the shipyard workers—the welders, the plumbers, the electricians, the fabricators, and the carpenters. They considered themselves artisans of their craft and were very proud of their work. They should have been. I wanted to get to know them and have them aligned with my goal—getting the ship out of the shipyard quickly and taking her back to sea.

Our crew hosted picnics for the shipyard workers and we singled out the ones who were doing a really good job by writing thank-you notes to them and their supervisors. With a smile, I would tell all the technical representatives who came aboard to fix our radar and combat systems that I would house and feed them as long as it took to fix the problem and that my crew was ready and willing to assist. I wanted to foster a sense of teamwork and motivate them with encouragement, not criticism. After all, we were somewhat codependent on this project to be successful and, as the saying goes, "You get more with honey than you do with vinegar."

I also wanted to make sure that the crew members were healing after the trauma of the mine strike. I wanted them to stay busy and focused on preparations for the examinations that the ship needed to pass and certifications that she needed to earn. Staying busy and active is as good for the mind as it is for the body, but I also wanted to make sure I spent time one-on-one with every crew member, taking the temperature of each person's emotional well-being. You wouldn't have found me in my office. I spent all my time on the mess decks (where the crew eats), in the engineering spaces, on the bridge, and topside on the weather decks. I wanted to be where the crew was working.

I have always been an advocate of maintaining a healthy work-life balance, even before this term became popular in the business world. I led by example, exercised regularly, and left my work at work so that I could maximize family time, and I wanted my crew to do the same. I also prohibited smoking on board *Princeton*, a few years before the Navy officially banned it in all interior work spaces. I instructed my executive officer to organize lots of social outings for the crew and their families. We went to concerts, sporting events, and theme parks. But I also brought in experts who provided training on nutrition and how to lead healthy lifestyles, and chaplains to facilitate spiritual discussions and deliver sermons.

When it came time for my sailors' evaluations, I provided individual career counseling and publicly recognized them for outstanding performance. When their tours of duty on the ship were nearing an end, I tried to get them the next assignment they wanted. Taking care of the crew's needs was my number-one priority.

We were able to repair the ship in six months and get back to the business of warfighting at sea. And two years later, we received several awards—the Edward Ney Award for food service excellence; the first Blue "E" for supply and logistics excellence; and the Marjorie Sterrett Battleship Fund Award for operational performance and readiness, an annual prize given to the two most battle-ready ships in the Navy. I learned a lot during this command about motivating employees to work better. And I found how to improve the culture of the workplace by changing the dynamics of my relationship with each one of my crewmembers and our collective relationship with the shipyard. I took those lessons to Navy Federal.

When you walk around Navy Federal's headquarters, you will notice lots of dates. Everyone's nameplate includes one—the date that he or she began working for the company. It is not unusual to see dates from the 1990s, 1980s, or even 1970s; long careers at Navy Federal are common. Also common are employees who have lots of family members who work at Navy Federal. One of the most legendary is Nel Ignacio, a member service representative at Navy Federal who worked at our call center for more than twenty years until she retired in 2012. She has twenty-six family members who have worked at Navy Federal and she personally recruited another twenty-five or more friends to work with us. She educated me early on about the importance of the Navy Federal family. I met her within the first few weeks of my arrival at the company. She was a petite Filipino woman with a large presence. She stuck her hand out to shake mine and introduced herself to me. A week later, I ran into her again in the hall and she tested me, asking: "What's my name?" I stumbled nervously until she reminded me: "It's Nel.

Don't ever forget!" We both laughed, but we both knew that she meant it.

Many years later, I was out in the field meeting with branch personnel. One of them asked me, "Is it true that you know every employee's name?" I had to be honest. I told her that I don't know everyone's name, but I work hard to learn as many as I can. (I also told her that it helps that branch personnel wear name tags.) But it says a lot about a company where the *perception* is that this is a place where everybody knows your name. It's a family.

Like every family, however, Navy Federal has its quirks. When I came to work here, it was already a very big company with a strong and ingrained culture. There was a passion for the mission of serving those who serve, but in many ways we *reflected* the people we served. The Navy is a big bureaucracy with a distinct "budget mentality." At Navy Federal, we had adopted the culture of the Navy budget, and it was hindering growth.

In the Navy's budget, you have a top line that Congress gives you and you have to make the budget work with that top line. In the Navy, the most expensive cost you have is people. If you add more people to your budget, you can't buy more ships, and then you have the people in your budget forever. To avoid this, I would see the Navy try to do more with less. Navy leaders had a budget and would try to do more things than they actually had the money to do. They would try to cram it all in and they would never give anything up.

Back in the 1980s, the Navy wanted to develop an improved gun projectile for its ship-based gun mounts. The project was called a Semi-Active Laser-Guided Projectile, or SAL-GP. The Navy poured out millions of dollars trying to bring this concept to the fleet. As of today, it still has not delivered a single round. The program should have been killed a long time ago. It is the same with Navy bases. The Navy has more bases than it could ever possibly use. Many of them have outlived their missions, yet they have not been closed. We have dozens of mothballed ships that have been sitting around for years, rusty and unused, which also costs the Navy millions of dollars a year. The Navy won't get rid of them to free up resources for things that are more important. (In some cases, it's Congress—not the Navy—that refuses to get rid of them. But the impact is the same.)

Following budget practices such as these means that the Navy does not put its money where it will get the most return. By contrast, Navy Federal is not constrained by a top line budget number as the Navy is because we have the capacity to generate more revenue. We can increase our top line. We can make investments that will generate even more revenue. We are also not dependent on the whims of Congress. If we manage risk appropriately, there is no limit to what we can achieve.

Navy Federal traditionally has been a conservative company, and that has paid off in some ways. The management has always been cautious about how many people it added to the payroll; as a result, Navy Federal has never laid anyone off. It also has been worried about other costs that can't be covered in an economic downturn or in the face of an unexpected reduction in our revenue. Cutting spending for any reason usually produces some adverse consequences. When you suppress the number of people in your budget, suddenly you have forty-five-minute wait-times on the phone. You have teller lines stretching out the door. You have a mortgage waiting-list of three months. Every proposed people investment is met with the comment, "Well, then, what are you planning to cut in order to afford this?" Every new idea is evaluated according to its impact on the budget.

I knew we had to change our mentality, or what I called the family "dynamics" at Navy Federal, but I did not want to change the family's traditions or values. One of the first places that needed some attention was the collections department.

When I took over at Navy Federal, I met with all the department heads to get to know them, understand their business, and identify their needs. Collections was at the top of the list. It was not the sexiest part of our business, and the group's morale was low, after a difficult time serving under a different leader. A new department head, Debbie Calder, had just been moved in to revive this vital part of our organization, and she had her hands full. I started visiting the collections team about once a week, wandering around and meeting the collectors and asking lots of questions. At first, the team members were a bit suspicious of my motives. Why was the CEO hanging around the collections department? But they soon learned that I wasn't there to play gotcha. I was there to learn about their business and to make sure they had the resources they needed to do their job well. Our lending department could increase our booked revenue, but the company had to be able to collect the money before it could use it. Collections is a critical *revenue* center for us, but it had been treated like a necessary-but-burdensome *cost* center. I made a point of telling everyone at Navy Federal how important collections was to the organization's revenue and its membership. Our collectors help our members work through their financial issues so that they can continue to make payments on their loans and credit card balances. This leads to success for everyone. If you can not collect your revenue, you will have less money to lend to other members. In fact, sometimes the collectors help our members just when they need it the most.

I was reminded of this when one of our collectors told me a funny story. We were celebrating his five-year anniversary at the organization. I held small employee forums for those celebrating their five-year, twenty-five-year, thirty-year, and thirty-five-year anniversaries—to recognize the employees and their contributions to Navy Federal. But it also was a way for me to get to know a wide variety of our team members and to listen and learn from them about our great company. At one of these meetings, the collector told me about a time he was stopped by a local police officer just a few blocks from our company headquarters. Our corporate offices are located in a residential neighborhood, and apparently our employee had been speeding. The collector admitted to the police officer, "You're right—mea culpa. I'm sorry I was speeding, but I was going to be late to a meeting at Navy Federal." (Of course, he thought to himself, "Now, I'm definitely going to be late!") The officer asked him what he did at Navy Federal. Collectors never know what kind of response they will get when they share their job duties with strangers, so he looked warily at the police-man and said, "I'm a collector." The officer then told him a story. Recently, his wife had lost her job and was having trouble making payments on several loans that she had with us. Our collections department had helped her restructure her loans so that she could begin to repay them when she got her new job. This allowed her to hold her head up high and was a source of much-needed relief for her. The officer then said, "I'm not going to give you a ticket today, but I want you to keep working in collections at Navy Federal."

Collectors became some of my favorite people. I talked about the importance of the collections department to the overall financial health of our company at small employee gatherings and big town hall meetings—every chance I had. The next year was a very good year for collections, and, consequently, it was a very good year for our overall revenue. As a result, we were able to give all our employees a really good bonus.

When I asked a branch manager at a town hall meeting if he knew why everyone was getting a good bonus, he said, "Because we're doing really well in business." I reminded him: "You can thank your collectors for getting you the bonus this year."

The collections employees heard about that comment through the grapevine. Their morale skyrocketed. They created lapel buttons for everyone at Navy Federal that said, "Have you hugged your collector today?" The Navy Federal family was intact, but the family attitude toward collectors was changed forever.

While most of the company's revenue growth has been organic, we acquired a few smaller credit unions while I was CEO. But we didn't call them acquisitions. We intentionally called them mergers because we wanted the acquired credit union to feel as though it was *partnering* with us, not being gobbled up. Although we did absorb the employees into our operations and changed the brand name of their branches, we wanted them to become part of our family and change the dynamics of theirs.

In 2010, a small credit union based in southern California and Nevada called USA Federal Credit Union was about to go under. The mortgage crisis and the recession had hit these two states especially hard. The regulators told them they would have to merge with another credit union or the government would take them over. We made a bid for them because they were strategically located in San Diego, where we had a lot of members and potential members. They had 19 branches, 200 employees, and 60,000 members. We thought that the merger would be good for our business as well as for theirs, since we could absorb their losses.

But apparently a lot of their employees were apprehensive about the merger and what it would mean for their jobs. I'm sure it was fear of the unknown, or maybe it was fear that a very big organization was about to swallow them up or lay them off. Indeed, there was some controversy in the credit union industry at the time because many of the big ones had acquired smaller ones and their managements had immediately laid off a large number of the workers. We didn't do that. In fact, we have never had a layoff in our company's history. I wanted to ease those fears and change their perceptions of credit union management.

I flew out to San Diego and hosted a big town hall meeting for all their employees, at which USA Federal's CEO introduced me. "We're going to welcome you into the Navy Federal family," I said, with a big smile. "You're going to be a full part of our team, but you're probably going to have a lot more work to do because we're busy and you're going to be, too." I also told them I was going to give all of them a signing bonus if they wanted to work for us and that I would be restoring their 401(k) matches. Then we passed out Navy Federal gym bags to everyone, a subtle reminder that, while we valued their skills, we also valued their health and knew they had a life outside of their jobs.

Getting out ahead of the merger to quell any rumors and dispel employee fears was the single most important thing we could have done to get the relationship between USA Federal employees and Navy Federal management off to a good start. We wanted to reassure them in person and introduce them to a new type of management—one that was open, transparent, and made *them* a priority. It had an electrifying effect and made the transition relatively seamless. Most of USA Federal's employees are still working at Navy Federal, and have enthusiastically embraced our culture. In fact, many have moved up the leadership ranks in the organization—eventually becoming branch managers, regional managers, and a vice president for branch operations.

Foot Stomper

Having a company that feels like family can be a double-edged sword. The benefits of Navy Federal's culture are obvious: people feel at home here and know that their coworkers and their boss have their backs. But there are cultural norms and habits that families develop, some of which help your organization and some of which don't. Both in the Navy and at Navy Federal, treating people well and reminding them that we value their contributions can make all the difference. In our case, it changed the family dynamics.

The War of 1812 battle between the American warship USS *Constitution* and the British vessels HMS *Cyane* and HMS *Levant* proved that changing the dynamics of a battle can fundamentally alter its outcome. Captain Stewart did not need a different ship to win the battle. All he had to do was take a different approach. Sometimes, as a leader, you don't need a new organization to improve your results. You just need to change its dynamics.

Chapter 6
CREATE A SAFE HARBOR

In the Navy you want your crew to be honest with you. As I always say, conditions are neither bad nor good. You cannot deal with a situation unless you create a culture in which these conditions can be discussed openly and honestly—without any adverse repercussions. You must create a "safe harbor" for your crew.

On the evening of November 8, 1998, I was in my cabin on the aircraft carrier USS *Enterprise* after dinner, catching up on some paperwork. We were three days into a six-month deployment to the Persian Gulf and were being sent to take part in Operation Desert Fox, a major bombing campaign that targeted Iraqi military and security installations. As the battle group commander, I was in charge, preparing to steam east toward the Mediterranean. We needed to be on site in the Persian Gulf by the middle of December. We didn't have much time to waste. We were on a war footing.

Every thirty seconds or so, I could hear the ear-piercing sound of an aircraft landing on the deck above my head. The noise came from the "arrested" landings of military jets onto the flight deck, the aircraft carrier's runway. For carrier operations, each plane has a hook hanging from its tail. As the aircraft approaches the flight deck, the pilot pushes the throttle ahead to increase speed. When the plane loses altitude and skims across the carrier, just inches above the deck, the tailhook catches a cable that has been stretched across the flight deck. This causes the plane to slam onto the deck and immediately stop in its tracks. The arresting gear, as the cable system is called, enables pilots to land with very little runway space. To take off from the flight deck, the planes are catapulted, as if they had been propelled from a slingshot. (The procedure actually is called a "cat shot.") This, too, saves runway space. In order to be good at it, military pilots must practice this touch-and-go process continually. It takes some time at sea before you get used to the violent sounds of the landings and takeoffs, but they are part of the daily—and nighttime—rhythm of life on board an aircraft carrier.

On our third night of flight operations, I heard something very different. It was more of a metal-on-metal sound, followed by an explosion. I immediately knew that there had been an accident. I raced up to the bridge and saw an S-3 Viking jet fighter on fire, surrounded by flight-deck personnel. They were all trained in firefighting, so they were able to extinguish the fire quickly. The wreckage of an EA-6B Prowler jet aircraft was cocked forward in the ocean below, slowly sinking. The ship had sounded the general quarters alarm, alerting all crew members to an accident and summoning emergency teams to the flight deck to help.

What had happened that night was that the EA-6B Prowler jet was cleared to land on the carrier deck while an S-3 Viking was still in the landing zone, blocking it. The Prowler should have been "waved off"—that is, instructed not to land and ordered to circle around for another approach until the Viking had cleared the flight deck. There is a careful choreography that takes place to prevent collisions of this kind, but it is not foolproof. In this case, the system broke down. The Prowler had no way to see the S-3 Viking that was parked in its way until it was too late. It was a tragic error.

All four of the Prowler's crew members and the two in the S-3 Viking ejected from their planes. One of the Viking crew members was dangling from the antenna of the carrier's island and the other was quickly rescued from the frigid ocean below. I went to the medical bay to check on their injuries, which were not life-threatening. We sent them back home to a hospital, just to ensure that they received extra medical attention.

But the four Prowler aviators were not so fortunate. Only one body out of the four was found and recovered. After a twenty-four-hour search, the other three were presumed dead. It was a devastating loss.

The next day I decided to call each one of the victims' families to express my condolences. I thought it was important that the families get a report directly from the admiral who was on board the *Enterprise* at the time of the accident. This is unusual for an admiral to do, and it was gut-wrenching, but I felt that it was the right thing to do.

I was also assigned to lead the official inquiry into the cause of the accident. In most cases, the tendency is to tell everyone, including families, that we can't talk about the investigation because—well, it's under investigation. But I'm also a big believer in telling crew members and families everything I know. I'm very honest and transparent with everyone. I give them the unvarnished truth. It may be bad news or good news, but it's the truth. It is what it is.

I told the families everything I knew about the accident and invited them to ask me any questions they wanted—and I promised straight answers. I created a figurative "safe harbor," where both the families and I could talk openly and honestly. I said that it was a dark night and there was a fouled deck. The Prowler just did not see the

Viking parked in its way until it was too late. The Prowler crew members had done nothing wrong. They had followed through on all they were asked to do. Others on the *Enterprise* had failed them. It was an honest mistake, but individuals were going to be held accountable for their actions that night. It was a chain of human errors—a breakdown in judgment—that had caused the tragedy. My investigation report said the same thing.

People *were* held accountable for the accident. We learned many lessons from this tragedy. The families needed to hear this information just as much as the Navy leadership in the Pentagon did. I told the aviators' families the truth, as hard as it was for them to hear. And I told them what the Navy was going to do to prevent it from happening again.

As I always say, I want to hear the truth, even though I may not always *like* the truth. I want to hear the truth, even if it isn't what I really *want* to hear. I know that the families of these sailors felt the same way.

I faced a similar situation when I was the CO of USS *Princeton* and we were performing a missile exercise off the coast of southern California. We were practicing shooting down aerial targets, but we were using live fire. It was expensive live fire. Each one of our targets cost $250,000. I was sitting in my command chair in the combat information center (CIC) on board the ship and gave the order, "Batteries release. You're cleared to fire on the incoming target." But nothing happened. Instead of that familiar *swoosh!* of a missile exiting the tube, I heard the roar of the missed target as it passed over the ship.

Instead of getting angry or becoming defensive or accusatory, I quickly called a meeting of the CIC team. As I walked to the wardroom, I thought about how anxious everyone would be about our failure to engage a very expensive target and what kind of tone I should adopt. I believed it was important for me to set a relaxed, confident tone so that we could discover what went wrong. I entered the room, and everyone stood up at attention and avoided my gaze. I told them to sit down. I looked around and saw a lot of chagrined faces. Some even looked scared. There was a lot of nervous energy bouncing around, but you could hear a pin drop. I said calmly, "Okay. We have to figure out what happened because, if not, we can't fix it." We had three more targets to engage that day and we needed to get the problem fixed ASAP. Way in the back of the room, one hand slowly floated up. A very young third-class petty officer cleared his throat and poked his head between two other faces in the room. He said, "Captain, I had my fire switch in the wrong position. I had it in the 'off' position." To which I said, "Thank you. You will be ready next time, right?" He said, "Absolutely, sir." "Okay, then," I replied, "let's get back to work." I had created a safe harbor for the crew, an opportunity to admit an honest mistake with no penalty. Our next three attempts were direct hits on the target. My message was clear: no reprisals for honest mistakes. It is what it is. We can't fix the problem unless we talk openly about it. We can't fix the problem unless we create a safe harbor for the crew to tell us the truth.

In the same vein, I always felt that it was important for the crew to feel comfortable to come to me anytime, unsolicited, with questions or concerns or good ideas. I tried to repeat that message early and often. I have seen too many COs retreat to their cabins, behind closed doors, and spend all their time on the computer and on the phone. They lose touch. In addition to spending a lot of time on the deckplates, I always kept the door to my sea cabin open. I remember one afternoon when we were in port, a young sailor was giving his visiting parents a tour of our ship. As he walked by my cabin where I was doing some paperwork, he said to his parents, "This is the captain's cabin. He has an open-door policy." He felt as though he could walk in anytime to chat with me about anything, and that's the way I wanted the crew to feel.

At Navy Federal, I expected the same kind of honesty and openness from all my employees, just as I was taught in military leadership training at the Naval Academy. We were told then that there were four acceptable answers to any question: "Yes." "No." "No excuses." And "I don't know, but I will find out." The first two are obvious, but the third is more nuanced. What it means is that, if you have made a mistake, you must own up to it and you must *own* it as well. In other words, you must be prepared to accept the consequences for your mistake. And number four? If you don't have all the answers, that's okay, too. As I frequently say, "It's okay not to know all the answers. But 'Hail Marys' are *not* okay." In other words, I won't tolerate guessing. I want to know what the actual facts are so we can deal with the situation. Why? Because, as a decision-maker, I expect you to give me accurate information. In the Navy, if my navigator told me that we were on a safe course to clear the harbor and we weren't, we could well have run aground—a serious situation for a warship. It was far better for him to say, "I don't know, but I'm finding out ASAP."

I remember a staff meeting that I held early during my tenure at Navy Federal. A manager and her boss were in the meeting. I started asking some probing questions to the manager, who worked in human resources, about some of our recruiting and hiring practices. The manager kept dodging the questions and shooting nervous glances at her boss at the other end of the table. I knew what was going on, and it frustrated me. I sought out the manager after the meeting for a short one-on-one conversation. I said to her, "Look, you weren't being forthright with me when I was asking you questions. And I wasn't getting the full picture." She said, "Well, my boss was in the room." I got it. She didn't want to put her boss on report. But I quickly told her that she was wasting my time. "I don't have time to play 'stump the monkey,'" I said. "I develop a picture of what is going on based on what you tell me. If I don't get the full story, it can be dangerous because I will make decisions with incomplete information." I needed for her to tell me the truth, not what she and her boss thought I *wanted* to hear. She promised me that it would never happen again. That manager is still with us, and she has been promoted several times, becoming one of our leaders in human resources. I also talked to her boss and told her that there had better not be any consequences for any of her employees being totally honest with me.

I had another experience on a visit to some branches in Pensacola soon after I became CEO. One of the branch managers picked my wife, Debbie, and me up and was escorting us to the branches around town. I started asking her some very pointed questions about Pensacola operations and branch performance. She had a look of horror in her eyes, and I could tell what she was thinking: *I don't have time to talk to the branch operations staff back at headquarters to find out what I should tell him.* I smiled and said, "Okay, I'm going to make this easy for you. I'm going to ask you questions, and you're going to give me the answers—to the best of your knowledge and in your honest opinion." At that point Debbie said, "Michelle, he really wants to know what you have to say. He wants to hear your thoughts. It's the way he learns." We all laughed and she said, "Okay, okay, I'll talk."

The point is that I really *did* want to hear the truth from everyone. It took awhile for everyone at Navy Federal to realize that I really meant it. It took awhile for them to get used to having the company's president stop them in the cafeteria line, the teller counter, the hallway, and the elevator, asking for their opinions on all kinds of things. It took awhile for all our people to understand that I really *wanted* their viewpoints.

When I became the CEO of Navy Federal, the chief financial officer was reporting to the chief operating officer rather than directly to me. I changed that because I felt I needed to be closer to the numbers. The CFO, Lauren Lloyd, was an accountant—a real pro at the numbers. She would present her monthly figures to me and she wouldn't mince words—something I really appreciated. She told it like it was. Sometimes they were good numbers and sometimes they were not-so-good numbers.

On occasion, Lauren would push me and our board of directors to make a decision that we really didn't want to make. In 2010, there were some new accounting rules that forced us to book all our estimated troubled debt in one year. In other words, we had to estimate how many bad loans we had at that moment and how many we projected we were going to have over the next several years. We were forced to write off all that debt in one year, even though many of the bad loans were just estimates. It was a big figure for us to swallow.

When Lauren met with me to discuss this accounting change and the impact on Navy Federal's net income, I said, "You know, I really don't want to do this." Maybe I was putting my head in the sand, but I tabled the topic and we moved on to other items. At the end of the meeting, I leaned way back in my chair and stretched and noticed that Lauren was staring at me. I asked her, "Did you get what you need at this meeting?" "No," she replied forcefully. "I need to make an adjustment to our balance sheet report. It is what it is, Cutler." I smiled and said, "I get it. Go do it."

I told her early on that I would thank her for every number she brought to me because I never wanted her to be afraid of giving me bad numbers or bad news. She appreciated this and always gave me an accurate assessment of where the organization was financially. Shortly before she retired, she brought me a plaque that I still keep on my desk. "It is what it is," it says.

Foot Stomper

Many leaders talk about the importance of open communications, but few actually demand it. Not many CEOs really want to hear the unvarnished truth from their employees on the front lines of their business. Some punish their employees for offering up the truth. Yet, it is imperative that we hear it. Leaders should never penalize someone who gives them a straight answer. Similarly, employees should always expect straight answers from their leaders. Always carefully consider honest mistakes. We all learn from them—leaders and teammates alike. Creating a safe harbor in which to talk about them is the first step.

Chapter 7

BE THE CAPTAIN OF YOUR OWN SHIP

As one of my first and favorite commanders said to me, "Do the right thing, and I'll back you up all the way." If you have carefully chosen and trained your crew members for the task at hand, you should trust them to do the job well—to "do the right thing." It is your ship. You are the captain.

Out in the Sea of Japan, the days underway are long and the nights are even longer. The sea has almost no tides because the small Japanese islands around its perimeter almost totally enclose this body of water. It has no major islands or bays or capes. The scenery can get a bit boring. When I was invited to take a helicopter ride over to the aircraft carrier USS *Midway* to have lunch with the admiral and other COs in our carrier group, I was excited about going. I was the CO of the frigate USS *Bronstein*, but I jumped ship that day, leaving my very capable executive officer, or XO, Lt. Cdr. Bruce Van Belle, in charge during my absence.

While I was gone, the XO had to perform some fairly complicated tasks, including an underway replenishment, or UNREP—the procedure used to refuel ships at sea. This one took place while *Bronstein* and an oiler were both moving along briskly. The XO had to maneuver *Bronstein* into place next to the oiler. Both ships had to be steaming ahead in parallel, close together—and avoid colliding—while the fuel hose was passed from the oiler to *Bronstein*'s crew. Then fuel was pumped through the line to *Bronstein*. It is a dangerous operation, but being able to refuel while at sea is vital; it enables ships to remain underway for longer periods of time.

The admiral had invited the COs of all the ships in the vicinity to the *Midway* for lunch. At the wardroom table, my fellow COs were surprised to hear that I had left the ship during an UNREP, with the XO fully in charge. If something had gone wrong in my absence, I probably would have lost my job. I was essentially missing a critical evolution, but I meant what I said. "Well, I trust him," I told the group at the admiral's lunch, and I wanted to demonstrate my confidence in him—both to Bruce and to the entire crew.

When I returned to the *Bronstein* and sat in my captain's chair on the bridge, Bruce came over and said to me, "Captain, as I was making my approach to the oiler, I turned around to see what you thought of the way I was driving the ship, and I realized you weren't there. It was quite a moment for me." It was the ultimate thank you from him. "I trust you implicitly," I told him, "and you will be captain of your own ship someday."

That same trust had been given to me by one of my first mentors, a crusty old Navy commander named Sydney "Sai" Manning. When I became CO of the oceangoing tug USS *Molala*, I had five years' experience in the Navy. He had thirty-two. He was a former enlisted sailor who had earned a submarine combat patrol pin in World War II. He was known as "the saltiest dog in the Navy." He was my squadron commodore, overseeing my ship and six others. He sat me down, with a pouch of chewing tobacco inside his cheek, a cigar sticking out of the side of his mouth, and his arms outstretched, and told me: "Cutler, I want you to have a set of 'you-know-whats' *this big*, and I'll back you up all the way." I was taken aback, but I instantly liked him. He was direct, plain-speaking, down-to-earth, forceful, and decisive. I had clear instructions.

Later, when a Navy chaplain visited the ship to check on the morale and welfare of my crew, he opined that it had been his experience that bachelor officers like me were particularly hard on their crews since they did not understand married life and sailors. Then he asked me for a sea cabin where he could hold counseling sessions. I said, "Well, chaplain, it's been my experience that chaplains who sit in an office and wait for the crew to come see them aren't worth a damn." The chaplain, who was a commander, just looked at me—a mere lieutenant. After an awkwardly long pause, he gave me a pleasant "good day" and proceeded to do his job without coming back to the office. He walked around and talked to the crew.

When he reported back to Commander Manning, he said the morale aboard USS *Molala* was sky-high. In his observations, the crew had a sense of purpose, and they felt valued. But, he also reported that the shaft alley could use a new paint job. To which Commander Manning pulled his cigar out of his mouth, pointed it at the chaplain, and said, "Chaplain, you worry about the goddam preaching and I'll worry about the goddamn shaft alley." It's what I call the Sai Manning Factor: "You do the right thing and I will back you up all the way." Manning cared about the condition of the paint in the shaft alley, but he cared about the crew's morale a whole lot more.

Soon after, one of my officers on *Molala* told me that his wife was expecting a baby, their first. We were scheduled to be underway when his baby was due. I told him, "Take some time off. Be there for your wife. You are not indispensable—no one is. We'll be fine in your absence." He stayed home while the ship got underway. He was not on board when we were directed to complete an emergency tow of a large amphibious ship. This was his area of expertise, and he would have supervised the evolution much more efficiently, but we completed the task without him and he was able to witness the birth of his son. Again, Commander Manning approved. We got the job done and I took care of my crew member.

At Navy Federal I wanted to give my employees the same sense of trust and empowerment that I had enjoyed with Sai Manning. We decided to give all our member service representatives the authority to return banking fees when and where they felt it was appropriate. What's more, they were authorized to "own the answer," so that they wouldn't have to pass the member off to another representative or a supervisor to get a question answered or a problem solved. Under the new system their goal would be to provide "one-touch resolution."

This type of latitude fosters an environment where employees feel empowered to make many decisions on their own. One of my branch managers, Carlos Perez, told me, "Here at Navy Federal, there is no black and white. We are more of a battleship gray. We are not tied to a particular procedure. We *do have* policies and procedures, but we are empowered to make exceptions." When these employees are making exceptions to do the right thing by our members, I back them up all the way.

Carlos related that one of his newer employees, Sylvia Jackson, was working with a member who had been charged an overdraft fee of $25. This member had been with Navy Federal for twenty-five years and had never before been overdrawn. She wanted to discuss the fee with a branch manager. Sylvia recognized the fact that this was a loyal member. She wanted to refund the fee to the member, so she came to ask Carlos for permission. At her previous employer, this type of refund would have required a supervisor's approval. Carlos said to her, "Go for it. You don't need my permission. I just ask that you note it in her file, so that the next employee who works with her knows what we did." Sylvia continues to be amazed at the authority she has. "I mean, at my former bank, we were only allowed to issue one fee refund a year. Here, I can issue a cashier's check of up to $250,000 without anyone's approval. Plus, we are not required to push products. At my other job, even if a customer had ten credit cards you were required to try to sell them another one. The pressure to meet your sales quotas was very stressful and felt wrong. At Navy Federal, it is different. We really *spoil* our members." Sylvia's comments are indicative of the value we place on doing the right thing for our members. Sylvia is right. We do spoil our members. And they like it.

A few years ago, an active-duty service member, his pregnant wife, and their two-year-old daughter visited our Portsmouth, Virginia, branch to cash a check from the Navy–Marine Corps Relief Society, a nonprofit that provides short-term and emergency financial assistance to sailors and Marines. Erin Wilcox, the member service representative who was helping the family, learned that they had just lost everything—including three family dogs—in a tragic house fire. Erin is also part of a Navy family— her husband is a sailor. She immediately offered to give them some of her daughter's toddler clothes and toys. The next day, she brought in an entire cart of clothes, toys, and books. Even more, her husband donated several of his Navy uniforms for the member, and he even took the time to sew on the rank insignia for him. Erin said it was just one Navy family helping out another.

More recently, the executive who runs our member service centers sent me a recording of a call that came in from a member. "Hello. Can I talk to a supervisor, please?" the member asked. The member service representative suggested, "Why, sure, ma'am. But perhaps *I* could help you?" "Well," she said, "there is no issue. I'm about to cry. Yesterday, I called to make my car payment and I was telling this girl how horrible my day was. I even sprained my ankle. Today, I get home and she had flowers delivered to my house. I've never had anyone be so kind to me. I'm blown away. I love Navy Federal. I just want to tell her supervisor." The best part of this story was that Kanessa Moyer, the member service representative who sent the flowers, did not ask anyone for permission to do it and she did not toot her own horn when she did it. It was just the right thing to do. In fact, we give all our member service representatives $100 every month to do the right thing by our members. In addition to returning fees, they can also use that budget to offer members little delights, such as flowers, chocolate, or gift cards.

Some employees are intimidated by this authority at first—especially new employees who come to work for Navy Federal from other financial institutions. They are afraid of making mistakes. But I told everyone at every opportunity that I had to engage with employees and managers that there *never* would be penalties for trying to do the right thing.

I also empowered our employees to refuse service to people whom I call "abusive" members. Our employees bend over backward to serve our members. They should be treated with courtesy and respect. I wanted all of them to know that I had their backs. Although we place the highest priority on member service, that doesn't mean that we have to do business with everyone—especially if they repeatedly mistreat Navy Federal employees. Navy Federal employees have the authority to deal with that kind of behavior as well.

I could always count on Nel Ignacio to make the right call on abusive members. Frequently, I would wander down to the member services department at headquarters to get her unvarnished opinion on a decision I was making and what impact it would have on our average member. She could take the pulse of these members because she was on the phone with them all the time. When I arrived at her desk on this particular morning, she was on the phone with a member—an irate one. I decided to wait for her to finish her call. There was an empty cubicle behind hers, so I sat down for a few minutes. She did not know I was sitting behind her. As I listened to her side of the conversation, I could hear her say over and over again, "I'm sorry you have had this experience, sir. I'm going to try to fix this problem with your account"—followed by a minute of silence. "Yes, sir. I am listening to you and I hear you. I'm going to give you my full name, my direct line, and my employee number. I'm making you a promise that I will fix this problem with your account before the end of the day." Another minute of silence. Then, I saw her stretch out her arm and hold the phone away from her ear. From my perch about four feet away, I could hear this member yelling and screaming at her and he was using all kinds of profanity. He was upset about his mortgage refinance rate. One more time, Nel said, "Sir, I'm going to fix the problem with your account. Please give me the time today to do so." The member sighed and said, "Okay," and hung up. I saw Nel set down the phone and get up and stretch, at which point she saw me behind her. She was startled, and started laughing nervously.

I said to her, "Nel, I appreciate how calm you remained with that guy, but you do not have to take heat like that from a member. I hope you know that you have my permission to close his account. No one should have to put up with that." As was typical with Nel, she insisted that she was not going to close his account. "Don't worry, Cutler. I can handle him and I'm going to help him."

I was proud of her for keeping her cool with this obnoxious man, and I applauded her dedication to providing really good member service. I would not have had that kind of patience with a member like that. But I wanted her to know that no one has to tolerate a verbally abusive member. And when the abuse turns into a threat, there is no debate.

One afternoon at one of our branches in Tampa, a big, burly guy came in to cash a check. He was in a hurry. The teller, who was probably half his size, noticed on his file that he had a delinquent loan. She told him she couldn't cash his check until he worked with Navy Federal on a payment plan for this loan. He refused and demanded that his check be cashed immediately. The teller stood her ground and politely told him no. She reiterated that he needed to deal with the loan first. He said, "I'm not going to do that right now and, you know, I come from a profession where we hurt people." The teller's eyes got really big, but she remained firm: "Well, that's fine, sir, but we can't cash your check and we can't continue to do business with you until you deal with your delinquent loan." He left in a huff.

Shaken, the teller alerted a staff member from Navy Federal's security force, who called the member a few minutes later on his cell phone and told him he was banned from ever again stepping foot into a Navy Federal facility. Now, some companies might not have given the teller the authority to refuse service to a member. She might have been required to call in a supervisor to deal with that bully. But not at Navy Federal. On my tombstone will be: "Cutler Dawson came to Navy Federal and started the Abusive Member Policy." I value our members, but I will not tolerate abuse toward our employees. We wanted that teller to know that I was watching and we have her back. She was doing the right thing.

One of the mantras I used in talks with my branch managers was: "You are the captain of your ship." Branches are something like a ship out in a big ocean. They might be far away from headquarters and some distance away from other Navy Federal support. I only gave our employees general guidance—not hard-and-fast rules and regulations. I told them I just expected them to do the right thing and take care of their people and serve the members in the right way. They knew that they had the authority to make their own decisions and I would have their backs—as long as they were doing the right thing. For many employees out in the field, it was liberating.

Even so, this concept can take some time to permeate through any large organization, especially one as historically conservative and heavily regulated as a financial institution. On one of my branch visits to New London, Connecticut, I popped into the manager's office to say hello to her. She was sitting with a member—a young, single woman. The member was crying because she had just been denied a car loan. She was a waitress and, although she had the sufficient income to get the loan, a significant portion of her monthly income came from tips and this income wasn't considered a reliable source. The branch manager had a really pained look on her face. She wanted to help this member because this hardworking waitress really needed a car to get to work, but when the branch manager had sent the loan application back to headquarters for approval, the lending department looked at the numbers and turned her down. The waitress did not meet our rules for a debt-to-income ratio because we would not factor in her tips.

I looked the young woman in the eye and told her that I was personally approving her loan. She was overwhelmed. And then the branch manager started to cry, too. What I told our lending team back at headquarters later was that we have to give the branch staff a vote in the lending decision. That branch manager is on the front lines of our business. She is the one making the human contact with our members every day. She was the one who would be checking on that member to ensure that the loan is repaid. Her vote is probably the most important.

Another time I was in a branch in Fort Stewart, Georgia, at the close of business. There was one couple left in the building—an Army first lieutenant and his wife. We asked the woman to snap a picture of me with all the branch employees. "Of course," she said. After she took the photo, I asked her, "I'm curious. What brought you into the branch today?" "Oh," she said, "I was trying to get a $3,000 personal loan." I asked her if she got the loan, and she said that it had been disapproved. "What was the loan for, if you don't mind my asking?" "Well," she said, "I need the cash to fly to Kansas to get custody of my children." *Oh, geez*, I thought. "I'm the president of Navy Federal and I'm giving your loan my personal approval," I said. "Come back tomorrow and we'll have the $3,000 check for you." She started crying and hugged me.

After she left, I said to the manager, "Let's look up her record and see if I made a good loan decision." Well, I hadn't. Her credit was terrible. The lending department back at headquarters was not going to be happy with me. But the loan was only $3,000, and she needed it for an urgent family need. I told the branch manager that when the customer returned to pick up the check, she should tell her that I was really happy to give her the loan but she needed to come through for me and pay it back. And, you know, that manager monitored the loan and checked in with that member for the next couple of years, and she paid every penny back—every penny. Sometimes, those folks at headquarters just needed to be reminded that our branch teams should and do have the authority to do the right thing—and that they can and will be held accountable for those decisions. And, when our employees do the right thing by our members, we at headquarters should back them up all the way.

When I sent one of my rising-star executives, Debbie Calder, to Pensacola to run our growing Navy Federal operational center down there, she came to see me—notebook and pen in hand—to ask me, specifically, what my goals were for her. She was expecting a long laundry list of specifics. Instead, I told her that I had two objectives for her: first, I wanted her to take the things from headquarters that she thought worked really well and implement them in Pensacola, and, second, I wanted her to find new and better ways to do business in Pensacola and tell us at headquarters what and how she did it, so we could implement them here. Eleven years later, our Pensacola operation has become a shining example of how to build a business *and* contribute to the regional economy. We are on track to create up to 10,000 new jobs and invest $1 billion in capital by 2026. Sai Manning would be proud of Debbie Calder.

For me, it was all about culture and delegation—preserving what's good about the culture at headquarters, but giving Debbie enough leeway to chart her own course. She was going to be her own CO, the captain of her own ship, and all she needed was someone like Sai Manning to remind her that if she did the right thing, I would back her up all the way.

Foot Stomper

I have a framed picture of Sai Manning on the side table right next to my office door. You can't miss looking into his eyes when you leave my office. And, of course, he is holding a cigar in his official portrait. He is a daily reminder that employees at Navy Federal are the captains of their own ships, and that if they do the right thing, I will back them up all the way.

Chapter 8

LISTEN LIKE A SONAR TECH

To understand the needs of your business, you have to have more than just excellent hearing. You also must have the curiosity to listen carefully. You have to listen to understand—just as Navy sonar technicians do.

In the wildly popular book and movie, *The Hunt for Red October*, a Soviet navy captain in command of the fictional *Red October*, described as one of the USSR's Typhoon-class nuclear missile submarines, makes a secret decision to defect to the United States. This newest of Soviet submarines supposedly has a "caterpillar" drive, making it extremely stealthy and virtually undetectable. Captain Marko Ramius orders his crew members to proceed briskly to the Atlantic coast of the United States under the guise that they will be conducting missile drills.

Fearing the threat that *Red October* poses, but unaware of Captain Ramius' intentions, the U.S. Navy sets out to find the boat, and a savvy sonar technician in the American attack submarine USS *Dallas* plays a pivotal role in the story. The sonarman has excellent hearing and is a master listener, which comes in handy when he is trying to find a single submarine in thousands of miles of ocean.

Detecting a "very faint low-frequency rumble—or swish," Sonarman Second Class Ronald Jones records it and runs it through a computer system, which identifies the sound as "magma displacement"—nothing manmade. Petty Officer Jones, trained to discern sounds of mammals mating and sediment movement, is convinced that the computer is wrong. The frequency of the sound is not low enough to be a natural ocean noise. He increases the tape rate to ten times its normal speed. When he does, he can detect a series of "thrums" in five-second intervals. Clearly, the sound is man-made: it is the *Red October*, the submarine that everyone thought was undetectable. Petty Officer Jones, or "Jonesy," as the boat's captain calls him, is promoted on the spot and heralded as a genius. But all he really did was listen.

Sonar technicians in the Navy are responsible for operating surface sonar, underwater sonar, and other oceanographic systems. The really good ones are legendary: they have been known to be able to identify individual mammals and distinguish among various models of Soviet submarines just by the sound of the boats' propellers. They are master listeners because they listen *to understand.*

I am a natural extrovert, and I draw my energy from being around and learning about people. Just like sonar technicians, I've been honing my listening skills for my entire career. But I learned most about how to listen when I was a commanding officer.

As the CO of a ship, one of your primary listening duties is receiving contact reports. Your most important responsibility is making sure that your ship doesn't collide with another one or with some other navigational hazard. In certain areas of the world, such as the Malacca Straits off the Malaysian Peninsula or the Dover Strait between the United Kingdom and France, the shipping traffic is intense, coming at you in all directions at all times of day and night. It can be dicey navigating through those bodies of water—especially at night.

As CO, you can't be on the bridge 24-7; sometimes you have to sleep. Plus, you have multiple responsibilities all over the ship that can take you away from the bridge. When you are not on the bridge yourself, you designate an officer-of-the-deck, or OOD, to be your eyes and ears. The OODs are instructed to call you in the event of any potential contact and tell you what that contact is, how far away it is, how fast it's moving, what the weather is like, and what the sea state is. When you receive these reports, you have to listen very carefully. You quickly have to develop a mental picture of what the OOD is seeing from the bridge to determine how much of a threat this contact is. Sometimes, an OOD will wake you up in the middle of the night to give you these reports. In those cases, you have to immediately shake off the cobwebs and listen even harder. Dealing with contact reports is the ultimate in listening skills.

The art of receiving contact reports is a balance between simply directing the OOD to make a course change (to avoid a contact) *and* teaching him or her how to make the right recommendation without help. When you are coaching junior officers, you are grooming them to be COs themselves one day. Your instinct might be to jump in and keep them from making a mistake. But, if you do that, they won't mature as ship-drivers. Young professionals need to go through the process of arriving at the right answers on their own. Gentle coaching, not prodding, is my style. I used contact reports as teaching moments to help me do this.

Sometimes you might receive a report that indicates that the contact is a little too close for comfort. In those instances, I would head up to the bridge and take a seat in my captain's chair. There, I would sit and observe. Some

COs will try to "stress" the OOD. I never did—I thought that was unproductive and demotivating. After all, we are on the same team. I didn't want to put the OOD on report and embarrass him in front of the rest of the crew standing the bridge watch that night. I wanted him to still feel like he was in charge. But I also didn't want us to be involved in a collision. So, I would just gently suggest to the OOD that we might just want to put a little more space between us and that contact.

My former shipmate and good friend, Capt. Kevin Campbell, has told me that I have a PhD in listening. Really, it is more of an intense curiosity for what makes people and things the way they are. When Kevin served as my chief engineer on the cruiser USS *Princeton*, he tested my listening skills. Our ship was homeported in Long Beach, California, but we were visiting San Diego to have the ship *de-permed*—a process designed to reduce the ship's magnetic signature by infusing her steel hull with bursts of electricity—to help her avoid detection and to minimize the attraction of a floating mine. We were in port for two to three days. There were rumors that we might be ordered to an early deployment for drug-interdiction operations in South America. This would be an exciting professional challenge for the crew, but it also would mean an unexpected, potentially lengthy period of separation from our families.

Sure enough, the three-star admiral in charge of all surface ships in the Pacific summoned me to his office, sending over a car and driver to deliver me to a meeting with him, where I was given orders to head south. When I returned to the ship a few hours later, I called a meeting of my department heads, the senior officers of my crew. I informed them that the rumors were true—that we were going to be ordered to deploy on short notice. Initially, my instinct had been to wait and tell the crew after we returned to Long Beach; I wanted them to stay focused on the de-perming job, and I thought there would be ample time to tell them about the impending deployment after we'd finished. My XO and most of the department heads agreed with me.

But Kevin did not. He argued that the rumors were rampant and that many of the ship's sailors had seen me leave in the admiral's car for the meeting. He was firm in his opinion that it was important for the crew to hear from me *now* to help quell the rumors. And he felt strongly that crew members would appreciate that I was entrusting them with this information.

He was right, and I was reminded that day of some advice that we had received as midshipmen at the Naval Academy. Before we were allowed to leave the Yard (campus) for an evening out on the town, we were instructed to call the school immediately if we got into any sort of trouble. We were specifically reminded that we should not wait until we returned at the end of the night or let the school learn the bad news from someone else, such as the police. In other words, "Bad news doesn't get better with age." The news about *Princeton*'s early deployment fell into that category. I immediately got onto the 1MC, the ship's intercom system, and shared the news with the crew. Effectively, Kevin reiterated to me that day the imperative of listening—listening to learn.

As I have said, one of the most important listening activities that a CO can carry out is getting to know the crew. I can't emphasize enough how important this is. I truly enjoyed meeting all my sailors, especially new crew members who came to work for me. I actually relished learning about them and what made them tick. I did this by listening to the stories about their childhood, their families, their hobbies, their aspirations, and their dreams. I often did this in *their* work spaces, not mine. I wanted to see them in their working environment, their own element. My rationale was varied. First, I wanted them to know that I cared about them as individuals; second, I wanted to see the world through their eyes; and third, I wanted to learn how to motivate them. You only achieve this by listening—listening to learn and listening to understand.

As I said at the beginning of this book, when I arrived at Navy Federal I knew what I didn't know, which was a lot. As I did whenever I assumed a new command, I asked a lot of questions and just listened. There is a tradition in the Navy that, when you take over as a CO, you don't change the set of the sails until you know the conditions of the sea. In other words, when you come aboard as a new leader, don't be so intent on changing the organization until you really understand the state of the organization. As my friend, Adm. Mike Mullen, former chairman of the Joint Chiefs of Staff, says, it is important to "Look. Listen. Learn."

Besides wandering around to talk to individual employees, I hosted small-group employee forums, held coffee chats with new vice presidents, and led town hall meetings with branch employees all over the country. Many leaders claim that they are in touch with their employees, but unless you are regularly meeting a broad cross section of them and hearing what's on their minds, you really are out of touch. Over the years, these small-group forums tend to flatten the organization and give people an opportunity to voice their views to top leadership. What did I do in these meetings? I asked questions and I listened.

That is where I found good ideas. Really great ideas. When we had a problem with fraud in our collections department, I was wondering how we could stop it. There was a family of brothers who were taking out car loans for cars that they never actually purchased. They would keep the money, but never hand over a car title to us. It wasn't until they had applied for and pocketed the money for six car loans that we caught onto their fraud. I was scratching my head over how we could prevent this. In talking with a small group of collections employees one day, I was discussing this case. One of our collectors, a young woman who had been working for us only a few years, piped up and said, "How about if we institute a policy where no member is allowed to get more than two car loans until they submit the titles for these cars?" Brilliant. It struck just the right balance of trusting our members to do the right thing *and* instituting some financial controls that would prevent future fraud. I gave her a $2,000 cash bonus for the idea. If I hadn't been listening, I never would have stumbled onto her and her good idea.

Another time I was visiting our New London, Connecticut, branch manager, who was married to a command master chief in the submarine force. Connecticut is the home of one of the Navy's submarine shipyards. Carey Boyd was a knowledgeable Navy wife and an experienced Navy Federal employee, and I trusted her implicitly. I always enjoyed spending time with her because she had really good instincts. On this particular visit, I asked her, "Who is our biggest competitor here in Connecticut?" Without missing a beat, she said, "That's easy—USAA." The United Services Automobile Association is a large insurance company that offers other financial services as well. Like us, its mission is to serve military members and their families. I asked Carey how we could be more competitive. Again, without missing a beat, she said, "Give our members with direct deposit access to their money sooner." According to her, USAA was clearing its active-duty members' direct-deposit paychecks a full twenty-four hours sooner than we were. That gave servicemen and women who had checking accounts at USAA full access to their paychecks a day before they would have received it with Navy Federal. Carey told me that twenty-four hours makes a big difference in our members' lives, especially if they have to pay the rent on the first of the month or they want some spending money for a long weekend.

I listened and I heard. I really had never considered how much of a difference twenty-four hours can make. I went back to our CFO, Lauren Lloyd, and I asked her to help me figure out how we could offer our members access to their paychecks more quickly. She gave me an analysis of what this policy change would do to our cash flow. The impact did not offset the value to our members. We made the change.

Sometimes listening to learn also involves having the humility to change your mind, based on what you hear. When I received a recommendation for increasing tele-working opportunities at Navy Federal, I initially opposed it. Maybe it was my Navy background that had conditioned me to believe that work was done alongside your shipmates—on your ship or in your office, not at home. I also believed that creating and maintaining a healthy work culture required working together as a team, and I feared teleworking would weaken that.

However, our tremendous growth over the past fifteen years had pushed our total number of employees beyond the office space that we had available to house them. At one point, the staff proposed that Navy Federal start a teleworking pilot program to help alleviate the space crunch, but I was skeptical.

That said, I love pilot programs. In my opinion, they always are a win-win effort. If they are successful and you implement them on a wider scale, you win. If you find out that they aren't going to work for the larger organization, you also have won because you have learned a valuable lesson at minimal cost. Pilot programs take away people's concern about failure. My H.R. team convinced me to authorize a pilot teleworking program involving a limited number of employees. A year later, a team of employees in our contact center received the prestigious Richard Cobb Award for Service Excellence. This annual Navy Federal award is given to a small group of the best-performing teams in branch offices and in our call center. When I found out that the entire team was made up of teleworkers, I changed my mind about the teleworking pilot, and I authorized expansion of the program, which still includes some of our brightest and most dedicated team members. If I had not listened to learn, I would not have been open to the decision.

Another pilot program that we later implemented across our organization was based on a discussion that I had with the then-commandant of the Marine Corps, Gen. Bob Neller. He sought me out at an event and related some anecdotes he was hearing from some of his younger Marines. They were being charged high interest rates on their car loans from Navy Federal and he wanted me to do something about it. Now, some leaders might have been incensed that the commandant of the Marine Corps was sticking his nose in other people's business, especially since the stories that he shared were only anecdotal. But I listened—and I understood. The message he was giving me was important to him: he wanted us to see if we could help his Marines. That is what a leader does. I told him I would look into it.

I probed our loan department and asked why these borrowers were being offered above-industry-average rates. It turned out that all of them were first-time borrowers. Our experience has shown that young, first-time borrowers with little or no credit history frequently default on their car loans. We thought about what we could do, and decided to start a pilot program where these borrowers could refinance their loans with us and get a lower rate if they had made twelve on-time payments. Essentially, we wanted to see a track record of regular payments, and then we would reward them with a lower interest rate. The program proved to be quite successful. Our young Marine members were able to get a lower rate after demonstrating their financial responsibility, and we were able to keep them as customers. If I had not really listened to General Neller, I might not have paid attention and would not have made the change.

Some of the decisions that I faced at Navy Federal were a bit harder to make. One provision in the landmark Dodd-Frank Wall Street Reform and Consumer Protection Act of 2010, known as the Durbin Amendment, put new regulations on the debit and credit-card interchange fees. These are premiums that retailers pay card-issuers, and historically they have averaged about 44 cents per transaction. Pushed by the merchants, the Durbin Amendment limited the fees that large banks (those with more than

$10 billion in assets) could charge, which was going to result in a net loss for us of approximately $100 million a year. It was a huge haircut.

We strategized over what to do about it. Many banks responded by reinstating checking-account fees. But what would happen if we charged a fee for checking when our members were used to not paying anything at all? Many of the people in my management council, my team of leaders at Navy Federal, had worked for us and other banks for decades and had seen lots of turbulent cycles and painful regulations during their collective tenure. I just needed to listen to them—really listen.

After looking across the whole company for ways that we could offset this lost income and analyzing a number of ways we could change our fee structure, my senior executives recommended that we *not* change anything; instead, they advised that we stay the course. They argued that this was more than about checking account fees. We wanted to send a message to our members that we are not like every other financial institution, beholden to quarterly earnings. We did not want to punish our members for some new government regulation that had nothing to do with them. Many of our members found our free-checking policy a real differentiator. My management council felt confident that this might be a way for us to capture market share. I agreed and I said, "We are not a 'fee' shop. You can use carrots or sticks with members. We are going to use carrots. We are going to *grow* our way out of this." And that is exactly what we did. Today, if you look at the growth of our checking account business, it is two to three times greater than the industry average.

Major retailers like Walmart and Walgreens had made the argument to legislators that with the passage of the

Durbin Amendment they would pass the savings on to their consumers with lower prices. I have not seen that happen. The fine print in the public disclosures for their stocks proved that the savings went right to their bottom line. Their shareholders benefited, but I don't think their customers did.

Foot Stomper

There are two types of sonar—active and passive. Active sonar emits sound pulses that produce echoes that then bounce off objects under water. Passive sonar merely monitors the sounds made by other vessels. Which type of underwater sonar enables the technicians to detect more submarines? You've got it: sonar techs have told me that it is passive sonar performs best. I've always remembered that fundamental lesson: being an exquisitely good listener is not just about being polite; it's also about *listening to learn* and *listening to understand*. Leaders will make better decisions if they learn to listen like a sonar tech.

Chapter 9
"GET IN THE BOSUN'S CHAIR"
★

To understand the perspective of your employees and the challenges they face, you need to stand in their shoes and take the same risks. You need to "get in the bosun's chair."

A s I mentioned earlier, one of the most dangerous maneuvers that ships at sea carry out is the process of refueling when they are underway. It's known as UNREP—an acronym for underway replenishment. While the oil tanker and the receiving ship are steaming ahead parallel to each other, the oiler's crew fires a pneumatic line-thrower, or shot-line, over to the receiving ship, where it is caught by experienced deck personnel, pulled taut, and used as a pulley to transfer a rig line from the tanker to the vessel that is being refueled. UNREP operations also are used to transfer munitions and supplies between two ships. And sometimes they are used to carry people from ship to ship—in a contraption called a bosun's chair. For the uninitiated, a high-line transfer in a bosun's chair might look like fun—something akin to riding in a ski-lift—but in turbulent seas it can be terrifying.

The secret to making the ride uneventful is the skill-level and knowledge of the line-handlers. If the line-handlers on each ship know how to adjust the high-line so that it has just the right give and take, you will have a smooth ride and you can just enjoy the view. And guess who the best line-handlers are? People who already have taken a few rides in a bosun's chair themselves.

I remember when we were in the middle of an UNREP on the frigate USS *Albert David*. I was watching my first lieutenant, Lt. (jg) Don Mathis, who was in charge of all the line-handlers during the maneuver. He was responsible for giving the orders to tighten or loosen the lines. He seemed nervous about the directions that he was giving his team. I wanted to boost his confidence and give him a different perspective. I surprised him and ordered, "First lieutenant—get in the bosun's chair! I would like to have you get in that basket and be transferred back and forth."

Lieutenant Mathis had a look of horror on his face, but to his great credit, he said, "Aye, aye, sir!" and jumped right in. I think taking the ride was a great lesson for him.

I wanted him to experience the consequences of his orders and how to coordinate better and more confidently the work of the people who were pulling on the lines. He needed to feel for himself what it was like to be hauled across. After he did that, he had a different—and improved—frame of reference.

I insist on the same standards for myself. When I took the destroyer USS *Harry W. Hill* out to sea for the first time as the CO, I told the personnel on the ship's bridge, "I have the conn"—meaning that I personally would be deciding what heading and speed the ship should take from minute to minute. Most COs expect their watch teams to maneuver the ship when getting underway, but I wanted to do it myself the first time. I will tell you that I was nervous, because the ship was a twin-screw ship—which has two propellers—and it handles very differently from a single-screw ship. But I tried not to show my discomfort. My crew members told me later that they had never seen a CO do that, but I wanted to show them that I would not ask them to do anything that I would not—or could not—do myself. Some call that "servant leadership." I just say that you have to "get in the bosun's chair." When I came to Navy Federal, I wanted to make sure that we had managers who had gotten "in the bosun's chair" themselves.

I always said that our "special sauce" at Navy Federal was that our employees are focused on providing top-notch service to our members. I think one of the reasons that we deliver such great member service is that many of our employees reflect our membership closely. Some 20 percent of Navy Federal employees and the majority of employees at our branch offices are or have been military spouses. Many of them are able to maintain their careers when their spouses change locations. And 10 percent of our employees are veterans. Many others are children or grandchildren of veterans. These groups of employees are one of the key ingredients of that special sauce. The military spouses and veterans who work at Navy Federal are especially qualified to advise our members on their financial needs and goals.

These employees understand the distinctive challenges of military life, which involve frequent moves, frequent deployments, and frequent family separations—all of which can result in missed bills, unforeseen expenses, expiring powers of attorney, unexpected home sales and purchases, and frequent job changes. Any one of these issues can cause financial stress. When you have employees who have walked in the shoes of your members, those employees are likely to be able to muster an unmatched degree of understanding and empathy. And because of that, they can provide the service and solutions to any financial problems our members have. They have been in the bosun's chair.

When we decide to make a big product or policy change, we always ask ourselves, "What is the impact on the member?" Indeed, Vince Pennisi, our chief financial officer at the time, told me that it was a distinguishing feature of our organization. Vince worked for several other financial institutions. In those, he attested, it was all about quarterly earnings. They focused first on improving the company's finances and *then* considered if the change would be an acceptable outcome to their customers. That's not how we thought.

We feel strongly that the best way to understand the impact on our members is to get in the bosun's chair and make sure that our employees are familiar with our products and services. I encouraged all our employees to use all of these services themselves so that they can understand the benefits of each—and the deficiencies as well. If your employees are *not* using your products, that may leave them less knowledgeable when it comes to serving your customers. I always said that I wanted our employees to be proud of what we offer to our members.

Consequently, when I learned that many of our employees did not have mortgages with us—especially those workers in California, where the cost of housing was much higher than at our headquarters in Virginia—I was determined to change our mortgage product. It turned out that we were not lending enough money to help our employees—and our members—in states like California. In response, we raised our loan threshold and we started offering employees a discount on their rate—enough to motivate them to get a mortgage with us, but not a significantly different rate from what we offered members.

I also noticed that many of our employees were not using debit cards when they paid for their lunch in the cafeteria. I asked our marketing folks to print up some tabletop cards to scatter around the cafeteria that reminded everyone that using Navy Federal products will only make these products better. Nowhere was that more obvious than with our credit card offerings.

In an effort to tailor our products to members' life stages, we had begun offering a variety of new credit cards—lots of them. All of our competitors were doing the same thing. The credit card industry is very diverse. We thought we had a balanced program: some offered low or no fees in exchange for modest travel rewards, and others offered really great rewards in exchange for a higher annual fee. All of them offered one point for every dollar spent, but the value of that point differed from card to card—in other words, not all the points were created equal. And the value of each of these points was not really that evident until you tried to redeem them. The benefits of each of our cards were not being explained in simple terms.

With so many different cards and so many different features, I had a hard time explaining them to my friends and family. I was sure that if *I* found it difficult to explain these differences, our employees were challenged as well. No wonder we were having a hard time expanding the program.

In 2010, a new leader named Randy Hopper took over our credit card business. He recognized that the sign of an overly complicated credit card is when consumers only use it for a short period of time. We had that problem. He initiated a comprehensive membership survey and conducted lots of focus groups. He wanted to dig into the issue. He found out that many of our members did not understand our credit cards, some were not happy about paying *any* annual fee, and many were using cards from other financial institutions more frequently. We could not expand a program that we could not easily explain and that people could not easily understand. It did not pass what I call the "Major Brown" test.

There is an old tale from the Civil War about a Union Army major named Brown. When U.S. Army Gen. Ulysses S. Grant wanted to issue orders to his troops, he would always tell his staff to take the order to Major Brown and ask him to review it. Finally, one of his staff members asked, "Why does Major Brown have to approve all orders?" "Because," said General Grant, "Major Brown is the dumbest officer in the Union Army, and if he can understand the order, then we all can."

With that in mind, we got to work simplifying the program. Randy and his team reduced our credit card offerings from six cards to three. We brought the value of all three cards *forward*—meaning that the rewards for each card were patently obvious to the member when he or she opened the new account. We also made it much easier for members to redeem their rewards. Now, they could even collect a *partial* redemption—using only a portion of their points.

The results were instant. Before we made these changes our Flagship® credit card had attracted only about 10,000 new account-holders a year. Sixty days after we launched the new version of the Flagship® card, members responded by opening 12,000 new accounts. By the end of the first year of the new program, our Go® credit card product grew to 200,000 new accounts—up from only 30,000 users over the previous seven years.

Unlike the membership of many other credit unions, many of our customers are young and are new military recruits. Their first transaction with us might be to take out a car loan. Many financial institutions might not want to take a chance on such a young person, often still a teenager. They might not want to offer a competitive rate for a first-time borrower with little or poor credit history. But we take the long view—that is, we want them to take their first loan with us, and we are willing to take the higher risk in hopes that they will always remember that they obtained their first car loan with us. We figure that if we earn their trust and loyalty early on, we will be their financial partner throughout their lives. In addition, if we want them to be members for life, we have to understand intimately what life stage they are in—what their needs are now, five years from now, ten years from now, and twenty years from now—so that we can grow *with* them. When we "get in the bosun's chair" and regularly use the products that we are offering our members, we can look at all our products, services, and processes through *their* eyes.

Around the first of every month, Navy Federal has a very large surge of members who come to our branches to get cashier's checks for their monthly rent. A significant percentage of our members live paycheck to paycheck, and when they get paid on the first of the month (the military payday), they immediately ask us for a cashier's check—the only form of payment their landlords will accept. About 40 percent of our branches' cashier's check volume occurs on the first of the month. It is significant and, because of the impact on branch traffic, labor, and resources, we considered imposing a nominal fee for cashier's checks. It was not unprecedented, since many other banks and credit unions charge up to $10 for each cashier's check.

After our savings and membership department conducted a thorough analysis, it recommended charging $5 per cashier's check. I thought about the recommendation for awhile and then rejected it. I was worried about the impact that it would have on our typical members, many of whom would be financially vulnerable to this monthly charge. In my opinion, the incremental income for the credit union was not worth the impact on these members. Our average member is thirty-seven years old and has an average checking account balance of about $2,000 and an average savings account balance of less than $2,000. The $5 fee that we were considering would total about 3 percent of their checking account per year. It also seemed a little unfair to charge them a fee to withdraw *their* money. If I hadn't lived in a ship for many months at a time, I would not have appreciated how much our typical members need every dollar they earn. If I hadn't spent so much time in our branches and heard time and again from our members that a cashier's check was the only way they could make their rent payment, I would not have appreciated how much this no-fee service meant to them. The only way I could appreciate this was to get in the bosun's chair.

When I arrived at Navy Federal, we still called our branches "member service centers" and we called our checking accounts and our debit cards "ShareChek" cards. These are credit union terms. We wanted to differentiate ourselves from banks, but what I soon found out is that most of our members didn't know what these terms meant. When I talked with them about the ways they can do business with us, I would mention the member service centers. Most of them gave me a blank look. They would tell me that they had never visited a member service center, but, then, they would tell me that they did use our branches. As an organization, we weren't really differentiating ourselves; we were just confusing our customers. We got rid of those names and started using banking terms that most people understand, like branches and checking accounts. It was a bigger change for our employees than it was for our members, but once they looked at the issue through our members' eyes they embraced the change.

Sometimes it took a little bit more understanding of our members' unique needs to embrace some of that change. On one particular branch visit a few years ago, I received a question from a teller who asked me why we had extended hours. None of the other banks in this particular town did. She said these evening hours were burdensome for her because it delayed her after-work workout. I said to her, "Well, let me tell you a story. When I was the CO of the frigate USS *Bronstein*, we were in the shipyard for repairs and my sailors had a little free time, but there was nothing for them to do on the shipyard. They had no cars, so they would walk or take the bus to the bars just outside the base—frequently a seedy one called The Pink Elephant, where they would get into fights and get arrested. I started to look for other activities they could do. I began to host more after-work picnics, baseball games, and basketball games, and I suggested that they go to the base library to get some books. Maybe it was naïve to suggest that they visit the library on their off-hours, but some of them took me up on it. However, they reported back to me that the library was closed when they tried to visit at the end of their work day.

"I said to the sailors, 'Well, I'll take care of that.' The next day I paid a visit to the librarian, who was a government employee. I told her that my sailors would like to come over and use the library after work, but they couldn't because she only opened the library from 9 a.m. to 3 p.m. She said, 'Well, those are the hours.' I told her that wasn't working for my sailors. She said, 'Well, that's not my problem.'" At this point in telling this story to the branch employees, the teller gave me a sheepish grin. I said to her, "Are you following me?" She said, "Yes."

The financial industry is famous for keeping "bankers' hours." But at Navy Federal, our mission is to serve those who serve. We needed a members' mindset. Our hours need to reflect their banking needs, which are usually more than 9 a.m.–3 p.m. Many of our branches open as early as 7 a.m. and stay open as late as 6 p.m., depending on the location and needs of the members.

Perhaps the best example of how we needed to think about the impact of our decisions on our members is our mortgage business. Believe it or not, a few years before I came to Navy Federal, we used to have a three-month waiting list. The mortgage business has always been cyclical, and if you go back into Navy Federal's history ours has been, too. There was a time at Navy Federal when they didn't want to add more people to the mortgage department because they didn't want to have a whole bunch of extra employees with not much to do when the demand for mortgages fell off, so during the busy times they would put members on a waiting list. At times, that waiting list contained as many as 10,000 members. You could have built a few good small businesses out of it.

Not only were we leaving a lot of business on the table with this policy, but—more importantly—we were not serving our members well. We needed to shift our thinking and get a different perspective. Many of our members are on active duty and move around the country—and in and out of the United States—frequently. It is not unusual for them to go on a quick house-hunting trip at their next duty station and make an offer on a house that weekend. In a good economy with a booming housing market, those members need to have a pre-approval letter from a mortgage lender in their hand, or they probably have only a few weeks to get a mortgage approved or settle on their new home. Are they going to wait in line patiently with Navy Federal for several months, or are they going to get a loan somewhere else?

Navy Federal needed to get in the bosun's chair. It was clear that the organization had to invest in more people in our mortgage business. But, first we needed to get rid of that waiting list as quickly as possible and get a better understanding of our members' mortgage needs. In 2003, everyone at Navy Federal was asked to help retire that waiting list. Executives from every corner of the organization were deployed to the mortgage department. There were product development folks closing the loans, marketing analysts processing the loans, and systems engineers taking mortgage requests on the phone. It was a collaborative team effort—with all hands on deck helping.

Besides learning more about our members' home mortgage needs and preferences, this triage effort also helped the team figure out where else Navy Federal needed to invest. To prevent this backlog from building up again, we needed a lot more mortgage professionals. We also needed better processing systems, better infrastructure, better technology, *and* a pipeline of new business. We weren't getting the referrals from real estate agents because they thought we still had a waiting list. Even several years later, this perception of our waiting list persisted because we had not been engaging with real estate agents or proactively selling our mortgage products. We needed to sharpen our marketing skills and change our sales culture concerning home mortgages.

We partnered with a network of real estate professionals and relocation services and courted them—going to their conferences, meeting with their leadership, and engaging with their real estate agents. We also empowered our loan officers to develop their own relationships with local agents. We encouraged them to take the business to the agents, not just wait for the incoming inquiries.

All these efforts fundamentally changed our mortgage business. We have become a leader in our industry, with a loan volume in excess of $14 billion. We are now a top-five lender in the nation for Veterans Administration (VA)–backed loans, with some of the most competitive rates. We just needed to think about the issue a bit differently. Getting in the bosun's chair helped all of us get that critical perspective.

Foot Stomper

Asking ourselves "What is the member impact?" has now become an ingrained mantra at Navy Federal. Every new product that we consider developing, every new technology that we plan to implement, and every new policy that we contemplate changing is never approved without our first doing a thorough analysis of the effects on our members. We know that the only way to really find the answer is to "get in the bosun's chair."

Chapter 10
BE A SEABEE AND FIND A WAY TO "GET TO YES"

You never want to hide behind the rules as a means to say no if the right answer is yes. In order to build a culture of people who insist on "getting to yes," you need look no further than Navy Seabees. Their motto is Can Do!

"The difficult we do now; the impossible takes a little longer." The Navy's Construction Battalions (CBs), known as Seabees, have a storied reputation for creativity and field ingenuity. The first three battalions of Seabees were formed in 1942, mobilized to build bases all over the Atlantic and Pacific theaters in World War II. In total, they built four hundred. They also protected the Atlantic convoys and supported invasion forces in the Aleutian Islands and in the Central Pacific islands—constructing or restoring harbors, airstrips, roads, and all kinds of facilities on the islands, many of which had been newly captured from the Japanese. They were some of the first to go ashore during the D-Day invasion at Normandy, and they joined the Marines during the invasion of Guadalcanal, Saipan, Guam, and Okinawa. There are very few World War II campaign battles in the Pacific that did not depend on the infrastructure built by the Seabees.

During the Korean War the military realized that it needed an air base at Cubi Point in the Philippines, but civilian contractors said it couldn't be done. The Seabees leveled a mountain in order to build it. In Vietnam, Seabees were called upon to carry out humanitarian missions as well as military ones, building schools, clinics, roads, wells, and bridges for local communities all over South Vietnam. In the Middle East, they have supported the military and the State Department, building where no one else will. They continue to amaze me: they are a combination of warrior, engineer, and humanitarian, all rolled into one. And they get stuff done. They know how to "get to yes." They never seem to let government bureaucracy get in the way.

When I say I want my crew to have a "can do" attitude, Seabees are my role models. In the Navy, I tried to view the rules imposed on us by the bureaucracy merely as guidelines, not hard-and-fast requirements. When I was the CO, everything depended on circumstances. This is a small item, but I would authorize my crew to wear flight jerseys and shorts on the ship when we were at sea, a practice usually only allowed for aviators. These long-sleeved cotton T-shirts were really comfortable. It meant a lot to the crew and improved morale.

I found that there were some things you could do at sea that had a high payoff for the morale of the crew. "Swim call" was one of them. Swim call involves stopping the ship dead in the water in the middle of the ocean and announcing to the crew that you are authorizing a free swim in the ocean for all hands. For safety, we would place a small boat in the water with a lifeguard and armed gunners—in case we saw any sharks. Crew members would stream to the fantail to jump off the ship. In fact, on occasion some sailors got so excited about the event that they jumped into the water, forgetting that they did not know how to swim. This is one ship's evolution that is not in the Navy's instruction manuals. It is done at the captain's discretion. If something goes wrong, no one will defend you. Some officers may regard swim call as a high-risk adventure, but I thought that the heightened morale and priceless memories that it spawned made it a must-do activity.

Most of the rules that I broke as a CO were minor, yet breaking them improved morale visibly. Sometimes my decisions to improvise were a bit more risky, but I always had a rationale for doing so. En route home from a six-month deployment in *Bronstein*, the steering mechanism failed, and we experienced a serious breakdown in heavy seas. Our only course of action was to divert to Guam to make repairs. Navy's rules dictated that I, as the CO, prepare a casualty report and send it up the chain of command as a message. It would cite the problem that we had encountered, pinpoint the cause of the mishap, and estimate how long it would take to resolve it. While we were in the ship repair facility dealing with the steering gear, we also encountered flooding in the main engine room that destroyed a main feed pump. The damage was more than just a mess—it also was a major engineering problem. My chief engineer was mortified: we'd had two engineering casualties on his watch in just a few days. I felt bad for him. He was really good at his job; it was just rotten luck. But I knew that if I sent a second casualty report back to San Diego it would reflect poorly on him. I talked to the shipyard's chief repair officer and asked him if there was any other solution to our problem. He stared me in the eye and said, "I can fix the main feed pump, too." What he meant was that he could fix it under the radar, without a second casualty report. He understood the implications of a second casualty report: it could be detrimental to the chief engineer's career. Instead, his team fixed our steering *and* our main feed pump and we got underway a few days later. I took a personal risk in not filing the report, but protecting the career of my hard-working and dedicated chief engineer was something that I felt was the right thing to do.

When Debbie and I were vacationing in Europe one summer, we took advantage of the Air Force's "space-available" program. When on vacation, military person-nel and their families may ride as passengers on a military transport plane anywhere the aircraft is going—so long as there is enough space for personnel who are on offi-cial business. Many military families such as mine have had fun—and saved money—by taking flight "hops" to Europe, Asia, or the Caribbean. Debbie and I found an available flight from Dover, Delaware, to Ramstein Air Force Base in Germany. Once we arrived at Ramstein, we decided to go to Frankfurt. We walked out of the terminal and were delighted to see an Army shuttle-bus in the park-ing lot that had a sign for Frankfurt. It was only about half full and it was leaving in five minutes. What luck!

We ran over, jumped on the shuttle-bus and headed to the back, high-fiving each other. Then this serious-faced military police soldier (MP) got on and said in a very loud and authoritative voice, "All right, everybody, I need a copy of your orders in order to ride this bus to Frankfurt." In other words, the bus was only reserved for those on official business. Well, I was on vacation and didn't have official business in Frankfurt. As he worked his way toward the back of the bus, I thought to myself, "Well, I can try to negotiate with him," but he had his instructions. No matter what I said, at the end of the conversation we were going to be off that bus.

Then, I remembered that I had a copy of some orders in my briefcase that had transferred me from San Diego to Washington. They had nothing to do with our European vacation. I handed him the papers, he continued collecting orders, and the bus left for Frankfurt—with us on it!

He got his set of orders and we got to Frankfurt. In reality, I thought the MP was implementing a dumb rule. The bus was going to Frankfurt whether or not we were on it and the bus was only half full. As I often tell my crew when I relay this story: "If they want a piece of paper, give them a piece of paper." Bureaucracy often has many rules like this.

In 2012, I was visiting a local military hospital, and I ran into the daughter of a friend of mine who was a brand new Navy nurse, just commissioned as an ensign. She was applying to get a mortgage loan with us to buy a townhouse near the hospital. I asked her how the process was going. And she said, "Well, to be honest, slow. They're asking me for a lot of information. They want a copy of my Georgetown University degree, to prove that I graduated from college, and a bunch of tax returns." To which I said, "What the heck? You're an ensign in the Navy; ensigns by definition are college graduates. Why are we asking you for that? And, I know that, as a new college graduate, you don't have many tax returns. Besides, if we want to know what you earn, we can find all military income levels published on the Internet."

Why were we asking for information that we should know ourselves? If we say we know the military, we should know what her pay grade is, what her stream of income is, and what her capacity is to repay the loan. We should also know that ensigns get promoted to lieutenant (junior grade) in two years and get a salary increase. All of this is pretty common knowledge. Perhaps Fannie Mae or Freddie Mac gave us some sort of required checklist that we were following, but clearly we were too worried about making a mistake in the paperwork and not worried enough about making the loan. I went back to my mortgage team and told them, "We can't be so rule-bound that we don't add some common sense to our processes. We want to 'get to yes' for our members." We had to simplify some of these processes.

A few years ago, Debbie and I were in El Paso, visiting one of our branches, and I popped into a cubicle to see how a member-service representative was helping a member. Sitting with her was this guy, a salty old retired Navy petty officer first class. I introduced myself and he started singing the praises of the branch employee who was trying to help him with a home improvement loan. "Oh, this lady that's helping me is wonderful," he said, "but I just got denied by Navy Federal headquarters for my home improvement loan. It's not her fault. I have terrible credit." I asked him how long he had been a member of Navy Federal. "Thirty-five years." I quickly found his file on our computer system and it told me that he had a mortgage with us and he always paid us on time. He *did* have a 510 FICO score—one measure of evaluating a person's credit risk—which in his case was terrible. But he had never caused *us* a loss.

I looked at him in the eye and I said, "All right, I'm the president of Navy Federal and I'm going to personally approve your loan today. I'm going to tell you what's going to happen if you don't pay us back. I'm going to recall you to active duty and I'm going to recall myself to active duty and I'm going to take you to admiral's mast." He laughed and pretended to beg: "Please don't bring me back. Don't take me to admiral's mast. I'll pay. I'll pay." And he got his loan and he paid us back. If we had played by the rules and just abided by our computer system's risk models, we never would have gotten to yes.

Foot Stomper

As a leader, think about "yes" as a mission accomplishment. Don't let the rules—especially the dumb ones—stop you from getting to yes, if yes is the right answer. Think like a Seabee—and figure out how to "get to yes"—for your team and your organization. It's a different approach, one that has made the Seabees legendary. *Can do!*

Chapter 11
FOLLOW YOUR NORTH STAR

Have a set of immovable principles that guide you. Be a leader who maintains a set of steadfast values and exhibits predictable behavior that is motivated by those principles and values. For me, my North Star has always been "Do the Right Thing."

Before the days of GPS, sailors at sea used the stars to navigate the world's oceans. When I was studying to become a naval officer in the late 1960s, we were required to become proficient in celestial navigation, which involved using an ancient mariner's device called a sextant to figure out where we were on the ocean and to determine what course we had to take to get where we were going. The most important star to find was the North Star, also called Polaris, because it is recognized for appearing to remain almost still in the heavens while the rest of the northern sky seems to move around it.

We all should have a North Star—a steadfast and immovable set of values that guides our behavior. Our North Star can help us determine what is right and wrong. Even as the world around us changes, if we have a solid North Star to guide our course, we will know what to do, and the people around us know what to expect from us.

Both my parents, Jim and Betty Dawson, served in the Navy during World War II. My mother lost her first husband in 1941 when he was killed in the Aleutians. A young, new widow at the outset of World War II, she decided to join the fight. A graduate of the University of Kansas, she became a naval officer in the WAVES (Women

Accepted for Volunteer Emergency Service)—which then was the women's component of the Navy. She first served at the main Navy building in Washington, D.C., and then was transferred to Pensacola, Florida, where she worked in human resources at the naval air station there. My father, a farmer from Virginia, was the valedictorian of his high school class, but his family lost its farm in the Great Depression. With no money for him to attend college and no farm, he went to work for the Internal Revenue Service in Richmond, Virginia. When World War II broke out, he became a Navy pilot in Pensacola. My parents met and married there.

After the war, they moved back to Richmond, where they raised me and my younger brother, Craig. My dad went back to work for the IRS and my mom became a homemaker. Craig and I grew up in a loving environment. We weren't a rich family, but we were comfortable. My brother and I attended Richmond public schools and took part in several sports—most notably tennis and basketball.

My first job was retrieving golf balls for my dad— collecting them from the driving range—for which he paid me twenty-five cents an hour. I would try to catch the golf balls with my baseball mitt. In those days, if you were too young to caddy, you could make some money chasing after golf balls. My parents, as children of the Great Depression, taught me that if I earned a quarter I should be very careful how I spent it. They both were very frugal, and never went into debt. As a result of their influence, I have never carried any credit card debt. I pay it off every month.

Mom was very athletic, and was accomplished in every sport she played—especially tennis and golf. She could move faster on the golf course than any person you have ever seen. At the time, female golfers were not exactly welcomed with open arms in Richmond. It was considered a man's sport, and women were interlopers. Maybe that is why she played so fast; she knew how to position herself around the golf course so none of the members could accuse her of being slow. She became her club's golf champion, and she mentored many other female golfers. I think she was way ahead of her time. But she was never vocal about it. She never expressed anger or resentment about what she, as a woman in the 1950s, was not allowed to do. She just quietly demonstrated her abilities and, in doing so, showed Craig and me how to develop ours. That was her North Star. She taught my brother and me how to compete in sports, and how to be gracious winners *and* gracious losers.

At the dinner table, my parents talked about the Navy a lot—how much they loved their assignments, how proud they were to serve, and how important military service is. Serving their country was also their North Star.

Both my parents made it clear that they wanted my brother and me to go to the Naval Academy. They believed that by attending the Naval Academy we would get the best possible education. They hoped that by becoming naval officers we would have great career opportunities—both in the Navy and in the private sector. I knew from an early age that I would apply to the Naval Academy, so I pursued an appointment and received one. At about the same time, I was also accepted to the University of Virginia, or UVA, as it is known.

Everyone has some self-doubts, and, with my acceptance letter from UVA in my pocket, I began to question whether I wanted to undergo the rigors of life at the Naval Academy. One morning, I came down to breakfast and announced that I was going to attend UVA. My mother and father had little to say to me, other than that it was my decision.

Over the next few days, when I came downstairs to the kitchen, there was no hot breakfast waiting for me. (Usually, my mom made me a custom-order breakfast.) This continued for a few days. It took me a while, but I soon realized that my folks were sending me a subtle message. They really wanted me to go to the Naval Academy. After thinking about it, I came down to the breakfast table and announced, "I have changed my mind. I'm going to the Naval Academy." My mother responded, "What would you like for breakfast?"

When I did arrive at the Naval Academy just a few months later, I was committed. My class had a high attrition rate—more than 40 percent—but I wasn't one of those who left. I had already considered quitting before I even arrived, but now that I was there I was going to finish. I had found my North Star. Serving and having a strong commitment to public service was at my core. It was in my DNA. I had just needed a little reminder.

Even though both my parents had served in the Navy, I really did not know much about it until I arrived at the Naval Academy. And, while the academic demands were rigorous and aimed at teaching us how to operate ships at sea, what the Academy really impressed upon us was the importance of having a North Star. Again, the words and deeds attributed to Revolutionary War captain John Paul Jones stuck with me:

> It is by no means enough that an officer of the Navy should be a capable mariner. He must be that, of course, but also a great deal more. He should be as well a gentleman of liberal education, refined manners,

punctilious courtesy, and the nicest sense of personal honor. . . . He should be the soul of tact, patience, justice, firmness, and charity. No meritorious act of a subordinate should escape his attention or be left to pass without its reward, even if the reward is only a word of approval. Conversely, he should not be blind to a single fault in any subordinate, though, at the same time, he should be quick and unfailing to distinguish error from malice, thoughtlessness from incompetency, and well-meant shortcoming from heedless or stupid blunder. . . . In one word, every commander should keep constantly before him the great truth, that to be well obeyed, he must be perfectly esteemed.

In other words, it's all about the people—taking care of them and setting an example for them, and being the type of leader whom you would want to emulate. It's not the technology or the firepower; it's the people.

In separate incidents in 2017 two U.S. Navy ships collided with commercial ships in the Pacific Ocean, resulting in the deaths of seventeen sailors. Unfortunately, these accidents were avoidable. In the after-action report on one of the collisions, it became clear that the commanding officer was not consulted in time to avoid a mishap. When I was a CO, I made sure that my crew members knew that if they were ever unsure of something they were to alert me *immediately*. There would never be any consequences for waking me up in the middle of the night. I was there to help and advise. I never wanted to be the CO the crew is afraid to wake up. As I've said, bad news doesn't get better with age. In the other 2017 collision, it was reported that either the crew members had ignored basic training in safety and ship-handling or their leader had not ensured that they had all the proper training and support. In my opinion, the problem was more endemic.

I felt as though the entire Navy had lost its focus on what should be its core competency—superior warfighting skills on warships at sea. Ships' crews were distracted by other priorities, such as excessive menial collateral duties, extraneous training classes such as motorcycle safety, unnecessary administrative accounting of trivial matters—all of which had become more important than warfighting. Seamanship is step one in the ability to fight your ship. It's the Navy's North Star, and the service had lost sight of it.

When it happened I talked to my senior executives at Navy Federal because we were being inundated with new government regulations that were consuming our time. I reminded them that *I* was the captain of the ship at Navy Federal, and that it was my responsibility not to overreact to and get distracted by the regulators. We needed to stay focused on our North Star—making Navy Federal a great place to work so that our employees could provide great service to our members.

Vince Lascara, who was chairman of Navy Federal's board for almost three decades, once said that Navy Federal should continue to try to grow—*but not for growth's sake*. He asserted that we should grow *as a result* of the good service and the value we provided to our members. Growth itself would not be the desired goal.

I really didn't know much about business or banking when I became the CEO of Navy Federal. I wasn't a certified public accountant. But I knew how to take care of people. I learned how to do *that* in the Navy. What I did know was that I was going to discover the business through its people. What I learned is that having employees who believe in what we're doing, along with members who place high trust in Navy Federal, makes for a terrific combination. This mix produces a spiral of success that contributes to both our members' financial gains and to the growth and health of our organization.

One of our member service representatives, Andrea Watson, recently handled a call from a woman whose sister had just passed away. She needed a loan for her travel expenses related to the funeral. Throughout the application process, she slowly opened up to Andrea, sharing that her sister lived in Pensacola and would constantly tell her how beautiful the beaches were. The member also confessed that she harbored a lot of guilt over the fact that she never found the time to visit her sister in Pensacola while she was alive. She mentioned to Andrea that she would only be in town for one day to settle her sister's affairs. However, she was going to make a point to stop at the beach, if only for a few minutes, to at least dip her toes in the sand.

While they were on the phone, the member's loan was approved, and the funds were auto-deposited into her account. She thanked Andrea for her help and for taking the time to listen. Andrea said, "It was my pleasure." But Andrea wanted to do more. She wanted that member to know that she truly empathized with what she was going through. So, she said, "You know, I live in Pensacola and I agree with your sister. We have the best beaches in the country. I know you said you planned to dip your toes in the sand, but I do hope you will stay a little longer. What I would like to do is place $25 in your account for you to have lunch on the beach, and take some time to think of your sister at the place she loved so much."

The member began to cry and said, "Andrea, I think God put you on the phone with me today." She was genuinely surprised that a financial institution could have so much heart. Andrea said later that it was wonderful to work for a company that empowered her to have this type of impact on a perfect stranger.

What is special about Navy Federal is how much our employees care about our members. You could meet a member service representative in Bahrain, a branch manager in Sacramento, or a collector in Pensacola and you would get the same level of care and service. Why is our culture so intrinsic and endemic in our organization? Because we value and care for our *employees*. You sustain a great culture by taking great care of your employees, communicating to them what a priority they are, and empowering them to make decisions.

Engaged employees make for engaged members. *That* is doing the right thing. *That* is our North Star.

Foot Stomper

If you want to be successful as a leader of an organization, don't focus on growth—find your organization's North Star. Stay true to that North Star, and it will guide you to success. Always do the right thing.

Appendix

Navy Federal by the Numbers

★

Between 2004 and 2019, Navy Federal Credit Union's assets quadrupled, from $22.8 billion to more than $100 billion. Its membership has more than tripled, from 2.5 million to more than 8 million. It has more than tripled the number of its branches around the world, from 106 to 335, and more than doubled the number of ATMs, from 290 to 671. Its total number of employees has increased from 4,500 to 19,000. Its facilities have grown exponentially—with three new buildings in Virginia and seven new buildings in Pensacola, Florida. Total loans have grown more than fivefold—from $14 billion to more than $76 billion. Total savings have grown by a factor of four, from $17 billion to more than $77 billion. The company has seen a gain of almost 12 percent in its combined annual growth rate between 2000 and 2017. During the great recession of 2008, it finished the year with $81.6 million in net income, and did not lay off a single employee. In fact, Navy Federal has *never* laid off any employees.

The organization has received numerous awards for exemplary customer service. The banking research advisory firm Javelin Strategy & Research named us the "Online Banking Leader in Ease of Use, Security Empowerment, Money Movement and Financial Fitness" and also recognized us as a "2018 Mobile Banking Scorecard Leader." In 2019, Forrester Research again ranked Navy Federal #1 for "Customer Experience among Multi-channel Banks/Credit Unions" and it was recognized as a "best-in-class" brand for customer experience, according to the company's U.S. CX index. KPMG has also ranked Navy Federal as #1 in Customer Experience Excellence.

In 2018, for the eighth year, *Fortune* named Navy Federal as one of the "100 Best Companies to Work For®," ranking it forty-second. That same year, *Forbes* listed us as one of the top "10 Best Employers in America," recognizing us as a great place for women, diversity, parents, and millennials. And, for the twelfth year in a row, the Department of the Navy ranked us in 2017 as the "Distinguished Credit Union of the Year." Finally, we earned the highest satisfaction rating among U.S. banks and credit unions, according to the 2018 American Customer Satisfaction Index (ACSI) Finance and Insurance Report. Navy Federal remains the largest credit union in the world and the twenty-ninth largest financial institution in the United States.

ABOUT THE AUTHORS

After a thirty-four-year career in the U.S. Navy, **Vice Adm. Cutler Dawson** served for fourteen years as the president and CEO of Navy Federal Credit Union, the largest credit union in the world and the twenty-ninth-largest financial institution in the United States. He and his wife, Debbie, live in Alexandria, Virginia.

Taylor Baldwin Kiland has written, edited, or ghostwritten eighteen books, including two about our nation's Vietnam POWs. A former naval officer, the third generation in her family to serve, she lives in Alexandria, Virginia, with her husband and their seven-year-old daughter.

Just DIE Already

Discover How Death to Self Produces Abundance in Christ

By *Jill Kight*

Dedication:

I dedicate this book to my husband, Brandon, and my mom, Sheila, who have always listened patiently to all my thoughts and ramblings and have offered encouraging insights. In addition, I dedicate these writings to my children, Blake, Dirk, Asher, Claira, Judah, and Finley who have provided numerous opportunities for my spiritual growth leading to ultimate abundance in a life for Christ.

Thanks:

I want to express my heartfelt gratitude to each and every reader who chooses to give this book their precious time. It is my great joy to pass on to you the message God placed on my heart, and it is my prayer that you grow in Christ in an ever-deeper way while always relying less on self and more on our Savior and Lord Jesus Christ. When you finish this book, may you find you have yielded to the Holy Spirit's prompting in whatever way He leads and have discovered grace-filled abundance in Jesus.

Editor: Pam Lagomarsino
Front Cover Designer: Brandon Kight
Formatter: Samantha Fury

Table of Contents

Chapter 1

The Rescue of the Dead

Small groups and one-on-one conversations ...this is where I thrive. Crowds? Not so much. Of course, I don't always get what I want and what works best for me. Therefore, crowds are a necessary part of life if I want to be at all social.

Often in a large crowd, I pause for a moment and think about the vast number of people around me: all with separate thoughts, all known by God, and all created with an eternal soul. I think of Jesus' words in Matthew 7:14, "For the gate is narrow and the way is hard that leads to life, and those who find it are few." As my eyes scan the sea of people even at something like a Christian concert or large church service, I am certain that all whom I see are not on the narrow path, Jesus' path, which begins when He places them there.

During these moments, my heart fills with gratitude beyond words for the salvation I received through my Savior while simultaneously aching for the "many" who are implied in Jesus' words. May the following anecdote I wrote possibly illuminate the dire situation of the crowds.

There was little to no hope. While their ship was sinking, the inhabitants had desperately searched for a lifeboat to climb into, but to no avail. Realizing there were no lifeboats, they flung themselves into the sea to swim quickly away from the pull of the ship as it descended into the depths of the sea. Incessantly and mercilessly, the ocean waves bombard the survivors frantically attempting to stay afloat. At the realization this was likely the end; one tired survivor recalled some Scripture his mother had taught him so many years before. He had rejected the truths as he grew, preferring to pursue the pleasures of the world, but now the Scriptures flooded his mind with clarity and precision.

"For all have sinned and fall short of the glory of God" (Romans 3:23).

Immediately upon remembering this verse, he mentally checked the box of goodness, that although he had sinned, he'd also been a good guy overall. His good definitely outweighed his bad. The sting of truth struck him again as he recalled another verse he was taught as a boy. "As it is written: 'None is righteous, no, not one; no one understands; no one seeks for God. All have turned aside; together they have become worthless; no one does good, not even one'" (Romans 3:10–12).

The thoughts that assaulted him were of desperation, fear, and condemnation. As the waves pushed him beneath the surface, another verse from childhood poured into his thoughts like a sweet childhood memory. "For the wages of sin is death, but the free gift of God is eternal life in Christ Jesus our Lord" (Romans 6:23).

2

He uttered a final cry before he sank deeper. From his memory, he whispered a prayer from the second part of Luke 18:13, "'God, be merciful to me, a sinner!''

What he didn't realize was a handful of other survivors all around were also feeling the weight of their sin, and they were being reminded of God's truth in their minds as well. Some remembered verses they had learned at home. Others recalled Scripture they had heard at Sunday school or VBS. Simultaneously, the Holy Spirit had been working on each one. Each had uttered similar cries for mercy. However, not all had been moved in the same way. Some hadn't ever heard truth, while others rejected it anyway and clung to their apparent "goodness."

Out of nowhere, all the survivors heard a calm, peaceful voice saying, "Come to me, all who labor and are heavy laden, and I will give you rest" (Matthew 11:28).

In the distance, they barely made out a lifeboat and they all frantically swam over and prepared to climb in. Right before the rescue, someone found an inscription on the side which stated, "Whoever loses his life for my sake will find it" (Matthew 16:25). The repentant survivors climbed in because they knew they were dead either way. While watching some find refuge in the boat, others remained in the water because of the bizarre and frightening inscription. They didn't want to lose their life to get in. In that boat, it was certain they would lose their lives, but in the water, there was still a chance of rescue.

Many justified their decision by reassuring themselves they didn't want the restraints of the lifeboat anyway, the lifestyle it would bring, and the annoying passengers they would have to be near within the long journey to shore. Anyway, they were sure they could swim. Others liked the idea of the boat and stuck close to it even though they didn't want to completely climb in. They really weren't sure they could trust the boat to carry them to shore. These survivors thought if it got really dangerous, they would just climb in quickly.

Once the excitement died down of finding the lifeboat, the relieved passengers now peered over and perceived what they could not take in before. To their horror, they discovered all those in the water were dead even though they could still hear their voices and observe their bodies moving. The voice again explained they, too, had been dead, but they were now alive. From this explanation, they understood that even though they thought they were climbing in on their own, they were not. The one who spoke to them over the waters was the same one who pulled them into the boat. At the realization they had no part in their rescue, they experienced a rush of thankfulness that overflowed in their hearts!

4

Ironically, the ones in the boat were alive even though they had been dead, and they could now rest from their striving for safety. Those treading water appeared alive even though the voice testified of their deadness, and yet to them, they were striving to keep their life. They were blind to their condition.

Over time, they could hear those in the boat praising, singing, and praying, and they joined in, and because they were doing what the people in the boat were doing, they thought there was no longer a distinction between them and those in the boat. As the relentless waves carried them farther from the boat, they even imagined there really was never a boat at all. They continued to tread water, but eventually, they succumbed to shark attacks, violent storms, and weariness. Through it all, they had reassured themselves with the whispers they heard that everyone, in the end, is the same, and it doesn't matter how you get to shore.

Now, let's talk about those who sought the refuge of the boat. They arrived safely on the shore, but not without passing through rough waters, storms, hunger, and much difficulty. Many in the boat could not get over their miraculous rescue. They focused their minds on this rescue, again and again, always praising the one who provided the boat. Others in this party let their minds wander in another direction. They didn't focus as much as they should have on the rescue or the boat, so they became preoccupied with the encircling sharks, which couldn't really get to them. They also forgot their boat was unsinkable. When they encountered the storms, they wailed as if there was not a firm boat underneath them carrying them through. Some even became so caught up in the goings-on of the ones treading water that they longed to do what the dead were doing. They were hot in the boat, the people were sometimes annoying, and the food was scarce. They forgot to continue to sing for joy for the boat and its provision. They had times that they remembered, and so they praised, but overall, their perspective was warped, so they didn't have the same experience as the victorious boat riders.

As time went on and they got closer to shore, they lost track of all those in the water. At last, they reached the shore and realized that no one who remained in the tumultuous sea made it. Those in the water had continued to ignore the call. The more they ignored it, the fainter it became. Their strength and efforts proved insufficient. Now those brought to safety would give praise to the life-saving boat forever as they knew it was the boat that got them to shore.

Did you see it? It is a picture of our life before Christ, salvation, and our eternity. The boat is Jesus. HE saves. HE pulls us up out of our deadness and gives us life. HE gets us safely to our heavenly home.

Just like the deceived ones in the water in this story, deception causes many to believe all is okay. This deception works itself out in a myriad of ways. Some believe a Savior isn't necessary. Others stake their eternity on the character trait of God's love covering all, believing everyone is okay in the end. Many naively trust that because they are in Christian crowds and involved in Christian activities, they, too, are secure. Some have uttered a prayer for forgiveness at one point in their life, thus "checking the box" that God "requires" for salvation.

In addition, deception also can work itself out in a true believer's life when they think salvation by grace requires nothing else of us. This is easy believism. It goes something like this, "I believe Jesus died on the cross for my sin. The Bible says I don't work for my salvation; therefore, I'm done. I can live freely, and by grace, I am and will be saved." This kind of attitude should cause us to prickle a bit. Is there some truth in it? Yes, but we have to ask ourselves, "What about the rest of the Word that tells us how to live? Shouldn't our lives reflect new birth?" If this is someone's attitude concerning salvation, there is a concern for their souls.

This kind of thinking should cause us to question the reality of a new birth in Christ. This is because when we are in the boat of Jesus, we follow His direction, instead of our fleshly desires (Romans 6). We are united with Him, and our old selves have died.

7

Our lives should not look like they always have. Growth in sanctification doesn't look the same in everyone, but God in His mercy doesn't leave us where we are for long.

We also see evidence of deception by a divided heart for God. There are true Christians safe in Jesus, but they get so caught up in what's going on around, and inside of them, they forget the mission and their overall purpose. Since they don't know who they are in Jesus and what they are to do with their lives, they find the apparent freedom of those outside of Christ appealing. There is deception for unbelievers against receiving the grace of salvation, and there is deception for believers to keep us from living out the fullness of our mission.

Overall, because of sin, things are messed up, and we tend to forget the life we have on earth is very temporary, and a spiritual war is going on around us. The battle is for our souls. In the boat illustration, hindrances kept some from climbing in and others from living and thinking like they were in. Likewise, there are other stumbling blocks for us to guard against in this life.

Although I am unsure of my conversion moment, I know when I saw a lasting change in my heart's desires. Within a year after graduating from college, I remember God drawing and bringing me to where I could do nothing but surrender. I didn't want to live for myself anymore. It hadn't satisfied me and instead brought me a lot of regret. He gave me the heart of surrender to His Lordship. Until that point, I thought I wanted a ticket out of hell, but I didn't want Jesus to rule over me. I wanted to rule over myself.

From my earliest memories, I remember hearing about Jesus. I accepted early on that I was a sinner. I never really struggled with that as I felt a burden and guilt for my sin. Repeatedly, throughout my childhood, I prayed the typical sinner's prayer, always hoping I had done it just right each time. It was as though I felt I had to say it just right for it to work.

I trusted Jesus had died on the cross for sin, but I felt little to no assurance I was actually His child. I didn't understand many things about the true Christian faith. Not understanding grace was probably the most detrimental. I wanted to please God, but I never felt my actions measured up—because they didn't.

I eventually did whatever I felt like, all the time experiencing guilt and fear. However, the desire to have fun superseded the desire for peace with God. Many times during this period, I knew I needed to surrender, but I was unwilling to take up my cross and follow Him. In His providence, grace, and mercy, He drew me to Himself and made me desire Him more than myself.

After He transformed my heart to submit to Him completely, accepting not only His sacrifice but also His rightful rule, I noticed over time that more of my desires were changing. I struggled with a lot of the same issues I had before, but I was crying out to God to change me so that I could get freedom from them. He did free me, and He opened up my spiritual eyes more so that I could perceive secret sins of the heart I wasn't even aware of before.

Over the next four years, I experienced growth in many areas. I read the Word, prayed, attended a small group, and memorized Scripture. Underneath it all, I felt this lingering feeling that maybe I wasn't a true believer after all. What if I just thought I was? How terrible it would be to appear before the Father someday only to hear, "I never knew you; depart from me." (Matthew 7:23). I battled with these thoughts for a long time and repeatedly asked God to show me I was His. I didn't want to be one of the deceived ones. Subsequently, I lacked joy in my Christian walk because I lacked assurance.

Finally, through a study I was doing, a simple answer came. Just look at the cross. I was His because of His completed work on the cross. My feelings couldn't tell me this. My feelings were always all over the place, but the truth of the cross could tell me. My Lord had regenerated my heart and gave me faith in His finished work. Assurance came to me when I looked to Him. Over time, I have been reassured in a myriad of ways that my faith is genuine.

The remainder of this book will have absolutely no purpose unless you first figure out where you fall in this story. Without Jesus, all Christian principles result only in moralism and good deeds that are nothing more than filthy rags (Isaiah 64:6).

Now, I want you to examine your faith. Is it genuine? Are you in the boat? If you are in Christ, are you the one praising your Savior, or the one looking at the world longingly thinking they get to have more fun? Do you desire God to receive glory and honor? Do you want the Holy Spirit to sanctify you and line up your life with the righteousness of Christ? These are absolutely essential questions. At any moment, a final wave could take you under.

Chapter 2

Hair, Trees, and Sticky Fruit

I'm forty-two years old. My natural hair color is what a friend termed "mouse-colored." Gray hairs poke through now and have been for a few years. I'm not yet ready to let them shine forth in all their brilliance. About every eight weeks, my stylist works her magic and covers all I want to hide. I walk away with a beautiful shade of brown with golden highlights. For the next month, one may observe I have pretty blondish hair. It is what is visible. It is what I want others to see and what I put forth. I know the truth of what lurks underneath. As the roots grow out, the truth of my hair color pushes to the surface, and I scramble to cover it again. I would argue we can draw a bit of a parallel with hair coloring, trees, and the fruit (or lack thereof) in our lives.

My children spent a good amount of time last year learning about trees. Appropriately, they even memorized poems about them, which kept my mind focused on them, as well. The Lord gave me deeper insights into trees besides just the basic knowledge of bark, leaves, and such. Verses in His Word concerning trees and roots began to really stick out to me. Did you know there are at least fifty-six Bible verses with a tree or tree reference in them? That blows me away! I don't know why this is so, but I know God does nothing because of chance. He chooses His lasting words with perfect precision.

From beginning to end, the Bible is full of seeds, trees, vines, and fruit terminology. Genesis 1, the first chapter of the Bible, recounts God creating trees and explains these trees produced seed-bearing reproducing fruit. To finish things off, Revelation 22, the last chapter of the Bible, boasts of the Tree of Life with its twelve kinds of fruit for the healing of the nations.

It was a tree and its fruit that was a source of temptation. It was because of a tree God kicked Adam and Eve out of the Garden of Eden. Noah required an abundant number of trees to make the life-saving ark, which carried eight people safely through a worldwide flood. A myriad of trees fueled the burnt offerings required in the Old Testament. It was a tree on which our Savior was crucified. It is a tree from which those who conquer will eat. It is a tree in the end that will provide the leaves for the healing of the nations.

So often in the gospels, Jesus gave analogies that pointed to deeper truths. He took the physical and related it to the spiritual. Perhaps the most significant meaning to me, besides the cross and the grace available to unbelievers, is the New Testament truths about us as believers being a part of this tree terminology. Jesus says, "I am the vine; you are the branches. Whoever abides in me and I in him, he it is that bears much fruit, for apart from me you can do nothing" (John 15:5).

This is a familiar verse to many Christians. We know we must stay close to Jesus to grow in Him and produce fruit. We may even believe this is true and is best for us. However, we could be operating under the mistaken belief it's okay if we don't produce fruit because God is love anyway. God is forgiving. We may believe that not producing fruit is our loss, but we're saved anyway. If this is our thinking, we may be overemphasizing grace. Grace is all over the New Testament. Our sin separates us from God. We are dead in this sin. The Holy Spirit brings about conviction, repentance, and conversion. We are saved by grace, but it's what comes after salvation by grace that reveals if there's been a true rebirth. Stopping at grace, we may miss the warning given before John 15:5.

John 15:2, "Every branch in me that does not bear fruit he takes away, and every branch that does bear fruit he prunes, that it may bear more fruit."

So, we understand from this verse that God takes away branches that do not bear fruit. Jesus then elaborates on this in the next verses.

"Already you are clean because of the word that I have spoken to you. Abide in me, and I in you. As the branch cannot bear fruit by itself, unless it abides in the vine, neither can you, unless you abide in me" (John 15:3–4).

Jesus tells the disciples here they are clean because of the word spoken to them. The word was a command to abide in Jesus. Our cleanness comes not through our acts, but through Christ's perfect life. His perfection has become our perfection.

If we are His, it is not even an option not to abide in Him. When we trust in Christ, we abandon our desperate, dead desires as being the foremost authority in our lives. According to Scripture, we no longer live. Our abiding/"living in" is in Jesus alone. We then actively line up our present lives with our already state of living in Christ. One way the genuineness or insincerity of an individual's faith demonstrates itself is through the fruit they produce. If an individual has no real life in Him, then there has been no rebirth, and therefore, no real fruit.

Sadly, some appear to be in the faith but are not truly in the faith at all. They are growing up alongside the vine with branches that appear similar to the vine's branches, but they are not truly from the root of the vine. If they were, the blood of Christ would have made them clean, and they would live and abide in the life-giving blood of Jesus. Their "blood" is from a different source.

Matthew 13:24–30 also comes to mind here concerning the wheat and weeds. Like the analogy of the vine and the branches, this parable compares Jesus' true followers to the wheat and the false ones to the weeds. They are left to grow up together, and then, in the end, the weeds, which are unbelievers who appeared so much like true believers, are gathered, bundled, and burned. The wheat is put into the barn.

This is where it gets pretty sticky. What we've seen so far from these passages and so many others is that true Christians demonstrate the authenticity of their root by obedience. You would think it would be easy then to differentiate between true and false converts since one could just look for those obeying Jesus' commands.

The chief difficulty here is false converts can also appear to produce fruit. They can give their lives to a cause, struggle financially while giving to others, serve in soup kitchens, and pour out their lives for their children. They may serve on church committees, tithe, and change diapers in the nursery. They are growing up next to and with the blood-bought "wheat." The weeds among the wheat may obey Christ's commands as do the wheat but be obeying for all the wrong reasons. They may obey to earn their way to God, to look good to others, or just to do the right thing morally.

Another complication is we often excel at appearing to be good people. Like dyeing our hair to cover up the true color, we paint bright colored acts over the darkness of our hearts to smother the truth of who we are, whether consciously or subconsciously. We hang on our trees the fruits of kindness, sharing, helping others, saying, "Please" and "Thank you," and smiling politely. By hanging those pretty fruits all over our trees, we appear so lovely as the sun shines down on us, and all is going well in our lives.

However, when a violent storm comes and the wind shakes the branches, the false fruit often blows away. Some false converts may scramble to rehang their false fruit and keep up the façade even after a storm. Others give up the act when trouble comes. Just imagine how persecution for following Christ has the potential for weeding out those growing alongside the vine from those attached to and abiding in it. Also, consider how one may find it easy to believe the truth of God's Word concerning salvation through Christ alone, but then befriend a Muslim, a Jehovah's Witness, or a Latter-day Saint, and subsequently decide there are other ways to God.

When unbelievers fall away, we see that what appeared to be good fruit is actually sticky, stinky, and spoiled from the inside out. In these cases, supposed Christians show their dead hearts through ultimately denying the centrality of the gospel of Jesus, the truth of the Word alone instead of feelings, or any other doctrine in Scripture. When someone walks away from truth, it is because there was never any anchor in Christ to begin with. Therefore, there is not a loss of salvation, but rather the revealing of what was never truly there. If we only look at the John 15 verses to understand this, it could appear that salvation can be lost. However, we are to always interpret Scripture in light of all Scripture. Whoever God the Father calls to Himself cannot fall away. His call is an effectual call without fail. A few passages that speak to the truth of this are:

- John 6:37 – "All that the Father gives me will come to me, and whoever comes to me I will never cast out."

- John 10:27–29 – "My sheep hear my voice, and I know them, and they follow me. I give them eternal life, and they will never perish, and no one will snatch them out of my hand. My Father, who has given them to me is greater than all, and no one is able to snatch them out of the Father's hand."

- Ephesians 1:13–14 – "In him you also, when you heard the word of truth, the gospel of your salvation, and believed in him, were sealed with the promised Holy Spirit, who is the guarantee of our inheritance until we acquire possession of it, to the praise of his glory."

- Romans 8:38–39 – "For I am sure that neither death nor life, nor angels nor rulers, nor things present nor things to come, nor powers, nor height nor depth, nor anything else in all creation, will be able to separate us from the love of God in Christ Jesus our Lord."

- 1 Peter 1:3–5 –"Blessed be the God and Father of our Lord Jesus Christ! According to his great mercy, he has caused us to be born again to a living hope through the resurrection of Jesus Christ from the dead, to an inheritance that is imperishable, undefiled, and unfading, kept in heaven for you, who by God's power are being guarded through faith for a salvation ready to be revealed in the last time."

Even though genuine believers are secure in the anchor of Christ, I must state that authentic followers of Jesus still mess up, forget truth at times, and screw

17

up royally. They still get angry, don and flaunt selfishness, disregard the exercise of self-control, and so much more. True converts sin, but they don't want to stay there and roll around in it. Their root is Christ, and they earnestly desire to line up their lives with obedience because of love for their Savior. True believers run to the cross, confess sin, and rest in Christ's sacrifice. Their fruit is not perfection, but it is rather a desire for obedience that honors their Savior.

I'm not at all asking for us to go around and question everyone's salvation. I am, however, asking us to consider whether the fruit in our OWN lives is from the tree of Christ or the tree of our own making. I'm also encouraging us to go after our sisters and brothers who are in sin. Because of love, we should challenge one with no fruit who believes they are in Jesus because of a prayer prayed at age seven. To come along someone and help them examine and compare the actions of their lives with the truth of Scripture is to show love. Jesus warns us about this very concept of believing we're right with Him when we're not.

> Not everyone who says to me, "Lord, Lord," will enter the kingdom of heaven, but the one who does the will of my Father who is in heaven. On that day many will say to me, "Lord, Lord, did we not prophesy in your name, and cast out demons in your name, and do many mighty works in your name?" And then will I declare to them, "I

never knew you; depart from me, you
workers of lawlessness"
Matthew 7:21–23

These verses in Matthew were always terrifying to me before I truly understood the gospel. At first glance, these workers appear to be followers of Christ since they refer to Him as Lord and have obviously been busy working for the kingdom. But if we examine closely, we see the reasons these workers of lawlessness gave for their right to enter heaven. They *claim* their works before the Father. *We did this* in your name, and *this* and *this*. They worked for their salvation to no avail. What you don't hear is an acknowledgment before the Father that *Jesus* did this and this and this… and because of what He did, they're forgiven and counted as righteous.

It is possible to have head knowledge about God with no true relationship with Him. We can do the activities of God, such as going to church, praying, Bible reading, serving, telling others about Jesus, and more, yet remain dead in our sin. Likewise, we can have little fruit and truly belong to Christ, which is an issue we will tackle in subsequent chapters.

Since all this is so sticky, we must find a way to really know the truth. Our eternal hope's genuineness is revealed as real or counterfeit only as we look at salvation and fruit as Scripture lays out. As stated previously, I have not always known with assurance I belong to Christ even after true fruit. There was a point early in my Christian walk when the Holy Spirit gave me the confidence of my belonging since it was through Jesus' work on the cross. He assured me of salvation, but not just through a feeling. He took me to the Word, reminding me of the cross and the finished work of my Savior there.

Rightly, I would caution here that we must be careful about relying on feelings alone without truth for assurance. I have friends who belong to other religions that emphasize faith plus works for salvation, who have "assurance" they are saved. Therefore, relying on a "feeling" alone is not necessarily an adequate indicator of rebirth. It is only as we measure our lives against the plumb line of the Word that we can know if we are in the faith.

> "But now the righteousness of God has been manifested apart from the law, although the Law and the Prophets bear witness to it—the righteousness of God through faith in Jesus Christ for all who believe. For there is no distinction, for all have sinned and fall short of the glory of God, and are justified by his grace as a gift, through the redemption that is in Christ Jesus" (Romans 3:21–25).

> "Repent therefore and be converted that your sins may be blotted out" (Acts 3:19 NKJV).

> "Then Jesus told his disciples, 'If anyone would come after me, let him deny himself and take up his cross and follow me. For whoever would save his life will lose it, but whoever loses his life for my sake will find it'" (Matthew 16:24–25).

Second Corinthians 13:5 commands us this way, "Examine yourselves, to see whether you are in the faith. Test yourselves. Or do you not realize this about yourselves, that Jesus Christ is in you?—unless indeed you fail to meet the test!"

We must ask ourselves some questions here. Is this me? Do I know I am a sinner without hope of forgiveness on my own or with my works? Do I know Jesus paid the penalty for sin by taking the wrath for sin in His body on the cross through His death? Do I believe His death was enough of a sacrifice, and there is nothing I can do to add to His perfect sacrifice?

If the answer to these questions is yes, then has this knowledge moved you to true repentance, which is a turning away from sin and a turning toward Jesus as your only hope for forgiveness? This rebirth causes a transformation in thoughts, attitudes, desires, and actions as following Christ leads us away from pursuing the flesh and self so that we pursue a life that loves to obey and bring glory to God.

Without thinking about the right answer, ask yourself right now what you would say to God if you were before Him, and He asked you why you should be with Him for eternity. If your mind moves to anything other than the death and resurrection of Christ, you may want to consider if your faith is truly rooted in Jesus.

The difference is always the root. A tree can't be anything other than what its seed determines. If we see an apple tree, then we would expect apples to form in the spring when the flower falls off. Likewise, true conversion demonstrates itself in the fruit of obedience to Christ. He tells us in John 14:15, "If you love me, you will keep my commandments." He doesn't say, "If you love me, you *may* keep my commandments." He clearly says, "You *will*." He knows this for certain because He tells us He gives us the Holy Spirit (John 14:16–17).

The same one who does the work of salvation for us is the same one who gives us fruit. Ephesians 2:10 adds to our understanding of this, "For we are his workmanship, created in Christ Jesus for good works, which God prepared beforehand, that we should walk in them." Not everyone will have exactly the same fruit, and the good works we accomplish through the Holy Spirit vary widely, but across the board, our lives as followers produce because He is the One doing the work, and He never fails.

Since all this is such a sticky issue, with fake fruit, real fruit, and no fruit, I would encourage you to ask God to reveal to you your heart's true condition through His Word, and in His faithfulness, He will. Ultimately, only God knows those who are of His seed and those who are not. Whether in this life or at the judgment, our true color rises to the surface and can remain hidden no longer. While we still have life, there is still time to repent of the true colors of our sin and trust in the crimson blood of Jesus for forgiveness, salvation, and rebirth into His life-giving vine.

Chapter 3

A Banquet of Junk

Sam plods to the mailbox after a long, stress-filled day at the office. His boss just moved up the deadline on his project, sales are down, his coworker is going through a divorce, and now he knows a stack of bills will greet him.

To his surprise, he discovers an exquisite envelope with gold lettering mixed in with the dreaded bills. He eagerly and carefully opens the envelope where he finds an invitation to a lavish banquet to dine on fine cuisine with a renowned man. He ponders how and why he was invited. It is true he knows this man.

It's a bit complicated, really, but he has essentially put all his hope in this one man. Oddly though, it's been quite a while since he's actually been close to him. As a result, the relationship is just not what it once was. Sam still reads about him when he has time, but he's just so "busy" that it doesn't happen often. He is blown away that this host actually desires his attendance at this banquet.

As the day draws near, Sam's eagerness to attend and sup until his heart is content intensifies. A week before the big event, he receives a package in the mail. He doesn't remember ordering anything. Any package he ever receives costs him something, and he feels a little unsettled since he's painfully aware of his meager bank account. He pushes past his thoughts of what this might cost him, and anxiously opens the package.

Inside, he discovers sophisticated evening attire; Sam is amazed to discover it fits to a tee. He falls back onto his bed and thinks it over. As he ponders the whole thing, he realizes he's really done nothing for the host to like him, and yet he has even provided appropriate clothing for Sam to wear so that he won't feel out of place.

When the big day arrives, Sam spends the day working in the yard, fixing squeaky doors, cleaning up dog poop, breaking up arguments between the kids, and paying bills, which are all necessary tasks, but they leave him feeling even more unqualified to attend the banquet. As it gets closer to the time to get ready, he decides he's not really feeling up to it. He's so tired, and he just wants to watch a movie and relax. He knows he should go, but it feels like so much effort and time to get ready.

Even though he doesn't feel like it, he reluctantly chooses to attend, but he resolves to keep his distance from the host. He justifies his thoughts by reassuring himself that he'll converse with the host another day when he doesn't feel so tired and worn out from all his work. He removes his dirty work clothes, showers, and dons his new attire, but doesn't feel worthy of it. He knows he has put on pure and beautiful clothing, but every time he looks in the mirror, all he can see is how he looked before he took his shower. He feels disgusted by his appearance, but now he knows he must go anyway.

By the time he arrives, he is famished from all the busyness of his day. When he is almost to the massive ornate banquet doors, another attendee opens the door in front of him, and he glimpses the host standing right inside the door beckoning him into the banquet hall. He can't believe his bad luck... that he has to walk in and be greeted by the host immediately. He knows he must think quickly! He wishes the host hadn't seen him. He just doesn't feel up to the time and effort it will take to talk with the host. Besides, even though Sam has put on what was sent, he can't see it. He's guessing the host can't either and will be upset with him that he came so filthy.

As if out of nowhere, Sam spies another room off to the side. Wait! That smells familiar. It's a little like the local diner. As he peers in, he discovers there's a spread of food in this room too.

If he enters the other room with the host, he'll have to sit down and wait. The meal will be delectable and nourishing, but he'll have to wait for it and be patient. Hmmm.... What to do?

As his stomach growls, Sam gives into his flesh and goes for immediate satisfaction at the buffet. He justifies his decision because he looks around and recognizes other people who were invited to the banquet as well. If they're doing it, it's got to be fine. The next thing he knows, he's gorging on nachos, french fries, hamburgers, chocolate cake, and ice cream. He's full and tired and decides to go home and watch TV. Popping some Rolaids to help with indigestion, he drifts off to sleep feeling guilty but reassuring himself that he'll attend next time he's invited... Next time will be different.

Obviously, this analogy breaks down a bit if we stretch it too far, but I hope you can still see its rightful application. On the surface, this scenario appears utterly ridiculous. What person in their right mind would think they were still dirty when they were obviously clean and well-dressed, consume crazy amounts of junk food when a delicious feast is coming, and pass up the opportunity to converse with this renowned host?

I would argue that many Christians do this exact thing regularly. We have turned to Jesus as the Savior of our souls because we are confident He is the way, the truth, and the life. We hope in Jesus' death and resurrection alone to save us from our sins. We have been clothed in His righteousness. All of Jesus' perfection has been applied to our accounts.

So, if all this is so, what's the problem? The problem is the disconnect between what we say we want and what we actually execute as Christians. The longer I read the Word, the more I discover the truths of a crucified life for Christ.

What I don't see in the Word is a confessor of Christ who does not have a radically changed life. With confession comes death, new life, rejuvenation, and fruit. We are told to taste and see that the Lord is good. The more we abide in Him and submit to His rightful Lordship, the more we will live in abundance. Why not run hard after what will actually satisfy? Why keep going to the junk food in the pantry?

Truthfully, in the moments of life, most of us go for the quick fix, which is the tangible, here-and-now solution that brings immediate satisfaction. Being impatient people, we settle for the "ok" solution instead of waiting on the perfect one. We impulsively reach for the sub-par (that thing we go to that we think will satisfy) when it will really, in the end, leave us with indigestion and bloating and a resolve to do better next time.

I have spent most of my life interested in food and nutrition. From about the age of ten, I was concerned with not becoming overweight. I read books on food and even decided when the "no/low fat" fad was popular that it was better to avoid meat and most of my mom's home-cooked meals. I justified eating fat-free candy, though, because clearly, it was a healthier choice since it had no fat.

During my high school and early college years, my interest in food turned into my obsession, and eating disorders ruled my life. Over time, God healed me of dysfunctional thoughts and behavior surrounding food. He has given me the right understanding of food now and the freedom to eat nourishing, satisfying food. I also feel free to occasionally eat junk food since I no longer allow any food to be my master. So, I give in to cravings here and there. i.e., turtle blizzards from DQ…Be still my heart.

I have discovered a strange thing with nutritious food. The more I eat healthy food, the faster my body burns through it. I'm hungry again within a few hours, and I want more goodness, which makes me happy because I truly enjoy eating nutritious and delicious food. Whenever I indulge in a fattening, carb-laden meal, I stay full longer. However, my stomach often hurts, and I feel bloated, sleepy, and uncomfortable. The adverse effects of the food on me make me run back to the yummy food my body is used to. I know what's good for me, so I put my knowledge into action by choosing healthier food.

I will say, though, that when I haven't prepared ahead of time and hunger strikes, I am way more tempted to just find whatever I can to stick in my mouth so that the famished feeling subsides. It will get the job done but in a sloppy, non-sustaining way. I have to plan ahead so that I have a healthy option to choose from.

I've also noticed with my children that the more they eat junk food, the less they want true food. They crave the high sugar-laden "food;" therefore, home-cooked meals don't hit the spot the way they once did since we tend to desire what we get used to eating even if we know it is not what is best for us. Also, when we get used to doing less to prepare our food and instead order quick meals and purchase processed foods, it can feel like too much time and effort to make a nutritious meal. We train our bodies and minds to just get the food in as fast as possible, and that quick fix becomes what we crave.

We intend and plan to do better, but the unfortunate truth for most Americans is they revert to the easy, quick fix. To break this habit, we must first decide that eating well is a high priority, and then consciously spend time on healthy food shopping, meal planning, cooking, and clean up. In addition, we must exercise patience to wait on the food, even if this is because we are out running errands and have no access to good food or fixing a meal at home. We make a choice to wait for what is better.

So, why the focus on food? I believe there is a helpful analogy here for our spiritual lives. We may be saved from our sins with our eternity secure, but we may be wasting our precious earthly time on wasteful activities, projects, movies, TV, trips, etc. We fill up on junk, and over time, we crave the junk. Scripture study, meditation and memorization, prayer, service, sacrifice, and evangelizing all feel like too much work and too much time. We may squeeze in some of these, just as we may eat some green beans along with fried chicken and mashed potatoes, but they aren't the main sustenance of our spiritual diets.

Despite doing this, we still sometimes wonder why we come to church and sit through the service with a distracted mind. After church, we rush home to feed our bellies so that we can relax and do what we want to do. By working all week, rushing kids around, keeping up with social media, cleaning the house, working out, mowing the lawn, and helping with homework, we are exhausted people who "can't" make it to the church prayer meeting, the weekly small group, or the move of someone in our church family. We go from one day to the next, taking in some of the Word and then feeding on junk for the rest of the day. We flip on Netflix at the end of the day to relax a bit. Drifting off to sleep while uttering a short dutiful prayer, we resolve to spend more time with the Lord tomorrow.

I'm not saying leisure and downtime are altogether detrimental, but rather they are an excessive pursuit in our society. I'm also not saying every Christian is the same in this, but many Christians struggle in having the desire to live for the glory of God. Instead, we are still living mostly for ourselves. Even if the desire is there, due to the busyness of our lives and the laziness of our flesh, we fail to put our desires for God's glory into action.

We were bought with the precious blood of Christ for more than a race-filled life that leaves us drained and unable to pursue what really matters. We are dressed in the righteousness of our Lord, our eternity is secure in Christ, and we remain on earth for a mission. We must live in the identity of these truths. In doing so, we will cease to feed ourselves with junk food that gives a sugar rush and a subsequent low sugar, sleepy dip when the lack of true nourishment wears off. The spread of food in front of us is fellowship with the body of Christ, a laying down of our lives, and true worship and a relationship with our King. It is the lasting food our spiritual lives crave.

Chapter 4

Take a Deep Breath

Christians like grace. We like thinking about this amazing gift, which we in no way earned, but rather received. When we can get our minds around it, we are blown away by the unfathomable love of our God, who would die a sinner's death when no sin was in Him to make a way for lost sinners to reconcile to the Father. We love these delectable chunks of meat. They taste so good to us, and by all means, they should.

Grace is mind-blowing. Our world is void of anything that compares to biblical grace. Rightly then, this grace should change us. Obedience comes from a blood system of Jesus. It isn't an option. It's assumed. It happens—always. Sanctification, or growth in holiness, comes from a life redeemed.

> "The hand of the LORD was upon me, and he brought me out in the Spirit of the LORD and set me down in the middle of the valley; it was full of bones. And he led me around among them, and behold, there were very many on the surface of the valley, and behold, they were very dry. And he said to me, 'Son of man, can these bones live?' And I answered, 'O Lord GOD, you know.' Then he said to me, 'Prophesy over these bones, and say to them, O dry bones, hear the word of the

LORD. Thus says the Lord GOD to these bones: Behold, I will cause breath to enter you, and you shall live. And I will lay sinews upon you, and will cause flesh to come upon you, and cover you with skin, and put breath in you, and you shall live, and you shall know that I am the LORD.'

So I prophesied as I was commanded. And as I prophesied, there was a sound, and behold, a rattling, and the bones came together, bone to its bone. And I looked, and behold, there were sinews on them, and flesh had come upon them, and skin had covered them. But there was no breath in them. Then he said to me, 'Prophesy to the breath; prophesy, son of man, and say to the breath, Thus says the Lord GOD: Come from the four winds, O breath, and breathe on these slain, that they may live.'

So I prophesied as he commanded me, and the breath came into them, and they lived and stood on their feet, an exceedingly great army.

Then he said to me, 'Son of man, these bones are the whole house of Israel. Behold, they say, 'Our bones are dried up, and our hope is lost; we are indeed cut off.' Therefore prophesy, and say to them, Thus says the Lord GOD; Behold, I will open your graves and raise you from your graves, O my people. And I will bring you into the land of Israel. And you shall know that I am the LORD, when I open your graves, and raise you from your graves, O my people. And I will put my Spirit within you, and you shall live, and I will place you in your own land. Then you shall know that I am the LORD; I have spoken, and I will do it, declares the LORD" (Ezekiel 37:1–14).

The Lord gave this vision to the Old Testament prophet, Ezekiel, concerning ethnic Israel. During their exile, the Israelites felt the Lord had cut them off from Him and His former promises. In His kindness and mercy, God gave Ezekiel this vision to show that Israel again would have life and even more so through the Messiah, Jesus, whom He would send.

Even though this was originally written to Israel, this vision applies to us today. In some ways, it's a visual picture for us and our conversions. We know we were dead and unable to come to Jesus. There was no life in us. Yes, there was physical life, but not true life in the sense of spirits awakened to the things of God. If we're born again Christians, it's all because the Holy Spirit opened our eyes to sin and our need of a Savior. He then removed our hearts of stone and gave us hearts of flesh (Ezekiel 36:26). He came into us. If we are in Christ, His Spirit is in us.

"And I will put my Spirit within you, and cause you to walk in my statutes and be careful to obey my rules" (Ezekiel 36:27).

We should note who is doing the work in this passage and so many others like it. God is the subject of this sentence. He is "putting" and "causing." He gives us new life and makes us a part of His family. We couldn't make ourselves to be reborn any more than we could make ourselves have life through physical birth. God is the author of all of it.

Psalm 139:15–16 captures this well for us, "My frame was not hidden from you, when I was being made in secret, intricately woven in the depths of the earth. Your eyes saw my unformed substance; in your book were written, every one of them, the days that were formed for me, when as yet there was none of them." All praise goes to Him! He gives us physical life, and then through grace, we receive spiritual life through Him.

We all know our hearts pumping in our chests is absolutely vital to life. If our hearts stop pumping, we die. God designed our bodies so that our blood systems continue to distribute life. As we breathe in, oxygen goes to our lungs, and then it oxygenates our blood and gets carried to our hearts. This oxygen-rich blood then gets pumped throughout our bodies so that our cells live. When our cells cannot receive this oxygen, they die. In God's perfect design, the blood flows back toward the heart through the veins after it picks up carbon dioxide and waste from our cells. The liver, kidneys, or intestines discards the waste, and the carbon dioxide is taken back to the lungs where we then breathe it out. It's a brilliant process we do effortlessly.

Upon our rescue from death to life, the Holy Spirit took up residence in us. He is like the blood pumping through our bodies, giving us life. We must breathe in vital Christian air to truly live to our fullest capacity. How do we get this pure Christian air?

We receive it from a life-giving sword, which is a bit of an oxymoron. Hebrews 4:12 describes it like this, "For the word of God is living and active, sharper than any two-edged sword, piercing to the division of soul and of spirit, of joints and of marrow, and discerning the thoughts and intentions of the heart."

The Bible is described as alive and moving. It is a living, active sword. A sword typically slices, exposes tissue, rips, pierces flesh, and causes life-giving blood to uncontrollably pour forth, thus resulting in death. Oh, how different God's sword is! His sword slices, exposes sin's roots, rips out the old patterns, and pierces strongholds in our souls, yet instead of blood pouring out, Holy Spirit sanctification pours in. Instead of this sword bringing death, it brings life.

The Word of God lines up our current spiritual state with our true, spiritual, justified standing. Christ brought us to live, and we are alive in Him. We must line up our flesh, the here and now, with the reality that we are spiritually alive. Little by little, our spirits are quickened as sin is actively put to death through obedience with the Word.

The Word exposes the innermost intentions of our hearts. It shows us sin when we think there is no more to be found so that we run to Jesus in repentance and praise. God's Word fills us with exactly what our spirits need. After reading, meditating, and putting God's Word into practice through the Holy Spirit, more and more areas of our lives become Holy Spirit rich. Just like our blood that brings vital oxygen to every cell and removes what we don't need, the Holy Spirit brings us life through the living Word and removes the junk in our lives that will cause us to be ineffective. As we continue to need oxygen all our lives, the sanctification process that God's Spirit works in us is also lifelong.

After having been a Christian for a little while, I felt pretty good about the amount of sin in my life (Even writing that now makes me almost cringe, since the very idea of it points to pride). The outward, visible sins in my life were no longer present, so I thought there couldn't be a whole lot more God wanted to work on in me. I couldn't have been farther from the truth. I prayed to the Lord to reveal other areas of my life where sin was present. Oh my, did the floodgates open up!

At this time in my life, I hadn't even considered the secret sins of the heart like jealousy, anger, bitterness, envy, pride, and selfishness. God, in His goodness, opened my eyes to these sins and other areas that needed sanctifying. His Word showed me how far short I always fell and how Christ's perfect life and sacrifice covered me. The knowledge of sin only made me love Him more and grow in greater thankfulness. I'm so very grateful for that time because this was the beginning of my understanding of the motives behind my actions.

Being all-wise and infinitely perfect, God doesn't just forgive us of our sins and then prevent us from being able to sin anymore in the flesh. If we immediately stopped sinning in every form upon conversion, my guess is we would depend on God less and love Him less than we do, since we see all Jesus saved us from.

The Holy Spirit often slowly shows us more and more of our inner wretchedness. I know a lot of Christians, including myself, who feel like worse sinners now than they did when they first came to Christ. It's just because they are aware of so much more of their flesh when they grow closer in fellowship with a holy God.

The moment we are converted and brought from death to life, we are justified. Our standing before God is of one who has never sinned (2 Corinthians 5:21, Romans 5:1). So we, who were dead and had no way of coming to God on our own, were brought to life. This life we received is not just credit as if we are brought back to zero again, so we are no longer in the negative in our standing before God. No, that's not our God. He does all that He does in an abundant, abounding way. He credited His Son's righteousness to us. We have Jesus' perfect, sinless record. That is our standing before Him. It's unbelievable—it's such sweet grace.

Ironically, even though our standing before God is one of being sinless, we still sin in our flesh right now. In and through Christ, we are already justified or declared righteous. Now, at present, we are being sanctified or made holy. We must ask ourselves, "How much of God do we want?" Do we want His kind of oxygenated blood flowing through our veins, or do we want to pretend as if we are still dead and not in need of Holy Spirit life?

When cells in our bodies become oxygen-depleted for too long, they die. Often, that dead part must be removed from the body so that neighboring cells are not adversely affected. Similarly, God instructs us in Matthew 5:29–30 about some drastic measures to take to avoid sin. "If your right eye causes you to sin, tear it out and throw it away. For it is better that you lose one of your members than that your whole body be thrown into hell. And if your right hand causes you to sin, cut it off and throw it away. For it is better that you lose one of your members than that your whole body go into hell."

These verses speak to the absolute weightiness of sin. Whenever God gives us these kinds of instructions, He is loving us. He wants nothing on this earth to be so precious to us that it keeps us from our eternity. To reiterate, if we are in Christ, we won't want to hang on to sin. The Holy Spirit will make us so uncomfortable in it that we will desire to let it go. If we are not truly Jesus' disciples, we may love our precious sin all the way to hell since we are unwilling to let it go.

God, in His infinite wisdom, knows a little sin in one area of our lives won't stay little. It feeds and deadens us to things of the Spirit. Therefore, we must take drastic measures to let the truth of God's Word make its way into every part of our lives.

It would be unfathomable to consider purposely cutting off oxygen to parts of our bodies, yet I wonder why it is we do this so often in our spiritual lives. This isn't something we would likely verbalize, but yet it's what so many do all the time. Imagine taking in oxygen for two hours every week and then calling it good. If the Word of God is like the oxygen we need for the Holy Spirit to sanctify us and give us life, then we should suck in the life-giving Word as if we were sucking in our last breath before diving deep underwater. Our fleshly temptation is to remain as we breathe in stale air, but instead, may we cry out as the psalmist did in Psalm 119:25, "My soul clings to the dust; give me life according to your word!"

Another helpful text to examine is John 10:10, where Jesus is speaking. "The thief comes only to steal and kill and destroy. I came that they may have life and have it abundantly."

Abundance means so many things for us, which we will cover in subsequent chapters, but for now, it means measuring our lives against God's standard and His instructions and finding that life in Him is freeing rather than constricting. It means putting off what inhabits the dead man and putting on what will make the live man thrive. It means hard work that results in a prolific yield.

For most of my life, I've been interested in exercise. I'm a disciplined person, so it's fairly easy for me to stick to something I think is important. My motives for exercising have varied over the years, but now, my chief motive is to stay in shape and be healthy. My husband and I have six children, so to have energy with them, I know I must keep myself in good shape. Since our youngest child is four, my guess is for the next thirty to forty years; we will have little ones around to play with. I want to have the energy to enjoy them, and I will continue to work out so that my body and mind function optimally.

Now, after having explained all that, I must state that working out is really hard. I rise early to accomplish this task before others awaken. Many frigid mornings, I would prefer to fix coffee and cover up with a warm, comforting blanket while reading by a fire. Even though that sounds appealing, I know that what is best is to put in the hard work first and then reap the benefits of it throughout the day.

I actively put off what I feel like doing for what is best for me to do. In the middle of a hard exercise, I sometimes want to quit. It hurts. Most of the time, I push through because I know the benefits outweigh the present discomfort. Also, moves that were difficult for me before have now become somewhat routine. Because I have put in consistent time working out over the years, I don't feel a lot different now at age forty-two than I did at thirty-two or even in my late twenties. I know my body will change as I age, but for now, I'm happy to feel healthy and active because of the consistency of working my muscles and heart.

Similar to working out and pushing through the uncomfortable to reap benefits, reading the Word feels foreign at first and extremely difficult. We tend to aim for small goals just to get it done. How many Christians feel justified in reading just one quick chapter of the Word per day? There are likely many reasons to explain why so many Christians choose not to feast on the Word, but I believe one of these is it is just plain hard. It's so much easier to fix coffee and cuddle up in a blanket, so to speak. We like the comfortable and familiar. Rolling around in what comes easy is what many of us do best. The more we intentionally spend time in God's Word, the more comfortable and familiar it becomes to us.

To sum up, perhaps it would help if we consider the easy here as oxygen-deprived and stifling. We are remaining in an environment with no air flowing through it. Slowly, but surely, we will lose valuable time and eventually die as ineffective Christians. To thrive, we must put in the hard work of studying, memorizing, and meditating on the Word. This is one way to live in the abundance Jesus describes. It is the oxygen the Holy Spirit longs to deposit throughout our spiritual cells. It is the sword that ironically cuts to truly heal and bring real life. It is the mind of Christ that transforms our wayward thoughts. Breathe it in.

Chapter 5

Want to Move Far Away?

I have watched my neighbor's two arborvitae trees by their driveway change from green to brownish green and then completely brown over the summer. The once-thriving trees have lost their lives, and there is no longer any hope for them. They were alive, and yet now, in such a short time, they are without life, and their root systems are dead. This eventually happens to all of creation. What was once alive, eventually dies.

Ironically, this is a bit opposite of the potential for our spiritual conditions. Before we were saved, we were dead. Our human bodies had life, but our spirits were dead—no life, no pulse, and no ability to do anything. Just like God breathed into the first man who had no life on his own, He is also the one who brings our dead spirits to life. Some verses that show us this truth are below:

"And you were dead in your trespasses and sins, in which you formerly walked according to the course of this world, according to the prince of the power of the air, of the spirit that is now working in the sons of disobedience" (Ephesians 2:1–2 NASB).

"Truly, truly, I say to you, whoever hears my word and believes him who sent me has eternal life. He does not come into judgment but has passed from death to life. Truly, truly, I say to you, an hour is coming, and is now here, when the dead will hear the voice of the Son of God, and those who hear will live" (John 5:24–25).

"We know that we have passed out of death to life, because we love the brothers. Whoever does not love abides in death" (1 John 3:14).

We also know with certainty from Scripture that we are reborn upon receiving Jesus as our Savior. New life comes to us where there was only death before. "Therefore, if anyone is in Christ he is a new creation. The old has passed away; behold, the new has come" (2 Corinthians 5:17).

We, as believers, have a new life system. What was fueling our dead souls before, won't work for souls alive now. Everything is different now because of our new birth. It may be helpful here to consider an analogy of our new birth and a move to a foreign country.

When we were reborn, our citizenship changed. The really crazy thing is we don't know anything about this country. Bizarre food, out-of-the-ordinary language, unusual people, and unheard-of purposes and focus of the inhabitants prevail. It is essential to adapt to thrive.

At first, we need to start with the basics and figure out the best food sources. Next, we would need to find adequate housing. Also, we must acquire the language. Lastly, we would need to know what to do in this new country with our time.

In the same way, our spirits that are alive in Jesus won't thrive if we keep everything the same. We don't come to Jesus for a "get out of hell free" card and then

43

go about the rest of our lives as if nothing changed. Contrary to popular belief, there is no separation in Scripture between receiving Jesus as Savior and making Jesus Lord. He is Lord—period! He has always been. When we come to Him for forgiveness of our sins through faith in His sacrifice, we are bowing to His Lordship.

When we ask for forgiveness for our sins, we are essentially seeking forgiveness for not putting Him first in our lives. All sin comes from the love of self rather than love of Him. Because of our sinful nature, we do not love Him and put Him first perfectly.

In receiving Jesus, we thus forsake our lives to find our life in Him. Coming to Jesus means finally finding life and its overall purpose. It means understanding we were made for a relationship with God, but we couldn't have it before. Once Jesus' life flows through our veins, everything about us changes.

The once-dead soul is now alive, and we need to feed it. A few people do not concern themselves with food regularly, but most of us have no problem feeding ourselves at regular intervals with snacks in between.

What if we approached Bible reading, study, and memorization with the same voracity and intentionality? Since our bodies will die, and our earthly lives are so short compared to eternity, wouldn't it make more sense to increase our focus on feeding our spirit? Too many Christians rely heavily on Sunday-morning teaching for their food, yet they would never dream of eating one meal a week. That would be absurd! They would eventually become malnourished and die. Our spirits need regular nourishment with lots of meat to chew on.

God has something to say to us in Hebrews 5:12–13 about this, "For though by this time you ought to be teachers, you need someone to teach you again the basic principles of the oracles of God. You need milk, not solid food, for everyone who lives on milk is unskilled in the word of righteousness, since he is a child."

Many Scriptures speak of the treasure and richness of God's Word, and it's available to us! We have a feast at our fingertips, but so often, we just want a little bite. "Oh, no thank you, I don't need a plate. I'll just grab a bite and run out the door. I'm not really that hungry."

We must train our appetites to enjoy this new food for our living souls. We want to grow up to maturity, and this is only possible with the real, nourishing whole food of the Word of God.

Second, with our living souls, we need adequate housing and a fitting environment. Again, life can't stay the same upon coming to Christ. As Christ-followers, it shouldn't feel comfortable to spend copious amounts of time with the world. Of course, we need to be around those who don't know Jesus, or else we could never share the truth of the gospel. However, we should enjoy the fellowship of other believers in the body of Christ more than the fellowship of unbelievers. If we fit in better with those outside of Christ, we should ask ourselves why this is since we should feel most at home with those in our family. We must all find a Bible-believing church where we can grow and mature in our faith and spur each other on in truth and love.

In addition, connecting with others in a small group setting can be very beneficial. When my husband and I were newly married and newly saved, we were six hours away from family. God, in His providence, surrounded us with other newly married couples in a gospel-focused church. We became like family to each other. We connected weekly with each other in a small group, and we challenged each other to put sin to death. We talked openly about struggles, and we prayed in real, specific ways for one another.

The church we attended highly encouraged at-home study of the Word and memorization. The prayers of mature Christians in the church were saturated with Scripture, and I knew I wanted to know Scripture in this same way. My husband and I, who had been brought to life from death, found new "housing" and a fitting environment for soul growth in our gospel-centered church and with like-minded believers.

Along with our new diets and new environment for our souls to thrive, a new language emerges from our rebirth. The more time we spend in the Word, the more we think about the Word. I have found that phrases come into my mind seemingly out of nowhere. (Thank you, Holy Spirit.) As we meditate on Scripture and roll it around in our minds, we process new truths and apply them to our actions.

What we think usually finds its way out of our mouths. I know for me I have been with a friend before, and I will share something I hadn't necessarily considered sharing. However, I had been thinking about it throughout the day, so when asked how things were going, I told them about my musings. Since this is such a reality, it just makes sense to actively focus on Scripture and God's goodness and faithfulness, so that praise naturally rolls off of our tongues.

Being around other Christians who also use the language of praise to the King of Kings rubs off on us, as well. When I am around other women who are obviously in love with Jesus and give Him praise, I praise more as a result. From all this, we can surmise our language acquisition or lack thereof directly correlates to our new environment and food sources.

People in different cultures use their time in a variety of ways. Staying with our country transplant idea, we would need to discover how to use our time with our new life. Surely, a new life would mean different priorities and an alternate use of time, right?

Since this is the case, we must be careful to keep what we consider as our priorities. We always make time for what is most important to us. If getting to work on time is important, we plan accordingly. If eating breakfast is essential, we work it in. If being in the Word is vital, we get up earlier. If we value the latest Netflix series, we make time for it. We have time, but we use it according to what we value as the most important. If I asked evangelical Christians what was most important to them, I would guess most would rank their priorities in order of God first, family next, work third, and friends after that.

Is this really the way it plays out in life, though, for most of us? Do we give God the first and the best of our time? This new life in Jesus demands (yes, demands) a new set of priorities and not just a new set of *stated* priorities—but a different *use of time*—kind of priorities. It means giving up something we value for something we value more.

This new culture's use of time means what we feel like doing at the moment may not be what we should do. It may mean turning off the TV earlier so that we can get up earlier to study and meditate on the Word and to pray and commune with our Father. It may mean using our lunch breaks to pray or do a Bible study instead of gossiping with our coworkers. It may mean serving a family with sick kids or someone in the hospital when we'd rather relax after a long day. It may also mean leading a Bible study with teenagers when you feel like hanging out with your spouse or curling up on the couch with a blanket and reading a book.

No matter what this new life requires of us and our time, we must remember it's absolutely for our good. Every time we say, "No!" to our old selves and, "Yes!" to the Spirit, it's a win for us spiritually. We grow and mature and lean more on our Lord all the time. Each time we obey, we bow to His rightful Lordship. Let's fully step into this new country and this new, unfamiliar culture. Let's embrace it all and quit thinking about the old life we left behind. The new in every way is exponentially better than the old, and the new is what will make us feel most alive.

Chapter 6
Inexhaustible Abundance

Are we satisfied? Are we content? Are we living in the fullness of Christ? I believe the answer to these questions is likely no. Perhaps this is because we run hard after the full cup that always asks for more, yet it can never overflow. We can think the next raise, next vacation, next new outfit, next completed home project, or the next child will somehow complete us and satisfy that longing inside us to be complete. As Christians, we know in theory that none of it brings true satisfaction, yet we often still pursue. Perhaps it is because we unconsciously think that even though every other pursuit leaves us unsatisfied, this is the one that won't.

The solution to this never-ending cycle of pursuing misguided satisfaction outside of Jesus is discovering who we are. It's that identity question again. Do you know who you really are? I'm not talking about how you describe yourself on your social media account—Jesus lover, wife to an amazing husband, momma to six, coffee addict, wine connoisseur, etc. You get the picture. Any of that could change at any time. I'm talking about the true you. The part of you that is left when all is pulled away is the true you.

Over the past few years, Brandon and I have enjoyed watching *The Crown*, a Netflix series about the British royal family. As Netflix releases more episodes, we have come to respect and understand the queen's position on so many issues. Perhaps the most remarkable takeaway I have pertains to Queen Elizabeth acting out of interest of the Crown despite her feelings. She fully comprehended her position and its entailments. With care and precision, Queen Elizabeth personified the Crown in every way. Her very identity was that of the queen.

As important as a title of royalty is on this earth, how much more is this title in the heavenly kingdom! Each of us in Christ has been adopted into God's royal family. We're not the foster kid who has just some benefits of family. Wondrously, we are blood-bought sons and daughters. We lack nothing of spiritual worth and value. It's almost like our time on earth is a giant play wherein we may act out a tragedy of poverty, hatred, and death, but when the show is over, we ascend home to our true family and our true Father. He defines us no matter what happens here.

Let's say that sometime in the next twenty-five years, persecution hits the country as we've never known. If religious liberty is removed from us, and true believers continue to worship Christ as He is due, we will be persecuted. As much as we hope this will never happen, we must consider the possibility. What if someone confiscates our property or removes our children from us? What if we are thrown into jail or shot on the spot? What if we have nothing left? No house, no family, no bank account, and definitely no coffee or wine. Then, how do we define ourselves?

We should define ourselves in the exact same way we should be defining ourselves now. We discover who we really are as we fix our eyes on Christ. When we behold Him, we discover His sacrifice demonstrates we are sinners through and through. Through the gift of salvation bestowed on us at conversion, we are the children of the King of Kings. We are justified, which makes us no longer guilty in God's eyes. We are being sanctified or made holy as Christ is, and we will be glorified. We are ambassadors for God spreading His message of reconciliation. We are secure and unable to be snatched from the Father's hand. We are sealed with the Holy Spirit. We are a chosen people and a priesthood. When all is stripped away, we will still have the greatest treasure of all. We can comfort ourselves with these sweet reassurances from Scripture:

> "What then shall we say to these things? If God is for us, who can be against us? He who did not spare his own Son but gave him up for us all, how will he not also with him graciously give us all things? Who shall bring any charge against God's elect? It is God who justifies. Who is to condemn? Christ Jesus is the one who died—more than that, who was raised—who is at the right hand of God, who indeed is interceding for us. Who shall separate us from the love of Christ? Shall tribulation, or distress, or persecution, or famine, or nakedness, or danger, or sword? As it is written, 'For your sake we are being killed all the day long; we are regarded as sheep to be slaughtered.' No, in all these

things we are more than conquerors through him who loved us. For I am sure that neither death nor life, nor angels nor rulers, nor things present nor things to come, nor powers, nor height nor depth, nor anything else in all creation, will be able to separate us from the love of God in Christ Jesus our Lord" (Romans 8:31–39).

Soak in that. Roll around in it. Bask in it. Absorb it. Let it affect every part of you. That description in Romans 8 is who we are. Persecution may come our way, but if we have Christ, we have everything.

This reminds me of the parable Jesus told of the hidden treasure in Matthew 13:44, "The kingdom of heaven is like treasure hidden in a field, which a man found and covered up. Then in his joy he goes and sells all that he has and buys that field."

When we have Jesus, we don't NEED anything else. He is worth any sacrifice we make and so much more. As we just saw in the Romans passage, since God gave us His Son, won't He graciously give us all things? We could be completely broke and without a source of income. Our family could all be gone. We could experience torture night and day, but we would still be secure in our Savior's arms. We would still have the fruits of the Spirit, as the seal of the Spirit in us cannot be broken. We would still have an unfathomable inheritance. What truly matters cannot change. Amen!

In and through Christ, we cannot even calculate our inheritance. It is like Jesus invested our inheritance in such a way that its dividends keep producing. This is the kind of money that seems to produce more as you give more of it away. This is abundance to the fullest degree. Therefore, it is absolutely ludicrous for us as part of this wealthy family, who has been promised this inheritance and investments, to then scrape by and live like we're broke. Now I know we have not yet tasted all the Lord has in store for us. Our full inheritance is coming, BUT, even now, we have God in us.

- The Holy Spirit dwells in us (1 Corinthians 3:16).
- He is enough (Romans 8:31).
- He guides, directs, and comforts us (Psalm 32:8, 2 Corinthians 1:3–4).
- The Lord gives us strength (Isaiah 41:10).
- He is our refuge (Psalm 46:10).
- He lifts us up (Psalm 145:14).
- He is a shield around us (Psalm 3:3).
- He rejoices with us and sings over us (Zephaniah 3:17).
- He promises never to abandon us (Hebrews 13:5).
- He is our provider (Phil. 4:19).
- He is our joy (Nehemiah 8:10).
- It's all about Him (Colossians 1:15–20, Psalm 24:1).
- He gives us treasure (2 Corinthians 4:7).
- Because we have Him, we have EVERYTHING (Colossians 2:2–3, Second Peter 1:3).

As I write this, I remember the ridiculous number of times I thought something else would satisfy me. It's not like I would ever verbalize that or even consciously think I need something else other than this amazing God. However, my flesh and my actions have shown it and still do show it when my thoughts are left unchecked.

When Brandon and I were first married, we lived in an apartment. I couldn't wait to eventually get a house as we knew it was wise to build equity and not just spend money on rent. Within six months of getting the house we really wanted, we began a kitchen remodel. We didn't really have the money for it, but we really wanted it. My husband learned a lot through this process since he had to do most of the remodeling for us to afford it.

The kitchen remodel was nice for a while, but after our second son, Dirk, was born, we were sure a new van fresh off the lot was what we had to have. Also, while at this house, we decided I would stay at home with Blake and Dirk. I made over half of our income, so it was tough to give up that money, but through prayer, we felt certain God would provide for our needs. He provided in all kinds of amazing ways, with one being a company calling Brandon about a job he had applied for a few months before. It was an increase in pay, and it really reassured us of God's provision and blessing.

We stayed in our first house for about three years before we got the itch to move on to bigger and better. Our starter home was built in the '50s, so we decided to upgrade to a new house in a new subdivision. I got cold feet just before the closing, but it was a bit too late to back out. We plunged ahead and definitely felt the strain on our finances. We were committed to not being in any debt besides our house, so we were unwilling to use credit for purchases.

Within the three to four year span we lived in this new house, we somehow came up with the money to finish the basement. Brandon spent most evenings during a six-month period working on finishing this basement. We only hired out what he could not do, so he again learned a lot about building and construction. At one point, he, with the help of a few great neighbors, even cut an egress window into the basement's concrete wall. During the time at this second house, I became pregnant with our third son. I pushed for the basement project to be completed before our Asher was born. Brandon accomplished this, and yet even that didn't satisfy.

An ache formed in us to return to the area where we grew up. With three sons, I prayed about God providing a job back home so that we could be closer to family. To Brandon's amazement, God did this. He even gave him the same salary (which was like a raise, due to the cost of living difference between an urban to rural area).

Having learned from our previous mistake of biting off more than we could chew with home costs, we searched for an older home with character. We eventually found one. Boy, did it have character! When we purchased it, dark paneling covered most areas of the house. Carpet was in part of the bathroom and lattice in the dining room. We began remodeling this house, but because it needed so much updating, we never quite got there. It, too, was a disappointment.

After having three children, we thought we were done. My husband is an only child, so three seemed plentiful to him. Having always had a close relationship with my mom, I longed for a girl to have this relationship with, as well. Even though I was close to my boys, I knew they would eventually become close to their future wives' families. I prayed for several years, asking God to change Brandon's heart about more children or asking Him to change mine. God answered. Brandon eventually came to me and said we should try for another baby. We were blessed within the year with Claira Marie. What a joy it was to have a girl to complete our family!

During this time, I continued to grow in the Lord. I was diligent about rising early to read the Word, pray, and memorize, but often failed to apply it during the day. It was hard with three little boys and a baby. I would long for the end of the day to just sit and relax with Brandon. In retrospect, I can see a lot of mental focus I wasted longing for rest when I could've just enjoyed the moments with the little ones God gave me. There were vacations here and there that promised peace and rest but sometimes left me even more exhausted.

After four years in the home full of character, God abundantly provided a rental home for us in our hometown because a higher-paying job opened. After fasting and much prayer, we believed God was calling us back to our hometown. We couldn't yet buy a home because the family buying our home of character needed to purchase it on contract. It would be several years before we would have the money to purchase another home.

During this time, God kept growing us spiritually and in our family size. He gave us a surprise son, Judah Wade, whom every member of our family adored. He gave me greater contentment to just enjoy the kids and focus less on my home. Since we were renting, there were no projects we could do. All we could do was enjoy our children and get plugged back into relationships in our little town. Eventually, we built a new, large home, where God gave us yet another addition to our family, Finley Grace. As I think back to my cries out to God for a girl, I'm truly in awe at God's incredible gift of not just one girl, but six years later, two girls in our family.

Before we moved into our new house, God had already taught me it too wouldn't satisfy. Over time in this home, there would be pictures to hang, things to move around as the family changed, paint color regrets, and landscaping needs, and so much more. We've faltered at times, even in this home, but overall, God has taught us to quit looking to what we own to fill us and make us complete. A house and possessions can't be brought to the standard we long for because that standard is perfection. We as Christians long for our perfect home with our perfect Father.

Just as Brandon and I sometimes looked for homes and projects to complete us, many Christians function daily as if we need something other than Christ to fulfill us. I now understand there is not a physical home, a vacation, a raise, a completed project, or a relationship that truly satisfies. What then? Should we never purchase a home, go on a vacation, rejoice over a raise, pursue an activity or project, or invest in relationships? Of course not!

That's taking it too far, but here's the tricky part. We can have, but not look to anything or anyone to bring us satisfaction or completion.

If someone needs a bigger home, and after prayer and an affirmative answer from the Lord, they should get the larger house. It is not necessarily the purchases or home upgrades that are sinful, but it can be the heart posture behind them. We must not pursue anything with the mindset that when we get this, do this, or have this baby, our life will be complete, and we will be satisfied. We must check our heart before we begin anything. In some cases, we should discontinue the action.

I have grown to become aware of just how often I run to a substitute to satisfy what only Jesus can truly quench. We run to so many other substitutes, such as: "I just need a coffee right now." "I really could use a break." "I wish someone would come and take these kids for a bit and give me a moment's peace." "When my house is clean, I'll be kind to everyone around me." "When this project is complete, all will be well." "We just need a vacation." The list could go on and on. Each person might run to something different. So, to reiterate, coffee isn't wrong, nor a break, nor a clean house, completed projects, or vacations. It is sometimes the motivation behind these activities where the sin lies.

Isn't this what so many of us do as Christians? We understand we are sinners without hope and no way of forgiveness on our own. We trust in Jesus' death and resurrection as our only hope of reconciliation with the Father. We are overjoyed at His gift of grace, and then we go on about our way, looking for something else to take care of our present need. Our bank accounts have received a deposit of an incalculable amount. We have all we need and more than we can even fathom or ask for.

Ephesians 3:20 says, "Now to him who is able to do far more abundantly than all that we ask or think according to the power at work within us."

We draw from the spiritual well of Christ taking out little bits of our wealth here and there, but never truly benefiting from all He offers us as His child. Wouldn't it be utterly ridiculous for a beggar, who suddenly received an inheritance giving him more money than he could possibly ever spend in a lifetime, to go back to begging because it's a quick fix? When he goes to the bank to withdraw money, he has to wait for thirty minutes or so to receive what he needs, so it's just easier to beg since it's the faster fix.

God answers us. He always gives us what we need, but often in a different time than what we planned. I have so often found that when I stop and pray and seek my Lord's solution, He answers. So often, though, it isn't an immediate answer. Life might feel overwhelming and chaotic, and when I sneak away and pray, the chaos doesn't necessarily go away. However, within about thirty minutes, I realize I no longer feel anxious and upset.

The quick fix would have been to call someone and complain about all there was to do and how the kids were so difficult that day. The friend, of course, would join in with me and tell me about her kids as well. Upon getting off the phone, I would possibly feel not alone in my day, but it's doubtful that phone call would change my attitude.

Ultimately, God's solutions satisfy. They change our perspective. They remind us Christ is more than enough, and He will give us more than we need to not only make it through but also do it in love to those around us and with thankfulness.

The reason this actually works is we're talking about the God of the universe. He doesn't do anything halfway, but fully and abundantly. When He gives to His children, He bestows gifts and help beyond measure.

John 10:10 says, "The thief comes only to steal and kill and destroy. I have come that they may have life, and have it abundantly."

In this passage in John, Jesus doesn't just tell us He comes to give us life. By using the adverb, abundantly, here, He tells us to what extent we are to have life. He isn't just referring to our life after death, but our life now. Most definitely, the adverb, abundantly, is not referring to Jesus plus all our hearts' wishes—wealth, fame, ease, and comfort.

Abundant life is a life of fullness in and through Jesus despite our circumstances, which may mean wealth or poverty, health or sickness, fame or obscurity, or completed projects or everything undone. Abundance is ours for the taking in any and every situation through Christ, who never changes.

So the real question is, "What do we truly want?" If we break it down and get honest, maybe too many of us are content to go for the quick fix and the tangible here and now. Going after God and understanding all He has for us and what is available to us is just too hard. When we go for the immediate, tangible fix, don't we really do it to have peace, joy, completion, satisfaction, love, and acceptance?

The very thing we are desperately desiring, we already have. In hypothetical terms, that hot coffee fix we thirst for has already been dropped off. The rest we crave in a vacation has already been given. The biggest project we would ever want to complete has been finished. It's all ours already in our Savior, Jesus Christ. We have the full bank account of peace, joy, completion, satisfaction, love, and acceptance in Him. Now, we must inexhaustibly draw out what belongs to us in Christ and live in abundance.

Chapter 7

You're on Fire!
(At Least I Hope You Are)

As part of my children's school curriculum this past year, we read a book titled *Parables from Nature.* I was amazed at how the author, Margaret Gatty, drew numerous parallels between nature and our spiritual journeys. I drew some similar parallels on a trip out west our family recently took.

We were so incredibly amazed by the beauty in all that we saw. When looking at it from a biblical perspective, I was also struck by the thought that so much beauty in the canyons and rock formations was likely the result of the flood, which we know was God's judgment on sin.

Now, millions of people have been able to gaze upon these wonders and marvel at their own small state because God brought beauty out of devastation. Perhaps the most significant sights from which I drew biblical parallels were the giant sequoia trees. Initially, I was just in awe at the sheer size of these trees, which are up to 311 feet tall with bases up to 40 feet in diameter. As we walked through the groves, I felt as though I was walking among silent giants.

After the initial shock of their size, I noticed they all looked like they had been burned. It turns out these ancient trees, some of them being over 3,000 years old, have survived forest fires because God made them to have chemicals in the wood and bark that insulate them from most fire. Before this was known, there was a 100-year stretch where rangers attempted to protect the trees from fire by working hard to put out natural fires occurring in the forests.

Through study and experimentation, researchers discovered the sequoias need fire to reproduce. Fire clears away the competing firs and cedars to expose bare mineral soil for the tiny seeds to reproduce. Mature trees may yearly produce 2,000 egg-sized cones bearing 400,000 seeds, which disperse only when the cones open. A few cones open without fire, but the majority need the heat for the cones to open and the seeds to disperse. In addition, the fire lets sunlight in and burns logs and branches on the forest floor to ashes, which is then used as fertilizer.

Hebrews 12:29 describes God as a consuming fire. Throughout Scripture, fire is often a symbol of God's presence. It is also spoken of as an instrument of God's judgment and a sign of his power.

I wonder how many of us err on the side of viewing the fires of life and things God wants to burn away in us in the same way the forest rangers once did. "Let's put it out! Put it out as quickly as possible for ourselves and for the people around us! Let's get back to ease and comfort because the fire is hot!"

If we're honest, we kind of like what's growing up around us. I know this is often my first response. "Make this stop! I like it when life's easy. I know I pray I want to grow in Christ, but I don't really want to have to give anything up. This should be easier. I dislike these growing pains!"

The problem with ease and comfort is it makes us coast. It makes us put on the cruise control and lets our minds wander. We tend to settle and become complacent over time. God definitely allows us to experience this ease at times, but He loves us too much to leave us there. If God wanted to give us ease, He would've saved us and taken us home, but He doesn't do that the majority of the time. In His great grace, He calls us to more all the time because He wants our all. And He wants our all because we are His, and He knows the more we surrender, the more abundant our lives will be in Him.

Isn't this the way we, as parents, relate to our children? As they grow and mature, we want to keep challenging them and giving them more responsibilities. Because we love them, we desire more for them than what they think they presently need or want. How foolish it would be to avoid challenging or giving them difficulties to preserve their apparent happiness or desire for comfort! In many ways, attempting to keep them where they are would be hating them. Since we as humans know how to prepare our children for their future, how much more does God know how to challenge and strengthen us for tasks ahead!

Again, Galatians 2:20 applies here. "I have been crucified with Christ. It is no longer I who live, but Christ who lives in me, And the life I now live in the flesh I live by faith in the Son of God, who loved me and gave himself for me." When we received Christ, we died. It's not about us anymore, which it never really was, but before Christ, we didn't know that.

Our lives take on a radical shift with our focus on His glory now and not ours. Colossians 2:6–7 says, "Therefore as you received Christ Jesus the Lord, so walk in him, rooted and built up in him and established in the faith, just as you were taught, abounding in thanksgiving."

When we received Jesus, our very root systems changed. The old root systems died, and our root systems are Jesus. Like little children playing dress-up, we can be tempted to drape parts of our old tree over our new one.

We try to tuck them in and think they can become part of us. We may talk and act like that dress-up costume we are in, but Christ won't let us pretend like that for long. He will allow the fire to burn away what does not line up with our identity in Him. The beginning of these verses start with "AS you received Christ Jesus...." How did we receive Jesus? BY grace through faith... complete and utter dependence on Him. In the same way, our Christian lives continue—by grace, we are fed and nourished with new roots and a new tree. We take the steps forward to obey the Lord. We choose to pray, meditate on the Word, and serve, but ultimately it is God's nudging for us to do so and His sanctifying work. We don't change ourselves, but rather he changes us through the obedience He gives us.

Trying to accomplish righteousness doesn't work. Already dressed in righteousness, we act in accordance with our clothing. Rolling around in grace, we are new. Our very tree is new, and it grows differently than the ones around us. Our tree, our root system, only gets stronger through fire. Trials and difficulties we go through in life, which threaten to undo us, which devour other trees. These difficulties, if we yield them to our Lord through thanksgiving and faith, have the potential to strengthen our tree, making it grow higher and reproduce exponentially.

The Lord is teaching me to quit trying to just make it through as fast as possible—to quit asking for what He's already given me, but to praise Him and thank Him in it. It changes everything. He gives us all we need to make it through the fire victoriously.

Have you ever noticed how we so often talk about people being blessed when they're doing well by worldly standards? Rarely would you hear someone say, "Oh, how blessed you are!" to a friend when her husband just lost his job. When your mom discovers she has cancer, you likely wouldn't utter praiseworthy blessing words at that time either. However, if what is most important is God's glory and eternity with Him, then we should view all He allows into our lives as a blessing. We might not understand it, but we know He is good, so He will use it for good. It may be the tailor-made "blessing" for our sanctification or for our neighbor's salvation. Whatever comes from it, whether we discover it or not, is a perfect fiery blessing through eternal eyes.

I frequently pray that God wouldn't leave me as I am, but He would keep sanctifying me. Even with praying this prayer, I still become annoyed when things aren't going "my" way. I recently realized just how many things in my life now are not as I would like them to be. I'm in a period of unanswered prayers and uncertainty of direction in some key areas. Additionally, different roles are emerging for me, and altered relationships have surfaced. During this, it seems God is silent. Of course, He isn't, since He speaks through His unchanging Word, but for me, at present, I need direction.

The tendency of my heart is to slip into discontented demands for help. In His kindness, He offers me a glimpse into my lazy heart that wants change without inconvenience. How foolish of me! The fire, the refinement, the burning away of chaff, was never supposed to feel good. It hurts. It destroys. It mortifies. Most significantly, this sanctifying fire burns away what holds us back from a truer, more abundant life in fellowship with our Lord Jesus.

Right before Jesus ascended into heaven, He gave the disciples the great commission to go into all the world to make disciples, and then He promised they wouldn't be alone, but He would give them a helper, the Holy Spirit. And do you remember the evidence of them receiving the Holy Spirit? Flames of fire above their heads and speaking in tongues.

The Holy Spirit used speaking in tongues to allow the surrounding peoples who had come to Jerusalem for Pentecost to hear the truth of the gospel that Jesus, the Son of God, had been crucified for sin and raised from the dead as proof of the Father's satisfaction. Because of this miracle of common men speaking in other languages and the clear presentation of the gospel, about three thousand people believed and trusted Jesus to save them.

Before the disciples had the flames of fire hovering over their heads, they had to go through some fire. The disciples had to die to self to reproduce, and, likewise, so do we. They had to experience the Holy Spirit's convicting power to show them their sin and their need for the Savior. They had to die to their identities, had to leave their occupations and families to follow Jesus. Then they had to die to their ideas of what Jesus would do. They had to die to their fear after Jesus was crucified that it had all been a mistake. After His ascension, they had to die to their doubt that He would give them help to complete the mission. They went through fire, and at Pentecost and beyond, they reproduced.

They also learned they had to continue to rely on the same Holy Spirit fire to give them guidance, boldness, and purpose as the fires of tribulation and persecution only continued and intensified. From start to finish, they believed, were sustained, and effectively used by God to accomplish His purposes. In Romans 12:1, Paul tells us to offer our bodies as living sacrifices. The sacrifices of the Old Testament were burned up with fire, but we are told here in the New Testament to be living sacrifices.

So picture this with me... Living Beings, Christians, walking around on fire and spreading the fragrance of Christ wherever we go. Do you know how someone who has been sitting by a campfire gives off that smell? It is clear they have been close to a fire. If we are constantly on fire with the Holy Spirit's presence, we should smell like it. When we've been through fire and trials and have known our Lord in a deeper way, we should testify of it to those around us.

Let's embrace the fire. Let's praise God for the fire and quit looking for the closest exit! Isaiah 43:2 says, "When you pass through the waters, I will be with you; and through the rivers, they shall not overwhelm you; when you walk through fire you shall not be burned, and the flame shall not consume you."

Let's walk through the fire, knowing He is with us. When we are in Him, when we have trusted in Jesus' sacrifice alone for the forgiveness of sin and peace with the Father, we are promised that **same Holy Spirit**. God is immutable. He is the same God today as He was in the years of the first-century disciples. If Holy-Spirit fire was available to them, He's available to us with the same boldness, power, and efficacy.

Chapter 8

I'll Surrender Some of It

I love worship music. I long for the feeling of the Holy Spirit, filling me up in Him. I look forward to worshiping in the presence of a group of believers praising Jesus with everything in them. Sometimes in the middle of an especially moving worship service, I will just be still and listen to the beauty in songs of adoration to our King. It gives me a small glimpse of what heaven may be like as we gather around the throne and praise and praise and praise. The four living creatures, as Revelation chapter 4 reports, never cease to cry out, "Holy, holy, holy, is the Lord God Almighty, who was and is and is to come!" (Revelation 4:8).

The twenty-four elders also join in this contagious worship as they "fall down before him who is seated on the throne and worship him who lives forever and ever. They cast their crowns before the throne, saying, 'Worthy are you, our Lord and God, to receive glory and honor and power, for you created all things, and by your will they existed and were created'" (Revelation 4:10–11).

The deeper we go into the depths of gospel truths, the more we earnestly desire to worship. Not only did this magnificent God create us, but He also redeemed us. We brought nothing to Him to be counted as a son and an heir, but yet we are, and it is all due to Jesus' payment of our sins.

When we really comprehend this, we are emptied of pride, and we just want to worship the One who did it all for us. We are like the woman at Jesus' feet pouring out expensive perfume in thankfulness and praise. She knew who she was and what God had made her. All praise had to go to Him at any expense to her.

When I'm in a worship service, and I look around at other believers pouring out their praise to God with hands raised, eyes closed, and mouths smiling, I do not doubt the sincerity of their worship. I believe they love Jesus and want to praise Him with their all. There is a posture of surrender in almost every part of them. They recognize they have been lost and found all because of grace. Who wouldn't want to give their life fully to the One who brought about their conversion?

As a whole, we sing lyrics about surrendering to Jesus, giving Him our all, letting Him take our everything, telling Him how worthy He is in all of our lives, forsaking all for Him, and so on. It is all absolutely true. As Revelation clearly stated, God is worthy to receive glory, and honor, and power (v. 4:11). He alone is worthy. Because He has redeemed us, made us His own, and given us His very own righteousness, we owe Him our all.

Unfortunately, I see in myself and others a real disconnect between sacrificial worship in song, posture, and talk when compared with real-life sacrifice and humility. I'm confident I'm not the only one who has praised the Lord in worship with hands raised and holy joy, only to leave church irritated that one of my kids did something embarrassing, ticked that someone uttered a crappy comment, and annoyed about the way something was done.

71

What happened to, "Lord, I surrender all," when that worship music was blaring, and "Lord, take my everything,"? Maybe instead of singing, "All," I should have really sung, "I surrender all to you, God, BUT my reputation and my pride," or "Lord, take it all, but my money, my house, my health, or my time." Now, of course, that's ridiculous, but yet, it is what our thoughts and actions sometimes show. They show we surrender to God a powerful song and the lyrics in the moment, but not a lot else. If we sing *all,* then we should mean *all.*

My life and yours should show an overall surrender, thus bridging the disconnect. Obviously, this occurs because we are not yet glorified. While still in our sinful flesh, we may feel one way and act another. We may sincerely want to give our Lord everything, but when our flesh kicks in and everything isn't going our way, we fail to surrender our all. Another way to think about our unwillingness to surrender is to consider how we make our plans and how God fits into them. More appropriately, we should humbly hold lightly every course of action and eagerly expect Him to rock our plans as He sees fit.

Even though this discrepancy exists in our spiritual lives, it doesn't mean we just accept and succumb to it. No! We fight it through the power of the Holy Spirit. Again and again, we repent, and we choose with His power to surrender our worship in all of life.

This lip service we give reminds me of the disciples' passionate surrender to Christ with their words, but a misalignment with their lives. When things became difficult, they scattered. If we only peer into Peter's allegiance with some of his words, we can get an adequate picture of this.

- "And Peter answered him, 'Lord, if it is you, command me to come to you on the water.' He said, 'Come.' So Peter got out of the boat and walked on the water and came to Jesus. But when he saw the wind, he was afraid, and beginning to sink he cried out, 'Lord, save me.' Jesus immediately reached out his hand and took hold of him, saying to him, 'O you of little faith, why did you doubt?' And when they got into the boat, the wind ceased. And those in the boat worshiped him, saying, 'Truly you are the Son of God'" (Matthew 14:28–33).

- "He said to them, 'But who do you say that I am?' Simon Peter replied, 'You are the Christ, the Son of the living God'" (Matthew 16:15–16).

- "Then Peter said in reply, 'See, we have left everything and followed you. What then will we have?'" (Matthew 19:27).

- "Peter said to him, 'Even if I must die with you, I will not deny you!' And all the disciples said the same" (Matthew 26:35).

- "Now Peter was sitting outside in the courtyard. And a servant girl came up to him and said, 'You also were with Jesus the Galilean.' But he denied it before them all, saying, 'I do not know what you mean.' And when he went out to the entrance, another servant girl saw him, and she said to the bystanders, 'This man was with Jesus of Nazareth.' And again he denied it with an oath. 'I do not know the man.' After a little while the bystanders came up and said to Peter, 'Certainly you too are one of them, for your accent betrays you.' Then he began to invoke a curse on himself and to swear, 'I do not know the man.' And immediately the rooster crowed" (Matthew 26:69–74).

What I have found to be immensely encouraging is Jesus actually kept using Peter for ministry! In Matthew 16, after Peter confesses that Jesus is the Christ the Son of the Living God, Jesus says to him, "And I tell you, you are Peter, and on this rock I will build my church, and the gates of hell shall not prevail against it. I will give you the keys of the kingdom of heaven, and whatever you bind on earth shall be bound in heaven, and whatever you loose on earth shall be loosed in heaven" (Matthew 16:18–19).

When Jesus prophesied to Peter about his key role in building the church, He foreknew Peter's betrayal. He was fully cognizant Peter would cowardly deny Him. Before the denial, we gather in the gospels that Peter certainly knew Jesus' identity. He previously confessed Jesus is the Messiah and Son of God, and yet he appeared ashamed of his connection with the God of the universe when things got precarious.

We have to contemplate what changed for the disciples to transform them from weak and frightened men to strong, bold witnesses for Jesus who were willing to die for the sake of the gospel. A miraculous metamorphosis manifested itself in them when the Holy Spirit came upon them at Pentecost. It was after the filling of the Holy Spirit that they did what they could not do before. After the filling of the Holy Spirit, the disciples spoke words of devotion and backed up those words with actions because they had the power to obey. They no longer just confessed they would follow Jesus anywhere and lay down their lives for Him; they actually did this.

We must ask ourselves: Is God the same today? Hebrews 13:8 says, "Jesus Christ is the same yesterday, today, and forever."

We know we receive the Holy Spirit upon receiving Jesus as Savior. "In him you also, when you heard the word of truth, the gospel of your salvation, and believed in him, were sealed with the promised Holy Spirit, who is the guarantee of our inheritance until we acquire possession of it, to the praise of his glory" (Ephesians 1:13–14).

He is the deposit until we are glorified. If the Holy Spirit transformed them, can't He do the same for us? Can't He give us the power to put actions behind our words of devotion? YES!!!

Upon the Father's rescue of our souls, the lifelong process of sanctification began. Sanctification continues in our lives until we die and are glorified. The Holy Spirit convicts us of sin through the Word. We then either obey and grow more into abundant life, or we ignore the conviction and remain people of lip service who live lives of spiritual scarcity.

Entering the Christian walk, I was somewhat expecting life to go as I planned, especially if what I planned was spiritual. Surely, God was on "MY" team, and He wanted exactly what I wanted, or so I thought. Through a long series of disappointments all packed in together, He has in His wisdom demonstrated to me that His thoughts are not my thoughts, and His ways are not my ways (See Isaiah 55:8).

Upon having children, I was sure there was a particular "formula" for turning them out right. Brandon and I have prayed for our children from the womb and pointed them to Jesus throughout their lives. I never expected perfection from them, but looking back now, I perceive I wanted nice, clean, neat boxes for their lives where everything fit in just so. God has shown me in a myriad of ways that Brandon and I are to be faithful in training them up in the faith, teaching them to avoid strong negative influences, and living out our lives of faith in front of them.

With this faithfulness, He has also taught me surrender. With each child, there is such anticipation and hope, and with each one, there is needed surrender. They fail, and they need a Savior, as do we. If I look to my children to satisfy me, I will forever be disappointed.

Keeping with that point, Brandon is an amazing husband. He loves Jesus. He works hard and provides well. He supports and builds into each of our children. With all that he is, he is not my Savior, and he cannot be all I want him to be. If I look to him to satisfy or if he looks to me to satisfy all he needs, we will both be disappointed. There is surrender of the marriage relationship to the Lord to allow Him to accomplish what He desires for our marriage. It may not be what I expect or think I deserve.

Surely, we don't need to surrender others around us, too, right? Maybe we have a close friend whose dependability is rock solid. That may be so, but ultimately friendships are a gift from the Lord, and as enjoyable as they may be, they won't fill or complete us. In hope, we enter some relationships planning that God will save that person through us. It often doesn't turn out that way. We are faithful in speaking truth, praying, and living out faithful lives, but we must surrender that relationship and all other friendships that God gives us into His hands. We keep praying, but we don't let our worship and praise change because of unanswered prayer.

Perhaps from time to time or always, we consciously or unconsciously seek out the admiration and praise of others. What a futile task! Even though we may gain some who approve, at the same time, we are likely inviting the harsh critiques of others. Inevitably, those who love us for a while will grow bored with us and move on to others they may admire. In addition, those who praise us may do it with insincerity and disdain in their hearts. We must hold and pursue all relationships with our hands open.

How quickly too we must surrender money into the hands of our King! We make plans for the money that comes our way only to have an unexpected bill come in the mail or a major appliance to break down. Maybe the extra money coming our way was a gift for that very purpose. Perhaps that bonus was for the persecuted family we read about in our Christian magazine. Regardless of the amount of money that comes through our hands, it never proves enough. The desire for more of it and more of what it can buy continues to remain. Perhaps this is because after we tithe and check that off of our list, we hold tightly to it and think about what we can get with the rest of "our" money. There will never be enough of it until we surrender it to the one who owns the cattle on a thousand hills (Psalm 50:10).

What's left if we hold lightly and surrender all else to Christ's Lordship? We are—our very selves. We may be tempted to believe God can have all these other things, but we get to decide what happens to us. We can pursue physical health by eating the right foods, exercising properly, applying the right creams, and taking all the necessary vitamins. By studying and staying up to date on the news, we can keep our minds sharp and clear. You know where I'm headed here. Even our minds and bodies may change in a split second. Being wise stewards, we should care for our physical and mental health, but ultimately surrender our bodies to the Lord. Even if it were possible for our bodies and minds to remain constantly strong, we will disappoint ourselves. We may have one idea of what we'll do and think and then react differently. We can't even rely on ourselves to satisfy. We too disappoint.

Being in Christ, we must rest fully surrendered. God doesn't owe us anything. We deserve nothing, but we received abundance. He bestows abundance in Christ, but it so often looks very different than our expectations. We expect things to be somewhat easy and go our way. Since we follow Christ and we know

He is good, we assume He will save our children and set them on fire for Him. We expect godly spouses who do almost everything right, fulfilling friends, abundant resources, saved people whom we witness to, peaceful families, hearty health, mental clarity, and so much more. We deserve it, don't we? ...That's laughable.

We deserve hell and separation from our Father. Instead, He's given us Himself. Anything else that "goes our way" is icing on the cake, or is it? Perhaps if we could see what God sees, we would want the broken family, the messed-up kid, the lack of finances, and more perceived difficulties. Isn't the point His glory? The surrender of our plans for His is to His glory and our good.

A lot of circumstances haven't gone my way. The sweet Holy Spirit repeatedly softens my heart through gospel truth. In the body of Christ, we are redeemed and have the righteousness of our Savior. When someone sins against us or when circumstances or people do not behave as "planned," it is so easy to forget what wretches we actually are. We can think we deserve more than unjust treatment. We know we didn't deserve Jesus, but after we got Him, we mistakenly believe everything should go our way. We raise our hands in praise and worship to our King because we know we received a relationship with the God of the universe all because of Jesus' sacrifice. Even with this knowledge, we carry on as if we're important people apart from the gospel.

It is imperative that we wake up, perceive the disconnect between our words and actions, and fight the flesh with the tools given to us with the power of the Holy Spirit. Only after realizing this, will we be willing to allow the Holy Spirit to work in us to line up works and faith. Knowing we actually have this power, we can worship our Lord as He is due with actions behind our undying words of devotion. Once we open our spiritual eyes to these truths, we will discern the many areas we are unwilling to surrender. Open surrender based on spirit and truth is authentic worship. May we find ourselves offering sweet surrender to our Lord in each and every situation! Depending on nothing else, but Jesus, we will worship abundantly. May the lyrics to the hymn, "The Solid Rock," sing out in our hearts and minds as all else proves to be unworthy of our hope and worship.

> "My hope is built on nothing less
> Than Jesus' blood and righteousness;
> I dare not trust the sweetest frame,
> But wholly lean on Jesus' name.
>
> On Christ, the solid Rock, I stand;
> All other ground is sinking sand,
> All other ground is sinking sand."

Chapter 9

You Brought the Ram, Right?

In the Old Testament, the Israelites were commanded to bring various animals to offer as burnt offerings. The Levites, who God designated as priests to Him, killed these animals and carefully followed instructions to prepare and burn the flesh as a burnt offering. Since the sacrifices offered only temporarily covered the Israelites' sins, they had to be offered repeatedly.

The Word tells us these sacrifices gave off a satisfying smell to the Lord. One place where God speaks of the smell of the offering is Leviticus 1:9, which states, "And the priest shall burn all of it on the altar, as a burnt offering, a food offering with a pleasing aroma to the LORD."

I brought up in a previous chapter that God wants more from us than lip service. He desires full lives of surrender for our ultimate good and His glory. Frequently in the Old Testament, the Israelites followed up their lip service with the required sacrifices to God, but so much of it was out of duty and not from their hearts. The Israelites were going through the motions, but their hearts were far from God. They followed a religion and not true love.

Since we are under the new covenant, which Jesus ushered in, we no longer sacrifice burnt offerings to the Lord. Jesus was the ultimate last sacrifice unto the Lord, so burnt offerings are obsolete. Jesus paid for our sins. We operate under grace and not the law in an attempt to earn God's favor. Jesus has earned every bit of it, and the Father has applied all of Christ's righteousness to us. This, however, does not mean we cease to give offerings to the Lord, although the motivation to do so has completely changed. Now love and gratitude for Jesus and all He accomplished for us motivate us to sacrifice with thanksgiving.

We are often quick to judge the Israelites and proud in our response that we would never do what they did, but it would be wise to evaluate if even today, while operating under grace and not law, we respond in similar ways. How often we praise the Lord with our lips, read our Bibles, pray, attend church, and serve others all the while having hearts cold toward the things of God! As true believers, we even have the Holy Spirit to empower us to obey and serve from the heart, yet it remains a struggle.

So, if lip service alone isn't true worship, and outward, cold actions aren't true worship, then we must consider again what true worship encompasses. As previously stated in the biblical definition in John 4:24, true worship is worship in spirit **and** truth. This type of worship comes from the Spirit since it cannot come out of the flesh. The Spirit uses the Word of truth to convict us, nudge us to repentance, speak what doesn't come naturally, and to empower us to obey. This combination of Spirit with truth starts with the right orientation to God. When this orientation shifts, we displace our worship, and we are tempted to offer lip service or go through the motions with our hearts far from God.

Have you ever wondered what caused Abraham to be willing to sacrifice the long-awaited son of his old age, the promised son who was in the line of Christ? Abraham knew His God, and he trusted when it didn't make any sense. His relationship with God did not allow for some sort of injustice or evil on God's part. In every way, God showed Himself to Abraham as good and faithful. Because Abraham knew His God through a close relationship, he trusted God with what was most precious to him. In a tangible offer of surrender, He obeyed God because He knew the truth.

If Abraham questioned God about why He would ask such a sacrifice of him, we are not privy to this in Scripture. He intimately knew His God through relationship, and he obeyed. God is not afraid of our questions. He can and does withstand them all. His character is unchanging. He is good ALWAYS even if what He asks of us does not feel good. We can never operate out of our feelings if our feelings contradict the Word of God since we cannot trust our emotions and our hearts. "The heart is deceitful above all things, and desperately sick; who can understand it?" (Jeremiah 17:9).

We would never even consider going to a mentally ill individual or a pathological liar and ask them for advice. It would be best for us to remember this when we consider following the leading of our hearts since they are gravely afflicted liars. We can never take our cues for disobedience or a lack of trust in God from our feelings. They are not a credible source. The Holy Spirit prompts and leads us in certain ways, but never in a way that contradicts the truth of the Bible. Only God's Word is trustworthy, and we should apply it to understand all that God calls us to do, no matter how difficult.

If we don't truly know our God as Scripture reveals Him, and if we aren't functioning out of a gospel-filled mindset, sacrifice doesn't make sense. Our insane, desperately sick hearts will tell us God wants us to be happy, and we need to pursue happiness at all costs. They will tell us we've worked hard enough. They will whisper that Christ accomplished it all on the cross; therefore, being careful not to add works to our salvation, we should relax and spend our time watching more Netflix. Our sinful hearts will always cater to our flesh and its comfort and ease.

Just as we draw closer to a crackling, well-built fire on a frigid night, we must draw near to the King of Kings to reconcile our feelings and the truth of who we are as a new creation with a new orientation to our Father. As soon as we take our eyes off our Redeemer, we are tempted to operate in a duty-based relationship to Him.

In his book, *The Cross-Centered Life,* C.J. Mahaney encourages believers to preach the gospel to themselves daily. There is so much wisdom in this practice, yet so many of us think we know gospel truths backward and forward, so we don't need to rehearse them again. However, upon meditating on gospel gems, we discover more facets of its treasure all the time.

If we truly spoke gospel truths to our cold hearts, then the warming of them would cause outward obedience and joy to pop out like exploding popcorn kernels. It is only as we constantly remember where we've come from, who we are now, and where we are headed, that we can rightly worship the one who made it all possible. It is only out of love and truth that we worship sacrificially.

One of the most essential truths we must remind ourselves of is we have been brought from death to life to live for Him. He didn't give us spiritual life so that we could hoard this life for ourselves. "Or do you not know that your body is a temple of the Holy Spirit within you, whom you have from God? You are not your own, for you were bought with a price. So glorify God in your body" (1 Corinthians 6:19–20).

"And those who belong to Christ Jesus have crucified the flesh with its passions and desires. If we live by the Spirit, let us also keep in step with the Spirit" (Galatians 5:24–25).

"But I do not account my life of any value nor as precious to myself, if only I may finish my course and the ministry that I received from the Lord Jesus, to testify to the gospel of the grace of God" (Acts 20:24).

These kinds of key truths must be the underlying foundation and cement connecting all parts of our lives. As believers in Jesus' death and resurrection, we were converted from spiritual death to spiritual life due to the Spirit's work in our hard hearts. We contributed nothing to this miraculous work but sin. Repeatedly, I have stated these gospel truths since they are so easy to know and believe, yet difficult to actually live. They must become the very underlying fabric of the foundation of our thoughts.

Once we are His, our Lord strengthens us through every weakness when we draw from His strength. He comforts us, protects us, and carries us all the way home. When we intentionally focus on these sweet truths and so many others, our hearts swell with love for our Savior. This love that finds its source in Christ works itself out in obedience both in speech and action.

In addition, when we know it's ultimately not about us, but all about the glory of God, we are freed up to consciously die to self. Why in the world would we promote the dead man and want the lifeless to receive honor and praise? Since Jesus brought us life and purpose, we seek His glory. In this way, our paradigm shifts to propel us forward to action for our King while armed with truth and hearts oriented to Him and not self.

Some of that action our Father God calls us to is fairly easy. Giving a ride to someone or taking a meal, depending on the circumstances, hardly seems like a sacrifice at all. That friend will likely thank us, and they may even tell someone else about our kindness. In this way, it is rewarded somewhat through the praise of others. Also, getting up to serve an adorable child who needs help is small obedience. Having friends over for dinner and games is also a reward in itself. This kind of service doesn't require a lot of lying down on the altar because we directly benefit. We tend to like "serving" in this way. It makes us feel good.

When we are required to truly give up something of ourselves, obedience to the Father becomes a bit more challenging. Harder obedience requires us to forfeit something we want to carry out what is better. Just a few examples of harder obedience are:

- Giving a ride to someone who smells and may have lice
- Helping a whiney child with dirt on his face

- Opening up your home for someone to stay with you for a while
- Babysitting a friend's children when your day is already full
- Giving money to a family in need when you have been saving for the new furniture for your living room
- Giving up your vacation to go on a mission trip instead
- Living below your means so you can be generous to others
- Talking to a friend about Jesus when she is opposed to your views
- Fostering a child
- Adopting an orphan
- Giving up your home and comfortable surroundings to live somewhere else and reach another people group who do not know the hope of Jesus

So often we know these are the kinds of things we should be doing. We discuss them in our Christian circles. We even do many of these things, but some we may deem as too extreme. It is tempting in many of these examples to think we deserve something more.

We shouldn't have to surrender our homes for someone else, or give money we have earned, or bother with that person. We shouldn't have to go talk to the needy individual at church when we would like to connect with so many other people. We shouldn't have to give up our Saturday to help someone move who has already moved ten times. And the list goes on and on.

These responses are the typical, fleshly ones coming up from the dead man. The only way to keep these automatic reactions from taking root and keeping us from abundance through obedience is to squash them with the gospel. My best life, from a worldly standpoint, is NOT now. I don't even live any longer. I've been crucified with Jesus. Christ lives through me.

What I deserve is eternal punishment, but what I've received is forgiveness, grace, and mercy. I extend to others what Jesus has freely given to me. If Christ so freely gave of Himself for me to live, then I, one with Him, am to give of myself in whatever way He calls me. It is only in the giving up of my life and my fleshly desires for comfort and ease that I find abundant life in Jesus. He is giving me new thoughts and new purposes.

At the forefront of our minds through everything should be the operating truth that it's not about us. Life is all about the glory of our Lord. If we love Him, we want to follow Him, and we desire for Him to receive the right glory He deserves.

I Feel Like….	I Replace My Thoughts/Will With…
• Piercing with my words	• As Christ did not retaliate, but trusted God, I will too.
• Having time to myself	• My time is not my own. I'm on a mission for Christ
• Keeping money for myself	• This is not my money, Lord. Use it as you see fit.
• God wants me to be happy.	• Happiness is found in obedience to Christ.
• No one appreciates me.	• I am complete in Christ and don't need man's praise.
• I don't deserve this difficulty.	• I deserve hell, but Christ paid for all my sins.

In Philippians, Paul writes about those in the church of Philippi. "Not that I seek the gift, but I seek the fruit that increases to your credit. I have received full payment, and more. I am well supplied, having received from Epaphroditus the gifts you sent, a fragrant offering, a sacrifice acceptable and pleasing to God. And my God will supply every need of yours according to his riches in glory in Christ Jesus" (Philippians 4:17–19).

Paul is comparing the help the believers sent to a fragrant offering to God. Likewise, as we give of ourselves in whatever way God asks, our worship is like a sweet-smelling fragrance to our King. Our Lord, who loves us beyond measure, will take care of us as we give of ourselves to Him, so we never need to fear we are giving up too much of ourselves for kingdom work. Our Father, who calls us to lie down on the altar, will give us everything we need to carry us to the end.

Finally, since Jesus became the final sacrifice and we are united with Him in His death and resurrection, we submit all we have in joyful surrender to our Father, too. It's like saying, "Not my will, but Yours, Lord," as Jesus cried in the Garden of Gethsemane. Every time we allow His Spirit to work in us instead of our flesh, we are, in essence, saying, "I receive Christ's work on my behalf. As He yielded to the will of the Father, I gladly yield. I lie down on this altar and choose His way and not what I feel like." Through all we are called to yield, as we listen and follow the Holy Spirit's leading, may we be to our God a sweet-smelling aroma of His Son.

Chapter 10

Use Your Head...The Dog Bites

I have often wondered why leaving sin behind just isn't an easier process. I may have a particularly productive time in the Word and prayer in the morning only to feel irritation in my heart shortly after the kids wake up and the day begins. Why can't God just take over? Why can't He just make me sweet and joyful? Why is it such an effort, a yielding, and a submission?

I don't really have all the answers to my musings, but I have a few guesses. If He took over and made it all easy for me, I would likely talk to Him less, think more highly of myself, forget my sin I was saved from, and fail to relate to those around me. I would likely imagine I had always been sweet and joyful. Of course, I was not and am not. The battle to line up the incongruence of my fleshly life with the spiritual reality of my righteousness and position in Christ is incessant. The battle is victorious as I yield to the power of the Holy Spirit.

Our powerful God is also a God of relationship. This is one reason He uses familial terms throughout the Bible. He wants to relate to us as a father with his children. When we are aware of our sin and our desperate need of Him, we talk to Him and depend on Him. He communes with us and gives us counsel. He calls to us to run to Him as we see in Jesus' welcoming words in Matthew 11:28–30, "Come to me, all who labor and are heavy laden, and I will give you rest. Take my yoke upon you, and learn from me, for I am gentle and lowly in heart, and you will find rest for your souls. For my yoke is easy, and my burden is light."

Since we are in this close family bond, the Lord gives us help through the Holy Spirit. Fathers help their children. They see their weaknesses and help support and grow them in strength. The same Holy Spirit who transformed the disciples is alive in us today as the Helper whom Jesus promised. Though it may sound preferable to us to have Him just take over and make our lives easy, that is not God's plan. Knowing His plan is perfect, we should learn to delight in the work of sanctification and cooperate with the Holy Spirit in it. He is in us, and it is essential to our spiritual growth that we live by the spirit and not the flesh. Romans 8:5–6 instructs us with these words, "For those who live according to the flesh set their minds on the things of the flesh, but those who live according to the Spirit set their minds on the things of the Spirit. For to set the mind on the flesh is death, but to set the mind on the Spirit is life and peace."

When we are adopted as children of God, His Spirit doesn't take over our minds and make us become different automatically. It is true God transforms our desires and convicts us in a way that makes us look at sin differently. But He doesn't just take over our thoughts for us. We must be active in this process of sanctification if we want abundance. This verse in Romans 8 implies action. We are to set our minds on the things of the Spirit. This would entail a deliberate conscious unification with the Spirit within us.

If we want our actions to give God rightful worship, we must start by getting our minds right. What we dwell on is what eventually comes out. The only possible way to walk in the Spirit is to set our minds on the things of the Spirit. Remaining plugged into Him, since He is our power source, we receive all we need to obey. An essential element of this is actively dwelling on Scripture. It's no wonder God speaks so often in Scripture about meditating on His Word. If we fix our minds on truth, we are, therefore, tapping into the power source of the Spirit.

Of course, to meditate on God's Word, we must actually know it. Part of worship is prioritizing our time to study the Word, memorize it, and spend time in prayer. In a difficult situation, when we are tempted to be upset and think the worst about something, we must have God's Word in our minds for the Holy Spirit to bring us truth.

Conversely, when we either don't have God's Word hidden in our hearts, or we choose not to lean on the Lord in the moment, we inevitably respond in the flesh. If I'm thinking about my agenda, my time, my wants, or my grievances, then I'm not walking in Holy Spirit power. We could devote all Scripture to memory and yet still respond in the flesh if we don't actively use what we have studied.

Imagine a power tool that can make a task ten times easier lying uselessly on a bench with its cord dangling to the floor. Obviously, without being plugged in, this tool is not being used as designed, and it really is useless. Now we know that is not the case with God's Word, but I believe that what it can do for our lives is so much more than we can imagine.

Because of this possibility, we must actively allow the Holy Spirit to use what we know.

Personally, I have been guilty of being in various Bible studies and growing in biblical knowledge without actively putting that knowledge to use. I've been in small groups for all of my Christian life. I've engaged in talks and conversations with others about the grace of God and marveled at His love and care, only to return home to act ticked about something that went wrong while I was away.

The only possible way to make our knowledge connect with our actions is to allow the Holy Spirit to actively use it and fight the flesh. We must break the old fleshly thought patterns by actively applying truth. This takes a ton of work. Since we are in the flesh and not yet glorified, the flesh is our default. It is what comes easy to us. Without thought or action, the flesh just naturally kicks in. We don't have to plan for the flesh. It's ready all the time to switch to cruise control at any weak moment, trial, or attack from Satan.

There's a lot of talk in certain Christian circles concerning the enemy's attacks. Christians tend to either overemphasize or dismiss Satan and his minions altogether. Some Christians think every single ill event that happens to them is from the devil. When this is the thought, they are talking about him frequently and how he's out to get them. We need to remember that God's hands have already filtered anything that happens to us. It does not surprise God when we have a trial, difficulty, a job loss, or a diagnosis of cancer. He has the potential to keep us from any and all these difficulties. James exhorts us about trials in verses 2–4 of the first chapter of his letter, "Count it all joy, my brothers, when you meet trials of various kinds, for you know that the testing of your faith produces steadfastness. And let steadfastness have its full effect, that you may be perfect and complete, lacking in nothing."

God is never playing defense, but rather He is and has always been in the offensive position. He's the one with the ball. He's scoring. He's fulfilling everything He has ever set out to do. Satan's schemes have not deterred God for a moment and have not caught him off guard. Since we can so often become confused about this, we must remember the lessons from the book of Job.

In the first chapter of Job, we are told about his abundant and prosperous life. Then it is described for us how Satan presented himself before God, and God drew Satan's attention to Job and his righteousness. In response, Satan explained away Job's faithfulness because of God's blessing upon him. Satan was certain that when the "blessings" were removed, Job's faith would reveal itself as bogus. God then allowed Satan to attack Job within certain limits by taking Job's possessions, family, and, eventually, his physical health. The end of Job's story recounted Job's faithfulness and God's blessings upon him.

As we ponder the story of Job's life, we glean foundational truths to process difficulties. God is always sovereign and in the offensive position. He is not a step behind Satan trying to bring good from his destruction, but, rather, God allows trials and limits Satan.

I have no problem speaking this way because I know my God. He is always faithful, sovereign, kind, loving, patient, and immutable. I don't have to understand all that He allows. I don't have to have a God I can completely figure out. I just need to trust who He is and what He has revealed in His Word. I don't need to know any more than that. As a child with her father, I can trust I don't always have to know all the details and the explanations (Deuteronomy 29:29). As a little girl trusts her dad's decisions, I trust my Abba Father. With this in mind, we can praise God for the difficulty, knowing it is not outside of His control, and His plan is always perfect.

Besides Satan's attacks, we must consider our sinful flesh and how it affects genuine worship to our King. Again, we examine wisdom from the book of James, "Let no one say when he is tempted, 'I am being tempted by God,' for God cannot be tempted with evil, and he himself tempts no one. But each person is tempted when he is lured and enticed by his own desire. Then desire when it has conceived gives birth to sin, and sin when it is fully grown brings forth death" (James 1:13–15).

I am not saying God allows difficulties to tempt us to sin. He is for us in every way. Just as no parent would purposely look for opportunities to tempt his children to do wrong, God doesn't tempt us to sin either. He is concerned about our good and His glory.

Drawing from these verses in James, we see our desires entice and lure us. If unchecked, this desire results in sin. Satan is clever, and he knows each of our weaknesses and temptations. The Word tells us he is a prowling lion seeking someone to devour. He searches for any crack to get in, and when he finds it, he puts a wedge in to pry open the crack and cause the most possible damage. The crack, so to speak, is our flesh, our desires, and our sinful tendencies. So, yes, he attacks, but he does it with what is already present and what he has permission to use.

Satan is like a mad dog on a chain who will sink his teeth into you if you get too close, but if you keep a safe distance, he can't actually harm you. In fact, God already posted a sign warning us to be aware of the dog. When all is going well in our world, we are aware of the dog's location, and we wisely know to keep our distance. However, when something happens to us, or something doesn't go our way, we often ponder the injustice rather than examining it in light of the gospel. In this way, we nurse, pet, and stroke the desires of our flesh, all the while forgetting our step and thus walking into the perimeter of Satan's chain. Before we know it, his teeth are piercing our skin, and we find it difficult to even recall the Word to fight back.

When God makes us His children, He gives us weapons to use to play offense. We choose if we will flee from the dog or step in a little closer so we can feel his hot breath. We're the ones in control of our response. The old man, the crucified man, likes the way the dog's breath feels on its skin, and the dead man beckons us to wander in closer to have the flesh nursed a little. The flesh relishes the thoughts of its importance and extreme significance in the grand scheme of things. It doesn't want to fight back with the weapons God has given because the flesh wants to roll around with the dog.

If we could see the overarching view from God's vantage point, we wouldn't want to change one trial in our lives. We don't have control over God's perfect providence, but we can exercise dominion over Satan by our responses even before a trial arrives on the scene. The only way to play offense and not defense here is to immerse ourselves instead in all God has given us. God promises us all we need for godliness in 2 Peter 1:3, "His divine power has granted to us all things that pertain to life and godliness, through the knowledge of him who called us to his own glory and excellence."

God has given us His Word. When we know the Word, we know that living in the Spirit far exceeds living according to the flesh. It doesn't matter how good that flesh feels in the moment; it's rotten meat that just promises sustenance from the outside. Whenever we, as followers of Christ, respond to a difficulty through angry shouted words, gossip, and a look that screams a thousand words, it is unfitting. It's like we've draped death over life. Only when the flesh comes out of its burial garments and parades itself around, do we smell the distinct odor of decay. Before it unveils itself, it promises such relief. After it has sprinkled decay on those around us, regret and discouragement are sure to follow. Thankfully, we know what to do with it. We repent and praise our King for forgiveness and His perfect righteousness. That flesh has no place for us anymore.

We must expect difficulties and utilize the new minds we have in Christ. First Corinthians 2:16 says we have the mind of Christ. We must know the Word to activate our new minds so that we think thoughts that line up with the Spirit. Part of intimately knowing His Word is accepting and believing wholeheartedly that difficulties are for our good, and they are from a good God.

> "The Rock, his work is perfect, for all his ways are justice. A God of faithfulness and without iniquity, just and upright is he" (Deuteronomy 32:4).

When assessing our thought lives as Christians, we need to consider Satan's attacks on our minds by his using the crack of our own weak, sinful, fleshly tendencies. As the Holy Spirit makes me more aware of my thoughts, I'm blown away by the myriad of wrong ideas flowing into my brain all throughout the day. In my flesh, I will let them ooze in. When I'm weak and tired, deceptive, negative thoughts ooze in like lava from the vents in a volcano threatening to erupt. At that moment, I can either let them seep in because it feels good to let off a little pressure, or I can go to the source of the leak by praying, applying truth, and worshiping my Lord. If I fail and cave to the temptation, I inevitably end up miserable due to the explosion of negativity that spews out into my mind and actions. Since I have been praying about growth in this area, the Holy Spirit has made me aware of thoughts that don't line up with a worshipful life of following Christ.

Therefore, in each situation, our thoughts then become, "What would be pleasing to God here? What is truth? What lines up with Scripture?" Paul tells us we are to "destroy arguments and every lofty opinion raised against the knowledge of God and take every thought captive to obey Christ" (2 Corinthians 10:5).

"I wonder what she meant by that comment?"

"I always have to do this. When will someone else see this need and take care of it?"

"This is overwhelming today. How will I get this all done?"

"I know why he did that. I have him figured out."

"Why can't this be easier?"

"Doesn't God love me?"

"Can't I ever just get a couple of minutes to think?"

"Why don't they just go to sleep! I'm done for today."

Vomit! Writing all that makes me want to spew! Notice all these thoughts involve the flesh. Every one of them is about ME. Pride is the overarching sin behind these thoughts. This pride presents itself in selfishness, judgment, sinful anger, self-righteousness, and more.

We must obliterate these thoughts! If we allow the enemy to squeeze in the crack, he'll stick in the wedge. A flood of outrageous thoughts will inevitably follow. Have you ever been thinking about something somebody did against you only to realize thirty minutes later that you were entertaining past injustices as well? Since the Holy Spirit has been making me more aware of my thought life, I have learned to retrace my negative thoughts to where they started. If I allow myself, then soon, I will think about an old, seemingly forgotten incident that had previously angered me because I first pondered some present injustice.

In God's kindness, He won't allow me to continue with this thinking for long. I comprehend that in those moments, I failed to seal the crack when I felt the windy draft passing through, and therefore a full wedge filled a gaping hole. That gaping hole allowed the dog on the chain to come in close to where I could hear his whispers.

As soon as we realize we are preciously petting our dead flesh, we must pull our hands from out of the grave and remember we are in the Spirit, and those fleshly thoughts are incongruent with the Spirit man.

The more I take the offense and immerse myself in Christ's thoughts, the easier it becomes to start with truth and immediately identify a lie or temptation when it creeps in. This isn't easy, but it makes me so aware of my dependency on the Lord. These kinds of thoughts make me run to Him for help. He is what I need. He is perfection. He is truth. He is righteousness. I AM NEEDY! Thankfully, He welcomes me to Him, and in Him, I find what I need.

Chapter 11

Sweating Praise

I like working up a good sweat. Well, I kind of like it. I don't always enjoy the getting-there part since it often involves hard work, but once the sweat is in full swing, it feels like its own reward. It turns out that it's actually extremely beneficial for us to sweat. An adequate sweat detoxifies and helps to regulate temperature. It may assist the body in healing wounds. In addition, when we produce sweat through physical activity, our body releases endorphins, which give us pleasure and help reduce the feeling of pain.

You would think that with the many benefits of exercise and the accompanying sweat it so often brings that everyone would want to get in on it. That isn't so because it just flat out hurts at times. We tend to "run" or walk away from the source of pain. The busyness of our lives gives us a great excuse to avoid exercise, and thus shun the sweat it produces. It always seems tomorrow will be a better day to fit it in. Tomorrow is just as busy, and so, we often push exercise to the bottom of the to-do list for another day.

In a previous chapter, we explored Old Testament sacrifices and our need to be a living sacrifice to our Lord. It stands out to me when I think about exercise and sweat that God clearly specified what types of animals could be brought as sacrifices. As we read in the Old Testament about what was acceptable, we discover pigs didn't make the cut. The Israelites were also prohibited from eating pork, as God deemed it unclean along with a list of other animals (Leviticus 11:1–8). Now, we know in the New Testament Jesus removed these prohibitions when He said, "'Then are you also without understanding? Do you not see that whatever goes into a person from outside cannot defile him, since it enters not his heart but his stomach, and is expelled?' (Thus he declared all foods clean.)" (Mark 7:18–19).

Pigs fell into the category of animals with split hooves and animals that do not chew the cud; thus, they were unclean. I believe it is noteworthy that pigs do not really sweat. To regulate their temperature, they have to wallow in the mud. I have no idea if this had anything to do with the grouping of pigs with the other unclean animals. Scripture does not tell us that; therefore, we do not need to know. For the sake of the illustration I want to give, I want us to focus on the fact that pigs do not sweat, and how it is essential to our Christian growth for us to avoid the behavior of the sweatless swine.

The alarm goes off at 4:50. I rise from bed, start laundry, get my workout in and sweat, start the coffee, get ready, switch the laundry, fix breakfast, and settle down for time in the Word and prayer. It will be a good day. The kids begin to awaken. Finley needs me. Dirk yells that he needs money to take with him today. Asher wants me to sign a paper. I remember Brandon and I haven't talked about picking up the kids tonight since I have to be thirty minutes away. Brandon still needs lunch to take. There's the laundry buzzer. Finley wants to cuddle on the couch. I need to get dinner started since we have a full day of school and lessons later. I have to text my friend about the meal train we're organizing for a family at church. Judah throws a ball and knocks over a glass of milk.

The list and issues go on and on. All day long, there are so many things to fit in and so many great activities to be a part of. Among all to accomplish, sin frequently pokes its ugly head out to see if it can get in on the action. I see its evidence in the whiney child, the orneriness of the young boy, the attitude of the preteen, the irritability of the teenager, and the selfishness of the adults. One would think that after forty-two years, I would no longer be surprised by its arrival on the scene, but I confess that from time to time, I am taken aback that my day is not going as planned.

Most definitely, I have grown in this area, but as a young mom, I was quite surprised by what I witnessed in my children and myself. I knew I was living with little sinners, but yet I somehow was still shocked by all the times they "ruined" my plans. It sometimes felt as though the anger that rose in me wasn't really my fault at all, especially since I could not remember ever being that angry before I had kids.

In God's grace, He didn't let me remain in this mindset for all my parenting days. He taught me this life of parenting was just the perfect breeding ground for my sin to sprout. It had always been there all along, but anytime something made me mad or seemed unjust, I would just find something or someone else that didn't make life so challenging, but with kids, it doesn't work that way.

As much as they may make our lives difficult, we wouldn't dream of walking away or getting out of our challenging situation. Love holds us with these sin stirrers of ours. And if we're honest, our children and spouses are exactly what we need to expose our sin and to propel us to the foot of the cross to both roll around in gospel truth that we are forgiven and to impart gospel grace to others God places in our path.

In fact, we must stretch this gospel-minded concept like a canopy over all the difficult people and situations we encounter. I remember being at a women's event as a young mom and hearing a speaker say we should never think that if a particular person was out of our lives, then our lives would be so much easier. She said that if a specific difficult person was out of our lives, someone else would be hard for us to be around. How true this is!

Since, therefore, we are certain we will come up against difficulties of all sorts, we should probably think less about avoiding them and more about how to respond to them. It is often in the disappointment that our days aren't filled with the ease we thought we deserve that sin simmers, comes to a full boil, and then spills over. As we have already explored, this starts at the heart level with unmet desires and is chewed on in our thoughts. If it's chewed on long enough, we will eventually become sick with it and spew it out on others around us in our words and actions. What if we instead started with the source and allowed the Holy Spirit to change our desires? If we apply the Word, we will welcome the ups and downs of the day, knowing sanctification grows best in that soil.

How do we practically apply the Word and welcome the yuck? First, we must label it something other than how we have identified it all our lives. Instead of distractions, inconveniences, issues, messes, and difficulties, perhaps we should count it all as the perfect condition for our spiritual growth.

If I asked any true follower of Jesus what they wanted during their time on earth, I would guess that many of them would vocalize the desire to grow in holiness and better line up their earthly lives with their already established spiritual position in Christ. Every single day, the Holy Spirit equips us with what we need for this growth. Maybe we just don't see it that way. If we did, we would be celebrating when we had bad days. We would say things like, "Wow! God was so incredibly gracious to me today. Let me tell you what happened... I spilled coffee on my shirt in the morning. I got a flat tire on the way to work. I was late for my meeting. I could only eat peanut butter and jelly for lunch since I didn't make it to the store. My friend smarted off to me. And I needed to scrape off my car when I came outside since it snowed while I was at work. There were so many incredible opportunities today for growth in humility today, dependence on God, and forgiveness. God is so good!!!"

Is this what we do? Perhaps some of us do, but for the most part, I'm assuming we would label this a bad day. Why? I would argue that we would think of it this way because it wasn't easy, and things didn't go our way. However, if truth be told, we deserve nothing. We have received a rich inheritance in Christ, and God adopted us into His family. We did nothing to deserve this. God does not owe us ease on this earth. He loves us too much to give us that. If He gave us ease and comfort, He would likely be allowing us to forfeit a close walk with Him and subsequent continuation of sin's tyranny in our lives.

What He requires of His children and what He knows will give us the most joy is thankful hearts for all He gives and allows. Thankfulness is all over the Word. We are repeatedly commanded to give thanks.

"Rejoice always, pray without ceasing, give thanks in all circumstances; for this is the will of God in Christ Jesus for you" (1 Thessalonians 5:16–18).

"Oh give thanks to the LORD, for he is good; for his steadfast love endures forever!" (Psalm 118:1).

"But be filled with the Spirit, addressing one another in psalms and hymns and spiritual songs, singing and making melody to the Lord with your heart, giving thanks always and for everything to God the Father in the name of our Lord Jesus Christ" (Ephesians 5:18–20).

"I will praise the name of God with song; I will magnify him with thanksgiving" (Psalm 69:30).

"Though the fig tree should not blossom, nor fruit be on the vines, the produce of the olive fail and the fields yield no food, the flock be cut off from the fold and there be no herd in the stalls, yet I will rejoice in the LORD; I will take joy in the God of my salvation" (Habakkuk 3:17–18).

Once we alter our desires to line up with the truth of Scripture, our thoughts should follow suit, and if they do rebel, we verbally conform them to the truth. We must open our mouths and thank our Lord for the difficulties and the troublesome individuals in our lives. We stop the lies Satan whispers to the lazy desires of our flesh for ease, and instead, we honor by praising our King in song and through prayer. We confess the character of our God so that we cannot entertain thoughts that God couldn't possibly be good since He allowed this in our lives. We audibly speak that God is good, perfect, gracious, loving, and sovereign.

We are told in Proverbs 4:23 (NIV), "Above all else guard your heart for everything you do flows from it." Okay, that sounds like a plan, but how? How do we actually guard our hearts?

In Philippians 4:4–7, Paul lays out a remarkable answer about how to obey the command in Proverbs. "Rejoice in the Lord always; again I will say, Rejoice. Let your reasonableness be known to everyone. The Lord is at hand; do not be anxious about anything, but in everything by prayer and supplication with thanksgiving let your requests be made known to God. And the peace of God, which surpasses all understanding, will guard your hearts and your minds in Christ Jesus."

Did you see it? God's peace guards our hearts. As we praise and honor our Lord in everything and give all our burdens to Him, His peace guards our hearts. We praise because we know and love the unchanging character of our God; thus, we surrender all to Him. We can trust Him with our all. With this, the wellsprings of our hearts are protected. Foul water from sinful desires is stopped at the dam of praise so that it is not permitted to mix with our fresh springs. The praise and submission of our hearts establish the dam of peace, and through it, we are growing in sanctification. First Thessalonians 5:23 tells us of the sanctification that comes to us through the God of peace, "Now may the God of peace himself sanctify you completely, and may your whole spirit and soul and body be kept blameless at the coming of our Lord Jesus Christ."

Because of who we are in Christ, a people deserving wrath, but receiving mercy, a people brought from death to life, a people with a secure eternal inheritance, our lips should be full of praise to the one who made it all possible.

"Shout for joy in the LORD, O you righteous! Praise befits the upright" (Psalm 33:1).

Praise is absolutely fitting for us as God's children, and it cannot be conditional. Knowing our King is perfect in all His ways, we trust and rest in His providence when events and people do not make sense around us. When everything changes, He is constant. Our salvation remains through it all. We are to still praise and trust Him.

Hebrews 13:15 tells us, "Through him then let us continually offer up a sacrifice of praise to God, that is the fruit of lips that acknowledge his name."

Notice the adverb, *continually* modifying the word, *offer*. Continually tells us how often we should offer a sacrifice of praise, which is without ceasing. In addition, notice our praise is termed a sacrifice, which is submission and dying of self. In the use of this word, *sacrifice*, we discover this is an effort for us. It goes against what comes naturally to us. Our fleshly tendency is to blame another when things don't go well for us and to question the character of another. This often happens when things are hard for us. We want to blame and criticize God all the time, forgetting He is always good, always perfect, always kind, and always merciful. We must completely shift our perspective to learn to praise God through everything.

Therefore, the overall question we must ask ourselves is, "What kind of sacrifice do we want to be to the Lord?" If we allow negative thought processes to continue and allow thoughts of, "Why me?" "I don't deserve this." "All I've ever done is serve the Lord, and this is what I get?" and "Why can't this be easier?" then we aren't sacrificing at all. That's the flesh, and it is our natural response. To go back to the pig illustration, when we respond in this way, we are behaving as the sweatless swine. We are holding onto our toxins and allowing the contaminated water to mix with the wellspring of our hearts. In this way, we attempt to cool ourselves off by scampering off to the mud of fruitless pursuits. Of course, the mud under us eventually warms up, and we forever have to find something else to cool us off.

The other option is to cooperate with the Spirit and allow Him to renew our minds with Truth from the Lord. Romans 12:1–2 says it best, "I appeal to you therefore, brothers, by the mercies of God, to present your bodies as a living sacrifice, holy and acceptable to God, which is your spiritual worship. Do not be conformed to this world, but be transformed by the renewal of your mind."

Since we're told in these verses to present our bodies as a living sacrifice, we should actively consider our minds and mouths as parts of this ongoing sacrifice. When we choose to praise, we cooperate with the Holy Spirit's work of sanctification in us. We allow the sweat to flow as we warm up, instead of running to something else to fix us and get us out of the pain.

May we be children of the Kingdom who welcome everything that comes our way with arms lifted high in praise and worship to our unchanging King. May our Tuesday afternoon praise be just as passionate as our Sunday morning corporate worship. Let's be people of God who profusely sweat praise.

Chapter 12

Spill It

So far, in our focus on worship, we looked at the incongruence of our corporate gatherings and our minute by minute actions, the yielding of our everything to our King, our thoughts and how they affect our behavior, and the worship of God through our speech. The last element of worship for us to think about here is worship through proclamation/multiplication.

When we are excited about something or if something amazing has happened to us, we talk about it. We bump into someone out somewhere, and we spill our news out onto them. Our faces light up, we speak quickly, and we gesture excitedly. If what we share is something the other person can take part in too, we encourage them to take the same trip, eat the same food, buy the new gadget, or splurge on the pool that gave us entertainment for the summer. Most of the time, we don't consider what the other person thinks of us at that moment. We just share.

I believe when most believers first repent and trust in Jesus' sacrifice, we are overjoyed to tell people around us. We don't yet know all the right words to use to share our rebirth, but we tell the news anyway. We are eager to tell someone else they need Jesus, too, because, "Why not?" It would be absurd not to tell of their default destination of hell and the possible alternative of life everlasting with their true King.

However, at some point, many of us shy away from evangelism. People don't always respond in the way we would've hoped. They may have asked a question we don't know the answer to, so we make a note not to be in that situation again. Over time, the wonder of it all fades, and we don't want to spill over onto those around us. It's old news. Every once in awhile, we hear a good sermon or watch a convicting movie that challenges us to share again. We pray for opportunities, share the gospel a few more times, and then prop up our feet in the Lazy Boy, relax, and doze off.

We don't share the best news in the world for numerous reasons, but I believe one key reason is we don't think about hell enough. Perhaps some of us even secretly believe it is nonexistent. The Father of Lies, Satan, loves to whisper that lie into our ears. I'm sure you've heard it from time to time. "How could a loving God allow people to go to a place of torment for eternity with no hope of ever getting out? That surely doesn't seem fair. It especially doesn't seem fair if they have never even heard the gospel. There must be something we don't understand." Yes, we listen to some of these lies and consider them in our minds. They are lullabies of lies, lulling us into a deep sleep. While sleeping, we fail to remember the mission. We miss the lost in our paths.

We "hope" the idea of hell is wrong because we cannot bear the thought of the myriad of lost souls who will go there for eternity. The deceitful devil has us right where he wants us, and we, so much like Eve, swallow the lies hook, line, and sinker. We're suckers for these lies because, in these lies, we are the heroes.

In our hero tales, we think, "Well, God said "this," but I would never do that. This teaching on hell obviously can't be true. If I were God, I wouldn't send someone to a place of torment for eternity." It isn't any wonder that so many buy into the idea of purgatory.

Purgatory is something humans would come up with as a good plan to punish sin. Yes, in our plan, all people get to go to heaven, but they have to pay for their sins first. An alternative to this plan we conceive in our wisdom may be the really bad people just die and cease to exist.

This idea of purgatory is erred in so many ways. First off, how could we even consider Christians paying for their sins? Either Christ died on the cross for our sins, or He didn't. If He did, how much of our sin did He die for? Was half of our sin atoned for or three-quarters of our sin covered? Jesus paid it all! When we die, we go to be with Him immediately. Hallelujah! Secondly, if there was another way to be made right with God, then it would not have been necessary for Jesus to be born as a human, live a sinless life, and suffer and die for sin. If people could just pay for their own sin, then Jesus' death was avoidable and unnecessary.

Purgatory or any form of this idea is a human concept to soften the blow to our consciences that most humans will suffer for eternity. We as Christians gird ourselves up against some of Satan's lies. We like to fight against the ones concerning ourselves and our position in Christ, and we do so rightfully. We preach the truth to ourselves as we should be doing. When we have thoughts such as, "I messed up again, surely God won't forgive me anymore. Surely, He can't love me after what I have done," then we must actively bring to mind truths of security in Christ.

If a friend tells us she has been thinking these kinds of thoughts, we are quick to quote the Word back at her and tell her to fight those lies. We remind her that, according to Romans 8:1–2, "There is therefore now no condemnation for those who are in Christ Jesus. For the law of the Spirit of life has set you free in Christ Jesus from the law of sin and death."

We then point her to Psalm 103:10–12, where we consider Christ's abounding love for her as His child. "He does not deal with us according to our sins, nor repay us according to our iniquities. For as high as the heavens are above the earth, so great is his steadfast love toward those who fear him; as far as the east is from the west, so far does he remove our transgressions from us."

We are really effectual at encouraging our brothers and sisters about false ideas about guilt and shame. We know what to do with that, and we see those lies labeled for what they are. Hell, on the other hand, we don't always treat the same way. Tempted to believe that hell is something other than what it is, we fail to slap truth on it and stop the doubt in our hearts. We like this lie a little more, so we keep it around. In fact, anything that doesn't sit with us well in Scripture, Satan seizes as an open door. He swings the door open, plants little seeds of doubt. If we do not pluck them out with truth, their roots go down deeper as they are watered by logic and sunned with emotion.

Satan has lost concerning the state of our souls as Christians. We cannot be snatched from our Father's hands (John 10:28–30), but we can be influenced in a way that renders us ineffective.

Think back to the garden again. Satan tempted Eve by the possibility of being like God in knowing both good and evil. She thought at that moment that what Satan was whispering to her was better than what God had given her. Satan appealed to her logic and the possibility of God holding out on her. The snake wasn't then (and isn't now) particularly sneaky. He just preys on our lack of true knowledge of the Word and on our logic and emotions. We consider the verses on hell and rationalize that we must not be understanding them correctly. Satan twists the truth that God is loving and makes us contemplate how love could punish someone for eternity. As always, Satan takes some truth and twists it.

Either we believe the Word and all that it discloses, or we doubt all of it. Either God preserved His Word for us through the ages so that it has reached us in exactly the way He intended, or He is too weak to keep His Word intact.

I know my God. Not even one word He utters returns to Him void. I don't have to understand all the ins and outs of everything. I just need to trust. It doesn't even have to make sense to me. I can't see the picture He sees. God does, and that's enough. We perceive one brush of a paintbrush, whereas God, as the master Artist, paints every last stroke to make a masterpiece. He sees the whole line—from eternity past to eternity future, but we can only perceive the minute dot on the line. God doesn't need our opinions and ideas on how things must be. Isaiah 55:6–11 sums it up perfectly.

Seek the LORD while he may be found; call upon him while he is near; let the wicked forsake his way, and the unrighteous man his thoughts; let him return to the LORD, that he may have compassion on him, and to our God, for he will abundantly pardon. For my thoughts are not your thoughts, neither are your ways my ways, declares the LORD. For as the heavens are higher than the earth, so are my ways higher than your ways and my thoughts than your thoughts. For as the rain and the snow come down from heaven and do not return there but water the earth, making it bring forth and sprout, giving seed to the sower, and bread to the eater, so shall my word be that goes out from my mouth; it shall not return to me empty, but it shall accomplish that which I purpose, and shall succeed in the thing for which I sent it.

How do we now get rid of the lies we may have pondered for so long? We blow them to smithereens as we look to the Word and the Word alone for our beliefs.

"This God — his way is perfect; the word of the LORD proves true" (Psalm 18:30). God says His way is perfect, and His word proves true. I believe it.

"Righteousness and justice are the foundation of your throne; steadfast love and faithfulness go before you" (Psalm 89:14). God says He is righteous, just, loving, and faithful. I believe it.

"But God, being rich in mercy, because of the great love with which he loved us, even when we were dead in our trespasses, made us alive together with Christ – by grace you have been saved -" (Ephesians 2:4-5). God says He is merciful and gracious. I believe it.

"And one called to another and said: 'Holy, holy, holy is the LORD of hosts; the whole earth is full of his glory!'" (Isaiah 6:3). God says He is holy. His Word is sufficient. I believe it.

"And just as it is appointed for man to die once, and after that comes judgment, so Christ, having been offered once to bear the sins of many, will appear a second time, not to deal with sin but to save those who are eagerly waiting for him" (Hebrews 9:27–28). God says after death comes judgment. His Word is sufficient. I believe it.

"But by the same word the heavens and earth that now exist are stored up for fire, being kept until the day of judgment and destruction of the ungodly" (2 Peter 3:7). God says judgment is coming. His Word is sufficient. I believe it.

"Then he will say to those on his left, 'Depart from me, you cursed, into the eternal fire prepared for the devil and his angels'…And these will go away into eternal punishment, but the righteous into eternal life" (Matthew 25:41, 46). God says hell is eternal. His Word is sufficient. I believe it.

When we believe once and for all that hell is real, and everyone we know is going there if they are not in Christ, we must then feel compelled to share the truth. Picture the people who you meet suffering eternally for their sin. Get that image in your head and let it propel you on to share the amazing news that Jesus loves them and paid for their sins on the cross (1 Peter 2:24). He suffered so that they don't have to. Repentance, which includes surrender to His Kingship, and trust in Jesus' death and resurrection, brings life and reconciliation to the Father.

Our role in sharing the truth of life and death is in so many places in God's Word. In Jeremiah 1:4–8, we are privy to a conversation between Jeremiah, a man called out to be a prophet by God, and God, who is reassuring him of his calling.

> Now the word of the LORD came to me saying, "Before I formed you in the womb I knew you, and before you were born I consecrated you; I appointed you a prophet to the nations." Then I said, "Ah, Lord GOD! Behold, I do not know how to speak, for I am only a youth." But the LORD said to me, "Do not say, 'I am only a youth'; for to all to whom I send you, you shall go, and whatever I command you, you shall speak. Do

not be afraid of them, for I am with you
to deliver you, declares the LORD."

A prophet's role was and is to warn and declare
future events. Although not in the exact same sense,
each follower of Jesus has similar words spoken over
us by God and similar callings to the prophet's calling.

"For you formed my inward parts; you knitted me
together in my mother's womb. I praise you…Your
eyes saw my unformed substance; in your book were
written, every one of them, the days that were formed
for me, when as yet there was none of them" (Psalm
139:13–14, 16).

"Even as he chose us in him before the foundation
of the world, that we should be holy and blameless
before him. In love he predestined us for adoption to
himself as sons through Jesus Christ, according to the
purpose of his will" (Ephesians 1:4–5).

God knew us before He formed the world. He
chose us to be in Him not because of anything great in
us, but all because of His mercy and love. God wrote
all our days in His book before He even formed us. In
light of all this, how could we possibly think our lives
are our own? We are here to love and point others to
our great Redeemer. We are here to warn of what we
are sure is to come. We are here to spread the fragrance
of our Lord onto those God brings to us to minister to.
We have all we will ever need in Him, and He equips
us with the answers to all the world's problems.

So many in the world wonder what their purpose
is. Foolishly, we as Christians sometimes wonder the
same thing whenever we are dwelling on what we
want and our glory. When we seek these things and

fail to be satisfied, as is certain to be the result, we end up in the same state of mind as unbelievers who are contemplating what it is all about. May it not be so of us any longer. Our purpose is certain.

"As for you, always be sober-minded, endure suffering, do the work of an evangelist, fulfill your ministry" (2 Timothy 4:5).

"All this is from God, who through Christ reconciled us to himself and gave us the ministry of reconciliation; that is, in Christ God was reconciling the world to himself, not counting their trespasses against them, and entrusting to us the message of reconciliation. Therefore, we are ambassadors for Christ, God making his appeal through us" (2 Corinthians 5:18–20).

"But you are a chosen race, a royal priesthood, a holy nation, a people for his own possession, that you may proclaim the excellencies of him who called you out of darkness into his marvelous light. Once you were not a people, but now you are God's people; once you had not received mercy, but now you have received mercy" (1 Peter 2:9–10).

We are to fulfill the ministry He has given us as ambassadors for our King by sharing the message of reconciliation. He has made us what we were not that we might spread His praises. The testimony of our salvation and the gift of salvation to others should be ready on our lips as we remember and focus on our mission.

Gospel mindedness will keep us ready to share as we always remember we are now a part of a royal, holy family, because of the new birth through Christ. It's all because of Him. As we think of that and go deep in those truths day after day, we cannot help but worship our Lord through spilling out onto others around us. May we dwell on truth and be Spirit-led to love others by telling them the truth of their lostness, their destination, and the U-Turn they can make because of Jesus. It all goes back to Him again and again. He will receive the glory and honor forever!

Chapter 13

Streams

It was pitch black. The darkness only lasted three seconds or at max five, but it was enough to give me a different picture than the rest of the women held in their minds. As we traveled back to our beds for the night, I heard chatter all around me about the kindness and love of so many people who came out to light the sanctuary. I, on the other hand, couldn't shake the feeling of darkness.

I had been at a women's retreat, and part of this retreat included a candlelight service where other Christians gathered to light the church for one service. After the service, candle holders left the church, and as the last one walked out the door, the lights were turned on. On this particular weekend, whoever was supposed to turn the lights on took a little longer than they were likely supposed to. I'm thankful for it now as I sense God gave me a unique perspective on the opportunities for unbelievers to receive Christ.

The once-lit church grew increasingly dim as each candle passed through the doors and out. My mind was overwhelmed by realizing a lost person's salvation opportunities stop once death takes effect. While in this world, the opportunities for salvation are all around us. Once we take our last breath, whether, after a long illness, old age, an accident while young, or Jesus' return, the lights are out, so to speak, and the opportunities are no more. This is the picture I got in my head. It was a thought of a person with no more chances to receive Christ's sacrifice on their behalf. Unlike the joy and love, which was the supposed effect of the attendees, uneasiness covered me like a heavy blanket.

Complete and utter darkness for eternity, along with pain and loneliness, awaits those who die outside of Christ's provision of forgiveness. I'm not sure why out of about sixty women, I was the only one I knew of who perceived the whole experience the way I did. Perhaps it was because the Holy Spirit had awakened in me, and continues to kindle in me, the reality of the biggest issue in life, which is the severed relationship of every man and woman with their Creator because of sin, which if left separated, results in negative consequences now and eternal consequences later.

I have attempted to speak truth to unbelievers and believers so that we may go beyond where they are. Personally, I don't want to be rocked to sleep in this life, but rather, I desire to be alert to the spiritual realities around me. I want to be far more concerned with a person's spiritual state than my well-being and comfort.

For this reason, I would beg you to examine your soul. Measure it up against what the Bible says. As we talked about the rescue boat already, I would revisit it again to ask you, "Are you truly in the boat?" Could it be possible that all along you have been swimming nearby the boat of Christ and doing what others in the boat are doing without actually having ever climbed inside? Repent. Climb into Christ. Submit to His Lordship.

Perhaps, you are certain you are a Christ-follower. Praise God! I would ask you, "Are you behaving like the ones swimming in the water?" The grace that saves us also sanctifies us. True salvation by grace through faith produces works. "Are you caught up in the goings-on of the world?" Worldliness does not line up with Scripture. Additionally, it won't bring you abundance. If ultimately, you have little to no desire for more of God, it may mean there has not been a conversion, and you too are not in the boat. Being caught up in the world does not coincide with dying to self and living in Christ (Romans 6).

"Do not love the world or the things in the world. If anyone loves the world, the love of the Father is not in him. For all that is in the world—the desires of the flesh and the desires of the eyes and pride of life—is not from the Father but is from the world. And the world is passing away along with its desires, but whoever does the will of God abides forever" (1 John 2:15–17).

If, however, when you read the Word, you are convicted, and you welcome the Holy Spirit's sanctifying presence in your life, rejoice! He is actively bringing pure, revitalizing oxygen to your cells while extracting the toxic, death-producing gas of sin. From this process, your life will bear fruit in keeping with repentance. May the fruit juice of rebirth and the Spirit's indwelling squirt out on all those around you in easy times, as well as during trials.

For a few years now, I have had the picture in my head of deepness with God. I have even prayed a somewhat strange prayer of, "Drown me, Lord. Drown me until I no longer come to the surface, but only You in me." My thought through all that is obviously not a cry for physical death, but rather a cry for spiritual life.

In reality, this prayer is a shout out to God for continued sanctification. In sharing some of these thoughts with some dear friends, I discovered they, too, had experienced some water thoughts and visions. One of my friends brought up the verse in Psalm 42:7, "Deep calls to deep at the roar of your waterfalls; all your breakers and your waves have gone over me."

In texting back and forth with my sisters in Christ, images of waterfalls, waves, and roaring waters bombarded my phone.

May we, as believers, be in the deep together, being drowned of ourselves and all the time being made more alive in Jesus. Consider the waterfalls as the gospel pouring over us repeatedly. Remaining under the waterfall, we cannot help but fall to our knees in worship with all God has given us. We experience joyful submission in this place. Our thoughts of selfishness and pride cannot remain here as they are measured up against who we are and what we deserve outside of the beautiful gospel. They are washed away while being replaced with submission and humility. Whenever the thoughts creep back in about how great we are and what we think we deserve and how awful it was that someone treated us in the way they did, we have only to step back under the cleansing power of the waterfall of the gospel.

In like manner, as life takes over, and we forget we are the blood-bought family of Christ, we tend to hold tightly to our time, money, talents, and reputation. As we continue to welcome the convicting power of the Holy Spirit in our lives, we will recognize our misplaced values, strip them off, and run under the refreshing water of the gospel.

126

As more gospel water pours over us, we change over time to have smoother edges and more of a solid footing. We don't have to remind ourselves as often to take our gospel bath. We find we are standing firm with roots reaching down near the stream. Enjoying our environment of stability in Christ, our lives become less about just going to God for the quick fix sometimes searched for in a concert, camp, or revival and more about the constant, steady waters of Jesus all the time. We metamorphosize into the plentiful trees of Psalm 1:1–3:

"Blessed is the man who walks not in the counsel of the wicked, nor stands in the way of sinners, nor sits in the seat of scoffers; but his delight is in the law of the LORD, and on his law he meditates day and night. He is like a tree planted by streams of water that yields its fruit in its season, and its leaf does not wither. In all that he does, he prospers."

We alter our priorities as we ground ourselves in the Word. Our roots continue to spread out into more Truth all the time, and we desire more of this lavish banquet and more fellowship with God through prayer. Through all this, we no longer look for junk to feed our roots because we have tasted the real food of Christ in His Word. We know He sustains us, so we don't have to search elsewhere for a little something else to satisfy. There's no more figuring out His will, His plan, our role, and our apparent happiness. The certainty of our identity and purpose in and through Christ is our theme. There is never a need to discover who we are. We find it all in our Jesus.

The abundance of our flourishing, confident, well-fed tree demonstrates itself through the heaviness of fruit on our branches. We submit to the Lord by yielding to His sovereignty in allowing any adversity into our lives, knowing He will ultimately wield it for our good and His glory. The worship of thankfulness through every difficulty produces succulent, tasty fruit that draws others near. We want them to share in this fruit and its source. Expectantly, we look for God to bring them into our paths so we can share and direct another weary, parched traveler to the wellspring of life found in our King.

There is nothing quite like all this. God takes a dead branch, gives it life through His Son, provides all it needs for growth and fellowship, and enables the once dead, but now alive, to spill over on all around. Only God could come up with this. Let's go deep with Him. Let's surrender our all to receive abundance. Let's burst forth in praise throughout all our lives to the One who is worthy! Praise be to our King and Savior, Jesus Christ, forever and ever!

Why I wrote this Book....

The ideas for this book came quickly when I finally decided to sit down and write, but as I look back now, I see that I have been pondering them for a long time. This book is the culmination of my thoughts and musings over a period of years as a true follower of Christ. Over time, I have felt a growing necessity to highlight the discrepancy between true and false converts. My heart breaks for those outside of Christ who believe they are forgiven and "good to go." My heart yearns for true converts to move from a stagnant Christian walk to a passionate relationship of abundance. It is my earnest prayer that false converts will repent and run to Jesus and that genuine believers will surrender all and find true life.

I would love to hear how God has used this little book in any way to deepen your walk with Him. Feel free to contact me at kight.brandon@gmail.com. Learn more about my books here at my website jillkightjustdiealready.weebly.com

CHASING BANDITS

by

LUKE J. ADLER
Deputy U.S. Marshal (Retired)

To OLIVIA

THE RELUCTANT BIKER BANDIT

10/02/2014

For the work-horses in law enforcement,
the men and women who do the job.

CHASING BANDITS

TABLE OF CONTENTS

PROLOGUE

COMING TO BE

"Nothing in this world can take the place of persistence. Talent will not; nothing is more common than unsuccessful people with talent. Genius will not; unrewarded genius is almost a proverb. Education will not; the world is full of educated derelicts. Persistence and determination alone are omnipotent. The slogan "press on" has solved and always will solve the problems of the human race."

– Calvin Coolidge, 30th President of the United States

It is the thrill of the chase, at least for me. My time chasing bandits spans more than two decades. I have brought every bandit I have chased to justice. These bandits are mostly federally charged felons, catching federal time. More than three thousand men and a handful of women bandits can personally attest to this achievement.

I don't feel every bandit is evil. That's why I call them bandits instead of bad guys, villains or what ever. In reality, most of the people I capture are not bad people, just people who make bad choices over and over again. Don't get me wrong; there is evil. I've seen that, too.

Bandits I've taken into custody have said to me, "Hey, man, you just don't understand what it is like on the street." Believe me, I do.

I could just as easily have become one of the bandits I hunted and jailed. If not for a few people in my life, my belief in doing right, and the insatiable calling for adventure, I really don't know who or where I'd be.

My family, the Adlers was a psychologist's idea of a blended family with seven kids and absent parents. The truth is, we never blended. My youth ended when I was fourteen. I left my volatile suburban St. Louis home and that world behind.

I spent the next two years, or "seasons," on the carnival circuit. I ate cakewalk-baked goods and leftover corn dogs. I survived. I watched what happened around me and chose to stay in control instead of getting lost to the drugs, alcohol, or chaos. I kept my childhood dreams alive to someday scuba dive and jump out of airplanes.

I breezed in and out of St. Louis after dropping out of school. I usually stayed with friends or camped in parks. I checked in on my grade-school crush, Tracy. Eventually, the police caught me. As a sixteen-year-old "delinquent," I was taken into juvenile custody and foster care.

There was already a hot-tempered older brother with unaddressed psychiatric issues in the juvenile justice system. My social worker, DeeDee Tate, cried the day she was handed my case file because she was "getting another Adler."

Ms. Tate was very wary of me and skeptical of my easygoing nature. She anticipated a "dark side." After our second visit, she realized I was salvageable from the system.

That year, I got my first exposure to the day-to-day world of good guys. Ms. Tate got me into a program called "Operation Ident." It was a feel-good "let's-get-juvenile- delinquents-off-the-street-and-in-with-the-good-guys" program. I did filing and general "gopher" work (go for this, go for that) at the St. Louis County Police Department's 4th Precinct. Little did I know that this minimum-wage filing job would get me into the

Marine Corps.

I focused on the options that would be available in my future, including the military. Sometimes exceptions are made and the military allows people to enlist at seventeen years old. I knew even back then, the sooner I got somewhere, the better.

With that goal in mind, I gathered letters of recommendation, with the help of Ms. Tate, from upstanding citizens willing to vouch for my good character, including foster parents I stayed with long enough for them to know me, the police officers, a precinct file clerk I worked with in Operation Ident, and the precinct captain.

The interviewing psychologist for the Marines was negative from the start. He wasn't excited to let me in because of my juvenile record. I prepared for the worst. He flipped through the stack of recommendations without reading them and stopped on the precinct captain's letter. "Okay, all these other people get paid to write these letters. I could care less about what they say. They're trying to get rid of you and dump you on us, but not a precinct captain. If he says you are good, I'll take a chance on you. He is the only reason I'll let you in."

And so it goes . . .

SEMPER FI

STORY ONE

"That which we persist in doing becomes easier for us to do; not that the nature of the thing itself is changed, but that our power to do is increased."

– Ralph Waldo Emerson

One thing about Marine Corps boot camp is that you can count on arriving in the middle of the night. I climbed off the bus at Marine Corps Recruit Depot (MCRD) in San Diego a little more than a week after my seventeenth birthday.

A few days into boot camp the platoon sergeant tapped me as "platoon guide," a leadership position. I held that position or the position of squad leader almost the entire time until we graduated.

After completing boot camp, I was assigned to the First Marine Division, or "1st Mar Div" as it's known in Marine jargon. My orders were to report to Camp Pendleton in California, located between Los Angeles and San Diego. Two of my older brothers had been Marines for very short stints, and they had been assigned "smart orders." The Marine Corps thought they were too bright to be wasted as "grunts." I, on the other hand, was assigned a general Military Occupational Specialty (MOS) of 0311. In plain terms, I was designated a grunt. Actually, it was exactly what I wanted to be—hands on, in the field, a combat infantry Marine. I wasn't sure what my future held, but if I was going to be a grunt, I wanted to be in Marine Reconnaissance.

All Marines are trained riflemen. Reconnaissance Marines are Marine Special Forces. All I needed to hear was that Recon gets to jump out of planes and scuba dive—the two dreams that kept me going through some very tough teenage years on the carnival circuit and in the juvenile justice system.

Even though there isn't much time to bond in boot camp, I was glad to see a familiar face when I reported for duty at the 1st Mar Div indoctrination building at Camp Pendleton. Private First Class Vincent "Vinnie" Wolfe and I were in the same platoon during boot camp. We had seen each other every day, but there was no getting-to-know-each-other bonding time in boot camp. He was the only familiar face in that sea of Marine green. Apparently, after boot camp, we had both opted for the thirty-day leave, so we arrived together at indoctrination and consequently bonded for life.

As if it were yesterday, I can still see the rocks painted scarlet red in the formation of the letters "HQ" for headquarters in front of the Indoctrination building. Looking around the sparse building, all I could see were olive drab uniforms in an old olive green, World War II-era, two-story frame building with barracks to sleep fifty people. There was a front desk where we were to drop off our orders, and a few rows of folding chairs lined up facing a plaque of the Marine Corps' Eagle, Globe, and Anchor on the far wall. The indoctrination building was filled with thirty to forty fresh-faced teens and a few seasoned Marines who were in charge.

The whole process of dispersing assignments among new grunts was arbitrary. For example, if there were ten available spots in a platoon, the next ten names on the list got orders to fill those spots.

It normally took a full day at indoctrination to be assigned to a unit. Vinnie and I huddled together and speculated about what was to come next for us. At our first opportunity, we told the staff sergeant on duty that we wanted to volunteer for Recon.

"Recon is for you if you like to eat nails and jump out of planes. You guys must be crazy. But that's fine with me," he said. He made the call to the 1st Recon Battalion to let them know they had "fresh meat."

Later the same day, another sergeant handed out orders to the rest of the young recruits waiting. Imagine our surprise when he called out Pfc. Wolfe and Pfc. Adler for infantry orders.

We informed the sergeant that there must be a mistake because we were going to Recon. "Shut up and get on the truck. You have your orders," he barked.

We grabbed those orders and headed out the door. I'm not getting on that bus, I thought. The Recon Orders that were coming trumped these orders in my hand. Once outside, I nudged Vinnie, and we veered away from the waiting trucks and circled the building. We came back inside through the rear door and found the staff sergeant who had called Recon on our behalf. We showed him our orders. He said, "That's no big deal, a simple glitch in the system. You Marines will remain here tonight and we'll cut new orders for you tomorrow."

The next morning, the company commander of Alpha Company, 1st Recon Battalion, sent over one of his platoon sergeants, Staff Sergeant (SSgt.) Schultz, to take a look and see if they wanted these two new young volunteers. SSgt. Schultz was fresh off the drill field. He was a fine example of a Garrison Marine—polished brass—straight off a Marine poster. When SSgt. Schultz came out to talk to us, we both jumped up and let him know we had volunteered. He looked hard at us and told the staff sergeant assigning duties, "Yeah, we'll take them."

The staff sergeant said, "You want them, you got them." Just like that, Vinnie and I went from 0311 Infantry to 0321 Recon Marines. We thought we were set.

The same barking sergeant who handed out orders the day before was back at it again later that morning. He again had orders for Vinnie and me to go to another grunt outfit. Out the door we went and back around again without hesitation. I kept faith that I had orders for Recon and SSgt. Schultz's affirmative response. Those orders were the orders I would follow. Vinnie quickly agreed.

We located the staff sergeant who called Recon on our behalf the day before. He was speaking to a young second lieutenant, so we waited until he saw us. Only an officer can change orders, so upon request from the staff sergeant, the second lieutenant crossed out the infantry battalion information and wrote, "1st Recon Battalion, OJT." With a few strokes of her pen, Vinnie and I had just been assigned to the premier company in the premier battalion in the 1st Marine Division. The "OJT," we later found out, meant "On-the-Job Training." This meant we got to skip three months of Advanced Infantry Training, which would have been similar to boot camp all over again.

Recon sent a truck over to the indoctrination building later that day for Vinnie and me. We got on. Little did we know it would be the ride of our lives.

For the next four years, Vinnie and I lived and trained together in all three divisions of the Marine Corps. We started in California. We also spent time in Alaska, climbing mountains and glaciers. We both went to Army jump school and Navy dive school. We transferred to the Third Mar Div in Okinawa, Japan, and traveled throughout the Philippines, Japan, and Korea for a year. We ended up in the Second Mar Div for our last year and a half. I spent six months on the "Med Float," while Vinnie remained stateside. I lived aboard ship, sailing the Mediterranean Ocean. On Easter Sunday, 1979, I was surprised by an unexpected opportunity to see the pope in Vatican City.

Vinnie and I spent our last six months as non-commissioned officers (NCOs) in charge of the scuba locker. We spent a lot of time diving in the Intracoastal Waterway in North Carolina and hanging out on Onslow Beach. The two of us have kept in touch (to Vinnie's credit) to this day.

Vinnie went on to work for the government as a contractor, blowing up stuff in the desert.

After a brief stint working odd jobs and as a commercial diver on the Mississippi River, I began chasing bandits.

STORY TWO

"People sleep peaceably in their beds at night only because rough men stand ready to do violence on their behalf."

– Attributed to George Orwell

Gotta love those Cardinals....

After serving fourteen years in the California state prison system, thirty-year-old Javier Allen thought he would move to St. Louis, the wholesome Midwestern town where his father grew up. He wanted to start his life over and, in the process, somehow feel closer to the father he never knew.

That's the romantic version.

Allen had spent almost half his life doing time in the California state prison system then chose St. Louis, he said later, because it was "out in the sticks" and he figured he could be a big player and "run the place."

"He was an OG, straight outta Compton," is what the gangsters say with respect. Javier Allen is an "OG"—Original Gangster—in "Gangsta Speak."

"Compton" is Compton Heights, a suburb in Los Angeles County, California. Birthplace of two of the most notorious gangs: the blue-wearing Crips and the red-dressed Bloods.

There is no other way to say it: Javier Allen was the real deal. He had earned the title OG. Allen was a full-fledged, blue-bandana-wearing member of the "Rolling Sixty Crips" when he got caught in the act of a drive-by shooting that resulted in his conviction of a triple homicide. The incident could have been more accurately described as a "stop, get out, and execute"—an ambush killing, really.

Allen was only sixteen years old when he pulled the trigger on those three men. He was tried, or adjudicated, as an adult. He spent the next fourteen years of his life in the California prison system doing hard time.

Allen's dad, James, had been a huge Cardinals baseball fan growing up in St. Louis, Missouri. James Allen had left St. Louis in the early 1960s for the Marine Corps Recruit Depot in San Diego, California. Between serving two tours in Vietnam, he settled in Los Angeles for a time. That's when he met and married Allen's mother, Sharon.

Javier Allen was born in an LA-area hospital in 1966. His parents named him after Julian Javier, the second baseman for the St. Louis Cardinals, who was in the midst of a stellar dozen-year career with four World Series appearances. James had big dreams of playing catch with his son and of Javier someday playing baseball.

James Allen was killed February 14, 1968, in Vietnam during the "Tet Offensive." His son was not quite two years old.

Allen grew up in the streets of Compton taking his lead from the older boys on his "set," or neighborhood. He had been "jumped in" when he was thirteen years old. In gang jargon, that means several of his gang friends beat the daylights out of him for exactly thirty seconds to prove they loved him like a brother. No hospital and no medical attention afterward. Busted up and bleeding, he was congratulated and welcomed.

At five feet nine inches and about a hundred seventy pounds, Allen was a big kid for his age at thirteen. He took the beating well and healed quickly. Javier was already well known by the Los Angeles gang unit officers by the time he was fifteen. He was a respected gang member by other Rolling Sixties, and he was feared by many of their street gang rivals.

His rivals were right to be afraid of him. Allen's police file was thick, as he had participated in numerous violent assaults, beatings, stabbings, and assorted shootings.

He had already been shot twice and stabbed three times in separate incidences prior to his sixteenth birthday. He lived and breathed violence. He had no hesitation in striking out at anyone who angered him.

Allen's "homie," known on the set as "Forty Ounce Loco," was standing outside his girlfriend's apartment building with a couple of "his boys," Javier Allen among them. They were waiting to get buzzed into the building. Forty Ounce Loco felt something warm on his back, then on his front. He likely thought someone had spilled something on him. Perhaps he was just confused. He was too numb to react and dropped to his knees, closing his eyes. He didn't know what hit him. He had been killed in a drive-by shooting.

Allen turned quickly and saw red—guns, a red car driving by, people inside wearing red clothes, and a bright red spray of blood onto the pavement in front of Forty Ounce Loco. Then he spun around and went down with a burning sensation in his arm. He had taken a bullet that missed his own chest by inches.

Forty Ounce Loco was his homie, his death worthy of retribution. Before the cops were finished with the crime scene, Allen, already a teen full of anger and hate, started putting his plan together. He knew who the shooters were. He also knew where he could find them. He didn't share this with law enforcement officers who spoke with him before he was taken away in an ambulance.

Three weeks later, "Dray," "Bud Man," and "Lil Tee" sat in their hooptie ride, a red Ford Mustang, smoking dope. They were parked on their favorite hillside spot next to a warehouse overlooking the city. They were high and still laughing about how those Rolling Sixties fools had "jumped about like clowns" when they were hit as the trio drove at them firing their "nines," or 9-millimeter pistols.

When the gang officers had questioned or "tossed them" about the incident a couple weeks before, they played dumb. The officer mentioned one homicide and said another kid, Allen, was in the hospital in critical condition and that he might not make it. Rumor was that no one had seen Allen on the street for three weeks now. It must have been a critical hit or maybe he was dead, they speculated. That would be "props," or recognition, for them and their crew. Allen was a dangerous adversary.

Allen's wound was actually classified as serious but stable. He had been hit in his left bicep, and one of his short ribs had been broken. Allen remained in the hospital for thirty-six hours and was released when his auntie picked him up. She took him to her house where he could recover, out of Compton, out of sight, for nearly three weeks.

The sheriff's department's helicopter unit was about three minutes out from the location given as a "shots fired" call in Compton Heights when both the pilot, Ivan Gomez, and his partner, Matt McGunga, noticed flashes on the hillside up ahead. One … It was too close to be … Two … their call but it appeared to be gunfire … Three … and it was right … Four … there. Another shooting was playing out in front of them.

The driver of the blue truck near the flashes, who was one of Allen's "home boys," saw the copter and freaked out. He floored the gas pedal and drove off amid smoke and the smell of burning rubber as the helicopter's spotlight came on. This left Allen literally holding the smoking gun in the police helicopter's spotlight.

In an instant, Allen tossed his "gauge," or 12-gauge shotgun, and ran in the opposite direction than that of his homie. The airship couldn't follow them both, he figured.

Gomez said, "Did you see that? The shooter just tossed a sawed-off shotgun over by that Mustang down there!"

McGunga, a seasoned cop with a decade working in the gang wars in LA, did see the gun thrown down. He was already calling dispatch to inform them of a possible homicide. The scene was clearly visible to the men hovering five hundred feet above, like a dramatic panoramic sweep in a movie scene. The red Ford Mustang's rear window appeared to be shattered, and part of a man's head and arm were sagging out of the driver's side window.

There was no other movement on the scene, save for the fleeing shooter.

Allen was sadly mistaken in thinking the helicopter might pursue the getaway car. Why would you chase the getaway driver, an accomplice, when you can bag the shooter who is on foot?

Allen was arrested minutes later by sheriff's deputies who arrived on the scene by patrol car. He was driven away shortly before Dray, Bud Man, and Lil Tee were all pronounced dead, each shot execution style in the head by a shotgun. He was charged with three counts of homicide.

The trial was a non-event. Allen was scheduled to be tried as an adult, but pleaded guilty to manslaughter, and received a sentence of fifteen to thirty years.

The next fourteen years of his life were spent inside the California prison system. That is less than five years for each of the men he had been convicted of executing in cold blood.

Allen, who was always big for his age, spent his time inside the joint getting bigger. All of his free time was spent at the weight pile. (I always wondered why they allow weights in the joint for bandits to come out stronger.)

When Allen was released from prison, he went straight back to his hood to get his life back in motion. He was now thirty years old and chose to shack up with his "baby momma," who he knew from the "set" where he grew up and who was now the mother of his child. "Cocoa" was her stage name now. She was an exotic dancer. She and Allen had hung out together when they were youngsters, and Cocoa had visited and wrote Allen letters when he went down to do his time.

"JA," as she liked to call him, had set her up with a little "something-something" to help her get by. She would pick up a package every now and again and mail it to Allen's auntie in St. Louis.

Cocoa received $800 each week for that errand and other odd jobs she did for Allen whenever he asked. She would put some of it on Allen's books when she visited him in prison. She never had a steady, dependable man in her life. For the fourteen years Allen was in prison, he was all of that for her. She knew where to find him every day. Theirs was a great relationship, right up until the day he was released.

Cocoa told me later that Allen was a changed man when he got out—and not for the good. She said he became "all demanding and what not," wanting to know where she was all of the time and who she was hanging out with. He even came by the strip club where she worked. Her boss didn't like that, and it was a violation of his parole "paper." She was irritated by his overbearing behavior. Within weeks of his release, she complained about this to Allen's parole officer, or PO. The violation of his parole gave her some breathing room from him again.

The parole violation would probably only carry a six-to-nine month sentence, twelve months at the very most, she figured. The version of the story that Cocoa told Allen was that his PO had called the house one day when he wasn't home. She told Allen that when the PO found out he wasn't home, he was enraged and threatened to give Allen a parole violation because he had been "seen" at her club. Allen apparently bought Cocoa's version of the story.

Allen decided he just couldn't do another twelve months' time in prison. He packed up Cocoa and their daughter, jumped in his Lincoln Town Car, and headed for St. Louis, Missouri. Certainly no one would find them in the Midwest, he thought. He had learned in prison that sometimes California wouldn't extradite parole absconders beyond the Continental Divide.

Allen was correct that most of the time California would not extradite beyond the Rocky Mountains, but he thought wrong about California not extraditing him. He had three manslaughter convictions. And he also thought wrong about no one finding him in St. Louis.

"Adler, I'm stumped," Andy Nielson announced as he stood in front of my desk with a smile on his face.

Nielson was on his way to being a great Marshal. He was a young Deputy U.S. Marshal in the Eastern District of Missouri office who wasn't afraid to ask questions when he didn't know something. He often came to me for advice when a lead dried up. Nielson was a hard worker, and he was eager to learn everything he could about hunting bandits. He also liked putting me to task and having me work through challenging files no one else would work.

He explained to me that he had received a "collateral lead" from the Marshals office in Los Angeles. A collateral lead was information one Marshals office put out to another office to follow up on leads that were traced to their district. He had two telephone numbers to check out and no contact information to check them against. So he came to me to see if there was anything to be done.

The local St. Louis telephone numbers he received from LA were both disconnected. Both of the numbers had been published numbers belonging at one time to the fugitive's aunt, Danielle Robinson.

We learned through a background check that Ms. Robinson had lived in St. Louis her whole life. Her younger brother James,

Javier's father, had left for the Marine Corps and was killed many years before. When their parents died, she inherited the two-family flat on Blackstone Avenue in St. Louis City.

Blackstone Avenue is located in St. Louis City's Seventh District. Ms. Robinson's house was near the intersection of Blackstone and Page Boulevard. It has always been a high-crime area and a "target-rich" environment for drug dealers, prostitutes, and bandits of all variety.

I placed a call into the St. Louis Metropolitan Police Department's intelligence unit. Those guys are really dialed in to what goes on in their city. They're a great crew to work with and an invaluable asset when chasing bandits in their territory.

Nielson and I kicked around the leads with them, and soon a picture emerged. Ms. Robinson hadn't lived on Blackstone Avenue for years. Since her parents died, she continued to rent the upstairs unit, but always rented only to family members. No one appeared to live in her parents' old unit on the ground floor. That seemed especially odd since she kept a working telephone there for many years.

Cellular phones were beginning to become more prevalent during this time, so it was no surprise that Ms. Robinson had recently disconnected the landline phone. A quick glance at Ms. Robinson's financial information revealed she lived way beyond her means.

The guys at the intelligence unit told me to check with Perry Jones, also known as PJ, one of their detectives who had recently been promoted to sergeant. As luck would have it, PJ was assigned to the Seventh District. He was a fit, lanky guy in his mid-thirties. I had worked with him before, and I knew he was a great cop.

Nielson and I drove down Blackstone Avenue by the house. We were in a vehicle the Marshals Service got from the Drug Enforcement Agency. The car was a Ford SUV with heavily tinted windows. This is not a typical "G ride," or government-issued vehicle. It screamed, "I'm a drug dealer!" It wouldn't stand out in this neighborhood.

During our first pass by the house, we noticed a white-over-blue (the fugitive was a Crip) Lincoln Town car with California plates. "I'll bet you those plates come back to the fugitive's girlfriend or a friend of a friend," I said to Nielson pretty confidently.

"No bet here," he said grinning.

He should have bet me, because I was wrong. The plates were actually registered to Javier Allen's Lincoln Continental. There was also a caution assigned: "Caution: Wanted Subject. Subject is known to be armed and dangerous. Proceed with caution."

"Are you kidding me?" I asked aloud to no one in particular. I couldn't believe the guy left his plates on the car and that the plates hadn't been run by any law enforcement during his drive from the West Coast to St. Louis. Cocky and stupid.

I called PJ.

"The best we can figure is that Javier Allen has been in your area for more than three weeks," I said without scolding. "An OG new in town didn't hit the cops' radar and none of your guys ran new California plates in this neighborhood?"

He didn't reply. He knew there was nothing to be said. I was getting a point across, and he would deal with the information and with his officers accordingly.

I then asked PJ if he was interested in arresting this bandit with us. I think he said yes before he hung up the phone, but he might have said it to me in person because he got there so fast.

PJ asked Nielson and me to meet him in a firehouse just up the street from the target's house. The firehouse was under renovation and was vacant at the time. We had a perfect perch from a second-story window to view the street, Javier's Lincoln, and the house in which he was living.

About forty minutes after we set up in the firehouse, two men exited the front door of the first-floor unit of the target house.

These guys were dressed in dress slacks, short sleeve shirts, and ties. They could have been detectives if they had been carrying guns and badges, but they weren't. I'm guessing the guys were door-to-door insurance salesmen or Mormon missionaries. As soon as the men were out of sight, Allen immediately walked out, got into the Lincoln, and drove off. We weren't prepared to chase him at that point, so we sat tight and waited.

Allen must have been checking the area for police once the visitors left. He made one loop around the block and pulled right back up in front of the house. He parked his car in the same place it had been just minutes ago. He scanned the area for a minute and walked back up on the porch. He stood there, arms crossed, for another minute, looking all around before he went inside. I thought, "Man, this guy just looks angry."

We climbed back down from our firehouse lookout. PJ and one of his officers grabbed some equipment from their car and got into the SUV with us. His other two uniformed guys were instructed to maneuver into the alley in a marked car and cover the back of the house.

PJ lugged a shotgun into the SUV. We had chased bandits together before, but he never came armed like this. I asked about the shotgun.

In his wisdom, PJ said we needed the shotgun because "Allen can relate to it."

"Listen, Luke, this OG has been shot with a pistol a few times already and he survived. A pistol won't mean squat to him," PJ said. "But when Allen went to commit murder, he killed with a shotgun. He won't want to mess around with a shotgun aimed at him."

Solid cop wisdom. Genius, really and a lesson learned.

I set the SUV's radio to the local R&B station and cranked up the radio loud enough, but not deafening, then I upped the bass. I saw PJ smile through the rearview mirror.

I needed to get Allen out of the house, but how could I do

that without him getting suspicious and arming himself with who-knows-what weapons he had stashed there?

Sometimes simple is best. I pulled in front of the house and laid on the horn, long and loud. We waited in the SUV with the song thumping. Nice speakers, I thought in passing. The marked patrol unit radioed to let us know they had taken up a position in the rear in case Allen bolted out the back door. I blew the horn two more obnoxious times before Allen walked out of the house and down the stairs of the front porch.

At six feet three inches and weighing about two hundred sixty pounds, Allen was quite a sight. He had twenty inches of biceps on each arm, a thick chest, and a neck barely contained in his skintight thermal shirt. He looked like he had learned how to protect himself in prison and spent a lot of time on the weight pile. He was an angry, violent force to be reckoned with, but we were ready for him.

Allen was glaring at the SUV from the sidewalk. He couldn't see through the dark tint on our windows, and the SUV looked like a drug dealer hooptie. While I was honking, PJ slid out of the rear passenger door under the cover of the loud music and masked drawing the door shut during all of the honking. He waited by the tire at the rear of the car. Nielson, PJ's street officer, and I readied our guns.

At my signal, PJ came around the rear of the SUV. He leveled the shotgun on Allen and simultaneous pumped the action of the shotgun.

The rest of us jumped out of the car. Allen was paralyzed— not so much frozen from seeing us and our three pistols lined on him as he was from the shotgun and the unique sound it makes when a round is pumped into the chamber. He still hadn't looked away from the barrel of that shotgun.

PJ said in a steady, quiet voice, "I will kill you when I pull this trigger." He also told Allen he would pull the trigger if Allen made a move before he was told.

I knew Allen would be familiar with the drill from his many interactions with the well-trained police in California, so I took the opportunity to begin giving him commands. "Face away from the vehicle, fingers interlaced, hands behind your head." He did as he was told. "Down on your knees, ankles crossed." Only then did he look away from the shotgun.

I slipped up behind him and got him cuffed. I quietly told him he could now relax and that we were just picking him up on his parole violation warrant from California. PJ kept the shotgun on him and stood on alert.

Cocoa came outside when she heard the commotion. She seemed unfazed by the scene. She started to back into the house, and I told her to freeze. She did. She was also familiar with the drill.

I asked her if anyone else was in the residence. She called to her daughter, who then came out of the house.

Allen was talking fast. "It's cool up in there, ain't no one else in there," he said. "You can look."

I was on my way to look anyway. It's what we call a protective sweep. Well within our rights. We need to make sure the residence is secure and that no one else is inside to cause us harm while we are securing a bandit.

I made a sweep of the residence with one of PJ's uniformed guys who came around from the back alley. I found a .357 revolver on a shelf in a back room. I unloaded the firearm and secured it in my vest pocket. Once the house was secure, we allowed Cocoa and her daughter back inside. We also brought Allen into the residence in order to remove his jewelry, empty his pockets and give his things to Cocoa before taking him in.

I read Allen his Miranda Rights straight off the card, like I always do, and told him again to relax. I didn't mention the gun I found in the back room. PJ, Nielson, and I took Allen back there to help him get a pair of slip-on shoes and a sweatshirt. He had calmly and politely asked if he could have those because he knew it would be cold in the jail. I watched him as he eyed the shelf where I had found the gun earlier. He seemed to relax and almost smirk when he saw the gun wasn't there. He told me later, that at the time he thought Cocoa had hidden it before we found it.

I asked Allen if we could search his car. He said we could, but his auntie, who wasn't there, had the keys and the car was locked. He didn't know we had seen him drive around the block in the car not long before we came to arrest him. He also didn't realize I had seen his keys hanging on a nail in the kitchen. The keys looked like Ford keys, and they were attached to a ring that had a Lincoln emblem on it.

That's what we call a clue.

I asked the two uniformed officers to take Allen to central booking in downtown St. Louis. This was a ploy to keep him relaxed and to get him out of our hair while we investigated. He didn't catch on, even when they booked him for safekeeping for the U.S. Marshals.

Once they were on the road, I turned and took a long, hard look at Cocoa. She was surprising, what I would consider a caricature of a Valley Girl. She was not the typical tough gangster girlfriend. She wore conservative jewelry, only had one visible tattoo, and was wearing a light blue pants suit with matching sandals. It was as if she was trying to emulate the look and dress of a safer environment, safer world, even though her life was made with a federal felon and she danced "on the pole" for money.

I read Cocoa her Miranda Rights off the card and paused for a few moments. She met my silence with silence. I told her I found the gun. She said loudly, "Pleeease! You know that ain't none of mines."

I politely asked her if we could search the Lincoln, and she said the car did not belong to her. She had heard Allen give us permission earlier and knew what that meant.

"You know that's my man's car and he said you can search it, but he ain't got the keys. I don't care if you search it." That's twice now I'd been told I could search the car.

With that, I retrieved the keys from the nail in the kitchen. PJ and Nielson went out to the car to search it. I stayed inside with Cocoa. They came back a few minutes later carrying a 9mm pistol, a thirty-two-round magazine, and a "Mac 10," a submachine gun that fires 9mm rounds at a blistering 1,100 rounds per minute.

"Wow," I said and whistled lowly. "OG straight out of Compton," I said out loud to no one in particular, relieved. I knew right then how lucky Allen was that we had surprised him without a gun. He was a dangerous, deadly bandit and not afraid to use guns as his tools for cold-blooded murders. If he had drawn a gun, we would have killed him.

Cocoa "saw the light" right away when she saw PJ and Nielson carry in the weapons. From the look on her face, the weapons may as well have been a train coming straight toward her. She stayed strong and started out by saying her daughter was only twelve and they didn't have any relatives in town. She began to plead her case with me.

I asked her where her daughter's dad was.

"You just arrested him," she said.

Cocoa could see I was having trouble with the mental math. Allen had been in prison for fourteen years. She assured me in no uncertain terms that Allen was her child's father. "Conjugal visits," she said and laughed, wiggling her assets.

Then she added quietly that Allen would understand that she was giving him up to protect herself and their daughter.

"So, now, what do you want to know?" she asked.

Cocoa told us she had driven Allen to the projects in downtown St. Louis where he traded some heroin for the two guns. He had the telephone number for a guy named Winkie Alberts.

Winkie was the "gun man". He was also a heroin junkie. With Cocoa's help, Allen had been sending cocaine and heroin to his auntie in St. Louis for several years. I later passed along that bit of drug information to the intelligence unit.

We charged Allen as a convicted felon in possession of a firearm. Two days later, I found out the Mac 10 had been modified to fully automatic. They tested it in the gun lab, and it fired full auto every time. The sere pin had been expertly altered to fire fully automatic on each pull of the trigger.

That bit of information changed the game dramatically. Allen was a convicted felon in possession of a fully automatic weapon that he had purchased in a drug deal. According to the federal statute, he could potentially face life in prison.

"Ouch," was all I could muster when we got that news.

What Allen didn't know was that we couldn't prove the guns were purchased in a heroin deal.

The Assistant United States Attorney assigned to the case, Jim Janson, was a former FBI Agent and a good all-around prosecutor. AUSA Janson demanded that Allen give up Winkie the gun dealer.

He did. He also gave up a West Coast music studio run by the Crips. The DEA shut down a huge money laundering scheme with that tidbit of information.

Allen also pled guilty and was sentenced to five years, this time to be served in federal prison. After which, he was transferred back to the California prison system for his parole violation.

A week later, we arrested Winkie without incident. He was strung out on heroin and barely coherent at the time. He was also a convicted felon in possession of a firearm—seven firearms, actually. All of the guns were stolen. When we were talking to him at the booking center, he looked around the room and then whispered to us that he could flip, or go to work for us. He said he could set up a heroin dealer from Los Angeles. He said, "This guy is an OG, straight out of Compton."

I told him I appreciated the offer, but we would pass.

Allen has since served his time in federal prison. He is no longer in the prison system. He is free and living in California.

POOKIE AND NAY-NAY

STORY THREE

"People always overdo the matter when they attempt deception."

– Charles Dudley Warner, American Author and Writer

Charles Dudley Warner was the gentleman who also so keenly observed, "Everybody talks about the weather, but no one does anything about it." A government program I have taken part in both cleans up criminally infested areas and helps rebuild safer neighborhoods.

The "Weed and Seed" program is a Department of Justice effort to clean up and redevelop high drug-crime areas in urban hot spots around the country. The "Weed" part of the program is federal funding to local police departments who are involved in clearing crime out of their districts, weeding out the bandits. The local law enforcement also gets federal law enforcement support and consideration for federal prosecution of the bandits captured in those areas. Once the community is cleaned up, the "Seed" part begins. Money flows in to businesses and grant funds for community services. The program is a solid deal all around.

During my participation with Weed and Seed, my supervisor was a fellow by the name of Bob Presley, one of the finest supervisors I have had the good fortune of working for. Presley was a man of good character and a hard worker. He has good common sense and good instincts. Plus, he liked chasing bandits, too. I always love that.

There was a period when our district was between Marshals; Presley was our acting chief deputy. He reported to another one of the good guys, Bill DeCosta, a chief deputy from San Diego who was our "acting" United States Marshal.

U.S. Marshals are appointed to their positions by the president of the United States. The rest of us, the Deputy U.S. Marshals, are civil servants. We hire on through the civil service process. There are ninety-five presidentially appointed U.S. Marshals, one in each of the ninety-four judicial districts, with an additional Marshal appointed to the Superior Court in the District of Columbia. There are a couple thousand Deputy U.S. Marshals.

Presley and DeCosta made a great team and, during their tenure, set some good things into motion in our district. One of their forward-thinking ventures was a cooperative effort between the U.S. Marshals Service and the St. Louis Metropolitan Police Department's (SLMPD) Weed and Seed program.

At the time, the SLMPD's Eighth District participated in the Weed and Seed program. The Eighth District includes some of St. Louis's lowest income, highest crime pockets and is located in the north central part of St. Louis City. Presley and DeCosta set up an arrangement for Deputy Marshals to take turns working with the Eighth District Weed and Seed officers one night a week. We would augment their manpower, and they would assist us on serving federal warrants in their district.

Not all Deputy U.S. Marshals worked this assignment. It was voluntary because we also had to work our normal shifts. I would be on duty for the Marshals from 7:00 a.m. until 5:00 p.m. and then head up to the Weed and Seed team, usually until 2:00 a.m. Then I'd grab some shut-eye before working my regular shift again the next day. That's why we only did this one night a week.

Other than the obvious drawback of missing out on sleep, there were mainly three other reasons not all deputies worked this assignment.

One, not all deputies like hunting bandits. It is dangerous and sometimes dirty work.

Two, not all deputies like work. Many look at their government job as a "gravy train."

Three, the Weed and Seed project did not mean paid overtime. The government developed a cost-effective solution for overtime known as "availability pay." If we worked extra overtime, we didn't get paid for it. So many deputies avoided it.

Under the leadership of Presley and DeCosta, their policy heavily favored spending the availability hours by working with Weed and Seed. We were also available for whatever else popped up, like making arrests. They tended to frown on stopping a chase exactly at quitting time, which I have seen happen.

It was no big secret; I loved to work the Weed and Seed assignment. I always felt a great sense of accomplishment when we bagged dangerous offenders who were preying on the community. Or if we brought in a thief or two who were destroying lives by stealing people's identities.

It was just such a night when Pookie and Nay-Nay came across my radar. I was working Weed and Seed with a new Deputy Marshal, Tom Franklin.

Tom was new to the Marshals Service, but he wasn't a youngster. He served in Army Special Forces before joining the Marshals. I had been in Marine Reconnaissance myself, so I appreciated his background.

I enjoyed working with Franklin. He had a quiet confidence and steady nerves, and he was a real professional. I never worried if he "had my back" in tense, critical situations, which were common on Weed and Seed.

That night, as we rode around with the Eighth District

officers, Franklin told me he had a "collateral" warrant from Atlanta, Georgia, on a guy named Pookie Montoya.

A collateral warrant means a warrant from another judicial district. When the Atlanta Marshals chasing Pookie found he had fled to St. Louis, they forwarded that information to our district. In the Marshals Service, we call that a collateral lead. I call it a poaching.

The arrest warrant for Pookie was for violation of his supervised release. In other words, when Pookie was released from federal prison after serving five years for a fraud conviction, he fled from his parole officer and started committing new crimes.

Tom also found out from the Deputies in Atlanta that Pookie had a twin brother, Nay-Nay. Nay-Nay was wanted on a federal warrant from the Central District of Illinois. There was no information indicating that Nay-Nay was with Pookie.

However, Pookie and Nay-Nay were twins, and they were both wanted on federal charges stemming from fraud, so it wasn't a far stretch that they would be together.

Franklin had worked up some leads on this case, including finding a name and address of a guy nicknamed "Pumpkin" who knew Pookie. The address for this guy was in the Eighth District as well, so we rolled by there to have a chat.

Franklin had run a criminal history on Pumpkin, and there were no felony convictions. However, Pumpkin was wanted in Jefferson City, Missouri, for a misdemeanor perjury charge.

There is a down side to that information. The county where he was charged would only have extradited him from surrounding counties. That means if he was located two counties away, they wouldn't come get him. As long as Pumpkin remained in St. Louis, the Jefferson City folks wouldn't come get him, but did Pumpkin know that?

On the way over to Pumpkin's house, I told Franklin that if we needed to, we could possibly use that warrant to our advantage.

Franklin said there were not booking photos of Pumpkin, but the warrant information listed him at six feet eight inches and 410 pounds. We both agreed that was probably a typo.

Imagine my surprise when we knocked on Pumpkin's front door and he answered the door in a little pink pajama outfit—all six feet eight inches of him and weighing every bit of 410 pounds.

Wow, he's a big boy and prissy to boot, I thought. He walked out that front door toward us—more accurately, you would say he sashayed out the front door—and asked us what we wanted.

Franklin, very professionally, launched into his spiel about Pookie's warrant and said that Pumpkin needed to do the right thing. I sat off to the side thinking about what to do tactically if Pumpkin got moody.

I realized after a few minutes that Pumpkin was just a cupcake. I assessed that Pumpkin was not likely to get violent, and he was the type to save his self. Of course, Pumpkin hadn't given us anything useful yet, and he claimed not to know anything useful, something you get used to hearing when interviewing.

I walked back to the "G ride" (government-owned vehicle) and studied our equipment. I gathered up a set of leg irons. Franklin continued the interview and then looked at me after a few more "I don't know nothing" responses from Pumpkin. I broke into the conversation and asked Pumpkin to take off his jewelry and empty his pockets.

Leg irons are really just handcuffs for your feet. They keep a motivated bandit from running. Or, as was the case that night, I figured they would have to double as handcuffs for Pumpkin.

I walked back up to the porch with this set of leg irons and told Pumpkin to leave all of his personal belongings in his house. He looked incredulously at me. Then he reminded me his warrant was only for a misdemeanor and said he knew they wouldn't extradite him from St. Louis City.

"I assure you that I understand the extradition process. I am prepared to and I volunteer to personally drive you to Jefferson City tonight," I said.

He thought I was kidding. It took him about half a second to realize I was not. Our one lead was not going to fizzle out because of a short drive. Actually it was about a hundred fifty miles each way, and with booking, etc., it would equal about six hours of my time. Well worth it I thought.

Even though Pumpkin's arrest warrant was a misdemeanor and they wouldn't come get him, it also stated his bond was ten thousand dollars secured. That meant, for him to be bonded out, it would take the whole ten thousand dollars, not just ten percent. Which would mean; that if he was delivered to Jefferson City, he would not be let out until someone posted the full ten grand in cash.

Pumpkin didn't look like he has that much cash on him. I was starting to get to him, and now he was getting nervous.

Pumpkin's mom, all five feet three inches of her—literally half as tall as her son—showed up while we were talking with him. She sadly told him she didn't have that kind of money, either.

I could tell Pumpkin was still hoping I wasn't serious about driving him to Jefferson City that night, but I had every intention of taking him if this didn't play out like I planned. I placed him in handcuffs (the leg irons, actually) and marched him inside to get rid of his jewelry.

He was wearing fuzzy house slippers when he met us at the door, so I needed to find him a pair of slip-on shoes without laces. When I opened his closet, I sat back on my heels and choked back amazement.

He lives here alone, doesn't he? Wait. Are they his? I thought. I was stunned to find dozens of colorful women's dresses and heels, sandals, and other women's shoes that looked like canoes but appeared to fit Pumpkin. He was watching my reaction as I looked at the clothes hanging in the closet and paused.

"I make my own clothing, thank you very much," he said haughtily. "Big and beautiful, loud and proud."

I wasn't judging. I was actually wondering where he found size fourteen EEE pumps to fit him. But I didn't voice that thought, either. It was amazing to me how many women's clothes and shoes were in this man's closet. And Pumpkin had made many of these outfits himself. He and his friends would go out to clubs dressed in drag. Imagine that. Pumpkin dressed like Zsa Zsa Gabor, fawning all over Pookie.

We outfitted Pumpkin with an approved kimono ensemble and made our way out the door to the G ride. Thank heaven we were driving a Ford Expedition. I didn't want to embarrass Pumpkin, but we would never have gotten that man into an Intrepid.

As we drove away from the front of Pumpkin's house, he broke and started crying. "Child," he said, "I just don't know what to do. I love him; he's precious!" He wiped his eyes with his fingertips. "But, I can't go to jail. I didn't think you were serious about taking me to Jeff City. It must be three hundred miles or more."

I told Pumpkin it was only about a hundred fifty miles, and we would be there in no time. I then asked him if Nay-Nay was with Pookie.

"Ooooh, child," Pumpkin said, his voice dropping an octave. "He's the devil."

"Excuse me?" I said. I had struck on something.

"That Nay-Nay, he's the devil. He scares me," he said, regaining his sassy voice.

"How can that be? They're identical twins," I said, pushing for more information. I glanced again at the Montoya brothers' files. Both Pookie and Nay-Nay's files had them at five feet ten inches and weighing maybe all of a hundred thirty pounds. Why would Pumpkin be afraid?

Pumpkin scowled and said, "I don't even care. I don't like

him. Nay-Nay's got the devil in him."

"Really?" I thought out loud. Now I could tell Pumpkin was going to talk. "Soooo, you're telling me that Nay-Nay is, in fact, the evil twin?" I asked.

"Oh, honey, you so right. I really don't like him. That's why they're not here at my house now."

Bingo. Franklin was quiet and listened to this conversation. He gave me a sideways glance and waited for my next move.

Okay, I thought. Now we knew the twins were both in town and had been here for long enough to make friends and enemies. With this ongoing good twin/bad twin scenario in play, I kept Pumpkin focused on Nay-Nay.

"Well, here's a thought, Pumpkin," I said. "How about telling us where Nay-Nay is?"

"Child, I'll tell you where he is right now. Just promise me you won't take me to Jefferson City!"

There it was, simple as that. We had struck up a deal with Pumpkin. We took him to the Eighth District holdover station instead of to Jefferson City, and he told us where we could find Nay-Nay. He never did tell us where his precious Pookie was.

We contacted the authorities in Jefferson City and advised them that we had arrested Pumpkin. They sternly admonished us and told us that if we had read the warrant information completely, we'd have seen there was extradition with adjoining counties only. I couldn't help but smile as I thanked them.

The area where Pookie and Nay-Nay were staying was located in a well-to-do area of Jefferson County. Jefferson County is two counties south of St. Louis City and not to be confused with the state's capital, Jefferson City, which is located about two hours west of St. Louis. A relieved Pumpkin and the Eighth District cops bid us farewell as Franklin and I headed to Jefferson County in search of Pookie and Nay-Nay.

The subdivision bordered St. Louis County near Interstate 44 and Highway141, prime St. Louis real estate. The subdivision had one main street, which wound downhill through a collection of stately custom homes. Toward the end of the street, it hooked a hard left and began a sharp incline for about two hundred yards.

It was almost 2:00 a.m. when we quietly glided the G ride to a stop about two hundred yards from the house Pookie and Nay-Nay had rented. The records showed the house belonged to a successful local builder. It seemed positively foreign that we were there looking for Pookie and Nay-Nay. Their urban track record didn't match this location.

At the end of this dark street stood the jewel of the subdivision. I took a moment to admire the magnificent house sprawled across the crest of a hill. In the dark night, with the lights on inside, the house had a diamond-like, sparkling beauty.

That vision was quickly shattered when we saw Pookie (or was it Nay-Nay?) running naked behind the big bay windows chasing another birthday-suit sprinter through the house with what appeared to be a feather duster.

The developer/builder, we would find out later, had a management company leasing his residence. He had no idea these wanted felons were now wreaking havoc in his home. He learned of this later when I contacted him and advised him of the illegal activity.

But, at that moment, we moved stealthily up to the house so we wouldn't alarm the frenzied nymphs inside. They were preoccupied and likely would not have noticed anything short of a bomb blast.

That night, all five Deputy U.S. Marshals assigned to Weed and Seed duty came out with us for the arrest. The other three took up positions near the rear of the house. Franklin and I went to the front door.

It wasn't until the third or fourth sequence of knocks, more like police pounding on the door really, that we drew the attention of some of the occupants. Pookie and his friend peered through the front window. Pookie immediately flew into flight mode when he saw our vests embossed with POLICE U.S. Marshals.

Pumpkin's precious Pookie was sprayed with pepper spray as he took off out the back door. One of his friends had unlocked the front door for us upon command.

Nay-Nay was rounded up in an upper bedroom as we performed a standard protective sweep of the premises. Nay-Nay was in bed … alone. He wasn't feeling well, he said, which immediately raised my eyebrows and my suspicions.

We handcuffed everyone, including the twins and three others. We herded all in a front room so we could sort through the mess and identify everyone present.

Nay-Nay lay quietly on a sofa without much fanfare. But Pookie was in full fight mode. One of the other Marshals found Pookie and his friend some sweatpants. Pookie was still suffering from what we call "Marshals cologne" (pepper spray). He was issuing threats and insults at us, like a grand dame, through his snot and tears. I would have sworn he was the evil twin! I thought.

After a bit, I'd had enough of Pookie's insults and needed to keep the situation under control. He was wild and not allowing the rest of them to calm down. "You gonna get it when Pumpkin finds out you been messin' around!" I said firmly. He shut up and glared at me, wiping his face on a sofa cushion.

Not only had we just successfully captured two federal fugitives, we had also discovered a counterfeit check-making operation in one of the rooms. Additionally, we recovered two stolen vehicles—a Land Rover and a Porsche 911 parked in the garage. State Farm Insurance would later take custody of those vehicles without so much as a thank you. Their files revealed they had already paid out more than ninety thousand dollars for those two vehicles. It was only 3:20 a.m., not too bad for one night's work.

To my dismay, Pookie and Nay-Nay were the only ones

who were wanted out of the group that referred to themselves as "Club Faberge." The others had clean records, so we booted them out into the night. They wanted to hang out with us inside until their rides came, but it was a crime scene and we couldn't allow it, unless they were part of the crime. So out they went, gladly.

Nay-Nay breathed a sigh of relief after they were gone and asked for his medicine from inside a safe. The safe was locked, of course, and was located in the bedroom with the counterfeit check operation. Pookie said he would get inside of it and told us he didn't want us looking in there without a search warrant.

"You are too bold," I told Pookie, using his vernacular to regain control of the situation yet again. "Besides, I get to be in charge today. I'll open the safe when you get me the combination or when the judge gives me a search warrant. I don't care either way. But, I will open it."

I then turned to Nay-Nay and said, "But if we wait on the judge, you wait on the medicine."

I turned back to Pookie, looking to diffuse what belligerence could come from his anger. Pookie was scowling at me. "And as sassy as you are, you might have a pistol in there and try to shoot me, Pookie," I said with a grin.

"You know I ain't got no violence on my jacket," he replied indignantly, referring to his police record.

"Regardless, I open the safe or it remains shut. End of story," I said.

Nay-Nay gave up the combination. He did have his medicine in the safe. We also found a stack of stolen identities in there. This discovery compounded their problems. But on the bright side, there was no gun.

The safe contained twenty Missouri driver's licenses and ID cards. All of them had different names and dates of birth, but everyone had either Pookie's or Nay-Nay's photograph on them. The twins were identical, but Nay-Nay had baby dreadlocks, and

Pookie wore purple contacts. That helped to determine who was who.

It turned out that Pookie was HIV positive and Nay-Nay had full-blown AIDS. They kept their medicine locked up so their friends wouldn't find out about their secret medical conditions. Now those are some good friends, I thought sarcastically. I wondered if AIDS was the secret Pumpkin thought made Nay-Nay the devil. I couldn't help but consider the potential health threat since these two had been hiding their illnesses from Pumpkin, the other three we sent home earlier this evening, and their other victims.

I spent the next several days cleaning up the mess from that night. The two cars had been stolen in Atlanta, Georgia. The twins said they had bought them from "Latin Kings" gang members for two thousand dollars each.

I called and spoke with a detective in the Atlanta Police Department's auto theft unit. He verified that members of the Latin Kings were involved in organized auto theft. He said he understood they were responsible for nearly a thousand stolen vehicles in the past two years, from Atlanta alone.

Apparently, once a month gang members would bring between six to eight cars to St. Louis and park them out at Lambert International Airport in a long-term parking lot. The cars would remain there until they found a buyer.

Once the cars were in place at the airport, these gangsters would frequent alternative lifestyle clubs throughout the area and market the cars. They would find buyers and sell the cars to people who were not only in the lifestyle, but who were also "in the mix," meaning they were bandits themselves.

The Latin Kings gang had someone working inside a license bureau in Georgia. The inside person would dummy up registration papers to make the vehicle appear legitimate. Each stolen car had what appeared to be valid Georgia license plates and registration. The vehicles were actually registered in the state's system.

Since 1981, vehicles have been assigned unique seventeen digit serial numbers. The vehicle identification number, or VIN, is a combination of alpha and numeric characters that identifies that specific vehicle. A VIN plate is located on the console of every car. It should be visible through the windshield on the driver's side.

When a car is reported stolen, the department receiving the report will enter the VIN into the National Crime Information Center, or NCIC. When an officer comes across a vehicle they believe may have been stolen, they run a check on the VIN through NCIC.

Some car thieves will take off the VIN plate and replace it with a salvaged or counterfeit VIN plate. More often, they simply cover the VIN with something thrown on the dashboard.

Upon closer inspection, I had noticed that the VIN on the registration papers was one digit different from the VIN plate. The gang's "inside guy" simply typed in a different number for the ninth digit of the seventeen-number VIN when he prepared the registration papers.

When checking a VIN, many law enforcement officers will look at the last six digits on the VIN plate and the registration papers. If they match, they often read the VIN off the vehicle's registration papers when checking on ownership. The night we arrested the twins, a local cop ran the plates and VIN and they came back clean. I couldn't believe with all of the counterfeiting equipment and stolen identities that the twins had actually bought those vehicles legally and outright. I went out to the garage and ran both the license plates and the VIN myself, to find out the cars were indeed stolen. I wrote down the whole number directly off the VIN plate on each dashboard. This time, by reading the VIN directly off the vehicle, I got a hit that the car was stolen. This information both shocked and angered the twins.

"We bought those cars!" they argued, indignantly.

They both started to talk, hoping for leniency by cooperating. During the day, the twins would drive around in their high-rollin' stolen rides and steal information regarding people's identities. Often times, they would blackmail patrons of alternative lifestyle bars into providing information they had access to from their jobs.

The twins were seeking prey in the Midwestern conservative culture who were not likely "out" or openly acknowledging their homosexuality. They found victims with connections, for example a guy who worked at a bank. The banker, for his own reasons, didn't want people to know he was gay. The twins threatened to expose his secret unless he provided them inside information regarding bank routing numbers or customer information.

Sometimes the twins stole their dates' identification. When the guy realized his identity had been stolen, he likely called the police. When the cops showed the victim a photograph of the suspect, usually one of the twins, the guy said he had never seen them before. What could he say? "Officer, that guy was a date of mine, a one night stand from a local gay bar. My wife just can't know!"

The twins were very bold in their criminal enterprise. They even stole—and got away with using—the identity of a local celebrity, a guy who owned a roofing company and who did commercials that aired on local television channels. His company had hired a "temporary" guy whose description matched Pumpkin. This temp worked in accounting.

I called the roofing company, identified myself, and told them they needed to audit the temp's work. They were completely surprised and bewildered. They found out later that several of their company checks had gone missing and that several counterfeit checks were passed through local banks.

The twins' main line of work was producing and cashing counterfeit checks, including cashier's checks. They produced the checks themselves and used stolen routing numbers with legitimate account numbers. They would spend the day driving across eastern Missouri cashing checks.

The twins had presented themselves to a local property management company as prospective buyers who wanted to lease the house for six months prior to purchasing. The manager at the management company called the twins' employer and asked for the name of the person the twins had used as a reference. The manager was then unknowingly transferred to "the temp" in accounting.

The temp, of course, verified everything the twins had said including their annual salaries, which were very good. But that was to be expected of regional vice presidents of marketing and sales.

The property management company was also a very well-known real estate company in St. Louis. The folks who dealt with Pookie and Nay-Nay later told me several times they knew something was wrong with the twins. "But hey," one person at the management company told me, "the twins paid in cash— nearly three thousand dollars a month—so the company let them lease whatever property they wanted."

The twins literally brought several thousand dollars in cash for the down payment and first month's rent. The property manager laughed as he told me he had instructed them to go across the street and get a cashier's check from the bank and bring it back to him. He had told them to do this every month thereafter as well.

I think the manager could sense that I wasn't amused. I asked him why he rented to them. He said he had no idea they were stealing from people. He actually told me, "I thought they were drug dealers. Personally, I wouldn't have given them change for a dollar bill."

Ironically, the bank across the street that received a lot of business from the property management company was also a victim of the twins. The twins had taken that bank for nearly one hundred thousand dollars cashing counterfeit checks, just not at that specific branch location, so the employees didn't recognize them.

Bank employees said they were not suspicious of the twins because the property management company directed other people with cash over to the bank for cashier's checks.

I also tracked down the owner/builder of the home where we had arrested the twins. He was also the subdivision developer. He was living in Arizona at this time and jumped on the first thing smoking to fly back to St. Louis. He was not a happy camper.

The developer couldn't believe the management company had leased his house to the twins. He filed a lawsuit against the management company. The developer's attorney contacted me a few days later. He wanted to pick my brain about the circumstances surrounding the twins' lease of the property.

It turns out the developer's attorney knew Assistant United States Attorney (AUSA) Tim Raven, who handled this case. AUSA Tim Raven is a fine Irish lad and staunch Notre Dame fan. Raven had told the developer's attorney to give me a call. I have spent time in court with Marshals duties of court security and transporting defendants who are in jail, and I have also testified numerous times in front of grand juries to get indictments, at preliminary hearings, and in both state and federal courts.

The attorney asked me a few questions, and I filled him in as best I could. He said he might need me to testify in state court if he filed a civil case. He was aware of the hoops he'd have to jump through to get that accomplished, but he just knew it was worth it.

I recounted my conversation with the manager at the property company to the developer's attorney. He was silent for a moment and then asked if I was joking. I assured him I was not. He told me that under state law they could sue for damages, lost rent, and damage to property. In reality, it was a loss or a wash unless they could prove negligence and prove punitive damages.

Here comes negligence: the old boy from the property management company telling me a half dozen times, "I knew something was wrong, but I thought they were drug dealers." That is negligence.

The developer's attorney laughed and said I could disregard. He would not need me to testify in court.

The attorney was confident the management company would settle out of court. They did. I never heard what the settlement amount was, but the civil case never saw the inside of a courthouse.

Here is a sore spot I have with the justice system: Even though both Pookie and Nay-Nay ran out on supervised release and committed all of these new crimes with so many victims, they were convicted but got less than three years each.

Since then, Pookie and Nay-Nay are no longer in the prison system. Pumpkin was never charged with any crime related to this case.

Occasionally, when I'm with my wife and she stops to shop for shoes, I'll wander through the aisles looking for size 14EEE. I still haven't found any yet.

STORY FOUR

Too often I would hear men boast of the miles covered that day, rarely of what they had seen.

– Louis L'Amour

Raleigh Baldwin was so distracted that he never saw a minivan with two men in suits on his forty-five-mile frantic drive to a White Castle of all places.

I kept the minivan gear in drive and had my foot lightly on the brake. I parallel parked on the street next to the busy fast food restaurant parking lot.

Raleigh, the man we were following, was in his late thirties but was acting like a scared kid. He was frantically willing the phone to ring—waving his arms, talking to himself, stopping every few steps to stare at the phone.

I could see the sweat dripping off his acne-scarred jaw in St. Louis summer humidity. Raleigh, who we had nicknamed "the son of Santa," was a grubby-looking man in dirty cut-off jeans and construction boots.

"Preacher Man, I bet he's afraid to pick it up to check for a dial tone," Chris Lovelace said smoothly from his typical spot on surveillance, the passenger's seat. I laughed quietly without taking my eyes off Raleigh.

Lovelace and I were both Deputy U.S. Marshals, but we could not have been more different. I was glad to be sitting comfortably in an air-conditioned car, unlike in Marine Recon days, being attacked by bird-sized mosquitoes and waiting on orders in some jungle or cane field for days on end. Lovelace squirmed uncomfortably in the passenger seat, readjusting the air vents toward him for the best effect to ward off the suffocating humidity.

He and I were both willing the phone to ring. When it did, we hoped to close the net on a most-wanted felon in a nationwide search. This bandit was known as "Santa," a jolly nickname for a nasty, drug-smuggling, dope-dealing bandit. We had discovered he was the ringleader of a nationwide drug enterprise. I stopped shy of describing his crew as "elves," despite the temptation. They were drug-dealing, gun-toting, hardened criminals who lived outside the law. They would do anything to stop us from interfering with their money making.

Lovelace shrugged his dark suit coat off gingerly, folding and laying it on the back seat.

"Big date?" I asked. Lovelace's cologne, a popular department store men's fragrance, was overpowering and offensive.

"I've got a date plus a backup late night happy hour lined up. Gotta keep fresh and keep my jacket nice. You see, Luke, we don't all run home to our grade school sweetheart," he sneered.

What a six-year-old, I thought. I figured he was crabby from the heat and worried he might miss his dating scam. True, I am smitten with the same girl I have been in love with since third grade. I was wondering if I'd get to see my Blue Eyes and the kids that night, or if this stakeout, like so many before, would go on all night. My wife is my greatest fan and is one strong lady. Lucky for me.

Lovelace lacked the patience for surveillance and typically pouted and fidgeted the whole time. We'd been put together on dozens of cases before. It had only been about fifteen minutes since we pulled up. This time we both knew this stakeout—waiting for this phone call, no matter how long it took—could close down this drug ring we had been chasing for nearly eight months.

I rechecked my Miranda card, stored in the minivan console, then reached back under my suit coat to undo the thumb break on my holster and unlock my Glock by feel. Just in case. Son of Santa was really nervous, and we didn't know what would go down.

I had a custom of reading straight from the Miranda card during arrests. This routine started from my first arrest. Back in the Corps, I learned to methodically check my gear before heading out on missions. This habit of preparedness had saved me many headaches in the field, underwater, and in the courtroom.

The anticipation of the phone ringing was palpable. Nine months into this chase could wrap up here and now. I stayed focused on the Son of Santa, playing out mental "What if ... ?" scenarios to keep my mind sharp and focused. Were we finally going to close the net on Santa?

The first time I met the notorious Santa, I was assigned to courtroom duties. U.S. Marshals have been tending court as another aspect of our duties since 1789 when George Washington appointed the first thirteen U.S. Marshals. Mondays and Fridays were typically heavy court days, so the court docket of the eighteen or so judges in the Eastern District of Missouri was full, and the Deputy U.S. Marshals, including myself, were busy moving around defendants between cells and courtrooms.

The Old Federal Courthouse in downtown St. Louis was built in 1926 and is a very majestic old building. The courtrooms are extremely large pretentious caverns with twenty-foot-tall ceilings. I liked being in this strong and quiet place that commands hushed voices. It is stately with beautiful hardwoods and Italian marble throughout.

The next defendant I was to escort was listed on the cellblock log as Roy Baldwin. I entered the holding cellblock area on the first floor of the courthouse. The distance was only six feet from my desk. The Marshals' office looked like the set from the sitcom Barney Miller. I greeted the detention officer, called out Baldwin's name, and grabbed handcuffs off the rack. As I prepared to handcuff him, I glanced through the cell door. "Santa," I hooted gleefully. "It's not Christmas night!" It was amazing how much this guy looked like Santa Claus. I could see where he picked up the nickname.

Baldwin's laugh was more of a wheeze as he took his time standing up to his full five feet seven inches. He waddled and scraped his tennis shoes like an old woman in house slippers. He shuffled across the cell floor to get into the handcuffs. I estimated his weight at around three hundred pounds. His skin was pasty with the ruddy-veined cheeks and nose of an alcoholic. He was an unhealthy-looking sixty-five years old with a long white beard and wire-rimmed spectacles. No kidding.

No red satin outfit with fluffy white fur trim, though. Instead he was wearing bib overalls, tennis shoes, and a flannel shirt. But other than the costume, he was the image of the winter legend himself. It's as if he had just stepped off the front of a Currier and Ives Christmas card.

At his slow, lumbering pace, I maneuvered him through the back corridors of the Federal Courthouse.

What did this embodiment of childhood delight do to end up in the federal court system? All I knew about this case was in the paperwork from the morning court docket.

As we entered Judge Meeks' courtroom on the third floor, I immediately spotted Baldwin's family members sitting in the row behind his attorney. Baldwin had claimed to be indigent, or a man of no means, and took the government up on the Miranda right to an attorney. The taxpayers footed the bill for a federal public defender. After sitting Baldwin down and removing his handcuffs next to his attorney, I sat down at the prosecutor's table next to Assistant United States Attorney (AUSA) Antoinette Diver, a sharp, young go-getter, keeping an eye on Baldwin while we waited for the judge.

"How's bandit chasing going these days, Luke?" Diver asked. I nodded and grinned as I said, "Business is good!" "I'm afraid we're a growth industry."

I leaned into AUSA Diver and quietly asked, "What's this guy looking at? Who's who here in the courtroom?"

Baldwin's family consisted of a scraggly-looking man I deduced to be about forty years old, and a young but hard-looking woman wearing cut-off jeans and a worn, oversized T-shirt. She looked to be in her early twenties and was holding a newborn baby in her arms.

AUSA Diver shrugged, uncommitted as she moved two stacks of files into place on the table. "This is a no brainer—a sixty-five-year-old guy caught with two kilos of methamphetamines in his possession at the airport. Mandatory minimum of fifteen years," she said.

I laughed, picturing Santa as a drug dealer passing out baggies of meth decorated with bright bows. "I don't suppose this is a bond hearing?" I asked. This is a polite way of asking if the case is tight enough to keep the guy in custody.

"No way in the world this guy is making bond," she laughed confidently.

Before court started, we speculated on the people in attendance. "Must be Baldwin's son, granddaughter, and great grandchild," I commented.

Back in the day, the U.S. Marshal in court would call out to everyone present in the courtroom as the judge entered.

I got the cue from the judge then stood and announced: "All rise! Hear ye, hear ye, hear ye! The United States District Court for the Eastern Division of the Eastern District of Missouri is now in session. All persons having business before this honorable court may now draw near and they shall be heard. God save the

United States and this honorable court."

Judge Meek walked briskly to the bench, his long black robe flowing behind. Good, I thought. He looks all business today.

"You may be seated," I finished.

We started off each session of court just like that for more than two hundred years. Federal court proceedings are very formal, and most of the old-time judges would tolerate no nonsense. At that time, tradition in our district dictated that the Marshals present would make that announcement. The recital is now made by the Clerk of the Court so the Marshal can focus on the prisoner and security.

Judge Meeks called the court to order and spent several minutes unapologetically silent, rummaging through papers and trying to get organized as though he had never seen the case before.

Then he announced the charges and said we were here today for a change of plea. In short, it seemed that Baldwin was on the naughty list this year. He had been arrested at St. Louis Lambert International Airport upon returning from a round trip to California—what I call the "Left Coast"—after apparently picking up dope from a well-known California motorcycle gang. He was busted by the Drug Enforcement Agency at the airport with two kilos of methamphetamine in his suitcase, known on the street at that time as "meth," "crank," or "go-fast."

Two kilos is about the size of a five-pound bag of flour and is worth about fifty thousand dollars in a bulk purchase like that or close to a hundred thirty thousand dollars broken out into individual doses. What he brought in was about ninety-six percent pure crystal meth—high quality and potent drugs. Once Santa "stepped on it" or "cut it" (usually with a couple pounds of ephedrine, commonly used for weight loss or as a decongestant), this batch would roughly be thirty-three thousand individual doses of meth he was bringing into the St. Louis area—in just one trip.

I wondered how many times he had made this trip, slipping cheerfully through security in Hawaiian shirts and shorts, life of the party. Who would think they would need to check his bag for anything other than a red suit and stocking stuffers while he was playing it up with the families, waving and ho-ho-ho-ing at the kids in the airport?

By law under the federal sentencing guidelines, Baldwin was facing a mandatory minimum fifteen years in federal prison if he was found guilty for being in possession of this huge amount of methamphetamine.

The public defender stood and announced to the court that two of Roy's children were present in the courtroom along with his fiancé. Diver and I exchanged glances and I did some quick mental math. So much for Mrs. Claus, I thought. That's right; the hard-looking twenty something was Roy's fiancé. The infant and the forty-something tired-looking guy were both his kids. The public defender announced that Roy would change his plea to guilty. He started into an unexciting and unimaginative tale, but he had everyone's rapt attention as we were keyed in on this old codger with a fiancé one-third his age.

The public defender continued, "Baldwin is sorry for his actions. Baldwin was a 'mule,' or a low-level drug courier, which he was forced into doing because of his indigent situation."

So, I thought to myself, the defender is saying Baldwin didn't willingly fly out to California and buy the meth he brought back to Missouri? It is terrible to be indigent; I was on the streets as a teen, making my way on the carnival, so I know indigent. But I never considered transporting drugs.

"Baldwin was traumatized by his participation in the Vietnam War loading cargo onto airplanes on bases located in friendly territories. Baldwin was also victimized by our society's lack of concern about his welfare," the public defender said.

So what they were saying was that Roy was pleading guilty, but it was our fault, society's fault, and the system's fault. We heard that a lot. Blame is apparently a lot easier than guilt and accountability.

Due to the severity of the crime and the mandatory minimum sentence to be imposed, Judge Meeks was mandated, or required by federal law, to hold the defendant in custody with no bail—unless he found extenuating circumstances. If so, the judge could allow the defendant to be released on bond. Federal judges are appointed by the president of the United States and often reflect the bent of that administration. Judge Meeks was an appointee of the Carter administration, and he was very liberal. My experience with federal judges is they resent being told what to do, and they resist mandates, especially liberal-appointed judges like Judge Meeks.

The prosecutor and I couldn't think of any extenuating circumstances for this bandit with the significance of his crime to be released on bond. However, fortunately for Baldwin, the public defender had thought of several.

Baldwin was a Vietnam veteran who was retired Air Force, which meant he had a monthly military pension, the defender said. AUSA Diver and I exchanged looks. This argument contradicted the whole "indigent-man-without-means" reason he had a court-appointed attorney.

Apparently that inconsistent line of reasoning did the trick today in Judge Meeks' courtroom. The federal public defender also included the new infant, Baldwin's fiancé, and their hardships as the extenuating circumstances. He told the judge the harsh mandatory sentence in prison was draconian and tantamount to a death sentence.

Okay, I figured I was on board with him on that point. Baldwin was every bit of sixty. He was facing fifteen years inside a federal prison. I was thinking his chances of living that long were dodgy.

The public defender pleaded with the judge to allow his client to be released on bond. He told the judge that Roy would need the time to get his affairs in order and marry his fiancé so she would have access to his military retirement and so on.

The judge enthusiastically agreed. He furrowed his generous eyebrows and sternly warned Baldwin that if he failed to appear for sentencing, he'd be facing an additional ten years in prison, to be served consecutively. Normally this might be a deterrent, but to a guy who thinks he's going to die during the first fifteen years anyway, it means nothing.

I looked across the way at Baldwin and could see that very same thought flash across his face. I shook my head in frustration. This type of case is the reason why the U.S. Congress mandated that defendants be held without bail, I think, frustrated by the loophole.

I sized up Judge Meeks. He was probably in his early sixties and likely saw Baldwin as a man of his age. Meeks empathized with Baldwin's dilemmas, likely realizing the downhill battle of age, his own aches and pains, and that time is precious and fleeting. He saw Baldwin as a guy who served his country and made some bad choices for the sake of money.

Then Judge Meeks told the defendant he was free to go. The gavel banged and plunked in the silence onto the bench.

That is what I call a head start.

With the court now in recess, Baldwin gained some spring in his step. He was free and headed for the door. He paused for a moment and turned toward me. He was all smiles now. With a nod of his head and a twinkle in his eye, he gave me a wink and then it was goodbye!

AUSA Diver and I were stunned. I quietly wondered why the judge didn't just buy him an airline ticket out of town, South America maybe.

Chasing fugitives had been my vocation for more than fifteen years at this point, and my instincts told me I had just watched one go out the door.

"May I please borrow Baldwin's case file and get familiar with it?" I asked Diver.

She gladly agreed and handed over the manila folder. "We both know Baldwin is not coming back to court on his own accord," Diver said.

"If he doesn't show for his next court date in thirty days, he'll have a month's head start and we'll have a cold trail," I said.

"He's clearly a fugitive now, and it's just a matter of time until he is formally wanted, Preacher Man," she said kindly and then sighed. "I can tell you are on to something and will be looking forward to the call."

The arrest warrant came down to the U.S. Marshals office four weeks later. I was waiting for it. I had my suspicions just from that short interaction with him. Based on his history, I knew there was more to Baldwin than being a drug mule for cash. The warrant charged him with failure to appear for sentencing.

Normally each fugitive warrant was assigned randomly in the "one for you, one for you, and one for you" style during the daily doling out process to Deputy U.S. Marshals in our district. The Deputy Marshal was then considered the lead on the investigation and responsible for apprehending that fugitive. Long before Baldwin's warrant came down, I had asked to be given the case. Those requests, as often as not, got lost in the system; Baldwin's warrant was assigned to a person in our office nicknamed "Back Door."

Law enforcement officers are notorious for nicknames with a catchy memory trigger like hair color, stature, or personality trait. I found there was enough truth to the monikers that the people on the streets picked up on them, too. In one of the small St. Louis urban neighborhood newspapers, the reporters actually referred to the officers of the Fugitive Apprehension Strike Team (the FAST unit) by our nicknames for their stories.

The FAST unit is a mix of local, state and federal officers who focus on apprehending fugitives throughout the five counties of the Greater St. Louis Metropolitan Area in "The Eastern

District of Missouri."

The nicknames are normally given by police officers in the FAST unit. I am not an ordained minister, but my nickname was "Preacher Man." It was given to me by one of the local newspaper reporters, but the FAST unit quickly adopted it. I like to think it was a moniker of respect. After two seasons with the carnival and four years in the Corps, I had never used profanity. I frequently would say, "Stop it," "Does your mother know you talk like that?" or "Do your kiss your mother with that mouth?" as a hint to lighten up on the trash talk. And I often said "Amen" to punctuate a thought; hence, the nickname.

Originally from the St. Louis area, my Midwestern "no-accent" speech doesn't give away much. Most people wouldn't know about my specialized training in the Marines Corps Reconnaissance Unit. Four years as a "super grunt" taught me critical tactical skills and instilled military discipline, training me to minimize my movement and to use situational awareness. I also picked up a couple moves as the youngest of three brothers, all relieved of a roof over our heads simultaneously by a stepfather. Then I survived the carnival circuit, up and down the Midwest, from the Gulf of Mexico to the Canadian border, during the carnival season. My time as a carnie taught me many things, not the least of which was survival.

Some nicknames are nicer than others, but overtly, Chris Lovelace was quickly and aptly named Back Door by fellow officers because he always volunteered to cover the back door of a building when we went to serve a warrant. Taking the back door was his way of staying out of harm's way while still being in on the bust to reap the glory and commendations. He would also stab you in the back or back door you if given a chance.

Everything about Back Door screamed Little Man Syndrome—he was small except for his ego and his attitude. Back Door originally tried to start his own nickname of "Love Lord," but the other officers had a good laugh and it never took.

Now, I'm not a big guy at five feet nine inches and a hundred eighty pounds. Back Door was about five feet six inches and a hundred forty pounds. He had small manicured hands and a mousy voice with an East Coast accent. He was athletic, and his prematurely gray hair was tightly gelled. He was a self-proclaimed ladies' man. You get the picture.

He constantly postured about being "a fed" and schmoozed with everyone he met. Sort of an Eddie Haskel from *Leave it to Beaver*. Anytime he sensed a camera around, he was in front of the lens. He spent more energy figuring how to get out of work than actually working.

Back Door would be the lead, but if this Santa character was as big and dirty as I suspected he was, he'd be a fun one to chase. I was all in.

It was a frosty early winter morning, and the skies were still dark as I walked to my U.S. Government-issued gray metal desk. It was one of twelve in the wide-open Marshal Service office. Ironically, every time I sat down there I was reminded that inmates in the federal prison system made our desks.

I reopened the prosecutor's manila folder I had kept in preparation for the now-official outstanding warrant for Roy Baldwin. I stood up and looked down at the cover, weighing the decision with a heavy heart. Baldwin was making two trips a month like the one the DEA caught him with; that was close to eight hundred thousand doses of meth pouring into the St. Louis area. On the other hand, there was the matter of working with Back Door.

Back Door played on several recreational teams at a time, but he was no team player in the field when it counted. He was definitely not a take-charge person or a leader. Working with him would be a daily pain.

I looked at the fresh stack of warrants that did get assigned to me that morning. I could pick one up and start the chase on any one of those other dozen federal fugitive warrants on my desk.

And … I would. I would get to every one of those soon, but my gut told me Baldwin was more than just a mule; he was a big time bandit. I wanted Baldwin off the streets. The chase was on.

I called over to the FAST unit to bounce the situation off of my mentor, nicknamed Red Dog. Red Dog was a red-headed St. Louis City police detective. He was one of the best. I knew he'd want in on the chase.

Through the phone I could hear his chair squeak as he leaned back, chuckling as I quickly filled him in on my dilemma. He knew the score with Back Door, having had experience working with him, too. The chair squeaked again as he leaned forward toward the desk to give his advice.

"C'mon, Preacher Man. Put Back Door in the backseat and let's go get this bandit. You are telling me you think he might be a big fish. I hear you. Count me in; I'm ready for this one," Red Dog said, knowing his commitment to the chase sealed the deal for me. "Catch 'em with ya later."

I smiled as I hung up. Red Dog is a good guy, I thought.

Baldwin wasn't a mule like his defense attorney said in court, but instead a major interstate drug trafficker of high potency meth.

I mentally committed to team up with the Lovelace aka Back Door.

Sighing, I picked up the folder and walked over to where he was reading the sports section of the St. Louis Post-Dispatch at his desk. I knew I was going to be spending what spare time I had lifting weights to work out the frustration of working with him.

He looked up at me from the paper and eyed me for a couple of seconds before he spoke. "I scored an interesting fugitive warrant. Maybe you've heard of it? Heard the dude looks like Santa," he said with a smug grin. "I was going to ask you if you wanted to assist me with it. I'm the lead on this one and am letting you in, get it? Keep me in the loop before you do anything cool."

I mentally gritted my teeth. "You bet," I said. Does he look more like a weasel or an opossum? I wondered to myself on the way back to my desk. His sneer was very sewer rat-like.

I sat down and pulled a Louis L'Amour book out of my center drawer. In between orders in training and operations in the Marines, we had a lot of down time. "Hurry up and wait" is what they call it for a very good reason. One of my fellow super grunts in the Reconnaissance Unit introduced me to Louis L'Amour western novels.

I had drifted through my teens because I am a survivor. I stayed alive on the streets and in the pack of misfits on the carnival, but I lacked a role model. I really took to heart the responsibility of the lawmen—and felt compelled to be more like the ones described by Louis L'Amour. I also feel a sense of camaraderie with Louis L'Amour. He hoboed his way across the country, was a boxer, traveled the world as a merchant seaman, and had said the inspiration for several of his characters were U.S. Marshals he had met. In times of frustration, like now, his work rang true. I flipped forward to a marked page. Louis L'Amour wrote, "Victory is won not in miles but in inches. Win a little now, hold your ground, and later, win a little more."

I nodded at Lovelace, who was watching me, waiting for my cue. With renewed enthusiasm, I grabbed the keys and Baldwin's file and said, "Let's hop in the G Sled and grab Santa." I drove over to the FAST unit to begin the hunt for Santa, humming the tune to "Jingle Bells."

With a refresher from the prosecutor's file, I made up a list of people Santa (AKA Roy Baldwin) knew and places he'd lived or visited. Baldwin had traveled all over the world during his thirty-year Air Force career. Since his retirement he had lived in a series of small towns throughout rural Southeastern Missouri. Mostly he seemed to favor unassuming, ramshackle mobile home courts. I knew he had drug contacts in California because he was on a return flight from there with the methamphetamine he got caught with at the airport.

We began by interviewing the people who knew Baldwin the best: his family. I chauffeured Back Door around without meaningful conversation on the hour drive to Farmington, Missouri, to meet Baldwin's family. Baldwin's fiancé; the son in his forties, Skip; and a younger son, named Raleigh, were pretty hostile and short with us, giving us the brief, standard answers about how they hadn't seen him nor had they heard from him and so forth.

All but one of them told me they'd be sure to call me if they heard from him. The younger son, Raleigh, appeared gleeful. He seemed to be enjoying the fact that we didn't know where Baldwin was. I suspected Raleigh was a dealer in his father's meth ring and was also, obviously, a client. He chuckled at us through rotted and missing teeth. He was agitated, and I suspected he was high based on his jerky movements and wide-open, wild eyes.

"You will never find my daddy," Raleigh said overconfidently as we walked out of the trailer back to our car parked on the weedy, patched gravel driveway. His Southern drawl reminded me of how Elvis sounded when he talked between songs on his later television specials.

Raleigh hopped off the chair and almost pranced out alongside us, saying in a whiny, grade-school, sing-song voice, "None of Daddy's family members will cooperate because they are all afraid of what he'll do to them." He laughed menacingly.

Apparently Roy had a mean streak.

I quickly discovered that one of Santa's co-conspirators and cousin, Frank Willis, the person rumored to have called in the tip on Baldwin to the police, was found dead the day after I watched Baldwin jingle out of Judge Meeks' courtroom. According to police reports, Willis' death was ruled a suicide. I spoke with one of the officers who worked the case, and he told me the law enforcement on the scene initially said it looked like the guy killed himself and ruled it that way. Then information started coming in that Willis was supposed to be Santa's driver from the airport the day of the bust.

The officers surmised that Willis had "dropped a dime" on Santa that day when he was drunk and feeling sorry for himself and not feeling like making the drive to the airport to pick up his rich cousin.

That's the story of how the DEA knew to grab Santa with his bag: his driver/cousin called in the tip. This was great grist for feeding the fear rumor mill but not enough to reopen the suicide case.

As I interviewed more people, the picture they painted of Roy Baldwin got more sinister. It was that of an evil, dangerous, and dirty old man. Being retired, he had a lot of time on his hands, and an idle mind can be the Devil's Workshop, or so it was with Baldwin. He was fond of traveling, chauffeured by a young, typically bleach-blonde, exotic dancer. He had an eye for the young ladies he found in exotic dance halls.

His military pension didn't go far after alimony split it in half with his first wife of more than ten years. When Roy retired, he made ends meet by doing odd jobs and spending the rest of his time enjoying the live entertainment at strip joints found in rural areas. Many of these clubs are small buildings, barely bigger than a mobile home on concrete pads. The one he frequented the most, called Fancy Free, was one of these cinderblock rectangles tucked behind a gas station less than a mile up a two-lane road from his Bonne Terre home.

Most of the girls wouldn't give Baldwin the time of day because of his age and his financial situation. But they would talk to him because of his charming resemblance to Santa. He soon found that many of the dancing queens in this line of work had "issues" from their childhood and they "self-medicated" with illegal drugs to get by.

Baldwin soon found he could manipulate these gals by supplying them with their drug of choice, while making good money and receiving female favors.

On his property, there were three dilapidated mobile homes situated in a row about twenty-five yards from his built-on mobile home where gals, down and out and strung out on his product would live and be at the old man's beck and call for all types of favors.

We found out no one beyond his family knew him as Roy Baldwin. Everyone he dealt with knew him as Santa. Bikers, dancers, and his fellow bar patrons all called him Santa. Even his "wicked elves," the drug dealers he supplied. We started following the dope and started uncovering them in droves. Dozens of dealers were all around Missouri and Eastern Illinois, and they all referred to him as Santa.

Another thing we soon discovered was that most of the people who knew him were deathly afraid of him. Even some of the rough-and-tumble bikers were scared of this old man. When we went to visit and interview them, they all told us what a dangerous reputation this Christmas-cheer-looking bandit had and that they weren't talking. No one besides a few of the dancers was afraid of him physically, but all of them said he was a cold-blooded killer.

One of the many rumors circulating around the community was that Santa was behind the killing of a young man found dead in the back of his pickup truck in a remote area of Ste. Genevieve County, Missouri. This kid, known as Quack, was a reputed drug dealer from De Soto, another small town about forty-five minutes southwest of St. Louis. He had been shot and dumped in the woods, and then he and his truck were set on fire.

The gist of the story was this kid was one of Santa's best distributors. As a good businessman, the kid went after a higher profit margin and started buying cheaper locally made meth, versus the more expensive stuff that Santa was buying from bikers and flying in from the Left Coast. Quack quit buying Santa's drugs, and the threat, "If you don't buy from me, you won't be in business," may have been made reality. This, as the story goes, was the kid's final undoing. Likely, no one will ever know. Another mother grieves.

Regardless of who was responsible for Quack's homicide, Santa's reputation as a dangerous man grew, and the legend was flourishing. People who had never met Baldwin personally were telling us what a bad hombre he was. My job was simply to find the guy and arrest him, but the fear of retribution among the locals was making it nearly impossible. We were being squeezed out. As the weather warmed up into summer, people got colder. No one wanted to talk to me for fear they would be killed in an equally gruesome way as Quack or shamefully like Willis. I was getting no cooperation, and the trail was going cold.

For weeks we heard rumors of Santa sightings, but nothing was firm and nothing panned out. We got the local media involved, put up posters, and canvassed local dives. It never failed that when we started chasing a bandit who had a unique description, we'd see people who looked like him everywhere. I mean, we were looking for Santa in the summertime. Everyone else thought they saw him, too. I was getting calls from all over Missouri from people who thought they saw Santa, including a tip from my wife's hairdresser and close friend. There was a real chance it could have been him, because Santa was known to spend time in several bars in that area. I did get a couple of good leads about him sneaking into town and continuing to drop off dope. The problem was that the tips came in after the fact, which didn't help too much because Baldwin was long gone again. People kept telling me he was driving back and forth from California twice a month in a blue minivan.

I was getting frustrated. It had been a couple weeks. I'm usually a laid-back kind of guy who doesn't get mad easily. However, I'm very strong in my beliefs with a rigid code of what is right and wrong—what the law is supposed to do, how it is supposed to protect people. I thought all of these people should see that they should be helping me catch this bandit. Baldwin was ruining lives and was rumored to be killing people! They just didn't see it that way. How could I help them to see reason?

One logical way would be to subpoena these people in front of a federal grand jury. The problem with that is there's a rule in the Department of Justice (DOJ) that says you can't use the power of the grand jury to hunt bandits. It is just a rule, mind you; it's not even a law. But they stick tight to it.

What a system. The G spends a ton of taxpayer money and effort, including grand jury time, to indict someone and prove they're guilty of a crime. However, once you know they're guilty, you can't use the same system to find them when they are in the wind.

I began June with a new tactic. I made up a list of the people who I knew were dealing Santa's drugs. In "legal speak," these were his co-conspirators and now known by those of us chasing them as his "wicked elf list." They probably saw themselves, like other drug dealers I've met over the years, as "independent retailers" or "successful capitalists" or "franchise business owners" taking care of themselves, but the federal conspiracy laws say otherwise. Once I established the list, I set about interviewing these folks and making them uncomfortable.

The key thing in these interviews is to try and catch the interviewees when they're "dirty." That is to say when there are any kind of outstanding warrants for their arrest or they're in possession of contraband items, any time—day or night—when they least expect it.

I had often gone to interview a witness only to find them in possession of narcotics, stolen property, or firearms. Shame on them when they're feeling cocky and all full of themselves, and they allow me into their home to talk, thinking they can toy with me and mishandle the truth. Human nature being what it is, Santa's elves were no different.

Over the next couple of months, I plowed through the "wicked elf list" and locked up several of them. Basically I went to interview them and caught them with guns, drugs, or outstanding arrest warrants. More than one of them was a convicted felon whom I caught in possession of a firearm. It is a violation of federal law to possess a firearm or ammunition if you have been convicted of a felony. The law contains a minimum sentence of fifteen years if you have three prior violent convictions. I guarantee you there is no better truth serum than that.

Many of their homes had bowls, bottles, and containers of ether, paint thinner, Freon®, acetone, anhydrous ammonia (a fertilizer), iodine crystals, red phosphorus, drain cleaner, battery acid, and lithium (extracted from inside batteries), which is mixed with ephedrine or pseudoephedrine to make crystal meth. Highly explosive combinations, materials just laying around in the kitchen and living room, mixed with ashtrays, magazines, and children's toys. Unfortunately for these families, by the time the U.S. Marshals come into the picture, the family situation has already disintegrated and the children are already integrated into the social system.

Unlike marijuana and cocaine, which are derived from plants, meth is a chemical compound. And with the addictiveness, everyone sees himself as an amateur chemist out to make big bucks.

I made a trip to the home of one of Santa's elves known as "Salvage Sammy." I found the trailer across the street, home to some local bikers who were breaking into the meth business. The trailer had exploded the night before, and literally nothing was left other than the concrete trailer pad and some gnarled metal. The local police told me later Sammy's neighbors were running a meth lab out of their kitchen and "they must not have gotten the ingredients mixed right that time." Fortunately for them, they had gone out to buy some more drain cleaner for their next batch. Whoa.

Apparently what these people were attempting was one of two ways to make meth. They were cooking up what is called "Nazi meth." It is a historically relevant name. Historical records show the Japanese first created methamphetamines and dispensed it to their soldiers to develop a new breed of killers who don't need sleep for days, don't eat much, and are homicidally aggressive and fearless. During World War II, the Japanese shared this secret with their allies, the Nazi Germans. During the Nazi revival of the late 1980s, the Neo Nazi skinheads, who researched their Nazi forefathers' tactics, discovered this way of making this chemical, which is "quick and dirty" to make. It can be created, start to finish, in less than eight hours. The chemicals, as previously mentioned, are very toxic and volatile. It can be made, as I have seen many times, in garages, outbuildings, kitchens, living rooms, and motel rooms. I've even seen labs in the back offices of strip malls. I once had two guys who were running a lab in the back of their van.

"Biker meth" is the other recipe for making methamphetamines. It is considered to be of higher quality and stronger, and it is made without the household chemicals. When Santa landed in St. Louis that day, "biker meth" was the norm, and the risk-to-profit ratio, according to Santa's choices, was worth running across state lines and flying commercial airlines halfway across the country.

Biker meth is named by the ride of choice of the gangs best known for the development and distribution of the substance. Hence the nicknames for meth synonymous with motorcycle riding like "go-fast" and "crank" (starting up a motorcycle). Biker meth is made in a laboratory with Bunsen burners, vials, droppers, and other equipment, including a special three-necked beaker. It is a felony to even possess that kind of beaker. The ingredients are less commercially available, pharmaceutical grade. It takes seventy-two hours, with constant watch, to make this meth.

There were a few "Nazi meth" labs cropping up in the rural areas around St. Louis at the time, many burning or exploding through the experimental phase while getting up and running. This is what Quack started buying instead of Santa's biker meth. This was Santa's new generation of competition.

Another frustrating aspect of this case was the fact that many of Santa's elves were their own best customers. Some of the people were so strung out on drugs they didn't know what day it was, or care. Meth gives a user a high that can last from a few hours up to twenty hours, and it is notorious for making people paranoid, homicidal, and incapable of sleep for days. Not to mention their teeth rot and fall out, and it causes damage to the brain, lungs, and liver.

I stopped at the home of a washed-up, nearly toothless, known dealer of Santa's dope named Kelly. She was eating up her own profits big time. She was living, freaked-out and high, in a trailer with a cocked AK-47 and a couple ounces of meth left.

High doses or long-term use of meth changes behavior and induces violence, hallucinations, depression, and psychoses. Kelly got clean while locked up on that arrest and wanted to help me, but she was cut off from the rest of the ring, who basically disowned her from the network the day I showed up on her doorstep.

Even though I caught and locked up six "dirty" dealers and they were facing substantial prison sentences, all of them refused to cooperate. That is, until they were in jail for a while and without drugs, needing a tweak (many people use alcohol or heroin to make the come-down off meth less painful). I would get a call from their attorney or the AUSA telling me "so-and-so would like to cooperate." By then, it was too late. They no longer had current information about Santa. Invariably, Santa would cut ties with anyone who he found out had been arrested.

However, my diligence finally began to pay off.

Word was spreading that this Federal Agent "Marshal Luke" was locking people up on federal charges because of Santa. The wicked elves were going to federal prison instead of getting probation from the state criminal justice system, like everyone figured would happen. I was showing up unexpectedly to interview people who were conducting illegal drug business. It was getting bad for business. Clients moved on; profits dried up. I was there because I was looking for Santa; therefore, he was the cause of their problems and the bad business. The sooner I caught Santa, the sooner they could get back to business, right? It was simple human nature, a matter of self-preservation. Telephone calls began to trickle in. In the beginning, they were anonymous, and people became more receptive to providing information.

One day in July while I was in Bonne Terre, the town of Santa's last known address, about an hour south of St. Louis, I was interviewing several of Santa's witnesses and neighbors. I stopped by the Fancy Free Strip Club, where Santa spent a lot of time before going into the wind. He had met his current wife there, the woman with the baby I had seen in court the day he made bond.

This was during the time when the U.S. Marshal Service shared the same dress code as FBI agents. I entered the front door wearing a suit and tie and dark sunglasses, looking like the quintessential fed. Immediately several of the patrons sloshed down the rest of their beverages, got up, and quickly exited the building without making eye contact with me. It was pretty funny. I began talking with the manager, who introduced himself as "Buckshot."

Buckshot was a large, rough-looking, middle-aged guy in a wrinkled, button-down cowboy shirt. The sleeves on his shirt had been torn off at the shoulders to show off his arms and tattoos. He wore generic-brand blue jeans and cowboy boots, which added more height to his six-foot, three-inch frame. A boxer, I summed up, and a severe alcoholic. His broken nose and cauliflower ears told me he'd been in the ring before. I guessed he'd need to lose thirty pounds to get back to his fighting weight of two fifty. I'm sure he was a menacing sight to dancers and patrons looking for trouble.

He was sweating profusely and was nervous as a kitten. He kept making the "safe" motion like a baseball umpire and assuring me nobody there wanted any trouble.

"What trouble?" I ask.

"Everyone has heard about all of the people you've locked up," Buckshot said.

"I only arrest people who are violating the law," I said.

He leaned in toward me and said conspiratorially, "A lot of people want to talk with you. They just don't want to be seen talking with you, and they don't want to get locked up. Or kilt".

"Now, we're talking!" I said. "Have them give me a call." I placed all of the business cards I had in my wallet on the bar.

My only fear was that his odor would knock me out. He apparently had given up on hygiene. His cologne was a mix of stale cigarettes and bourbon. The sleeveless shirt exposed his eighteen-inch arms that were looking saggy, and I observed tattoos that indicated he'd been in state prison. He was sweating like he'd just finished ten rounds in the ring, and his hands were trembling. He leaned in close to me and whispered, with decaying and broken teeth, the name of a stripper. Buckshot had long since lost use of a toothbrush, and his breath hit me like a stiff uppercut. He said I should talk with this tiny dancer, Candy, and he told me where I could find her.

I drove in the direction of the trailer court to find "Tiny Dancer." Ten minutes later I pulled up to the trailer, but it turned out to be vacant, a dry hole. An elderly neighbor woman peeped her wrinkled, chicken-looking head and neck out of her trailer door and hollered to me, without me even asking, that Candy had moved out about a week ago.

"Good riddance," she croaked loudly. "If you ask me, I'd say she's a hussy." With that she slammed the door shut.

I headed back to the club and called the St. Francois County Sheriff's Department and asked them if they had an available unit in the area. I believe the sheriff's departments are often the best contact for information on where to find locals.

As I waited on the parking lot for the deputy, one of the dancers opened the door to the club, squinting at the sunlight. The smell of heavy, designer-label perfume, sweat, and stale cigarette smoke carried out the door and overtook the heavy sweltering summer air. She looked around and held up a black cordless phone. "Hey, Luke, you've got a telephone call inside," she hollered in a husky smoker's voice.

How about that for cooperation? I thought, grinning. I had never seen this woman before in my life, but it was apparent word was getting around there; people knew who I was and what I was doing there.

I walked in the building and scanned the bar, sizing up the crowd for potential threats and recognizable faces. The girl who had called out to me in the parking was nowhere in sight, but the cordless phone was sitting at the end of the bar. Buckshot was leaning heavily on both arms over a fresh drink at the far end of the bar. He watched me warily as I picked up the telephone.

"This is Luke," I said.

The woman on the phone hurriedly said, "I'm Candy. I might know something." Her voice was soft and quivering, but her tone was hard-edged. She was nervous.

I told her I needed to talk with her in person regarding Santa. She agreed and gave me directions to her new address. The music had gone quiet, and the dancer was standing by the speaker, talking quietly to another girl. Buckshot was nowhere in sight, and the once busy room was empty but for a handful of people sitting outside the rings of light hanging low above the cocktail tables.

A young sheriff's deputy was out in the parking lot when I walked out. The music geared up again almost on cue as the door closed behind me. I told him what I was doing and invited him along. He didn't have much new news about Santa's crew. He was happy to come with me on the interview.

We followed Candy's directions and arrived at the new address a few minutes later. Her new place was similar to the previous one: an older, poorly maintained trailer in the backside of a run-down trailer court. It was approximately five miles from Fancy Free, where she was currently employed.

She invited us in. I bet Candy was once a pretty girl. Now her skin was very tanned, and several scars were visible. She had several visible, petite, girly tattoos of roses, a unicorn, hearts, and a fairy. The light through the shades was enough to show her nose had been broken at least once. Her blue eyes were lifeless and without joy. She carried herself like a woman forty years her senior.

Candy started talking immediately, rushing the words like she had been practicing what she was going to say.

"I don't know how much help this is, but Buckshot says I need to talk to you. I want to get this over with and get me off any list I heard you got going on. I'm gonna talk to you and get this out of the way since you are knocking on everyone's doors these days." She lit a cigarette, took a drag, and held her breath for a second. Then the words poured out like a confession, the smoke coming out as she spoke.

"Yes, I know the guy everybody calls Santa; he use to come into Fancy Free a lot. I don't do meth, so I'm not his type. He has hooked up with a couple of girls who buy what he sells, if you know what I mean. He even got one pregnant." She half-giggled then shuddered. "I can't quite figure out how that would've happened. But anyway, he hasn't been around the club for a while. That's what I know."

She gasped in a breath of air, gathered herself, crossed her legs, and daintily flicked the ashes like a pro into a red ashtray that I recognized a lot of bars use.

She flourished her cigarette like a '50s movie star, holding it up by her ear. She said she heard that Santa was living in California and that he returned occasionally to drop off more drugs for his dealers at bars at places between the airport and Bonne Terre. This was her scoop? We already knew this, but I was grateful she met with us. As she was talking, a shotgun shell laying on a countertop caught my attention.

I waited until she paused for effect with this bit of information. I changed direction. "Are you a hunter?"

She giggled coyly at that and said the shell belonged to her roommate, Ben. "I bet you like hunting, don't you? Ben's not home now; he went to meet his parole officer."

Getting more comfortable with us there, Candy said Ben was paroled from the Missouri Department of Corrections about five months ago. He served fourteen months on a five-year sentence for the distribution of methamphetamine, which meant he was a convicted felon.

I asked Candy if Ben knew Santa.

"Oh, yeah, I'm sure he does," she said. She seemed relieved to be talking about Ben, not Santa. "He and Raleigh, Santa's son, hang out and are real best friends."

I drew a line from Raleigh to Ben on my mental chart of the drug ring. Raleigh, I recalled, was the son of Santa who thought it was so funny that we couldn't find his dad.

I asked Candy if she owned any guns. "No," she said, "I couldn't hurt animals and I am afraid of guns." She smiled. For a flash, I could see the pretty girl she must have been. I asked her if Ben was a hunter.

"I don't think so, but maybe, because he has several guns," Candy said. One of them she described as a sawed-off shotgun.

"You know, Ben owns this trailer. He bought it before he went to prison. I just rent a room from him. He's not my boyfriend or anything," she said, looking back and forth from the deputy to me, waiting for some kind of reply.

The sheriff's deputy grinned and kicked the floor and found something of interest in the workings of his shirtsleeve.

"Thanks, Candy," I said. "You have been very helpful, and we appreciate it."

As I stepped out of the trailer, I knew I was on to something. We walked to the car, and the deputy, who hadn't spoken since we left the strip club parking lot, thanked me and asked shyly to be part of the team as much as possible.

I knew Candy the Tiny Dancer was short on information but connected by association—she was possibly the wick on the dynamite.

I suspected Buckshot had his own little dealings going on at the club, and me showing up so often was messing up whatever small-time thing he was running. If by sending Candy in my path he was able to get me to stop snooping at the bar and on track to find Santa, he could continue doing his thing and keeping the niche he had carved out for himself.

I returned to Ben and Candy's trailer a few days later with Red Dog and a search warrant. Back Door wasn't interested in going; it wasn't the big bust. He knew it wasn't Santa, so he said he would stay back and do paperwork, he had a hot date lined up.

Ben was home this time and was likely asleep when we initially knocked on his door. We knocked twice more, and the third time the door popped open. We entered, guns drawn, and Ben, wrapped in a blanket, was stumbling toward us a few feet away, still half asleep. Candy wasn't at home.

Ben was stunned by our visit. But he was also unmoved by our findings. The search of Ben's trailer revealed several firearms, which included the sawed-off shotgun. He also had several ounces of marijuana packaged for sale in baggies and trace amounts of methamphetamine.

He never said a word to us. He just quietly went his way to federal prison to do his time. He pleaded guilty to being a convicted felon in possession of a firearm and in possession of a sawed-off shotgun. The government didn't charge him with the drugs.

Raleigh, "Son of Santa," didn't think everything was quite as funny as he had before his best buddy was plucked off the party train. I visited him a couple times a week, but I still didn't have Santa.

Ben went straight to prison in less than five months. He pleaded out without speaking for himself. He spent less than three years in prison for being a felon in possession of an unregistered firearm. By maintaining his silence, Ben kept his honor with Santa and Raleigh.

What Ben and Raleigh didn't know was that during the search of Ben's trailer we also found some telephone numbers. One of them was an 800 number for a pager.

While we were processing Ben through his quick re-entry into prison, we also concurrently subpoenaed the records for this pager and analyzed the telephone numbers. The result was an overlay of the master list of Santa's wicked elf network. It also revealed several calls from California, specifically San Diego.

I took a hard look at the California numbers and found four pay phones that made calls into the pager. I mapped the address associated with the pay phones, and it turned out they were all located in San Diego within a mile of each other. Those pay phone calls were all of longer duration than the other calls. It appeared that the caller was retrieving messages from the pager voicemail system. Who would that be?

Candy got us closer to Santa than any time since we started this investigation," I thought.

Now that we had a general location of where we believed Santa was located, we just had to catch him at one of the phones.

There was no schedule or routine that I could see from the records, and waiting wasn't always a good tactic when the trail was finally warming up.

The question now was, how would I get him on the phone?

I met up with Red Dog to lay out a plan. It wasn't like on television with big, computer-generated organizational charts with pictures on the walls, lab equipment on the other side of the glass wall from the strategy room, and people running in with mystery-solving addresses just as we suited up.

I couldn't help but think of Son of Santa, Raleigh, who repeatedly mocked us and laughed at our attempt to track down his daddy as the key to the whole thing. "Raleigh has been completely uncooperative," I said.

"Baldwin's mix of business and family points to his son, who I bet would likely be in contact with Santa," Red Dog agreed. "He seems to have stepped up in the ranks as the main connection for the wicked elves in his father's absence. And he is loyal to his father."

There was a problem with setting up Raleigh as the target. Raleigh was not bright and was a meth user himself. He indicated everyone was afraid of his dad, including him. I figured he wouldn't make a move without talking with his dad.

"I can't imagine Ben having the pager number for Santa and not Raleigh," I said.

Red Dog shrugged and smiled. "I got a line on the location of a bank robber working out of South City. Catch 'em with ya later," he said as he headed out the door.

Here's the thing: I neither laughed at nor ridiculed the bandits or anyone else. However, when we were in a tense situation with guns drawn, anticipating the worst, I commanded their attention and respect. I believe that is what kept me out of situations, like in so many cop shows, with foot chases over chain-link fences, landing in alley trash cans, and having shoot-outs when the bandit thinks he can take the cop.

I told many a bandit, "Don't you make me shoot you. If I shoot you, you will die." Some folks aren't afraid of getting shot. But most folks are afraid of dying.

Then I got calls from prison from these bandits after I'd put them away and they were doing hard time, and they'd still call and give me tips because they respected me for keeping things from getting messy and for treating them with respect.

I'd been nothing but respectful with Santa and the gang, but their lack of cooperation was taking up a lot of our time and taxpayer money. Almost eight months at this point.

The day before I set off to re-interview the Son of Santa and stage the plan, I called a friend of mine, John Salducci. John was based in San Diego with the U.S. Marshals Office. I had previously called John with a heads-up when we found the area code from the pager records.

This guy, Salducci, was a bona fide U.S. Marshal Service stud and, of all things, he was also the supervisor of the fugitive crew in the Southern District of California where we believed Santa was.

Salducci and I met during our training to be in the Marshals Service Special Operations Group (SOG). SOG is the Marshals Service's tactical group, our "SWAT" team. Salducci and I had been together on several SOG operations all around the country. I knew I could bring him in on this. Salducci was a natural leader, and he loved to catch bandits. I knew I could depend on him. He was the real deal.

I updated John regarding our find with the pay phones. It turned out John was very familiar with the area. "It is a bandit-rich environment, Luke," he said then laughed as a tip of the hat to me calling fugitives bandits.

"It is so much nicer than 'bad guys,'" I said.

"I will send out several teams of fugitive investigators to familiarize themselves with the areas around the pay phones. I'll survey the area myself. You never know, Santa in the summertime in San Diego?"

The fugitive apprehension teams in San Diego began hunting Santa with us.

I dialed up Back Door at the office. He was sitting at his desk and waited until the third ring, like always. He believed it made him appear engaged in something but that the call was important enough to interrupt him. He had an angle for everything he did.

"You want to come along on something interesting on the Baldwin case?" I asked.

"Who"? He asked, sounding irritated. He was definitely more shrew than opossum today on the phone, I thought. I could hear Jack Buck calling the St. Louis Cardinal's game on his desk radio in the background.

"The Santa Guy, Lovelace," I said, positively annoyed.

"Wasn't listening, sorry," he said. "Do you think we would be back in by quitting time? I have a hot date lined up with a girl I met at a bachelor party last weekend. Best looking one in her group, and she wants me!"

I would love to get home to my wife and kids, I thought. But getting this guy off the streets and his crew out of business would help us all sleep better.

Because we had started taking down so many of Santa's crew on federal arrest warrants, our local U.S. Marshal had been in contact with our headquarters in Washington DC. The decision was made to make Roy Baldwin a "Top Fifteen Most Wanted." It was obvious this case was a very big deal to our office and the agency.

Uncovering this huge network had caught a lot of people's attention. Roy Baldwin was the head of a large criminal enterprise.

I headed south again to Bonne Terre with Back Door, filling him in on the investigation since the last report as we drove. I was going to find the Son of Santa and see if I could startle him into contacting his dad.

"The plan is to talk with Raleigh and let on that we are close to catching his dad," I said. "He doesn't know if Ben has flipped on them or not and if he's begun to inform on them. I figure if we plant that seed, it will grow into panic, and the kid will call his dad."

Back Door, clearly clueless as to what I had just said, shrugged and agreed with the plan. He then pulled down the passenger's visor to check his hair in the mirror.

We found Son of Santa in a bar down the street from his house, an old diner turned pool hall. As I entered the bar, I had a similar effect as I did in Fancy Free, Buckshot's place. Several of the patrons immediately finished their drinks and headed out around us, mass exodus style, for the door. Raleigh sat there silently as I talked, and he looked quizzically from Back Door and back to me several times. Back Door stood with his hands clasped together just behind me, sunglasses still on, Men in Black style. I could hear him exhale loudly, cheering at the Cardinal's score on the television above the bar.

Raleigh knew I had locked up several of their dealers, including his buddy Ben, cramping his style. I could almost hear him wonder about Back Door. I could tell Back Door's presence was disruptive.

"Our guys in California, out in Los Angeles, are very busy," I said. Which was true. Our folks in Los Angeles were always busy. I watched closely for Raleigh's reaction. I saw the side of his mouth twitch. I figured he was having a good laugh at that comment, since he knew his father was in San Diego.

"You know you need to cooperate. Your time is running out, and this is the last offer we'll make," I said simply. "Turn in Roy Baldwin and save yourself some time in prison."

"Yeah, less prison rape time," Back Door said with a laugh.

Raleigh just sat there smoking and drinking, staring at the window. I reached my hand in my back pocket, and he flinched.

Good, I thought. He is on the defensive. I slowly pulled out my wallet and put a business card on the bar next to him. I turned to walk out the door, waiting for Back Door to take my lead. I looked over my shoulder, and Back Door was standing for an extra moment to give Raleigh what I assumed was a tough-guy stare. It was kind of hard to tell, since he still had his sunglasses on. Raleigh just looked at him, confused.

It was a gamble calling Raleigh's bluff, but any move from him would be in our favor.

What Raleigh didn't know was that I had other units set up on surveillance north from Bonne Terre up Interstate 55 all the way to the airport in case he jumped. I had also obtained a federal court order to trace a potential telephone call.

Sure enough, Son of Santa bit. Not long after we left the bar, our surveillance unit at the bar called in to inform us Raleigh was seen walking to his car. He closed the door on his car, hard. He started the car and gunned it, then pulled off the lot and headed north toward St. Louis.

The area Raleigh lived in was very rural, but they did have pay phones at convenience stores and restaurants. Regardless of this local convenience, he drove to St. Louis. Could Santa be in St. Louis? I wondered to myself.

After a forty-five minute drive, Raleigh pulled off the highway and into the lot of the first fast-food place he found past the reflective green rectangular "Entering St. Louis County" sign. As far as we could tell, he didn't make us on the trip. We started tailing him from the parking lot of the closest pay telephone from the bar.

We stayed back and surveyed the White Castle.

Good idea, Son of Santa, I thought. I pulled out of traffic and into the first spot on the street, ready to block in the lot if need be. He walked around the lot looking at the other cars there, scoping out the area. After he was sure no police cars were in the lot, he went inside. Like I said, he was distracted enough to miss me and the Men in Black fed parked less than twenty yards away.

He went into the bathroom and, less than two minutes later, reappeared and headed straight for the outside pay phone.

Our friends at the local phone company were great. I had worked with these folks for years, and they had helped us catch more bandits than you can imagine. They were consummate professionals and very dedicated. They were our silent partners in our effort to get these bandits off the streets.

I was immediately on my cell phone to the phone company, letting them know the phone call we had been waiting for was likely being placed from this address. The technical end of this hunt now began in earnest. I then called Salducci in California to let him know what was happening.

I was eyes on Raleigh as he was calling Santa. I could see him place a call that was very brief, squinting his eyes and deliberately punching in the numbers of the pay phone long enough to hear the tone with each button he pushed.

"Son of Santa is dialing a pager," Back Door said gleefully.

Then Raleigh started waiting. He paced around and smoked like a fiend. He was a nervous wreck.

I was alternately talking to the local phone company, Salducci in California, and the St. Louis Marshals' office, keeping everyone up to speed with what was happening.

Raleigh was wilting in the heat. The minivan panel showed the temperature to be ninety-nine degrees. The humidity must have been over eighty percent, so the "feel" outside was well over a hundred degrees.

He started his car and turned on the air conditioner but left the window open so he could hear the phone. I slid the minivan's gear into drive and kept my foot on the brake, in case he started moving.

It had been close to twenty minutes when the Son of Santa jerked straight up in the seat, put his weight into shoving the door open, hit the yellow concrete post next to the phone—dinging a good sized dent in the door—and leaped for the phone.

One of the phones in the minivan rang, startling us. We were focused on the scenario in the parking lot, trying to hear or somehow understand how the conversation was playing out on the pay phone.

I grabbed the phone off the console and answered it. It was my friend at Southwestern Bell. They were in the process of tracing the call, but there were some "hiccups." Raleigh had used a calling card, which was routed through a call center somewhere. The call center was then forwarding the call. It was going to take some time. I thanked him and placed the phone back in the console.

Bottom line: at this time we didn't know who was calling the kid or from where. The only thing we did know was the first call went to the mystery pager.

The same cell phone rang again. It was the telephone company again with more bad news. One of the other telephone companies they were dealing with didn't think the court order pertained to them.

Gee, thank you, Judge Green, I thought sarcastically. He wasn't the judge who signed our court order; he was the judge who handled the breakup of the telephone company. He ruled on the case of a suit filed against the telephone company in the 1970s, ruling that the alleged monopoly hurt the consumer. The end result from Judge Green's handling of the case was the telephone company shattered into the baby "Bells." Then everyone and their brother got into the telephone business.

Personally, I believe that break up hurt the consumer in one very big way—it crippled law enforcement's technical advantage over the bandits and hurt our national security, because these telephone companies just won't work together on this very time-sensitive and needed legal service. Not to mention that, as a consumer, my local telephone bill immediately doubled and the service suffered.

From a law enforcement viewpoint, it became a nightmare dealing with wiretaps, telephone traces, and simply asking for records. I was experiencing some of that nightmare now.

My friend at the phone company assured me he was on it, and the phone companies would try and work through this thing and find us a location of the caller. He said he'd call me back after he spoke with his legal department. I hung up the phone in frustration.

Son of Santa was still on the phone. He was just standing there. I could see his profile. His right elbow was on top of the pay phone box, and he was rubbing his hand through his hair over and over again, listening to what was being said.

I immediately called the Assistant U.S. Attorney who was working with us on the case. He assured me he'd call the judge and they would get things worked out.

Five minutes later my phone rang again. I was thinking it was my guy at the phone company with more bad news.

"Hello?" I answered.

"It's John. Merry Christmas! We got him," he said in a rushed and excited voice.

"Are you kidding me?" I asked.

"For real, Luke. Baldwin is off the street."

Well, how about that? Santa was in the bag.

"Finally, Santa really is in custody in California." I smiled and turned to Back Door, relaying the news. His smile widened. "I get to take the sure-thing hottie out tonight after all," he said.

"As soon as you called while you were tailing him back up to St. Louis, Salducci said," we moved four teams from the fugitive apprehension crew. They rolled up on the pay phones you had discovered and mapped earlier. There he was, the Santa wannabe, in the flesh, all red-faced and yelling into the pay phone."

The Deputy U.S. Marshals there said they recognized

Baldwin right away when they pulled up. They jumped out of the car, guns drawn. They pistol paralyzed him and cuffed him up. "Apparently Santa hung up the phone without saying goodbye to his son," Salducci said.

While Salducci was telling me the story, I could still see Raleigh at the pay phone. He had finally hung up the phone, but he just stood there staring at it, hands at his sides. John told me he'd call back with the details, and I thanked him on a great job and hung up. I wheeled the minivan through the parking lot toward Son of Santa.

I pulled up alongside Raleigh, who was still standing by his car, now head down and staring at the hood. He moved his head to look up at me, dazed. I wasn't sure he recognized me.

"We arrested your dad in San Diego," I said quietly. "I will be asking the Assistant U.S. Attorney for an arrest warrant for you."

He just stood there, frozen in the blistering heat. Then I drove away. He wasn't laughing now. I watched him in my rearview mirror. He just stood there, staring back at me.

Salducci called me later and filled me in with the details of the arrest.

"Baldwin looked just like Santa, still with the beard, and was dressed like a tourist, in a Hawaiian shirt, shorts, and sandals. He gave up with no resistance. He even allowed the deputies to search his apartment, which was located a short distance from the pay phone," Salducci said. No guns, drugs, or money were recovered.

In his last minute of freedom, Baldwin hung up the phone when the Deputy U.S. Marshals jumped out of the car. When he hung up the telephone, the call tracers couldn't fully process that phone call; it couldn't be verified. We couldn't charge Raleigh—couldn't prove his full involvement.

Baldwin was taken to the Marshals' office in San Diego, where he was processed and he received his initial appearance before one of their magistrate judges. They ordered him to be returned to the Eastern District of Missouri for sentencing on his original charge.

Baldwin arrived back in St. Louis three weeks later via "Con Air," the Marshals' Service prisoner airline. I've flown Con Air assignments in the past. While it's a no-frills airline flight and very efficient, it's nothing like the Hollywood version, except for the severity of crimes the passengers carried out. It is, though, a very cost-effective way of transporting dangerous bandits across the country in a safe and timely manner. As a taxpayer, I have to say, "You gotta love it." The courts certainly do, too. Before Con Air, it took forever to get a bandit from one place to another. Imagine driving cross country with a serial killer in the backseat.

I picked up Santa from the airport on a breezy day in September. He was among several dozens of bandits who were also being moved on Con Air. He was no longer sporting his Hawaiian shirt. Now he was wearing tan slip-on tennis shoes, a plain, white T-shirt, and tan pajama-style pants that he had been issued for his cross-country flight. Roy recognized me straight away and was all smiles when I picked him up from the airport.

I once again escorted Roy Baldwin into Judge Meeks' courtroom on the third floor of the magnificent old courthouse the next morning. I sensed him stiffen when we entered the room. The defendant's side of the courtroom was empty. He was clearly indigent and alone now. He had lost everything. Now, truly as a man of no means, Baldwin stood there with only his public defender as the judge pronounced his sentence.

Judge Meeks berated Roy for fleeing and went on about how no one can escape justice, blah, blah, blah. In the end, the judge gave him the original fifteen-year sentence with only nine months more added for failing to appear—just a month more than it took us to chase him down.

I thought to myself sarcastically, Wow, judge, that'll teach him and anyone else paying attention to flee justice. The judge apparently didn't really factor in that it was a big deal for the

Marshals and everyone involved. We spent months tracking down this bandit and breaking up an established drug ring. At least he was off the streets, as were six of his crew.

As we left the courtroom, Roy said out loud to all within hearing distance, looking over his shoulder toward me, "That wasn't a bad deal after all."

"Merry Christmas to you, Santa," I said without glee.

Back in the cellblock, all was said and done except for Baldwin doing his time. I talked with Baldwin about his adventure. Of course he wanted to know how we caught him.

"You know, all of the bandits ask me that," I said. "And of course I never tell them."

I asked him about the kid murdered in De Soto, and he gave me "the look." He straightened up, paused, and said, "Another time. Not here in the cellblock."

He clammed up after that and never spoke of it again.

He offered to sign a copy of his wanted poster for me. It read: "To Luke, from Santa. Ho, Ho, Ho."

Back Door accepted a special commendations award along with us for catching Baldwin. He was there for the photo shoot. I was satisfied with shutting down a drug ring that had been putting out thousands and thousands of doses of crystal meth.

The government decided not to prosecute Baldwin's son, Raleigh, which I think was a shame. I saw him a few years later at a state-run halfway house. I drove by on the way during an investigation of another bandit and recognized him walking out the front door. He looked soulless—rotted and lost. He wasn't laughing.

Santa's young, former stripper bride and baby disappeared off our radar. I was told they likely disappeared with a substantial stash of "mattress cash." I hope they found a more wholesome life.

A little more than a year later, I received a Christmas card at my office with a return address from a federal prison in Texas. It was from Santa. It said, "Don't forget to leave milk and cookies out this year. Ho Ho Ho!"

FERRARI

STORY FIVE

"'Give me your tired, your poor, Your huddled masses yearning to breathe free,... Send these, the homeless, tempest-tossed to me....' And I'll get them all stoned".

- Emma Lazarus, as quoted by the dope man

Would you kill yourself to escape justice? I know of several bandits who, in one form or another, have done just that. Most of the time the U.S. Marshal Service will believe it, but occasionally we will exhume a body just to make sure it's really you. The fact is, we prefer a body to go with each of our arrest warrants. It keeps things tidy. If we don't have a body, the case remains open until you appear. If we hear of you again, we will chase you until we find you.

Sean Ferrari, a twenty-year-old kid from northern Virginia just outside the Washington DC area, figured suicide was a better way to go out than spending the rest of his youth in federal prison.

At the age of eighteen, Ferrari had quickly built and run a large drug distribution operation just outside of Washington DC for more than a year. When federal law enforcement officers on the original case arrested him, he reached a plea agreement and made bond. He had paid close attention to people working in the legal system: how they worked, what they said, the forms they used, everything about the process. He asked questions along the way. He learned. Not to straighten up and fly right, but to beat the system next time.

Ferrari was caught with the psychedelic drug lysergic acid diethylamide, commonly known as LSD or acid. More than one million doses of it!

Michael Jones was born in Spokane, Washington, the son of a prominent attorney. When the time came, Mike headed east to Georgetown University, just like his father had in his youth.

Michael walked toward a car that was off the road with tread marks in roadside gravel like it had been driven erratically and stopped. He was in the George Washington Memorial Park near Great Falls, Virginia. Michael walked around to the driver's side of the black Ford Mustang. He caught a whiff of alcohol or maybe men's cologne. The driver's side door was open, and the car was running with no one inside. Inside the tape player was a cassette playing a familiar melody over and over: "Suicide Solution," by Ozzy Osbourne.

Michael was careful not to touch anything, which made him smile. He thought to himself, would it really matter anyway? A suicide note was left on the driver's seat. There appeared to be droplets on the page that blurred some of the words as though the author had been crying when it was written. A nearly empty bottle of vodka had fallen or been thrown on the passenger floorboard, saturating the carpet.

Inside the car a thick wallet was flipped open on the dashboard with a Virginia Class F Driver's License with the photograph of Sean Ferrari visible through the plastic film.

Michael stepped away from the car and followed a trail of clothing that led toward "Difficult Run," a murderous stretch of waterway that leads down into the Potomac River. The Park Police have pulled out many, many bodies downstream from here. Many thrill and death seekers tempted fate and didn't make it through the turbulent run of water. This stretch is illegal to swim in and filled with signs and warnings. But that day, to a twenty-year-old kid facing more than twenty years in prison, it looked like a good alternative.

Michael shoved his hands deep into his pockets to fight off the brisk autumn breeze as he walked away from the scene. Clearly the scene of a suicide, he thought; anyone could see that. Michael never called the authorities. He couldn't very well remain as a witness, could he?

Besides, he told himself, the Park Police would probably find it themselves. They did find the car, but not until six and a half hours later. When they processed the license plate they would find the vehicle was registered to Sean Ferrari, who was currently out on bond from the United States District Court in the Eastern District of Virginia.

Michael was long gone by then.

I'm not an office guy. Desks are good for holding files. I don't do well with people all about office politics. I always catch the bandit I'm after and I always complete and close a file. I am at my desk as little as possible and am out on the street, tracking bandits and capturing as many as I can.

During this time, I was assigned to the Fugitive Apprehension Strike Team (FAST) unit, a multi-jurisdictional team encompassing federal, state, and local officers. There were Deputy U.S. Marshals, FBI Agents, Missouri State Highway Patrol Officers, and St. Louis City and County officers, as well as officers from outlying counties and smaller municipalities. People rotate in for about a year. When local law enforcement officers are assigned to the unit, the Chief Marshal or one of us deputize them as Special Deputy U.S. Marshals.

In the FAST unit, I was out on the street doing what I love the most—catching bandits. Our mission was to chase down and apprehend St. Louis City's most violent fugitives. We were assigned warrants for federal bandits, and the unit chased them with endless vigor. As a team we averaged a thousand to twelve hundred arrests a year, which is an incredible feat for a six-man unit.

One afternoon I actually was at my desk finishing paperwork and answered a call at my desk phone at the FAST unit office. It was another Deputy U.S. Marshal, "Wild Bill" Parsons, from my district. Wild Bill called to say that we had a big case coming out of headquarters in Washington DC.

"Luke, we received word that one of the U.S. Marshal Service's Top Fifteen Most Wanted fugitives is in the area," Parsons told me.

No "Hello" or "How's the wife and kids?" from Parsons. I'm okay with that. He knows time is against you on manhunts and that I am all business. Orders were for me to drop everything and catch this guy, Sean Ferrari. "Ferrari is now the FAST unit's new immediate priority," he said.

A few hours before, a match to Sean Ferrari's fingerprints popped up in the Missouri State Highway Patrol's Criminal Identification Section. The second set of fingerprints was tied to the name Joey De Mutt who was recently arrested in St. Charles, Missouri, for violation of the Missouri Controlled Substance Law (VMCSL). He was arrested for selling more than half a pound of marijuana to an undercover cop. This fingerprint match meant they were right: Ferrari was someone who Washington DC law enforcement didn't really believe had committed suicide. They had been trying to pick up his trail for more than a year.

The fingerprint match happened in a miraculously short turnaround time of ten days after the arrest of De Mutt. This matching process normally happens when the prints reach the FBI's national fingerprint center, then go on to the state systems.

The two U.S. Marshals in Washington DC working to track down Ferrari knew the typical time for matching up fingerprints to bandits is ninety days or more. The fast turnaround was due to their hard work and diligence. Ninety days feels like an eternity when you are chasing a bandit who can be two states away in a couple of hours leaving little or no trail. They took the initiative to send copies of Ferrari's prints out to each state's identification bureau. It was a lot of work for them, but seriously sped up the process.

Ferrari would tell us later that he had researched the fingerprint system. He'd obtained a book from one of those underground, anarchist bookstores. Ferrari figured he had at least four to six months before we would get a match from the St. Charles arrest, so as Joey De Mutt, he knew he still had a few months.

It is certainly a good thing the U.S. Marshals Service makes more arrests than all other federal agencies combined, somewhere in the neighborhood of eighty thousand arrests annually. One of the things that keeps me motivated is imagining all those bandits on the streets. If not for those arrests, we'd be neck deep in bandits, crime, and chaos.

US Marshals are very resourceful with what they have, a kind of "make-do" inventiveness I learned as a Reconnaissance Marine.

In the Marines, if the helicopters that were supposed to pick you up for maneuvers were grounded because fuel hadn't made it to them yet, you took the trucks to get to them. If the trucks broke down on your way there, you marched. You found a way to complete the mission.

The Marshals Service is not nearly as well funded as the FBI. We use a lot of old-fashioned ingenuity. Most of the time, it is hard work, long nights, and street smarts. When funding is an issue, I remember Albert Edison's quote, "The three great essentials to achieve anything worthwhile are, first, hard work; second, stick-to-itiveness; third, common sense."

The Drug Enforcement Administration (DEA) funds Metropolitan Enforcement Groups or MEG units to which they are commonly referred. MEG units are made up of state and local law enforcement officers who concentrate on getting drug dealers off the street.

Any time the MEG units or any state, county, or city law enforcement come across a kingpin, a "high-roller," or someone dealing in weight that meets the federal guidelines, the DEA "adopts the case" from the state prosecutors and the bandit gets federal prosecution. This means federal charges, federal prison. Career criminals know these guidelines that attract the feds and try to stay off the federal radar.

The St. Charles County MEG unit is located west of St. Louis. They had been hearing rumors about a new dealer in the area, a young guy selling pound weight of pot. Pound weight is a bigger dealer than someone dealing joints or nickel bags (enough for a three to four joints), with street value of less than twenty dollars. A pound was sold for about twelve hundred to fourteen hundred dollars to the dealers who then divided it down to joints and nickel bags and sold it to users. This type of dealer was a bigger fish but certainly not going to catch federal attention. When local law enforcement catches this level dealer, they try to flip him to give up information on someone higher up the drug chain—the bigger dealers who feed him product. So the MEG unit started to focus on this new kid.

The St. Charles MEG unit developed an address in old town St. Charles City, an aging area with older homes and rental property. They made a plan to go find the new kid and immediately executed a search warrant. What they had no way of knowing at the time was that this new kid, Sam Smith, was actually the target of a federal manhunt for someone named Sean Ferrari.

When they executed the search warrant, no one was home. Since the search warrant was specifically for the search and seizure of marijuana, they went for the drugs and didn't take the time to do a search for related documents in the apartment.

The cops at the St. Charles MEG unit figured they would process the evidence, apply for warrants on Sam Smith, and pick him up later. What they didn't know was that Sam Smith no longer existed.

We would find out later there had been a file at Ferrari's "Sam Smith" apartment that they missed in the desk drawers. In one of the drawers, there were least a dozen false identities. Each of them had the photograph of Sean Ferrari. That was a near-miss that would have caught Ferrari a lot quicker.

A couple hours later, Sean Ferrari, whose current identification belonged to Sam Smith, returned to find his apartment had been "tossed" by the MEG unit. Ferrari, already a seasoned criminal with nothing to lose, didn't lose his cool. He realized there were no cops around his place then, so he calmly inventoried his apartment and assessed the damage. His dope and some of his cash had been seized and a copy of the search warrant had been left on the kitchen table. The law mandates a copy must be left at the residence when executing a search warrant. Ferrari, who already felt superior to law enforcement, realized his precious file containing his fake identities had not been disturbed. So Ferrari scooped up the file, a few belongings, and into the wind he went ... again.

As he left Sam Smith's apartment for the last time, he dumped his wallet in a trashcan outside a fast-food place and slid into his wallet his next identity with a Missouri Driver's license that read Joey De Mutt.

Sean Ferrari was an extremely intelligent, calculating kid with a bad attitude and a superiority complex. He had a serious chip on his shoulder. He painted himself as a sad, lonely picture, the victim of a divorced family. He played up this "poor me" scenario to the kids buying his drugs, many of whom could relate. He channeled his anger from his parents' divorce into destroying as many lives as he could with drugs. He wanted to make everyone else as miserable as he was.

He had been accumulating false identities since his original flight from justice in Washington DC. Once a week or so, Ferrari would go to the local library and read through various newspaper obituaries. Whenever he found a person near his age, he would research those records to see if he could make it fit and add that name to his list of identities. At this point he had more than a dozen, for which he would procure driver's licenses, identification cards, library cards, insurance cards, etc. Each of Sean's identities was contained in a separate envelope. He would simply empty his wallet and refill it with a new one each time he was arrested or stopped by the police.

Ferrari always kept a few lives running at the same time. He still had a small amount of dope and cash stashed at another safe house he had set up for emergencies. He knew the cops had not seen him yet, and he figured they were so lame at doing their job that he could chill out with his friends for a couple of days and sell out the rest of his inventory before he blew out of town. And there was a girl.

Joey needed money fast. So, as he had done several times before, he set up a quick dope deal with a guy he bumped into a while back to sell him a half-pound of pot. The dope deal was set, and Joey arrived to the prearranged parking lot with his stash. What he didn't know was his buyer was an undercover cop with the MEG unit. The MEG unit swarmed him, cuffed him, read him his Miranda rights, took him into custody, and transported him directly to their office.

Once they returned to the office, they ran Joey's identification through the system, and no records appeared. The MEG unit officers thought they just had an average, scared, twenty-year-old kid without a record about to wet his pants because he got caught with a half-pound of marijuana.

The St. Charles MEG unit cops interviewed Joey. Since no previous records popped up and he was a first-time offender, they made him an offer they felt he couldn't refuse: If he would give them someone bigger, they told him they would go easy on him; maybe they could even process him and let him go home that night. In the course of the talk, they asked him if he knew Sam Smith, the new kid in town who was selling pound weight. How funny is that?

Ferrari was clever and smug. He quickly came up with a plan to play the cops and wiggle out of this mess quickly and cleanly. "That's who I got my dope from," he taunted them. Joey De Mutt played the game for all he was worth. He told them everything he knew about Sam Smith. They thought they had gotten this Joey De Mutt to flip, or to give up his dealer and cut a deal with the cops himself. The fact was, he was mocking and laughing at them the whole time. The cops were completely entranced by his story, chomping at their bits, listening for the juicy piece of information. They wanted Sam badly, and they thought this kid Joey was the key. He seemed to know everything about Sam. He even described Sam's apartment with keen detail. They figured he must have been telling the truth because his information regarding Sam's drug operation was so accurate.

Joey told them he could "hook up" with Sam and do a "two-pound deal," but he would need to be let go and on the street. "It's a done deal then," he told them. The cops agreed to let Joey go free that night, but he was to call them once a day before noon and give them progress reports on what was going on. They told Joey he had to set up the deal with Sam by the next weekend.

Ferrari was already planning before he was out of the police station doors. He could keep the identification of Joey for another week. Barely able to contain himself for totally playing and getting one over on the cops, he solemnly assured them he could do it—and he disappeared into the night.

What the St. Charles cops didn't know was this kid "Joey," aka Sean Ferrari, had been arrested by the DEA in Virginia in possession of approximately one million doses of LSD or acid.

As Joey was booked, his prints were taken and placed into the system. They were processed locally at the St. Charles County Sheriff's Department and then forwarded to the Missouri State Highway Patrol's Identification Section. There the prints were reviewed and hit a match: a set of prints the lab had received from the U.S. Marshals Service about a year earlier. The unique fingerprints were those of Sean Ferrari. The fingerprint examiner contacted the U.S. Marshals identification service in Arlington, Virginia, and notified them of the match.

That call stirred a flurry of activity at the U.S. Marshals Service headquarters in Virginia. Until now, there had been no new leads on the Ferrari case for more than a year. The lead investigator on the case placed a call to our St. Louis office to advise us a very wanted Ferrari was in our neck of the woods.

Joey was out on the street now planning his next move. He was now working for the police (as far as they knew) so he had some time to relax and regroup. He knew the cops weren't looking for him as Joey. They also weren't looking for Sam, because Joey was going to set him up for them. He was free to plan.

So, each day at about noon, "Joey" dutifully called the cops and told them he had made contact with "Sam," but that Sam was a little nervous because of the search warrant and all. Joey told them he was not sure exactly where Sam was staying now, but he was sure he'd find out soon. Joey even brazenly met with the cops a couple of days later. Again he told them he was scared of Sam, and he asked what would happen if Sam got wise to the setup.

The cops reassured Joey that everything would be okay, and he just had to make good on the deal in order to work off his case. Joey hesitantly told them he would "suck it up" and just do the buy. He told them he thought he could set up a deal in the next couple of days. Joey told them it was hard since he didn't have any cash. Naïve to the game, the cops even gave him a few bucks and sent him on his way.

He called them a couple of times and outlined the deal he had set up with Sam. It had been nine days since Joey's arrest and release. The cops thought they were about to swoop down on Sam Smith the next day.

On day ten of this plan, a call came into the St. Charles MEG unit. They were there to answer the phone and scrambled every time the phone rang. This time it was me calling, asking them about this kid "Joey De Mutt," whom they arrested ten days before. The supervisor told me the kid was working for them trying to set up a bigger fish.

I didn't even let on that I was surprised by this arrangement or that it was worth a point of discussion. I gave him the rundown on Joey's real identity and asked them how I could get in touch with Joey. He told me Joey called them every day at noon. Since it was about two thirty in the afternoon and they had not yet heard from Joey, I was guessing they wouldn't. The supervisor told me they didn't have a number or address for Joey, but he could have his guys look for him and they would give me a call when they got him. I thanked him as we hung up. I started hunting, too. The chase began.

How do you find a guy who has been a ghost for the past year and a half? I wasn't daunted. I knew that you just start looking in his latest haunts.

That was where I started. I worked up some lists. First a list of people Ferrari knew in St. Louis. That was easy: zero. Next I looked at Sam Smith's and Joey De Mutt's associates. Both of those lists were a little bit longer. I looked at the addresses he used and cross-referenced other people associated with them. I now had a little bit more than nothing to go on.

I called our office in Washington to give them the news. Of course they wanted to know why we didn't have this kid in custody yet. I was then advised that they were sending out two deputies who were familiar with the Ferrari case. These were the guys who took the time to mail out Ferrari's fingerprint cards.

I don't know anyone who likes to work with someone looking over his shoulder. I certainly don't. But, as it turns out, we got a couple of great deputies who flew into St. Louis. The leader of the two later became one of the top people in the U.S. Marshal Service. To this day I admire and respect that man more than I can say. He's a quality person and a good leader in our agency.

In the meantime, we hadn't slept for the past twenty-four hours and knew time couldn't be wasted on sleep. This guy was getting away. During this time we'd made some progress with Ferrari's old addresses and associates. I say "we," because I was working with two of the finest St. Louis City detectives I've had the pleasure of knowing, Red-Dog and Jarhead, both on assignment to the FAST unit. These guys were workhorses. They didn't bat an eye at working the next thirty-six hours straight "just running and gunning," chasing the bandit.

As we interview some of Ferrari's "kindred spirits," it appeared that he was somewhat of a cult hero to the young anarchists who had been buying his dope and hanging on every word of his controversial rhetoric.

They all raved about what a wonderful human being Ferrari was and what "great dope" he had. His followers had no idea who he really was, and when we told them the rest of the story, Ferrari's stature with them sky rocketed. "Damn the Man!" "Down with the government!" these people would interject during the interviews, empowered by their one degree of separation to Ferrari's celebrity. They all wished him well and told us they hoped we would never find him.

We pressed on anyway, continuing to check addresses and interview more lost souls as we encountered them throughout the night. We were beginning to develop a list of people who were the inner circle of Ferrari's world in St. Louis. As we began to interview and focus in on them, our guest Marshals from Washington arrived. We picked them up at the airport the next day. I liked them both straight away.

We didn't ask for the help to come in from Washington. The deputies realized coming to St. Louis to posse up with us might be seen as an invasion of our territory, stepping on our feet, taking over our case. I did see this as the case, but we did what we needed to do to get this guy off the streets. The deputies were already doing a great job with it. Their distribution of the fingerprint cards was Ferrari's undoing.

Right away they told us they were here to assist us and obtain whatever resources we might need in this hunt. "Straight up, this is your backyard, and you know the lay of the land. We didn't fly in to run this operation. We are simply here to work together and lend a hand," the lead Marshal said.

They did that—and more. These guys were no "empty suits." Empty suits are people I define as the employees who are physically there, punching the clock, shuffling paper, but not invested or passionate about their job. These guys even had something to sweeten the deal. They informed us we were authorized to offer a five-thousand-dollar reward for Ferrari's capture. I had never paid a dime in reward money before that day. I was excited. Now I was thinking, Five grand? How can we not catch this guy!

The U.S. Marshals Service often makes arrests, and the FBI ends up receiving the credit. Both agencies vie for precious dollars from Congress. Part of the problem is marketing. When the public hears "feds," they assume FBI. I've had to laugh many times when I've identified myself as a U.S. Marshal and the person says, "So are you guys with the FBI?" The U.S. Marshals Service didn't want to read that the FBI had captured one of the Marshals Service's bandits. Especially not a Top Fifteen Most Wanted!

For their reasons, my headquarters sent word they did not want an FBI agent along, and we were to capture Ferrari now.

So, T-Mac, the FBI contributor to our task force, wasn't with us on this chase because of that old agency rivalry thing. This was a U.S. Marshal Top Fifteen, and we had priority orders. Personally, I couldn't have cared less about the rivalry; he's a good man and good on the chase, so I would have brought him along. Instead, T-Mac just jumped into the pile of bandit files we had stacking up while we were chasing Ferrari.

With the additions to the team on board, we continued to focus our attention on Ferrari's inner circle. We finally made some headway and found someone who was more interested in staying out of jail than they were loyal to Ferrari.

This guy was a major space cadet. We found he had some weed in his possession. I think "Space Cadet" had not been on terra firma for some time, a Cheech and Chong kind of cloud-of-smoke "duuuuude," if you know what I mean. He just seemed to stay high.

We quickly discovered how to turn Space Cadet against Ferrari. The key factor in his cooperation was jealousy, a "big bummer." Space Cadet and Ferrari were sweet on the same young lady. The young lady was, of course, "goo-goo" over Ferrari's guitar playing, poetry, good looks, and drugs. So an unrequited Space Cadet bitterly filled us in on Ferrari's travels over the past twelve months.

Ferrari, it seems, had arrived in St. Charles County, Missouri, shortly after his faked suicide in Virginia. He brought some cash he had stashed and a little bit of pot with him. Ferrari had an established drug network behind him. He knew the business well, but in Missouri he would have to build a new operation from scratch. He couldn't risk contacting anyone in Virginia for help. He just couldn't trust anyone in his old life. He was wanted on federal charges that carried serious prison time. Besides, he was dead to them.

Ferrari figured selling acid was what got him caught up with the DEA in Virginia. So once he was established in Missouri, he decided to deal marijuana exclusively. He thought marijuana was a much more tolerated drug, and it wouldn't bring him much attention from cops. Ferrari was familiar with how cops work from his Virginia drug bust and incomplete trip through the legal system. Ferrari later told me he was confident he could manipulate any police he might encounter in the future.

He forged documents on copy machines at local print centers. Everything from W-2s and 1099s to falsified rental agreements with fictitious landlords. This kid, not old enough to order a beer, printed up pay stubs, rental receipts, and birth certificates with embossed county seals. Ferrari used many of these forged documents to procure fraudulent drivers licenses using the names of deceased people in multiple states. He was way ahead of the curve in identity theft.

Ferrari was a young, clever, and fearless buck. He thought he was unstoppable. He didn't respect law enforcement or think we were very smart. He was sure the Marshals couldn't catch him. I, on the other hand, was confident we could.

Once Ferrari established a safe house in the St. Louis area, he decided to sell marijuana. He found out how much pot cost on the street by simply asking around like he was looking to score some. Then he traveled to Texas, avoiding areas with contacts from his previous incarnations, in search of cheaper pot. How funny is that? This young rebel who preached anarchy to the kids to whom he sold marijuana was a pure capitalist at heart. Buy low and sell high. He created privileges for some of his anarchy-absorbing followers by "sharing the adventure." He selected a few to take along—a couple of his inner circle friends—for his trips to Texas. They thought this was a wonderful adventure, and they were proud of the fact that they were chosen from the group for these missions. In reality, Ferrari needed "patsy" material, someone along for the ride with him on whom he could shirk blame in case the police stopped them. Most of these kids had rap sheets involving drugs of some kind. Ferrari had an identity without a record. Who would have to take the fall if they are busted? Regardless, it was handy for us that he had chosen to take Space Cadet with him on multiple occasions.

Apparently Ferrari made several runs to Texas and brought back ten to twenty pounds of marijuana each trip. Space Cadet learned a little more about Ferrari's operation each trip they made. So, upon questioning, he was able to give us a good picture of who, what, when, and where in Texas. He also told us that was where Ferrari was at that very moment. Ferrari hadn't taken Space Cadet with him this time.

It seems Ferrari was making one last twenty-pound deal before he went into the wind again. We figured he was looking to make about twenty thousand dollars on this last load. Money he would need to go on the lamb again and get re-established in another city under yet another identity. We uncovered later that his plan was to settle in Los Angeles and melt into the mass of lost souls there. It reminded me of what Frank Lloyd Wright, the famous architect, said, "Turn the world upside down and everything loose will land in Los Angeles."

Our Marshal brethren from DC were euphoric over this new information. They jumped on Space Cadet's leads and the new information on where Ferrari was. They thanked us and saddled up again, this time for Texas. We bid them farewell and safe hunting as we dropped them off at the airport. They said they'd keep us posted on the hunt and let us know when they arrested Ferrari. We went back to hunting our other bandits and tying up loose ends on the Ferrari case.

We caught up on our paperwork, which certainly piles up when you chase someone for forty-eight hours straight. We got some sleep. I spent an evening with my wife and kids. We found a few more addresses Ferrari had been linked to and a couple more people in the area who knew him by yet other names. We stayed focused on capturing Ferrari while he and his patsy crew did their deal and road tripped back from Texas.

We found an apartment Ferrari was currently renting under another one of his pseudonyms and investigated it. Inside the apartment we found county seals, blank birth certificates, blank W-2s, insurance applications, etc. I knew we were closing in!

Toward the end of the week we heard from The DC Marshals who were now on Ferrari's trail in Texas. They confirmed Ferrari had picked up the twenty pounds of marijuana and he was headed back to Missouri. The FAST unit teamed up again and headed out on the chase. For the next forty-eight hours without break, we pursued leads to capture this brash, young bandit.

Space Cadet told us about two other friends and confidants of Ferrari's. We had yet to find those two, so it made sense they must be with Ferrari. We finally made contact with the kids' parents to see what they could add and let them know the gravity of the situation.

The first parents we contacted told us they didn't know where their kid was or whom he was with. However, the parents of the other one told us their son, "Junior," was in Texas with some friends. They described one of Junior's new friends to us and added that he seemed like such a nice young man. The description fit Ferrari.

We had asked the parents not to mention us contacting them or the pursuit of Ferrari to Junior, on the off chance he called them. We were concerned for the safety of the kids with Ferrari. We didn't know how dangerous the situation could get if Ferrari knew he was being closely pursued. During the drive back to St. Louis, Junior called his parents. Since the parents thought they knew better than we did, they blew us off and told Junior as much as they knew, including everything we had told them regarding Ferrari's history and how dangerous he might be.

Junior, in turn, told Ferrari everything he knew. So now, everyone knew as much as we did. As I think back, maybe Junior's parents wanted to get rid of their kid and thought a federal prison would be a good place for him to stay.

Ferrari asked Junior not to talk with us for twenty-four hours after they got back. Junior promised he would wait and kept his promise to Ferrari.

We waited for Junior's parents to call on Saturday. They had told us Junior was expected home early Saturday morning, and they assured us they would bring him to our office first thing so we could talk with him. Sure enough, Junior apparently did arrive home early Saturday morning. Junior told his parents he was not going to talk with the Marshals until the next day, because he promised Ferrari. Unbelievably, Junior's parents went along with it.

Sunday afternoon rolled around, and Junior's parents called to let us know they were on the way to our office. I sat Junior down at a table in an interview room, and his dad took a chair next to Junior on his side of the table.

I set the stage for focusing and getting down to business. "Do you know what time it is?" I asked. "It's time to talk."

I told Junior about all of the various violations of federal law he had committed. The Assistant United States Attorney (AUSA) was in the interview with us. Our goal was to get his story, get a lead, and get back in pursuit of Ferrari quickly.

At the beginning of the interview, we offered Junior the five-thousand-dollar reward money. The entire deal was predicated on this kid cooperating fully. The Assistant U.S. Attorney told him he wouldn't be prosecuted if he told the truth, the whole truth, with nothing added and nothing left out. The Assistant U.S. Attorney told him several times: "You must be truthful, and if your information results in the capture of Ferrari, you are home free without prosecution."

Junior's dad was very excited about the prospect of receiving a five-thousand-dollar reward. Too bad he hadn't been as eager and engaged about Junior's friends and future.

Junior launched into his version of reality. He told us from the start that he waited until Sunday to talk with us because he promised Ferrari he would give the guy a twenty-four-hour head start. Ferrari had assured Junior that we'd never be able to catch him if he had a twenty-four-hour lead on us. So Junior waited until Sunday before he contacted us—and his parents had gone along with that. His dad added nothing, just shrugged.

Junior said the last time he saw Ferrari was at a bus stop in south St. Louis. Ferrari boarded a city bus carrying a duffle bag. Inside the bag was twenty pounds of Mexican marijuana that Ferrari's Texas source had "fronted" him, or given him without payment in advance, since he was such a good customer. He waved goodbye, and Junior watched him roll out of sight.

I was furious when I found out. I couldn't believe Junior's parents had gone along with this plan by a drug dealer, leaving their son to "clean up" the situation with law enforcement. We had clearly explained to them how serious Junior's predicament was. Good grief, I thought. As a father of two, I know the delicate balance of friends and family. It was obvious to us who had control in this relationship. It certainly was not the mom and dad. Regardless of how mad I was, the government had made a deal with Junior, and I needed to get the information from him. I'm normally a pretty even-keeled guy, but I sat there fuming as we interviewed him.

We sat with Junior for hours, going over Ferrari's life for the past year since Junior had known him. Junior's story jumped around a lot and took a lot of sorting out. Eventually, he laid out the entire drug operation, and he informed us of everyone involved … almost.

Space Cadet had told us two guys went with Ferrari to Texas on this last trip, Junior and some friend of his. Apparently Junior had left out a few crucial details and the involvement of this other person.

According to Space Cadet, Junior and a friend he had grown up with had accompanied Ferrari on this latest road trip. The friend was scheduled to report to the United States Naval Training Center Great Lakes in a few days.

I was already at a slow boil because they had waited a day to contact us, and Junior's father kept interrupting the interview and bugging us about the reward money.

I uncovered several inconsistencies during the interview. Junior's story was not consistent with Space Cadet's version. When he had finished his version, I confronted him with the fact that we knew he'd left out a player in his story—to name one thing.

Junior figured there was no reason to bring his almost-military buddy into this, and the Marshals wouldn't be any the wiser if he didn't. Oops! His jaw dropped, and he got that "deer in the headlights" look.

"I'm sorry I lied to you," he said somberly. "Can I start over?"

We had just spent several hours going over Junior's story, and it appeared we would be spending more time going over it again. Ferrari's trail was cooling all the while. Still, it was music to my ears. I leaned over close to Junior's face and told him evenly, "You just threw away five grand and immunity!"

I looked at Junior's "Father of the Year" loser and repeated to him that the reward money was no longer part of the deal.

I spoke slowly and clearly and looked at both the father and Junior to make sure they were getting it. "Now, Junior, you are going to tell us the whole story in order to stay out of federal prison—IF you get it right this time and the AUSA agrees not to prosecute."

It amazes me every time how people sit down and talk with federal investigators, figuring they can lie and no one will find out. The problem with lying to the Marshals is this: it's a felony offense. If you get caught, it can mean a felony conviction and prison time. Truth be told, we typically already know the answers to some of the questions before we ask them. The interviewee doesn't know which ones and has to guess. It is a huge risk to take, and Junior blew it big time.

Here we went again with the story, but this time, Junior got it right. He went back and filled in the blanks where he had previously omitted his friend's involvement, and he added a "proud-to-be-an-American" spin to justify his previous omission. He told us he was just trying to keep his buddy out of trouble since he was getting ready to go serve our country.

However, at the end of this version of the story, we were no closer to Ferrari. In fact, Junior's retellings had caused us to lose even more time.

At this point I was ready to arrest Junior and prosecute him. He was beginning to catch on now and started the water works. It was finally sinking in. The tears were a sign the games were over and I was finally getting to him. Finally, after all these hours, this kid got it. Maybe now I could get somewhere.

"You know, you may be headed to prison even before Ferrari." I paused for effect to let that sink in. "One more question," I said, raising my voice above the noise of his bawling. "Who would Ferrari go to with this much weed to sell?"

Junior looked up at me between sobs, sniffled big and loud, and his eyes lit up. He only knows one guy who could buy this much dope. "It's gotta be Pat the Brat," he said.

Of course he didn't know exactly where Pat lived or what his last name was. That would have been too much to wish for. But Junior was now scared to death, and he told us as much as he knew. He was convinced—one hundred percent positive— that Ferrari would go to "Pat the Brat" to sell this amount of marijuana.

It was late Sunday evening. Junior and his dad were long gone. So were their hopes of the five grand.

No big-strategy-room meeting with white boards and bright lights for the FAST unit. We gathered around a fast-food restaurant table, a common way we developed game plans. Most meetings were either over a quick meal or through open windows between cars. We were seasoned veterans who had worked together a long time and knew what worked for us. I shared the results of the Junior interview with the rest of the

FAST unit. We went over what we knew about Pat, which was not much. We knew his name was Pat and that he was apparently a brat who lived in St. Charles County, Missouri, a short fifteen-minute ride west of St. Louis. Junior mentioned Pat worked on or made neon lights. Red Dog, a very competent and reliable St. Louis City cop assigned to the FAST unit, was with me in the pursuit. We made a great team.

I recalled a business card from one of the addresses Red Dog had visited early on in our hunt for Ferrari. We reviewed our notes, and bingo! Pat's Neon Lights. We had a potential address and telephone number that fit.

I am sure nobody likes to have Marshals knock on their door asking about federal fugitives. I am certain no one likes the knock at 2:30 a.m. I always choose to be as respectful as possible in any situation, but there we were, again. Ferrari had evaded capture for more than eighteen months. We were ten days behind him from the fingerprint match. I had been on this case a few days. Any more delay, and the trail of leads would dry up again. Hence the middle-of-the-night visit.

I knocked very loudly on the front door, what is called the "police knock." After the third or fourth time, the lights in the house came on. A very small man and woman in their mid-forties answered the door together and asked politely what we wanted. We identified ourselves, and I asked them if Pat was home and if we could speak with him. They were naturally in shock by this visit and, almost robot-like, they invited the two men wearing bulletproof vests into their home.

We waited in the living room area as the dad went to get Pat. Mom, on automatic manners, offered us something to drink and we declined. It's hard to play good cop/bad cop when someone is serving you tea and scones.

The father returned to the living room, and Pat appeared a few moments later. Pat looked about sixteen years old and was wearing thick glasses. His brown hair was disheveled, and he was wearing superhero pajamas! He towered over his five-foot, three-inch mother and father by about two inches. Are you kidding me? Do we have the right house? I thought. I was surprised this twenty-something-year-old guy who looked and dressed like a little kid was a big-time drug dealer. I had to swallow a laugh and was beginning to understand the name, "Pat the Brat."

Pat just stood there, looking barely awake, likely trying to figure out if he was dreaming this. For the longest time, he said nothing. He stared at the floor, unwilling to look at us. We started asking him questions rapid-fire style. "How do you know Sean Ferrari? Sam Smith? Joey De Mutt? Where is he? Do you know how to contact him?"

Finally, Pat spoke. He admitted he knew Ferrari. "But I haven't done anything wrong," he whined, directing his statement more to his parents than to me. Mom and Dad then chimed in in Pat's defense, bolstering what Pat said.

They can't believe "Patrick" would be involved with "those kinds of people." I repeated relevant bits of what Junior and other folks (including Space Cadet) had told us about their son being one of Ferrari's biggest clients. This line of questioning, followed by Pat's denial and his parent's defense on his behalf, went on for half an hour or longer. He clammed up.

I changed tactics. I asked Pat's mom and dad if they'd escort me to Pat's room to see if he had any telephone numbers, cards, letters, etc., from Ferrari. Pat's dad began stomping angrily toward Pat's room, and immediately the son began to whine in protest. In a very meek voice Patrick said to no one in particular, "Don't you need a search warrant?" The question just hung there like someone hit the pause button.

I stopped dead in my tracks. I turned around and walked back to Pat. I was confident about how he had earned the name Pat the Brat. I asked his dad to sit down next to the soggy-tissued mom on the sofa. As calmly as I could, I explained to everyone present that I needed either a search warrant or permission to search the premises. I further explained that we had enough probable cause to obtain a search warrant, and that I could call the federal prosecutor and request one if need be.

I said that we could bring in a drug dog but, since I could smell the odor of marijuana myself from out there in the living room, it was not necessary. I simply told Pat and his parents that I believed we would find drugs in their house.

I turned to the parents still seated on the sofa and told them my best guess was that the drug dog would "hit" on the parents' room also, which would mean they were part of the operation, had possession of drugs, or were at least knowledgeable of Pat's drug-distribution operation.

"If there are drugs present, which Pat is distributing from the premises, the house might be seized by the government for forfeiture and sold at auction," I said.

Mom, who had been fidgeting like a maggot in hot ashes, immediately started screeching loudly at Pat that he'd better start cooperating. I brought it down a notch and gently asked Pat and his mom and dad if we could search the house. Pat's mom lost it and began screaming, half toward me giving us permission, half spouting off angry epitaphs at Pat. Pat meekly said, "Okay." Pat's dad hopped off the sofa and showed me to Pat's bedroom. I believe he was glad to leave the room with that commotion going on. It was about 3:45 a.m. by then, and I knew if we were to catch Ferrari before he skipped town, the window of opportunity was quickly closing.

Patrick's bedroom décor was something between early superhero and 1960s anti-government chaos, things you would expect in the room of someone much younger. But then again, he was wearing superhero pajamas. Immediately visible as we entered the room, or to use the legal term "in plain view," was a scale with what appeared to be a baggie full of marijuana sitting on a dresser. On the walls were posters of good guys: Superman, The Justice League, and the Green Hornet. There was also a poster of the Sex Pistols, which I expect was part of Ferrari's "anarchy meets punk rock" influence.

Some things were much older. We discovered two Samozaryadnyi Karabin Simonova or SKS assault rifles. The guns were almost as big as Patrick. Frankly, I was surprised to find the weapons. We also found psychedelic mushrooms, three hits of acid, and some hashish.

We secured the weapons and regrouped in the living room. Pat's mom had regained her composure. I then began to interview Patrick.

I started by asking Patrick how he contacted Ferrari. He still wouldn't look at me and mumbled his answers. "He calls me. I don't know how to get a hold of him," he told me defiantly. After several more questions and disrespectful mumbled replies, I was fed up.

"You still don't get it, do you? We have you. You are finished!" I exclaimed—part out of exasperation from his obstinacy and part out of exasperation from the lack of parenting that had been going on here.

I explained that we had him with this dope and these guns (emphasis on the guns), and he still would not cooperate. "In a few hours the courts will be open, and we can charge you with federal crimes," I said matter-of-factly.

Like a sassy grade school kid, he quietly said, "The guns are legal, and there's only a pound of dope."

What a punk, I thought. What he didn't know and what I happily explained to him was regardless of the fact that he may have purchased the guns legally, he used them as part of his drug-distribution operation. This violation of federal law carries a mandatory five-year sentence. The sentence has to be served "wild" or consecutively to any other sentence he receives. Patrick just sat there with a very puzzled look on his face.

I turned to his mom and dad now and asked them if they had any other place to stay. They gave me a quizzical look and asked why. I began the explanation of the government's forfeiture process. I told them the government would not allow them to remain in the house, because they were part of the drug-distribution conspiracy. I paused to give them a minute to digest this information so they could come to their senses and cooperate.

I heard a soft, almost childlike whimper come from Patrick. "He's in room 211 at the Dusty Motel."

"Excuse me?" I sputtered, now taking slow, deep breaths.

Patrick repeated himself, this time with more emphasis. "He's in room 211 at the Dusty Motel. He called me yesterday and asked me to pick him up from a bus stop in the city. He said he'd give me a pound of dope if I would do like he said."

Patrick then told us that Ferrari wanted him to scrape together the money for the other nineteen pounds and meet him again that day at 9:00 a.m. inside the coffee shop across the street from the motel.

It was now about 5:45 a.m. on Monday morning. I told Patrick to get dressed and accompany us to the motel and show us exactly what room Ferrari was in.

Patrick started to protest, pout, and cross his arms. "Why do I have to go?" he asked.

Frankly, I was enraged and didn't know how much longer I could keep my cool with this kid. I explained to him, "Because you're his dope buddy, because you helped put him in the motel, and because you know what room he's in. I'm not risking any mistakes at this point. We're too close to ending this thing!"

"What if he sees me?" Patrick asked, wide eyed, losing the attitude and finally getting scared for himself.

Ah, I thought. This strategy was working with him and just might work for the brat in the long run, so I stayed with it.

"Oh, he'll see you, Slick! I'm going to show you to him. He's going to know it was you who gave him up. He's going to prison for twenty plus years, and your dope career ends now. Do you hear me?" I said.

Patrick looked pleadingly toward his parents for some support, to save him from his choices that had led him here. His dad said, "I'll get your coat."

Normally I would never let a bandit know how we caught up with him or who gave him up. However, the circumstances in this case dictated we proceed as we did. We decided to burn that bridge, actually for Patrick's benefit. Maybe Patrick could get on with his life and give up the dope nonsense before it consumed him and his family completely. I was pretty certain his parents were "scared straight" at this moment, and it would be a good time to start.

Ferrari told Patrick in his farewell speech that the Marshals might visit him, but it wouldn't be for several months. Ferrari also told Patrick it was for the best that Patrick not know what name he used. Ferrari said that by then, Patrick's memory would be "vague." But still, he didn't want those Marshals to know what identity he had used.

We drove slowly into the motel's parking lot. Room 211 is in the rear of the building. The room is located on the bottom floor, about three doors down from the corner. Patrick verified the man at the front desk was the same one he had seen through the window who checked Ferrari in the night before. Ferrari had told Patrick to wait in the car while he went inside.

According to the man at the front desk, Ferrari had paid cash and had used yet another name, Joe-Joe Beans, that we were not familiar with. Ferrari told him he would be leaving in the morning and asked for a seven o'clock wake-up call.

It was actually about 6:50 a.m. when we woke him. We still had Patrick in the back of one of our cars, and we had been watching the room for over an hour. We planned to hit the room right away, but the AUSA wanted to get a search warrant to keep it an airtight case. So we waited until we knew the warrant was signed, and then we hit the room.

My supervisor, Moe the Empty Suit, was personally bringing a copy of the warrant to the scene. He screamed and cursed me, demanding we actually wait for him to arrive, another thirty minutes or more. We had plenty of manpower on site and were ready. I was concerned because we didn't know if Ferrari was armed and, knowing he was dangerous, I didn't want to risk taking down Ferrari by surprise and hopefully without any shots fired before he woke up and potentially made us. The sad thing was that even though Moe had little if any involvement with this chase, he just wanted to be on the scene when we arrested Ferrari so he could tell headquarters he got his man—a Top Fifteen Most Wanted. The dilemma I was facing was between office politics and safety. All for someone's ego.

We had never heard of Ferrari carrying a weapon. But Patrick had two guns, and there's always a first time. You can't ever play a bandit cheap.

People were starting to stir, banging open doors, stumbling for free coffee in the lobby. We knew we didn't have much time. We had confirmation the warrant was signed, so we moved forward. I'd catch trouble from Moe the Empty Suit, but this chase needed to end now.

We had a key for the room and quietly unlocked and opened the door. It stopped. Ferrari had used the chain lock on the door. This foiled our surprise wake up. We had to force open the door by popping the chain. I prefer to sneak up on bandits and catch them sleeping. It catches them vulnerable, off-guard, and not likely armed.

We could see Ferrari asleep, alone, in the bed farthest from the door, as soon as it opened. We yelled, "Police! U.S. Marshals! Freeze!"

So we "pistol paralyzed" him and got him cuffed up. Pistol paralyzed is the "deer in the headlights" fear that stops you in your tracks when you find yourself looking down the barrel of a gun, with a lawman at the other end and his finger on the trigger ready to use it.

At first he was panicked and thrashed around on the bed. It really didn't take him too long to calm down once he was handcuffed, and soon he just sat there resigned to his fate. I watched him transition to thinking of what to do next. We tossed the room and were soon confident he was unarmed.

The smell from the marijuana just about knocked us out. I couldn't believe all the drug dogs in the St. Louis metropolitan area hadn't come by to pee on his bag. The heavy, earthy stench was nearly overwhelming. He had nineteen individual eight-by-ten-inch envelopes of marijuana, each with a pound in it. The pot wasn't in baggies like we usually find it. Drug dealers mostly do that to help with containing the smell. No wonder the dope was so pungent. He also had his file with a dozen or so unused false identities inside.

After a few minutes, Ferrari was back to his bold self. He began telling us how lucky we were to catch him. I laughed.

"Yeah, that's right," I said sarcastically. "It had nothing to do with the hard work we put in over the past two weeks. Two Marshals from Washington flew down to Texas and were right behind you."

Then I showed him the vehicle Patrick was sitting in and said, "Junior and Space Cadet also gave you up. That's the way it always happens. We always win, and we always catch our bandits." Ferrari hung his head. He was crushed because his minion anarchists had given him up.

We drove Ferrari to the Marshals office where he was processed on the original charges from Virginia. We didn't prosecute him or anyone else involved with him or his nonsense in Missouri. The dope certainly didn't meet the federal guidelines, and the AUSA hoped and believed they were all scared straight. Strangely, Ferrari seemed relieved when I told him no one else would be charged federally.

Like most bandits I've chased, I truly believe Ferrari was

not a bad kid. He simply made some bad decisions and didn't stop—just compounded them with worse ones. He said he had been the product of a messy divorce, and he took out his rage by trying to get most of the Eastern seaboard high. Before Ferrari was shipped back to the District of Columbia to be tried, he signed his Wanted Poster for me: "Luke, it's nice to be wanted, let's do it again real soon."

The Washington Post interviewed me for their feature story on this incredible chase.

I flew to Virginia to testify in Ferrari's case, but instead he pleaded guilty. He was sentenced to twenty years in federal prison. In the courtroom he told me he would escape federal prison at some point and would leave the United States for Europe. He told me I would never find him again. I called the folks in the federal prison system and shared that little bit of information with them. Occasionally I'll check with the prison just to make sure he's still there. He is.

BONUS BANDIT

STORY SIX

"It looks like the street just fell in. Just at the wrong place at the wrong time."

– Larry Nelson, Professional Golfer and Vietnam Vet

"United States Marshals Service, Deputy Adler. May I help you?" I answered my desk phone at the Fugitive Apprehension Strike Team (FAST) unit. The perks to this assignment were hunting bandits with great local, state, and federal law enforcement officers.

"Yeah, you can help me. Get off your butt and catch this bandit I'm sending you," Deputy Marshal Dan Flair said gruffly then started laughing.

Some things never change, I thought.

Flair was a great Deputy Marshal and a good man with an obviously dry sense of humor. He worked out of the U.S. Marshals Office in Springfield, Missouri. We had met during a high-threat mob trial in St. Louis we both worked some years earlier.

Flair filled me in on the history of the case:

Apparently a Missouri State Highway Patrolman, or Trooper, stopped a guy on eastbound Interstate 44 near Springfield, Missouri. The guy was doing ninety in a sixty. Trooper "Too Tall"

Thompson had a nose for dope.

Trooper Thompson pulled the vehicle to the side of the highway to talk about the speeding violation. While talking with the driver of the vehicle, he noticed the guy's heart was pounding out of his chest and he was sweating profusely. It was a cool October evening and there was a chill in the air. The driver, Leonard Combs, wouldn't look at the trooper.

Thompson asked him for his license and registration.

"Why'd you stop me officer? I don't have anything," Combs said, holding the steering wheel tightly and staring straight ahead out his front windshield.

Thompson explained to Combs that he felt obligated to pull over anyone driving faster than sixty-four miles per hour in a sixty-mile-per-hour speed zone. Since Combs was doing ninety miles an hour, Thompson felt compelled to "light him up," which means turn on the lights and pull him over and give the person a ticket or summons.

Combs was too scared to get the sarcasm and Trooper Thompson was in no mood to explain.

"Step out of the vehicle, sir," Thompson said. "Keep your hands where I can see them. Step back to my vehicle, please."

"Am I under arrest?" Combs inquired.

"Is there something I should arrest you for?" asked Trooper Thompson.

"No, I was just wondering," Combs replied.

Thompson noticed Combs was wearing a black jogging suit and designer running shoes. Which really came in handy for Combs at that moment, because he took off running like an Olympic sprinter—not so much sprinting as flying.

An eighteen-wheeler blew by, blasting his air horn. Thompson had bent over slightly and held on to his "Smokey Bear Cover," a nickname for state trooper hats that resemble the hat on the famous fire prevention bear. Trooper Thompson didn't want his hat to be gone with the wind, but that was exactly what had happened to Combs.

By the time Trooper Thompson looked up, Combs was already forty yards into the grassy knoll on the other side of the patrol car. He was quickly slipping out of sight into the dark. Thompson considered chasing him, but he thought better of it. Where could this guy go, after all? Thompson knew he needed to stay with the vehicles. He was sure he'd find drugs when he inventoried the vehicle. Boy, was he right. There were three hundred pounds of marijuana and a kilo of cocaine in the trunk of that car.

He radioed in the situation regarding the fleet-footed Combs. Thompson was sure Combs would be caught on foot and in the custody of his backup unit soon. He had no idea the other troopers and county deputies were working with a major accident that had just occurred three miles north on the Interstate.

Deputy Flair finished the case history by telling me Trooper Thompson recounted the facts of the traffic stop to the Assistant United States Attorney in the Western District of Missouri in the Springfield Division. Combs was charged with possession and the intent to distribute three hundred pounds of marijuana and one kilo of cocaine, estimated street value of three hundred sixty thousand and forty thousand dollars respectively, and there was a federal warrant out for his capture.

"So, I thought I would send you the lead on this guy. Do you think you can find him?" Flair taunted, knowing my track record.

"Son," I said. "This isn't Whisky Grits, Missouri. This is the big city. We believe in law and order here. Combs is as good as caught right now."

"Yeah, yeah, cowboy," he said. "Since we are all in the Show Me State, shut up and show me." With that, he hung up.

I began a work-up on Combs right away. This guy was making quite a career of being a bandit. One thing I noticed quickly was that Combs didn't stray far from home. All of his prior arrests and former addresses were all within an eight-block area. I was glad to see those eight blocks were right in the center of St. Louis Metropolitan Police Sergeant Perry Jones' District.

I had known Jones, as "PJ," for a long time. We had chased and captured bandits together in the past. He had cop smarts enough for a whole district and he always ran a great crew of officers. I knew it wouldn't be any different this time.

At the time, PJ was still new to working in the Seventh District of St. Louis City and he didn't know all of the "regular players" in the area yet. Officer Rodger Gibson was one of PJ's best guys. He had been working the night shift in the Seventh District for many years. I knew he chose to work overnight so he could work a secondary job during the day to provide a better life for his family.

You see, Gibson looks like Mr. Clean and can bench press his squad car. He is also a jovial guy with a great sense of humor. However, he doesn't put up with nonsense or rude behavior. He is handy to have around when someone is misbehaving.

Gibson is also a great communicator. He is the guy law enforcement calls when a message needs to be communicated to residents in the District. He is accepted as part of the community. Everyone, solid citizens and the bandits alike, all respect Gibson's skills and good nature.

When I asked him about Combs, Gibson said Combs had been seen recently in the company of a young lady near the area of Hamilton and Page Avenues. Gibson said he wasn't surprised Leonard had finally caught a federal case. "It was simply a matter of time," he said disappointedly. "He has made the big leagues now."

I showed PJ and Gibson the possible address I had from a telephone number Leonard used to call his bail bondsman in the past. The number was listed to a house on Hamilton just off of Page Avenue.

Gibson immediately protested. "No way. That house is never a problem. In all of my years in the Seventh, I've never even been there. I'm not even sure who lives there," he said.

The only thing I knew was that Combs had called the bail bondsman from the telephone number at that house.

"Well, let's go have a talk anyway," I said.

We arrived at the nicest house on the block. It was very well kept, and the yard was tastefully decorated, a nice change from the others on the block. PJ and I knocked on the front door. Gibson and another Deputy Marshal were watching the back door in case Combs should suddenly choose to make a run for it.

To my surprise, a woman I recognized answered the door. It was Millie West, a very nice woman who worked at the intake center at the St. Louis County Jail.

"What are you doing here?" we both ask in unison, laughing.

"I live here," Ms. West said.

"I'm looking for a bandit who used your telephone," I said, almost apologetically. She had a puzzled look on her face until I showed her Combs' photograph.

"That's the boy dating the girl who lives next door," Millie explained. "They don't have a working telephone, so I let them borrow my cordless phone from time to time."

Millie told us she saw him at the house next door just twenty minutes ago. I thanked her. I appreciate people who are pleasant, cooperative, and tell the truth, something rare in the business of apprehending fugitives.

We passed the information to Gibson, and we all shifted our focus one door down.

Again, PJ and I knocked on the front door. The girlfriend's grandfather answered the door. He told us she and her beau stepped out to go to the "movie rental store" about ten minutes ago. He invited us in, but we politely declined and told him we would wait outside.

PJ and I discussed strategy. PJ and his guys would watch the house. I went with the other deputy to the "Movie Rental Store" to track Combs. If I missed him at the store, PJ would grab him at the house. It made sense. The store was about eight blocks away, outside of the Seventh District, so PJ and Gibson stayed in their district.

We were only five blocks away when PJ "hit me" on the police radio, informing me he had a guy wearing a black running suit heading for the target house. I could see the movie rental store ahead as I turned around and headed back toward PJ.

PJ was parked about a block from the residence. Gibson was parked around the corner. Marked police cars are a common sight in this neighborhood, so it didn't raise any suspicions by the bandit. When the guy got up the stairs and near the front door, PJ pulled up in front of the house and called out to the guy.

The chase was on. The guy took off running. PJ called his location and direction over the radio.

I was driving toward them in the direction the suspect was running. He's running right to us with PJ hot on his heels, I thought. About the time I turned onto the last cross street, PJ called out on the radio calmly, "The suspect was abruptly stopped by Officer Gibson."

Now, as I said, Gibson is a tank. He was not built for foot pursuits, but he was built for stopping fleet-footed bandits. And he did so … abruptly.

When I got there, Gibson had the bandit on the ground and was applying handcuffs. The bandit was screaming, "What'd I do? What'd I do?"

I got a good look at the guy. "Hey," I said, shocked. "That's not Leonard Combs. This guy looks shorter."

PJ came running up about that time and said, "He tossed these."

PJ was holding a Glock .45-caliber semiautomatic handgun in one hand and a baggie with one ounce of "rock" crack cocaine in the other.

"Dude," I said to the bandit. "Timing is everything. You're not even who we're looking for, but you made the team today." Gibson, a huge sports fan, loves the sports euphemisms and laughed.

As it turned out, the guy they chased down was Jimmy Black III. We ran his rap sheet and found out he had six "Suspended Imposition of Sentences" (SIS) and one Suspended Execution of Sentence (SES) on his record. These were nothing more than a smack on the hand. The guy was a career criminal who had never been to prison. Coincidently, he had one of those arrests with the fugitive I was hunting, Leonard Combs. Black's one SES was a conviction for unlawful use of a weapon and possession of a controlled substance, with no jail time served. The other SIS's really don't even count.

I read Black his Miranda rights and asked him to talk with us. He looked at me and said, "Pound sand."

He let me know in many four-letter-word combinations that his attorney would have him home before we could finish our reports. I just smiled.

"Au contraire," I assured him as I dialed up my attorney, Assistant United States Attorney Paul Richards.

AUSA Richards told me to bring Black into the office the next morning and he would be charged accordingly. Black appeared to be unsettled when I told him I would finish my reports in the morning and he would still be locked down.

"Whatever, dude," he replied, glaring at me.

PJ and Gibson took Black to the city lockup. PJ also made sure the evidence technician folks knew the evidence needed to be processed ASAP. As they saddled up to leave, I told PJ I was going with the other Deputy Marshal to make one more pass by the house, since Combs was still out there, although I couldn't imagine he would stick around after all of this commotion a couple blocks away.

As we turned onto Hamilton Avenue, I saw a guy walking

hand in hand with a cute little lady, halfway up the block. "I cannot believe it," I said.

Sure enough, Combs was walking straight toward us. He was so into his girlfriend, he was blinded by love and oblivious to the two men sitting in the family car (we were driving a maroon Ford minivan with tinted windows). I pulled up to the curb and just sat there. He came right to us.

We jumped out on Combs and his gal; both of them just about wet their pants. We pistol paralyzed him and got him cuffed. Who would have thought we would get this bandit with all of the activity Black had caused with the chase earlier?

In custody, Combs was in a talkative mood. The only problem for him was that we had the guy he could give up already in custody. Namely, Jimmy Black III.

I dialed up Dan Flair the next morning. "Hey. You guys have any more bandits you need caught?" I asked.

I gave him the run-down on Combs and told him about our bonus bandit, Jimmy Black. We shipped Combs back to Springfield, Missouri, via the prisoner air transport—or ConAir as it is commonly known.

Later that morning, I took Jimmy Black in for processing. Now remember, this guy ranted about how his attorney was going to have him out before I finished my reports. At that time, he wasn't out yet. But I wasn't finished with my reports, either.

AUSA Richards hammered out a criminal complaint charging Black with being a convicted felon in possession of a firearm, possession with the intent to distribute crack cocaine, and possession of a firearm during the commission of a drug crime.

Frankly, Black was looking at a whole lot of prison time here. The felon-in-possession charge was a ten-year prison stay by itself. The cocaine charge carried up to twenty years in prison. Possession of a firearm during a drug crime carried a mandatory five years that would run consecutive to his other sentences.

Sentences can either run concurrently or consecutively. Concurrent sentences means serving time for multiple crimes together. Consecutive sentences are what the bandits call "wild." In other words, Black had to do the time for the first two sentences before his time would even begin to run on the five-year sentence. He would also do the full five years, no chance for probation or parole.

On the first two sentences, he could be sentenced to prison time ranging from one year to the statutory maximum each offense would carry, and they could run together.

The coup de grâce on the deal was that AUSA Richards petitioned the court to hold Black without bail. In the federal system a bandit can be held without bail if the government can prove the person is a flight risk and/or a danger to the community.

The first point in the government's petition was that Jimmy had shown himself to be a career criminal. All of the SIS convictions demonstrated that Black was a slow learner. His behavior didn't change. He just had a good lawyer.

The second point in the petition was that Black fled from the police when questioned. He just didn't flee very well.

Thirdly, he was "slinging," or selling, crack cocaine. I may sound like I'm on a soapbox here, but crack is killing our society and is clearly a danger for our community. Black did this all the while in possession of a firearm. We all know that firearms can be dangerous, especially in the hands of guys like Black. Also, the firearm turned out to be stolen.

The last thing the court took notice of were the many failures to appear for traffic violations. If Black didn't pay attention to a court on minor issues, why would he follow the court's instructions on a major issue?

Black was held without bond. He didn't get out until a very long time after I finished my reports. Since he wasn't released on bond and the federal court system works diligently for speedy trials, Black went to trial quickly.

We arrested Black the beginning of March, and by May fifth, he was on trial. He didn't like our jails and he wanted to get out of there as soon as possible. He said he believed he could beat this case.

Black was given a court-appointed attorney this time. It seemed the legal wizard he used in his previous state cases wanted too much money to represent him for the federal case. Since Black was locked up, he couldn't sling dope, so he wasn't making any money. Therefore he was indigent and an attorney was provided for him.

Black's court-appointed attorney was a woman I knew from my time around the courthouse on many other cases. She was a very good, competent attorney and a very nice lady. She was very well liked and respected in the courthouse. But she was not a magician. Old Merlin himself could not have done anything to get Black out of trouble this time. Black really should have made a deal (plead guilty).

The trial only lasted two days. The first day they picked a jury of Jimmy's peers and the AUSA gave his opening statement. The defense attorney chose to withhold their opening statement, which it is their right to do.

AUSA Richards waxed eloquently about what the facts of the case would show. This is why this man is called the "Dean of Prosecutors."

There were a couple of highlights during the trial. AUSA Richards had me visit Jimmy's house prior to trial to speak with the young lady with whom he lived. She allowed me into her house to chat. While there, I observed and seized a box of .45-caliber bullets that she said belonged to Jimmy. Hank Sterling, the firearms examiner, later said those bullets were an exact match to the bullets in Jimmy's gun.

The gun itself was a large weapon, but it was very lightweight. I know because I owned a Glock that was the same size. I testified that I sometimes carry mine in the waistband of my shorts and cover it with a T-shirt to conceal it. You wouldn't know I had it on me "unless maybe I ran from the police and threw it down in a vacant lot." I don't know, but I think the jury really liked that little tidbit of information.

The final nail in Black's coffin came when Black took the stand against the advice of his attorney. He told the jurors he didn't know who those guys were who chased him that night. He thought they might be robbers. He was going to a friend's house. He said he didn't have a gun or drugs. That was his story, and he was sticking to it.

AUSA Richards brought out the fact that Black had been in possession of drugs and or guns on numerous prior occasions for which he had received several Suspended Imposition of Sentences. AUSA Richards also pointed out that Black's friend, Leonard Combs, was also wanted by the U.S. Marshals for a similar drug charge in Springfield, Missouri. That was the reason we were already at the house Jimmy visited that night.

At the end of the trial, the judge excused the jury to deliberate. The jury panel stood and exited the courtroom. The judge then turned to Black to speak with him. The judge said, "Dude, please. You've got nothing coming after that testimony."

But he did. A guilty verdict. The jury was back faster than Jimmy could run. I think they set a new record.

About ninety days later, the judge sentenced Black to seventeen and a half years in federal prison. The federal judges give their sentences in months. So when the judge said, "Two hundred and ten months," Black focused on the "months" part and said out loud, "That's not so bad."

Then I said, "Dude. That's more than seventeen years."

When I used the "Y" word—years—it hit him like a ton of bricks.

Black started whining and crying in the courtroom. He had never been incarcerated before, and now he was staring down seventeen years. He started saying to me, "Luke, why didn't you talk to me? I could have helped you out, man. I could have given you someone big."

"I did try to talk to you, Jimmy," I reminded him. "And you told me to 'pound sand.' And that your attorney would have you out before I finished my reports. I told you it wouldn't happen that way. You didn't believe me."

About three weeks later I transported Jimmy Black III to the United States Penitentiary at Terre Haute, Indiana. That was the prison he'd been assigned to by the United States Bureau of Prisons (BOP).

I was there on the street the night Jimmy came into custody. I walked him through the federal judicial process from start to finish. I testified at all of his pretrial hearings. I testified again at his trial, and I was there when the judge sentenced him. Then I drove him to his new home in federal prison. I took Jimmy from the street to the joint. It's not very often that happens in law enforcement, certainly not at the federal level.

I left Jimmy Black III at the receiving and discharge area of the United States Penitentiary. I told him to say hello to Leonard for me.

Several years later I checked, and Combs and Black were both still serving their sentences.

DR. FAÇADE

STORY SEVEN

"Never interrupt your enemy when he is making a mistake."
— Napoleon Bonaparte

Willie Peters was nothing more than a two-bit thief. A nickel-and-dime guy, really. A street hustler at best, certainly not typical of a fed case. When you read in the newspaper, "Savvy Guy Bilked Investors Out of Millions," that's not Willie. Willie was more like a two-thousand-bucks-and-change kind of guy.

Don't get me wrong; I'm not going soft on crime. If I lost a hundred bucks in a scam, I'd want blood, and I'd want the rascal to get his day in court. I certainly think taxpayers deserve that and more. That's why I chase bandits.

Peters was not a sophisticated schemer. He acted on impulse, at the spur of the moment. His choice in prey one day came back to haunt him.

Peters had the misfortune of crossing paths with an attorney, Trevor Higginbothams. Higginbothams was a successful lawyer, and Peters thought it might be fun to assume an attorney's identity. So he did. He also damaged Higginbothams' credit and committed bank fraud and mail fraud along the way.

The United States Attorney's Office has guidelines they follow. A certain dollar amount of loss must be reached for a crime to be filed and prosecuted federally. If you took a look at Peters' rap sheet, it would be no surprise that he caught another fraud case. It is, however, quite surprising the case made its way into the federal system.

Nearly any fraud related to identity theft is a violation of some federal crime or other. Using someone else's Social Security account number is a federal crime. If you commit the crime against a bank, it's bank fraud, also a federal crime. If the fraud you commit causes something to be mailed, you have mail fraud, etc. However, getting the federal prosecutors to take the case is not always easy.

When Peters' case came up, Higginbothams, the lawyer whose identity he had stolen and ruined, had become the U.S. Attorney for the Eastern District of Missouri. He had the power to get the case issued federally—and made sure it was. Peters ended up serving time in federal prison for ten months. Let's just say the charges typically wouldn't have earned federal attention if the U.S. Attorney didn't have Peters on his personal radar.

This was Peters' first time in prison and where his real criminal education began. He began learning about fraud from some real pros there. In prison, Peters was a bit of a hero for having messed with a U.S. Attorney. The U.S. Attorney is the presidentially appointed person who heads up the federal prosecutors' office. So, in theory, he's responsible for all federal prosecutions in his district. Peters was a legend for ripping off the guy who had put them all behind bars.

When a federal bandit is released from prison, he reports back to his sentencing judge. The judges are busy being judges, so they have Supervised Release Officers (SOR) who report to them. The SORs keep watch over their "flock," similar to a Parole Officer. When a member of the flock goes astray, the judge slaps them with some more time in prison. The sentences are all in accordance with the standard federal sentencing guidelines.

The thinking behind replacing Parole Officers with

Supervised Release Officers is that the judge who heard the case against the bandit originally knew more about him than a bureaucratic parole commission.

Like many small timers who use prison as a training class, when Peters hit the streets again, he was ready to get busy with some real fraud. He checked in with his Supervised Release Officer for a few weeks. It was just enough time for him to get on his feet and erase his trail, or so he thought. He stopped reporting for his supervised release and disappeared into the wind.

The judge uses the "long arm of the law" to bring a bandit back into the fold. In the federal judicial system, that long arm would be the U.S. Marshals.

This is where I came into Peters' life ... again. His warrant came across my desk one day, and I started making preliminary inquiries. I remembered dealing with Peters during his first go-around with the feds. I went and had a talk with a buddy of mine—let's call him "Friendly"—at the Postal Inspection Service.

Postal Inspector Friendly was involved with Peters' original case. He filled me in on what he knew about Peters' old case. What he neglected to tell me was that the Postal Inspectors were working a new case on Peters and they were looking for him, too. Do you sense a little "Friendly" competition here? When I have a warrant, I say, "Let's all play catch the bandit." It's best played as a team sport.

Peters, not unlike many other bandits I have chased, lived an alternative lifestyle. He also had a bad habit of dating people and either stealing from them or assuming their identity. I don't blame Peters for wanting a new identity. His real one was the pits.

I found out Peters was changing up his pattern since his stint in prison. He began stealing identities from people he didn't know. Complete strangers. Peters apparently began stalking the grounds of a very large metropolitan university hospital in St. Louis, looking for a new victim. Apparently he figured he had been a lawyer, so why not be a doctor? He stole a white lab coat, a stethoscope, and began making his rounds.

To get a snapshot of where this was happening, St. Louis City has an urban area referred to as the "Central West End." It is a great location—lots of upscale older homes, a great variety of restaurants and businesses, walking distance to Forest Park, which is a several-hundred-acre park and a very short commute to a prominent university hospital. It is a preppy, avant-garde neighborhood of the trendy and well-to-do.

The Central West End has attracted folks from alternate lifestyles for years. It has several coffee shops, antique stores, commercial mail offices, and art galleries. I thought it might be a perfect fit for Peters.

I began making my rounds on some commercial mail services in the last area I knew Peters had been living. These are places where you can rent a mailbox. I also checked out some of the coffee houses nearby. I remembered Peters was a sucker for a good latte.

I got lucky and hit pay dirt with the first commercial mail outfit I visited. I showed the young lady behind the counter a photograph of Peters and asked if she had seen him. Her nametag read "Susie," a perky name for a perky girl with a subtle nose ring and tongue piercing.

"That's Dr. Façade," she said with teen angst. "I already told your partner all about him."

"Excuse me?" I said, confused. "What about Dr. Façade and my partner?"

"You know, Postal Inspector Friendly," Susie told me as she reached under the counter and produced a business card belonging to Postal Inspector Friendly. Real nice, I thought. My "pal" Friendly forgot to tell me he was here looking for Peters, too. "You are with the Post Office, aren't you?" Susie asked.

Normally when I show someone my credentials, which are clearly labeled "Deputy United States Marshal," inevitably people say, "Oh, you're with the FBI?" Not today. Today was the first time I had been asked about being a Postal Inspector.

As I identified myself to her for the second time, I explained to her that I was with the Marshals Service and I was federal law enforcement.

Susie filled me in regarding "Dr. Façade." She said he was living in an apartment down the street while doing his residency at the hospital.

"He seems like an okay guy," she said. "He's a little pompous, even for a new doctor. He'll probably be terrible to deal with once he finishes his residency." She was quiet for a moment and cocked her head while in thought. "He is always kind of nervous, you know? He's really suspicious of everyone and everything."

I went ahead and told her that Dr. Façade was not really a doctor and that was not his real name. I told her he was a thief and that he stole things from people. I also told her that Peters was wanted by the United States Marshals Service.

"Is that like the FBI?" she asked. I did a mental eye roll and wondered how some people get through the day.

Susie said she hadn't seen him since the Postal guys came by. They hadn't told her why they were looking for him.

"I thought that was kind of funny that Postal Inspectors wanted to talk with a doctor. I couldn't imagine why," she said. "They left in a hurry when I told them where he lived."

She told me that Dr. Façade—Peters, that is—received mostly credit cards and bank statements in his mailbox.

"I don't suppose he ever came in here with anyone else?" I asked.

"No, not really," Susie said. "Once or twice he came by with a girlfriend, but she waited outside."

I asked her if she was sure the other person was a woman, because I didn't think Peters would have a girlfriend. She spent the next several minutes explaining to me in great detail the difference between a female friend and a girlfriend.

"I knew he was gay right away," she said. "His friend drove him by our office. She parked in front and waited for him in the car. I also have seen them out a couple times when I stop with friends for happy hour after work at local restaurants or bars on my way home."

"I don't suppose you saw what kind of car his friend drove or a license plate?" I asked.

"No, I don't pay much attention to that kind of thing. It's probably a BMW. But, it might be on the security tape."

"Security tape? I didn't see a security camera," I said.

"It's a secret," she whispered conspiratorially as she leaned forward over the counter toward me. "The boss put it in about a year ago when a local business was robbed. It watches the front door outside, the inside of the office, and the back door."

I suggested to Susie that she call her boss and let me speak with him. He told me he would review the tape and download a photograph of the car if they could. He said it might take a day or two, but that he would call me if he got anything.

In their haste to chase down this bandit, the "Postal guys" as Susie called them, had neglected to find out about the security tape and the mystery girl, who was his friend.

I thanked the young lady and started for the door. I stopped, turned back, and asked her how she knew he was a doctor.

She rolled her eyes and smiled. "He comes in wearing his white lab coat and stethoscope around his neck. His name is embroidered above the pocket, over the top of the hospital name." I thanked her and left.

I reviewed Peters' file. He had grown up in Webster Groves, Missouri, an upscale quaint little village in the creeping suburbs of St. Louis. He had graduated from the high school there and soon after had been estranged from his parents because of his lifestyle choices. The parents were now deceased. He was a "late-in-life" baby, an only child born to parents in their mid-forties. It didn't leave me much to go on for family interviews.

I headed back to the office to do some telephone work. The first call I made was to the hospital. I wanted to track down the "doctor" lead.

I called the information desk at the hospital, and they connected me with Dr. Façade's office. I spoke with his receptionist. There was no way I thought I would get through to the doctor. But she sounded excited when I identified myself and said, "Oh, honey! He's going to want to talk with you. I'll get him and put you through."

A few minutes later, a man's voice greeted me. The guy sounded young, but also stiff as a board. I informed him of who I was and why I was calling. He asked for a call-back number and said he would get back to me. I told him the Marshals' number is in the blue pages of the phone book if he'd rather look it up. He said he would do that, and he abruptly hung up.

"Wow!" I said aloud to no one in particular. "This guy is Mr. Personality. I hope he has a better bedside manner." I had such high hopes when I spoke with his receptionist. My phone rang and I answered.

"Hi, Deputy. Dr. Façade here." The guy sounded like a different person, very personable and relieved. He explained to me about his apprehension in talking to a stranger over the telephone.

"About six weeks ago, I was in surgery. When I came out, I showered and began dressing. I had a funny feeling that something was wrong or different. I just felt like someone had been in my things. I couldn't quite put a finger on it."

The doctor said he then looked through his wallet and his belongings. He still had cash in his wallet, though he had no idea how much he had to start with. His license was there and his credit cards seemed okay. His watch and chain were there. Still, something seemed amiss.

Two weeks later he received a call from a local car dealership. There seemed to be a problem with the cashier's check he had given them. Dr. Façade told me that he agreed with them that there was a problem. He wasn't in the market for a car, and he hadn't given them or anyone else a cashier's check. And no, he said vehemently, he didn't have their BMW.

The doctor said he called the police in a panic and reported the incident. He spoke with a detective who handles fraud investigations. The detective assured him they would look into it. In the meantime, the detective suggested that the doctor contact his credit card companies and his bank.

Dr. Façade put a hold on all of his credit cards and notified his bank. The bank informed him there was a high level of activity in his account recently. Mostly, checks that had been cashed and withdrawals. Dr. Façade told me he felt sick. He went back through his wallet and realized one of his credit cards was missing. He called the detective back and told him about the missing credit card and the activity on his bank account.

A week later, Dr. Façade received a call from a Detective Smith in the fraud unit in the St. Louis City Police Department. Detective Smith said he needed to review some of the notes on the case. The young doctor said he could be available the next day at noon to meet. Detective Smith spoke sternly with him, letting Dr. Façade know this was "his" case now. Smith was in the fraud unit now, and the doctor would be wasting precious time. The detective assured Dr. Façade it wouldn't be necessary to meet if he could just give him five minutes now over the telephone.

Detective Smith went over some of the notes on the case the previous detective had. Dr. Façade told him he had already discussed much of the exact same things with the police just the other day. Dr. Façade said he found himself getting agitated with Detective Smith by the end of their conversation.

When Dr. Façade asked Detective Smith if the police were close to catching the guy, Smith told him they had no idea who the "perp" was.

Dr. Façade repeated Detective Smith's quote to me: "This guy is very good! He's a pro. He's brilliant and he may never be caught."

The doctor said Detective Smith came across as egotistical, snobbish, and effeminate. He told me that as he hung up the telephone with Detective Smith, he realized the detective had asked a question that struck him as odd. "What's your mother's maiden name?" Smith had asked him.

"Why would he want to know that?" he asked me.

Dr. Façade had a hard time admitting he may have made a mistake, even to me now. He had apparently given "Detective Smith" his mother's maiden name. "He was so annoying I would have given that guy anything to get rid of him. Now I started getting calls from my bank again. They said my new account was overdrawn, and there were numerous ATM withdrawals. I kept asking them, 'What new account?'" he relayed to me, exasperated as we finished our conversation.

In the following days, my footwork uncovered some more of Peters' continued antics. He had called into the bank, again posing as Dr. Façade. He informed them that all of this "nonsense" had been a mistake. He told them he had found his credit card, which he had thought was stolen. He also found that the missing funds and withdrawals were actually done by a former lover. Peters, posing as Dr. Façade, told the bank that he would make good on everything, but he did want to open a new account as a safety precaution. He also called his credit card company and did the same song and dance. They reactivated his cards and credit line.

The bank and credit card companies told me they had verified the caller was indeed Dr. Façade by requiring him to provide his mother's maiden name. Peters had complied without hesitation, having eked out that info from the real Dr. Façade (posing as Detective Smith).

A local jeweler called the real Dr. Facade and told the doctor that his check had bounced. They sternly insisted he return his Rolex or make good on the check.

The doctor's financial life was in ruins, he was becoming paranoid, and the stress was killing him. He said it made him physically sick when he called the St. Louis Police fraud unit to give them the update and found out his suspicion was correct—there was no Detective Smith.

Now I was up to date with the case, and Dr. Façade was confident I was who I said I was, because he looked up the number himself in the front of the phone book and called me back at my office.

I told him Willie Peters was the man who had stolen his identity and created this mess, and that I would let him know when I caught him.

Dr. Façade gave me the name and telephone number of his hospital's security guy, whom I would call next. Before we hung up, the doctor said angrily that he's a surgeon and he'd like a chance to operate on Peters. Whoa, I thought. This guy has really been pushed to his limits.

I called hospital security and asked them to go through any surveillance tapes they might have and look for people around the operating rooms or doctors dressing rooms on the given dates. The security guy informed me the hospital has fifty thousand visitors on any given day. He assured me, with a hint of sarcasm, that they would review everything and get right back to me. I never heard from them again. He probably wondered why I would bother them with such a request. I wondered why they bothered to have security cameras and video recorders if they can't even use them to find a felon posing as a doctor being pursued by federal law enforcement.

I did hear back a couple days later from the boss at the commercial mail office. He had found the picture of Peters' mystery girl and the car she was driving. It was a Ford Mustang, not the BMW as Susie had thought. The photograph also gave up a Missouri license plate number.

How cool is that? I thought. A security camera helping with security. I knew this lead was going to close the loop on this bandit.

I ran a check on the license plate. It came back to a Mickey Smith in Webster Groves, Missouri. She lived on the same street where Willie grew up. Mickey was about the same age as Peters. Childhood friends? I wondered.

I called the real detectives at the fraud unit. They told me they had a good lead on Peters about a week ago, but it "went south," which means it went bad for some reason. The detective filled me in on the details.

After Peters had called the real Doctor Façade, posing as Detective Smith, he opened a new account with the doctor's identity. He immediately began running up more fraudulent charges on credit cards and started bank withdrawals. He had even taken the time to pick out a nifty new watch from an exclusive jeweler.

Peters called the bank's Chesterfield, Missouri, branch, just west of St. Louis, and inquired about his new account. The questions he asked about the account made the teller suspicious. The teller was very smart and had played along with Peters so as not to spook him. Peters said he would come by the bank later to cash a cashier's check from his hospital. He said he would need the cash since his bank account was a wreck. The teller assured him that the request would be granted in light of all his recent problems. She immediately notified her bank security. Security, in turn, called the St. Louis City Police fraud unit detective.

The detective contacted Inspector Friendly at the Postal Inspection Service. The two of them raced out to the Chesterfield branch of the bank to catch their bandit. Problem is, in their haste, they both parked their unmarked police cars next to each other by the curb. It was a no-parking zone.

What would you think if you pulled up and saw that? Cops maybe? That is what Peters thought as he drove by in his new BMW.

So what did he do? Run? Not exactly. He calmly drove across the lot and parked at a little Mexican restaurant where he could watch the bank.

Inspector Friendly was inside the bank when the head teller told him a "Detective Smith" was on the telephone and urgently needed to speak with him.

Inspector Friendly picked up the phone. "Hello?"

"You'll never catch me; you're too stupid," a voice said from the other end of the phone connection. It was Peters calling from across the parking lot to the bank where the real detective from the fraud unit and Inspector Friendly were awaiting his arrival.

Peters sipped a margarita and grinned as he watched the law enforcement officers fume and storm out of the bank. He could tell they were upset because of their animated gestures. They didn't speak on the way to their vehicles then both sped off. This pleased Peters a great deal.

He was very proud of himself at that moment, and he believed no one could catch him. He was wrong.

During that time, I slowly drove down Peters' old street in Webster Groves. The houses there looked much the same as they had when Peters played there as a child. The neighborhood was now changing, a mix of young married couples and a few older widows and widowers.

I stopped and spoke with an elderly woman I found working in her front yard. I introduced myself, and she told me she was a retired schoolteacher who recently lost her husband, Frank, to cancer. Frank had been a police officer for a short time after he got out of the Army. "He was in World War II, you know," she said proudly.

She thought police work was too dangerous, so Frank became

a mailman. He had retired from the post office in 1983 after more than thirty-five years.

She seemed appreciative of the time we spent in conversation. She did most of the talking. I just listened patiently. She had a sharp memory; I knew the answers would come soon. She recounted the old neighborhood to me and educated me about her neighbors without prompting.

"Do you remember Willie Peters?" I asked her when she had paused.

"I sure do. He was in my classroom at school one year and lived three houses down. I always thought that boy was a little funny, you know. He was a momma's boy for years. His parents were older, and they spoiled and pampered him," she said, shaking her head while leaning on her shovel.

"My Frank used to say Willie Peters was a sissy. I told him to stop that. The boy is an only child." She paused, saddened. "We couldn't have children, you know. That's one of the reasons I loved to teach. I loved to spend time with my children."

She also told me about Mickey Smith. "The Smiths were Willie's neighbors. The two of them were inseparable. It used to make Frank so mad when he'd offer to play catch with Willie, but Willie would choose to play dolls with Mickey instead."

Mickey Smith's father had passed away a number of years ago. Her mother was in a retirement home somewhere in the city. Mickey still owned the house, but she rented it out now. "She's too good to live here anymore," the woman said, irritated.

I thanked the woman for the time she spent with me and started to leave. "You should find another job. Being in the FBI is too dangerous. Your wife must be frightened all the time." I smiled at that. Even a schoolteacher doesn't get it. Then she added, "I don't know why Mickey doesn't just sell that house; she works in real estate."

Easy enough to track down, I found Mickey Smith worked for a real estate company located in Chesterfield, Missouri. It caught my attention because it was the same suburb where Peters tried to cash a check as Dr. Façade.

I called an officer I knew at the Chesterfield Police Department. As it happened, he knew the office manager at the real estate company where Mickey worked. "He is a memorable character," was all he would say.

Fifteen minutes later, Rex the real estate office manager called me. He was a good ol' country boy selling real estate in the rich suburbs. I asked him to keep this investigation to himself, "on the down low." I told him I was looking for a friend of Mickey Smith. I told him I didn't think Smith was involved in the crimes, but I couldn't be sure. He said, "Boy, I hope not. She's one of our biggest earners."

Before I had a chance to start with follow-up questions, Rex asked me, "Are you looking for that homosexual feller?"

"Willie Peters?" I asked calmly.

"Oh, I don't know his name." Rex said. "I've only met him once. Didn't care for him. He's uppity. Thinks he's special, better than everyone else."

"I don't suppose you know where he lives?" I asked him.

"Nope, but I'll bet you a hundred dollars and a bottle of good bourbon I know where you can find him tonight at 6:30 p.m.," Rex said.

"Well, I can't take your bet, but I do hope you can tell me where I can find him."

"Not a gambler, huh? I thought all you men wearin' black suits were," he said.

Rex told me he had overheard Mickey Smith talking with "that what's his name." She told him she would pick him up at six thirty this evening, after she showed her last house. Then they could get a bite at the Mexican restaurant near the mall.

I made a call to Kathy Steen and Cal Simpson, two of our newer Deputy U.S. Marshals in the office. I asked them how they'd like to have dinner at a Mexican restaurant tonight. They both always accepted when I invited them to accompany me on captures. They were on their way to meet me at a local fast-food restaurant parking lot to go over the details of the plan.

In an abundance of caution, I didn't want to be seen in the restaurant. I had dealt with Peters during his first go-around in the federal system. I didn't want to risk him seeing me and slipping out a back door.

Deputy Kathy Steen is a Mississippi country girl. She's a little gal, but very athletic. Cal, on the other hand, is a big guy. He played football for a nationally ranked college team before joining the Marshals Service. Cal was on the front line. I think he was the entire front line. I thought it might be quite a funny scene to see if Willie would try to get by him.

I pulled into the strip mall parking lot at about 6:45 p.m. I was driving an older Ford Explorer at the time. I told Kathy and Cal to drive together in one of our minivans, to give the appearance of a husband and wife. I told them not to get there until seven fifteen. Hopefully Peters and Mickey Smith would be inside by then.

Sure enough, I spotted Mickey's Mustang straight away. As luck would have it, I got the parking space next to hers. I sat there and waited for Kathy and Cal.

Cal pulled the minivan onto the parking lot in a light, cold drizzle. He pulled up near the front door to let Kathy out. What a gentleman! I thought. She waited for him under the awning then they walked into the restaurant together.

I hoped they wouldn't sit down and order a big meal. Not five minutes later, I saw Cal walking out the front door with Peters in tow. Kathy was behind him fending off Mickey.

When the two deputies entered the restaurant, they spied Willie and Mickey straight away. The fugitive and his friend were sitting at a table near the entrance. They were chatting away like two little grade school kids.

Peters almost wet himself when Cal walked up to his table

and told him he was under arrest. At six foot four and an athletic three hundred pounds, Cal was an imposing sight. He reached down and grabbed Peters with his big meat hooks. Mickey, in shock, started mumbling something about how they hadn't eaten.

I jumped out of my ride and ran to meet them as they came out the front door. "Dr. Façade" was berating Cal and threatening him with a lawsuit for this horrendous injustice.

I said, "Hey, Willie, don't you remember me?"

"I don't know who you are, sir," he said haughtily, trying to turn and twist out of Cal's grip.

"Come on, man, the jig's up now. You're in handcuffs and going to jail. We're not going to let you go; you can relax now," I said.

"I am Doctor Façade, sir, and you'll regret this, I promise you. My attorneys will (yak, yak, yak . . .)."

I am a patient man. I deal with all sorts of lying, cheating, stealing, maiming, and killing on a daily basis and not necessarily in that order. Peters was desperately trying to keep with the act; his voice was getting higher pitched and whiney. He was just making it harder on himself.

"I thought you used to be an attorney, Willie. That's right, you just played one at the ATM machines," I chuckled. This is one way I "help" bandits adjust to the situation of being surprised, cuffed, and whisked away. I keep steady and in control but with a sense of humor. They seem to sense they are passengers on this trip and have lost control but are okay with it because I am confident and "just doing my job." It doesn't mean Peters wasn't getting on my nerves; I would just never show it.

Mickey was over being shocked, and now she was just plain mad. She was screaming unintelligibly about civil rights.

I reached into my credentials case and got out my "Miranda Rights" card. I began reading them their rights straight off the card. I told her, "You need to listen to these, too."

"Me?" She said. Then Mickey immediately shut up. She turned a pasty white and said, "I think there's been a misunderstanding."

"I'm sure there has!" I announced like a game show host.

"May I go?" she asked weakly.

"Please do," I told her. She opened her car door and left without any delay or fanfare—or even looking back at her lifelong friend.

As we neared the Jennings City Jail, Peters' protests grew weaker. He had been housed there years before, and he knew it well. The Marshals office in the Eastern District of Missouri had contracted with Jennings City Jail for many, many years. It was a very well-known place to our bandits.

A little known fact is that the Marshals Service contracts with jails to house federal bandits. We don't actually operate any jails of our own. That's one of the biggest differences between the U.S. Marshals and a county sheriff's department. The feds do have a few jails. They're called Metropolitan Corrections Centers (MCC). But, the MCCs are operated by the United States Bureau of Prisons (USBOP).

As we pulled up to the jail, Peters finally admitted who he was, said he wished he were dead, and began howling and crying.

I laughed and told him, "If that was what you wanted, you should have tried to get away from the big guy, Cal, who cuffed you. Maybe you would be. Now since you've said that, I have to tell the folks at the jail to put you on suicide watch."

Peters didn't see the humor in that. He tightened his face into a grimace, but he pulled it back together and stopped the wailing.

As I wrote up the paperwork for the arrest, I realized how surprised I was that Peters kept up the act as long as he did. Also, he didn't remember me from his first go-around in the fed system. Not that I am so memorable, but most bandits remember the person who caught them. I have been recognized several times while at restaurants and baseball games. I have a good memory. I always try to remember them first.

I called the real Doctor Façade the next day and told him we had arrested Peters. He was very appreciative, but I could tell he knew this whole mess with Peters was far from over. I knew that, too. The effects from these cases can linger for years. I told him he could contact the Victim Witness Coordinator in the U.S. Attorney's Office. They might be able to help him sort out his credit mess, and they could let him know what would happen to Peters.

About six months later, I happened to be in that same hospital on another case. As I walked down a corridor I heard a page: "Dr. Façade, line 2312. Dr. Façade, line 2312." I stared up at a surveillance camera and shook my head. Then I smiled and waved.

PLAYING IT CHEAP

STORY EIGHT

"Well, of course a boxing match is hard because boxing isn't set for you to do good. You have to force your will upon someone, but dancing you don't have to force your will. It should be a lot easier [to take up dancing] because if I make a mistake I don't get hit."

– Evander Holyfield

It was one of those autumn days in St. Louis when the temperature fluctuated from below freezing in the morning to the mid-fifties in the afternoon. Not too uncommon, and most people are just relieved to be rid of the brutal summer heat and humidity.

I was assigned to St. Louis County Police Department's Combined Urban Fugitive Force, the "CUFF" unit. The unit was made up of three St. Louis County Detectives, a Deputy U.S. Marshal and two or three officers from the various municipalities located in St. Louis County.

St. Louis County surrounds the City of St. Louis like the letter "C." However the city is not located inside the county as most cities in the United States are. Due in large part to the Civil War, the City of St. Louis and St. Louis County are two separate entities with nothing in common. This ridged separation often spills over into the social-political arena. This often leads to political infighting throughout the "Greater St. Louis Metropolitan Community."

St. Louis County is home to more than a hundred municipalities of which approximately seventy have their own police departments. The CUFF unit commander would dip into these departments like a reserve, requesting officers from municipalities to serve for about one month. Voila! A couple teams emerged: "North County" and "South County" regions with three or four law enforcement officers each on assignment to do nothing but chase bandits full time.

The team concept was less formal than it sounds, and while both teams typically operated separately, we could augment each other or work together as one team if needed. The concept was a good one, and the results were excellent.

The CUFF unit's number of arrests was not as large as St. Louis City's multi-jurisdictional Fugitive Apprehension Strike Team, or FAST unit, whose number of captures was huge. This was due to the area of operation. The FAST unit operated in a much more condensed inner-city high-crime area, while the CUFF unit was spread over an area three times as large.

I know I had my dream job, and I have always loved working with state and local law enforcement officers. I have been fortunate to work with some of the best. The detectives who made up the CUFF unit were a stellar example of professional law enforcement officers.

On this particular chilly-then-warm-then-cold fall day, I was working with two such great officers from small North County municipalities. Our CUFF unit was down to three members. Because of a rash of armed robberies and shootings, many of the local departments detailed their officers to work with the local FBI. The FBI had a task force of more than thirty agents dedicated to catch those bandits. In this type of situation, municipalities recall their officers from special duty to work an investigation.

A "stick-up" crew was operating throughout the region. They were believed to be responsible for about thirty armed robberies and several shootings. In one instance, they drove through a fast-food restaurant in the city's south side and shot a young cashier in the neck. Miraculously, the young man survived. The FBI and local law enforcement were working feverishly to identify these guys.

My CUFF unit team was busy working through the stack of our assigned arrest warrants. We started at 6:30 a.m. that day and had made our first arrest in St. Louis County before 8:00 a.m. We got slowed down at booking and didn't get back on the hunt until after noon.

When you make an arrest, you are also required to transport your bandit to the St. Louis County Jail's booking center.

I tried for quite some time to work out a "bigger picture" system so we could take the bandits to the local precincts or municipalities and book them there. This would save us a trip to central booking, which could mean a trip of thirty miles or more. My system would make use of St. Louis County's "pickup" van. The pickup van travels around and picks up bandits who are wanted by the county but who are arrested by other jurisdictions.

The local precincts resisted this process because some folks thought we were doing the fun part and making extra work for them by dumping our bandits on them. To me, it just made sense and would have saved considerable time so we could go catch more bandits. No such luck. As if we were fisherman, we were told, "You catch them; you clean them."

We had a warrant for a "lady bandit" named Mildred. Her file showed she was a white gal and known as a "biker broad." Apparently, Mildred worked as a stripper when she wasn't selling large amounts of dope for her motorcycle crew, which is what the warrant alleged.

I was behind the wheel, driving the three of us through St.

Louis City, heading toward a lead on a location for this lady bandit in St. Louis County. We noticed a building on fire ahead, about four city blocks in front of us. It appeared to be a four-family flat and was engulfed in flames.

Straight away I noticed two things: first, several fire trucks were blocking the street ahead of us in front of the fire. That made sense.

The second thing I noticed, which seemed very curious to me at the time, was a white guy who had all but flattened himself out, like Silly Putty, on a brick wall. The guy was leaning against the front of a building immediately ahead of us on the right side of the street. He appeared to be watching the fire and trying to hide at the same time.

"Behold, the guilty flee, thou no one pursues".

The neighborhood we were in is a notoriously high-crime area located in the near north side of the city. The area is racially mixed; however, it is predominantly black. So the presence of this white guy was not necessarily out of place. But his behavior certainly commanded attention and set off my "bandit radar."

I made the next right turn and circled the block. As I turned back onto the street, we were a block behind the guy. He was now directly between the fire and us. He had moved further along the building toward the fire so he could get a better look. He was half squatting behind a six-inch pipe that ran up the side of the building.

"Oh, yeah, this is our Sparky," I said as I pulled our car to the curb.

We quietly slipped out of our car, which that day was a black Mercury station wagon with wood paneling on the side. We affectionately nicknamed this G ride the "Wally Wagon."

Sparky was so focused on the fire that he didn't have any idea we were there.

I drew my gun and said, "Hey, Sparky, what's up?"

Sparky immediately stood up. He was shaking like an autumn

leaf in a gale wind.

There were three of us standing around him. We were all wearing body armor with bold "POLICE" in yellow across the chest. We identified ourselves to him and began to ask questions in rapid succession.

"Where are you from? What are you doing here? What's your name?" Sometimes if you ask a silly question mixed in, you will get an honest answer, so I started asking, "Do your friends call you Sparky? Do you have a light? Do you like barbeque?"

Once the questioning started, Sparky dropped his head and started staring holes into the ground. He wouldn't look at us, but after the barbeque questions, he started answering.

"I have a friend who lives here, sir," he said quietly.

"In the building that is on fire?" I asked.

"Yes, sir," he replied.

"Sooo, you just came from that building that's on fire?"

"Yes, sir," he said again.

"Can you show me some identification?" I asked.

He took out his wallet, which was virtually empty. He reached inside the wallet and pulled out a small piece of newspaper clipping. It was an obituary. He began reading it to us and said it was his grandmother's obituary. He said he was the guy listed as the grandson.

"I'm sorry to hear about your grandmother," I said. "I was kind of holding out hope for a driver's license, a picture identification of some kind, a library card, you know, something like that."

As we were talking with him, we noticed a stringy, wood-shaving-like substance on his shoes and pant legs. It resembled sawdust.

"Hey, Sparky, what's with the sawdust on your feet?" I asked. He started shaking his feet and legs to get the debris off and told us he worked in a "sawdust factory."

"Sawdust factory?" I asked. It was so ludicrous, I didn't even laugh. "And why is it you're standing right here at this very moment?" I asked.

He looked up from the ground, right into my eyes, and said, "I like to watch the fires, sir."

Sensing a confession, I added, "I know you set this fire, but how many other fires have you set?"

With that his head and shoulders slump downward and he said, "You're right, sir. I did it."

"Hold that thought," I said. I pulled out my Miranda card and read him his constitutional rights.

I then asked him to go on.

Sparky continued his admission about having set the fire. He told us his real name and we began addressing him accordingly. We cuffed him up at that point and contacted the fire department and police department's arson investigators to swing by and pick him up.

It was about 2:40 p.m. by now, and just as we were wrapping up, one of the officers got a call from his municipal department. They needed him to come back in for something or other. So we took off our vests and climbed into our G ride and headed for the office so he could grab his car and go.

There were just two of us from the CUFF unit left on that day. We began to arrange our warrants for the next day's hunt. I picked up Mildred the lady bandit's warrant and placed it on top.

We had been looking for this gal for about a month now. I had tried a telephone number we had developed for her. No one had ever answered when I had called over several weeks. I dialed the phone one more time. After about the third ring, I heard, "Hello?" A man's voice.

"Hi, is Mildred home?" I asked casually.

He told me she just stepped out, but she'd be back in five minutes.

I then explained to him who I was and why I was calling. The guy said he was Mildred's husband, they knew about the warrant, and they'd been saving up money for an attorney. He promised they'd be in and surrender to us the next day.

That is not likely, I thought as we amicably disconnected.

I asked the officer if he wanted to run out and get one more. "Of course!" he replied.

Fifteen minutes later, we were outside the door of the address we had on Mildred. There was a real beater of a car in the driveway.

The house was a single-story ranch style with a carport instead of a garage. It was located in a quiet neighborhood in North St. Louis County near the airport. The area was typically hardworking blue-collar folks. The houses in this block were all well kept, except for Mildred's.

The day was now uncomfortably warm, and it had turned out to be a long one. This last warrant of the day was for a lady bandit—easy enough—so we left our bulletproof vests in the car.

We approached the house for a knock and a talk. We had already called the local municipality from the car and advised them what we were doing. They said a marked unit would be on the way in the next twenty minutes or so. We told them we would make contact with the residents in the meantime.

The residence was really in a state of disrepair. The yard was un-kept. Large, fresh oil stains covered the driveway. The paint was peeling, and several windows were cracked. It was indicative of a family experiencing drug abuse, as were so many of the houses we visited.

I knocked on the door, and a woman appeared a few minutes later. The gal was wearing a man's button-up shirt like it was a robe. The shirt was a mechanic's shirt with a man's name embroidered over the pocket. Mildred's husband had told me earlier that he worked as a mechanic. The woman's hair was disheveled, but it was the same length and color as Mildred's. This woman had no makeup on, and the photo we had of Mildred showed her all dolled up, stripper-style. So, I was very confident that we now had Mildred to take into custody.

The woman protested that she was not Mildred. She said her name was Myrtle, but she didn't have identification with her. This seemed at odds with the purse I could see on top of a table across the room. The residence was all but empty of furnishings. A wooden crate had been flipped on its side, and a board was placed on top for the dining room table. There was a folding lawn chair on one side and one of those bright orange plastic molded chairs that was popular in the 1950s on the other side.

I could hear other voices coming from inside the residence, and I asked her who else was home. She claimed she was there by herself. This clearly didn't make sense, since I had talked with her husband twenty minutes before and now I heard voices.

The list of people who think I'm an oddball is probably fairly long. However, I don't normally hear voices unless there are people to go along with them. So at this point, we placed Mildred in handcuffs.

I drew my weapon and called out, "Police! Is anybody here?" in a loud, commanding voice.

My partner remained in the front room with a cuffed Mildred, but placed himself in a position to watch my back. The house was small, about a thousand square feet total. I made my way down the hall toward the voices. As I got close, I could make out that the sounds were coming from a television. However, I continued calling out, which is protocol, while doing a protective sweep. There was no answer to my commands.

The courts recognized the inherent danger of police work and fugitive apprehensions specifically. There is case law, which allows us to conduct what is referred to as a "protective sweep." It's not exactly a search; it's more like a brief walk through to ensure no one else is present who might cause us harm or present a danger. It also allows us to look in the immediate area around the fugitive, for weapons.

I observed a duffle bag in the center of a bedroom that is

otherwise empty. I passed another bedroom and the hall bathroom. All empty. I moved along toward the last bedroom. As I entered the room, I noticed a television on top of a cardboard box. Next to the television there was a spoon, a lighter, a screw-on soda cap, and a syringe.

I was guessing someone in the house used heroin. The heroin kit might have been Mildred's, but it might also have belonged to the fellow I just discovered in the room.

As I neared the room I observed a mattress on the floor. There appeared to be a pair of boots hanging off the side of the mattress with a pair of feet still inside of them. I again called out, "Police! Is anyone here?" No reply.

I used a technique we call "slicing the pie." It's when you slowly move around an obstacle slicing the scene into small pieces at a time. The method allows you to remain concealed while you make observations. I continued these slow movements until I had the guy in full view.

The guy was just lying there, staring at the television set. He appeared to be very relaxed, almost catatonic, and he hadn't said a thing so far.

Perhaps I'm being rude, I thought, annoyed with him already for not responding. So I introduced myself to him over the top of my Glock semiautomatic pistol.

I personally like the Glock pistol. It's lightweight, reliable, and carries more than fifteen rounds of "bandit repellent." Which, comes in handy in situations such as this. I called back to my partner to let him know Mildred had lied to us about being alone.

The guy finally looked up at me and asked, "What's wrong, boss?"

In prison, inmates often address guards as "boss." I was very wary. I told the guy to stand up, interlock his fingers, and place his hands behind his head. He was very compliant with my commands. However, as he stood up he kept his left leg stiff and got up in a very awkward motion.

I called out to my partner that we were on our way up to the front of the house. I positioned myself behind the guy, and I grabbed his hands tightly with my left hand. I noticed the handgrip of a revolver sticking out of his left rear pants pocket. I immediately commanded him to stop and put him down on his knees with his ankles crossed. I placed him in handcuffs and removed the revolver from his pocket.

"Why the gun?" I asked him.

He calmly responded that he found it in a vacant lot. He said he was going to turn it in at the gun buy-back program for some cash. At the time, the St. Louis City Police Department was purchasing guns with no questions asked.

The gun was an "Ivor-Johnson" five shot .38-caliber revolver. The weapon was a very old gun and was loaded with five "lead nose" rounds of .38-caliber "short" ammunition.

I asked the guy his name, and he told me he was Oscar Blasing Conner. His name didn't ring any bells with me.

I asked him if he had identification and if there were any warrants out on him. Oscar said he shouldn't be wanted, because he just got out of the joint three months ago and hadn't committed any crimes since he had been out.

Now, I'm a life member of the National Rifle Association (NRA), and I believe in the right to keep and bear arms, especially by law-abiding citizens in their own homes. But ole' Oscar here just admitted to being a convicted felon in possession of a firearm and fresh out of incarceration. I quickly unloaded the gun and secured it.

Oscar told me his wallet and identification were in the duffle bag in the other bedroom. I retrieved the bag, where I found his wallet, as well as four "00" buck shotgun shells inside.

In the meantime, my partner searched the purse on the table and found identification showing that the woman we had in custody was likely not Mildred. Her name was Myrtle. I have found a lot of false identities over the years while chasing bandits, so once I got Oscar to the front room, I called dispatch and ran both Oscar's and Myrtle's information.

A few minutes later dispatch advised us that Myrtle was wanted for felony bad checks from St. Louis County, and that Oscar is not wanted; however, he was currently on parole for armed robbery.

How about them apples? I thought. This gal was not Mildred, but she was wanted. I asked them both about Mildred, and they both swore they didn't know her. I found out later that Mildred and her husband had moved out of that address two weeks earlier and had forwarded the telephone number to their new residence. That tidbit of information would have been nice to have from her husband when we spoke a few hours earlier.

The local police unit we called for had still not arrived. It was now 4:10 p.m., roughly an hour after we had requested backup that was supposed to have arrived in twenty minutes.

I contacted the United States Attorney's office. I talked with Assistant U.S. Attorney Richards, who was nicknamed the "Dean of Prosecutors" and who was the supervisor of "The Gun Club." This is the unit in the U.S. Attorney's Office that handles violent offender cases.

I briefed AUSA Richards about what we had and gave him a quick rundown on Oscar's history. I told him that I could book him in as a "hold for safe keeping," and we could bring him in tomorrow. AUSA Richards gave me the okay and said he'd begin working up a "criminal complaint."

A criminal complaint initially bypasses the grand jury process. The U.S. Attorney prepares an affidavit regarding the facts of the criminal violation alleged. The agent or law enforcement officer swears that the statement is true and correct to the best of his or her knowledge and belief. If the judge finds probable cause to believe the subject has committed the offense, you then have an arrest warrant.

The CUFF officer and I are headed to the St. Louis County Jail with Oscar and Myrtle in tow. As we neared the jail I got a call from AUSA Richards. He told me to go ahead and bring Oscar downtown to the Marshals office. He had spoken with the Magistrate Judge, who wanted to see the defendant now instead of tomorrow. Richards told me he'd work up a criminal complaint before I arrived.

We dropped Myrtle off at the St. Louis County Jail in Clayton, then with Oscar still in tow, headed to downtown St. Louis to the Marshals office.

We had Oscar, his ID, his revolver, and his four shotguns shells. I brought them because they were evidence of the crime of being a convicted felon in possession of ammunition. That's a separate charge under federal law.

As we dropped off Oscar in the holding area, he told me he would be getting "heroin sick" in a few hours. Heroin addicts suffer from withdrawal syndrome if they go without the drug for too long. I thanked him for the information, and I could see he was beginning to get agitated. I passed the information along to the detention officer.

I met up with AUSA Richards in his office and we went over the complaint. It was perfect, without need for any editing. Richards called the judge and we were instructed to come down to chambers. As we arrived at the judge's chambers, two FBI agents I knew were leaving. They had "John Doe" warrants for the arrest of the two bandit robbers who had been terrorizing the local community.

In rare cases, the FBI will obtain John Doe warrants for the arrest of persons they know have committed a crime, without knowing the bandits' true identities. Later I found out that, in this case, they had bank surveillance photographs of two subjects robbing a bank. They just didn't know the bandits' true identities yet. Since the FBI had a team of some thirty agents and other officers waiting for these warrants, the two agents kept power-walking right by us with a polite nod.

The judge came out of the office and said he wanted to see Oscar because he'd be working overtime tonight anyway. It was now 4:50 p.m., and the FBI planned on working late on their investigation today. They told the judge they might need search warrants later that night, so he chose to stay there and keep working.

The judge took the complaint into the front office and waved for us to follow him into his chambers. He read as he walked. He took a seat in his brown leather chair behind his massive desk. I stood in front of the desk while he read, a residual behavior from standing at attention in my Marine Corps days.

I glanced down at the judge's desk. Directly in front of me was an 8x10-inch glossy black-and-white photograph of a guy holding a sawed-off pump shot gun.

It was the surveillance photo of two guys robbing a bank. I figured these were the two guys the FBI just got John Doe warrants for.

I pointed to the guy on the left in the photo. "That's Oscar, Judge."

"Excuse me?" he said, looking up from the complaint.

AUSA Richards laughed out loud. "That's a good one, Luke," he said. He knew the Marshals Service and the FBI sometimes compete against each other and don't always get along.

They think I am kidding, I realized. The judge started chuckling also, getting the joke. I reached down and picked up the photograph. I tapped on the picture, looked at them dead serious, and said, "Really, gentlemen, this guy is Oscar, the guy in my complaint. He's the guy I arrested with the gun in his pocket this afternoon."

They realized I was not kidding now. The judge, still smiling, picked up his telephone to call the FBI.

The two FBI agents quickly returned, and we worked up a search warrant for the address where my partner and I had arrested Myrtle and Oscar. They also sent agents to the county jail to interview Myrtle. She got a sweet deal, I'm sure. Myrtle "came in" on Oscar and also identified his partner, who the FBI guys went after and arrested later that night.

Myrtle and her husband were semi-homeless heroin addicts who had met Oscar and his partner while scoring dope. Oscar and his cohort used Myrtle to rent the house we found them in. They were one big happy family for half a minute.

The judge issued a warrant on the complaint we filed charging Oscar with being a convicted felon in possession of a firearm and ammunition. We later had to amend the complaint because the gun he had on him was old enough that it qualified as an antique. Oscar must have thought he was an Old West bank robber, so he needed an Old West gun. But the bullets and shotgun shells were modern enough to convict him. The government also charged Oscar on both of the bank robberies.

I testified against Oscar in both state and federal court. He was convicted on everything including the attempted murder of the young man shot in the neck in the fast-food restaurant incident. Oscar Blasing Conner received a life sentence in state court and the maximum ten years confinement in his federal case. Both of the judges ordered his sentences to run wild.

As I sat in the witness chair during one of the trials, I thought about that warm autumn afternoon when I met Oscar. Myrtle's husband and Oscar's partner were not there that day. The sawed-off shotgun in the bank robbery picture was missing, too. Likely Oscar's partner had it on him while they were running whatever errand. Our odds would have gone way down with four bandits, three guns, extra ammunition, and me without my vest.

I had left my body armor in the car because it was late in a long day, and I underestimated what we would find while we were chasing a "lady bandit." I thought about how fortunate I was that the Lord was watching over me that day. I have never left my vest in the car again ... ever.

WILLARD E. BYRD

STORY NINE

"It ain't what you don't know that gets you into trouble. It's what you know for sure that just ain't so."

– Mark Twain

St. Louis City Police Detective Benny Gary hung up the phone and turned to his partner, Bill Frailly. "He's there now. My guy said he's in room 106."

The "he" Gary was referring to was checked into Silkey's Hotel under the name Sam Watson. He was selling "buttons" of Mexican black tar heroin.

Gary had instructed his informant known as Slicko to buy two buttons of heroin from a new guy who had been showing up at Silkey's Motel. This new batch of black tar heroin was rumored to be good stuff among users and dealers alike. Two out of ten known users to date had visited the emergency room on their way to the morgue. It was that good.

Slicko had scored three buttons from Sam Watson just ten minutes before. He used one of the heroin buttons shortly before he called Gary, but before Slicko got crazy high he called the detective as instructed. Some folks snort the stuff, but Slicko "rode" a needle or injected it straight into his veins. The plan was to meet Slicko in the alley behind the England and Son's

Wing House, located near Grand and Page. Detectives Gary and Frailly would jump out on the informant and appear to be "rousting" him, or stopping and frisking him. They would let Slicko go on his way a few minutes later after slipping him fifty bucks on the sly for his help. He would give them the two buttons of heroin he had purchased. He wouldn't mention the third button he bought for his own use.

Detectives Bill Frailly and Benny Gary had been partners for three years. They were the only "salt-and-pepper" crew in the Sixth District's Detective Bureau at the time, meaning one white officer and one black officer. They worked well together. Even the other officers would joke that Frailly and Gary seemed to be everywhere and know everything. The bandits hated them because they worked so well together and were successful.

The St. Louis Metropolitan Police Department's Sixth District Station was located on West Florissant Avenue at the time, in the Walnut Park neighborhood. The Sixth District's commander, Captain McDonough, stopped Bill Frailly in the hallway. The captain told Bill he wanted the guy selling the "killer heroin."

"Enough said, Captain," Frailley responded. Frailley was already on his radio to Benny asking him to leave the shooting range and head back up to the Sixth District.

That had been four days ago.

Slicko was a new informant and worked with Detective Frailley. He seemed pretty good and had already provided some good stuff on his own. But, like all heroin junkies, he could be a little shaky at times. At Frailley's request, Slicko had gone into Silkey's Motel and asked if they had a room available near the center of the back building away from the street.

The man behind the desk opened the register and placed his finger halfway down the page. "One-oh-six," he said in his heavy Punjab accent. Slicko was checking out the names on the list. He saw the name Sam Watson written in next to 108. Slicko said he would like to see the room's location to see if it would suit him before he paid. He walked around the side of the building where the two detectives were waiting and gave them the news.

Detective Frailly called dispatch asking for three Mobile Reserve Officers to meet him down the street from Silkey's. Mobile Reserve is a unit of seasoned officers who are used for special assignments or to back up district officers in high-crime areas. Mobile Reserve Officers wear a special patch with lightning bolts. They aren't assigned to a specific district, and they don't handle routine radio calls.

Frailley didn't have time to apply for a warrant. Sam Watson would sell what was left of his buttons and be out of there soon. They would conduct a "knock and talk" to see what developed from there.

The big red-headed Irishman from Mobile Reserve almost knocked the door from its hinges with his first knock. The guy staying in room 108 poked his head out of his door to see what was going on. Detective Gary asked the man to get back in his room and close the door. Instead, the man bolted from the hotel room past Gary and ran across the hotel's parking lot toward Natural Bridge. As he rounded the corner of the motel's front office, he ran headlong into the third Mobile Reserve Officer.

During the search of Sam Watson's hotel room, the officers discovered a pistol (stolen), a shotgun, and seventeen buttons of black tar heroin. Captain McDonough would be pleased. Detectives Frailly and Gary had his guy.

Detective Gary wrote the report exactly as it had happened. He was stunned when the Circuit Attorney's Office refused to issue the case. The Assistant Circuit Attorney at the warrant office argued the search was illegal and the evidence would be suppressed.

"No way am I going to bring this case in front of a grand jury," the ACA said sternly.

Too bad Watson wasn't a convicted felon, Frailly thought.

Maybe the feds would look at him if he was. Otherwise, there was no way the United States Attorney's Office would issue a warrant on seventeen buttons of heroin with just an SIS on his record.

It was just as well. Sam Watson had pleaded guilty to three burglaries when he was just seventeen years old. But that had been nearly twenty years ago. Since then he hadn't been in any trouble. It appeared that Sam had been rehabilitated, from his record.

In reality, Sam Watson had been dead for nearly twenty years.

At 3:12 a.m. the next morning, the man from room 108 in Silkey's Motel walked out the front door of the police headquarters at 1200 Clark Street a free man. He was very pleased with the outcome, and he smiled as he made his way across Tucker Boulevard. A gray Lincoln Town Car was waiting at the curb, its engine idling. The driver was a petite woman who waited patiently for her passenger.

The Lincoln was parked behind the Federal Courts and Customs House at 1114 Market Street. The man chuckled as he climbed into the waiting car. He knew the federal courthouse intimately. He'd been convicted of federal crimes inside a courtroom in that very building eighteen years ago. As the Lincoln pulled away from the curb, the man laid Sam Watson to rest for a second time.

I flipped through the fresh stack of warrants on my desk and I came across Willard E. Byrd's file. Byrd was wanted for violation of his parole. He'd been out for a while and hadn't bothered to see his federal parole officer.

This case seemed interesting. Willard was an old-time gangster from the city's north side. He had grown up learning his trade in the ghetto of the housing project "Pruitt-Igo." Pruitt-Igo was an island of high-rise public housing buildings near Jefferson Avenue and Cass Avenue on the "near north side" of St. Louis. A gangster by the name of "Slim" Stones controlled most of the crime on that island: murders, robberies, beatings, heroin sales. Many of his prodigies would later become notorious gangsters in their own right.

According to his file, Byrd started out as a burglar and petty thief. He had three convictions for burglary by the time he was nineteen years old. Those convictions landed him eleven months in the city's workhouse, a place to warehouse young men while they awaited their trials. The liberals convinced themselves it was a nice way to help rehabilitate young men instead of sending them to prison. These were a rough eleven months for Byrd, and his dark side exploded. He'd been sentenced to three years in state prison, but a deal was made and the judge gave him time served and placed him on probation. Byrd walked out of the workhouse a very changed person.

Byrd's burglar buddies, Sam Watson and Kenny Jackson, had both rolled over on him. Jackson was just the lookout man and he was the youngest of the trio, so he wasn't charged. Watson was charged, but he received a Suspended Imposition of Sentence (SIS) and he never spent a night in jail, just like the cops had promised him.

When Byrd was released from confinement, he convinced Watson and Jackson that all was forgiven. He had even lined up a new score that would make them all very rich. He ensured them this would be the last burglary for all three. Well, it was the last for two of them. Both Watson and Jackson disappeared after that night. Byrd gave up burglary and branched off into the drug trade.

Byrd wasn't any more stealth at selling drugs than he had been at burglary. He caught a federal case a few months later. Byrd was convicted of possession with the intent to distribute heroin and being a convicted felon in possession of a firearm. This firearm was a fully automatic submachine gun. He spent the next sixteen plus years in various federal prisons.

Watson and Jackson were distant cousins who had moved

to St. Louis with their families when they were both in grade school. Their families would occasionally make the trek back to Mississippi to visit relatives. It was rumored that the two would-be burglars had moved back to Mississippi to start new lives. It was also rumored by some that Byrd had made them disappear.

I took a copy of Byrd's fingerprints to the St. Louis Metropolitan Police Department's (SLMPD) identification unit. Lieutenant Rob Hanson was in charge of the unit at that time. All of the officers and units of the SLMPD are great to work with—no kidding. Lt. Hanson's unit was no exception. I relied heavily on them for photographs of bandits I was chasing, fingerprint matches, and other tools of the trade.

Lt. Hanson was great to work with and to work for. I would later work under his command in the Fugitive Apprehension Strike Team (The FAST unit) when he was promoted to lieutenant colonel. Hanson later became the chief of police, and I lost contact with him for a while. I would work for him again when he retired from the police department and became the United States Marshal for the Eastern District of Missouri.

I dropped off Byrd's fingerprints and picked up a booking photo of him. His booking photo wasn't of much use since it was nearly twenty years old. However, the booking photo of Sam Watson was great, and it looked very similar to Byrd's mug shot. Watson's photo was a fresh one.

I reviewed Willard's file and tried to figure out this puzzle. I put together that Willard had been arrested using the identity of Sam Watson. Both Byrd's and Watson's fingerprints were old enough that they were not in the Automated Fingerprint Identification System (AFIS). The arresting officers were Detective Bill Frailly and Benny Gary. I knew Frailly and I'd heard of Gary. I gave them a call to find out why the case went south on them.

Watson's case was never issued due to evidentiary problems. His booking photo and fingerprints went into a file under his name. Watson's fingerprints were mailed to the FBI's fingerprint identification section. Case closed. The firearms and heroin were destroyed six months later.

A month later, Lt. Hanson's unit was notified the fingerprints for Watson matched Byrd's. The two files were reconciled, but no case was pending and Byrd wasn't wanted by the feds yet, so there had been nothing else to do.

I contacted the Missouri Department of Revenue (DOR) and requested a copy of the drivers licenses for Byrd, Watson, and their other partner, Jackson. Several days later I received the licenses of all three subjects. All three of them were current and contained a picture of Byrd.

Detective Gary told me they had recovered a vehicle from in front of Watson's room that night. The car, a gray Lincoln Town Car, had been left there with the keys inside. Gary ran the plate and contacted the owner, Ms. Ebony Lewis.

Ms. Lewis told Gary she did not know Sam Watson. She said her son had borrowed the car the night before and hadn't returned home yet. She thanked the detective and assured him that her son would pay severely for his actions. Gary thought it was odd Ms. Lewis hadn't asked about the well-being of her son. She then went to the motel and recovered the vehicle.

I did some research on Ebony Lewis and found out her son, Willard Lewis, was seventeen years old. Now how about that for coincidence? I also found out she worked with Tonya Byrd, who was Willard Byrd's sister and also the owner of Silkey's Motel.

Lewis had recently moved into a townhouse complex in North St. Louis County. Her townhouse was near the intersection of Highway 367 and Redman Road. It became my new favorite hangout.

I cruised by the townhouse any time I was in the area. Several times I had seen Lewis and her son Willard Jr., come and go from the residence in a white Mustang. I hadn't seen Willard Byrd or the gray Lincoln.

One evening while I was out chasing other bandits, I made one of my routine passes by the complex. There it was. Parked across the street from Lewis's townhouse was a gray Lincoln Town Car. I ran the plates and they came back "not on file," which was no surprise. I quietly exited my G ride and looked inside the Lincoln. I felt the engine; it was still warm. A copy of the latest P.M Swirl newspaper was sitting on the front passenger seat.

The P.M. Swirl was a St. Louis neighborhood newspaper that specialized in posting bandit photos and bandit stories. I had often used the newspaper with excellent results. I had placed a photo of Willard Byrd in the paper, but I left out the story about what happened at Silkey's Motel so he wouldn't catch on.

As I looked through the windshield of the Lincoln, I could clearly see the photo of Byrd in the newspaper. I called Jeb Graves, a deputy from my office, and asked him to come out. He in turn called in two more deputies.

Graves and I went to the front door, and I put the other two deputies to watch the back door. I had spoken with a neighbor a few weeks before who confirmed Willard Byrd lived there. I had a federal arrest warrant for Byrd and I knew everything was in good shape legally. I didn't have a search warrant but, you see, I didn't need one. "The Supremes," those nine black-robed justices, told me so.

When you have an arrest warrant for a subject, you can enter their residence at any time if you have a reasonable belief they are present. You can't randomly search for contraband, but anything you find in "plain view" can be used against them.

I used my neighborly knock on the front door. I could hear a woman's voice from inside asking who it was.

In a conversational tone I said, "It's the police. We're U.S. Marshals."

"Who is it?" I heard her say from right inside on the other side of the door.

"Police, U.S. Marshals, open the door," I loudly commanded.

She shouted, "It's the police!" and I heard thundering footsteps running from the back of the house to the front and up the stairs. I kicked in the front door, and a moment later I was standing in the doorway. Graves, who also had his gun drawn, covered the woman and a young man seated on a couch in the front room. I caught a fleeting glimpse of Byrd at the top of the stairs.

I ran to the top of the staircase as Byrd threw something into the closet and became pistol paralyzed when he saw me and my gun.

"Don't you make me shoot you, Byrd. If I do, you will die, and you don't want to die today. Not like this, not in front of your woman and your son."

He was looking at me, checking for any waiver. He realized I really meant it. With that he surrendered, and I placed him in handcuffs.

We sat Byrd on the couch in the front room with his girlfriend and his son. When I conducted the protective sweep of the rest of the house, I found the leather bag he tossed into his closet. The bag had his dope, a Glock semiautomatic handgun, and an Ohaus brand, three-beam scale. The bag also contained his identification in the name of Kenny Jackson, several casino receipts, and several keys.

Byrd was in a rage for the rest of the night. I had read the Miranda Rights off the card, and let's just say he didn't say anything nice to us. After a while, we packed up the evidence and called it a night. I drove Byrd to the Jennings, Missouri, City Jail and dropped him off for the night. Graves followed me since we had driven in separate cars. The other two deputies were long gone.

As I neared the jail I conversationally said to Byrd, "I hope you didn't have that pistol to use on us!"

He looked up at me and said, "No, man, you know I had it

because of all of them home invasions."

I wasn't completely surprised when I found out Willard was fighting the case. He wouldn't plead guilty because he was facing a fifteen-year mandatory minimum sentence in prison. He hired a defense attorney who was a complete jerk and who would later end up in federal prison himself.

I was surprised when he decided to take the case to trial without a jury. That's what is referred to as a bench trial. The defendant proceeds to trial without the benefit of a jury to hear the case. Typically, that's what we call a "slow guilty plea."

The judge who tried the case was one of the best, most respected judges on the bench in our district. There was no denying he was certainly one of my favorites. He took charge of the courtroom, did not tolerate nonsense, and let common sense rule the day. He has a nephew who is a syndicated conservative radio talk show host on the East Coast. I was very surprised Byrd opted for a bench trial in that court.

At the end of the trial, Willard was found guilty and sent to federal prison for twenty-seven years. The following week I happened to be in that judge's courtroom on another matter. During a recess the judge called me to the bench. He told me that Byrd's attorney had called me everything but a nice guy. Sore loser. We had a good laugh over that.

Two weeks after his sentencing, I had the pleasure of transporting Byrd to the federal prison in Greenville, Illinois. It's unusual in federal law enforcement for an officer to arrest someone on the street, take him through trial, and deliver him to federal prison. I have had this happen at least twice in my career.

That was the last I saw of Willard E. Byrd, but not the last that I would hear from him.

About two years later, an attorney named Jack Boatswain (JB) from the St. Louis City Counselor's Office contacted me. JB asked me if I remembered a case involving Williard E. Byrd. I assured him I remembered the case and asked him how I could be of service.

Since Byrd had a lot of time on his hands in federal prison, he thought he would spend it suing the City of St. Louis and various other entities. That was what he did to fill time between filing baseless complaints with law enforcement agencies such as mine. (I was notified of the latest one twelve years after I had arrested him.)

I ran down some old files for JB and filled him in on as much as I could remember about this "jail Byrd." As an attorney, JB was a stud. He did all of the work to get Byrd's case quashed in federal court. I hope my assistance helped him in some small way.

Each time I drive near Highway 367 and Redman Road, I think about that not-so-free Byrd still serving time there and I smile.

PROFESSOR NORMAL

STORY TEN

"I fear there will be no future for those who do not change."
— Louis L'Amour

At precisely ten minutes after one in the afternoon, the telephone rang in Manfred Zietzer's office. Zietzer was the bank president of Sveriges Riksbank, the Swedish national bank.

"Good morning. Is this Manfred Zietzer?" the caller asked in English with a British accent.

"Yes, sir, it is. How may I help you?" Zietzer replied in perfect English with just the hint of a Dutch accent.

"Good day, sir. I am Charles Bedford of the investment firm Kingsford, Holmes and Bedford of London," he offered as an introduction.

After an uncomfortable pause, while wondering how this stranger had gotten through on his direct phone line, Bank President Zietzer inquired, "Please excuse me, sir, I'm not familiar with your firm, but how may I assist you?"

"Yes, yes. I see," Bedford flushed and stammered, glancing up at the man across the desk from him. "I was calling in regards to the American citizen Alfred Normal and the fifty-million-dollar letter of credit issued to Mr. Normal from your bank."

"Excuse me, sir, but I'm quite sure I have no idea what you

are talking about!" gasped Zietzer, unable to contain his shock.

Bedford glanced quizzically at Normal.

Alfred Normal could tell from Bedford's body language and his half of the conversation that something was going terribly wrong.

Normal glanced at his Rolex watch and verified the time was now exactly 12:12 p.m. Greenwich Mean Time (GMT). He casually stood and excused himself to use the facilities. He whispered that he would be right back.

Normal hurried down the hallway past the restrooms. He used the rear stairwell to exit the building and come out onto Strand Street in London's financial district. He couldn't imagine what had gone wrong with his plan. He would have time to think about that during the twelve-hour trip back to the Isle of Man.

Normal would have walked away with a fifty-million-dollar letter of credit if he had only remembered one thing—there is a one-hour time difference between the United Kingdom and Sweden.

The Sveriges Riksbank Bank president was as precise with his time as he was with accounting for every krona. Normal's inside man at the bank had verified that Manfred Zietzer left his office at exactly twelve o'clock noon each day for lunch. Zietzer would be gone precisely one hour. This was more than enough time for Rudolph "Rudy" Heinz to waltz into Zietzer's office, pick up the telephone when it rang, and verify the information Bedford would provide about the letter of credit for Normal.

Heinz had been working at the Sveriges Riksbank for about nine months. Each day at exactly twelve noon, he would wait for Zietzer to leave his office before he entered and emptied the trash cans. Heinz had been able to provide Normal with copies of the bank's letters of credit along with their accompanying documentation.

On this day, Heinz had waited by Zietzer's desk until the last minute for the telephone call that never came. Was something wrong? He wondered. Had Normal pulled the deal off without Bedford making the confirmation call? Heinz couldn't imagine Bedford not calling to confirm a five-million-dollar letter of credit. Heinz might have flown into full panic mode if he had known Normal was actually setting his sights for ten times that amount.

Heinz smiled, reassuring himself. Yes, that must be it. After all, Alfred Normal was a slick one, wasn't he? This would be Heinz's last day working as a janitor for the bank. He would wait until Sunday and then he would catch a flight from Stockholm to the Isle of Man where he would meet Normal to pick up his cut of the money, two million dollars plus a ten-thousand-dollar signing bonus. Normal had told Heinz to stay with the bank another two or three months to not arouse suspicion, but Heinz didn't see the need. With that kind of money, a man could disappear into the sun and sand, he assured himself.

Heinz had met Professor Alfred Normal, PhD, by chance in a tavern near the bank where he worked. The men had hit it off right from the start. Heinz had never really known a "Yank" American before then. This one was very friendly and was buying the drinks.

Heinz learned that Normal had tired of working in his field of chemical engineering. He quietly and conspiratorially told Heinz he had made a large sum of money during the past decade working for American oil companies. He loved traveling, but his investors had squandered a good portion of his savings.

Normal easily convinced Heinz that he had begun managing his own investments and he had made substantial gains in recouping the millions he'd lost. The financial field was his true calling, Normal sadly told Heinz, but he needed major backing to make a real impact.

Normal said he liked the way Europeans used "letters of credit" to guarantee financial investors. But he would need to work in the field for ten years at least before he could garner the backing of a large bank. The letters of credit themselves had worth and many investors traded them like currency. If only he could get ahead of the game somehow, Normal said as he fretted and stared desperately into his drink.

The letter of credit, he explained, was simply the bank's guarantee that they would back his financial decisions. Heinz didn't want to come across as stupid, since, after all, he worked in a bank. Heinz listened as Normal seemed to cook up a plan on the spot. Normal told Heinz that he could make them both rich if he had such a letter issued on a large bank such as Sveriges Riksbank.

The scheme Normal proposed to Heinz was that they would make up a "pretend" letter of credit from Sveriges Riksbank made out to Normal. No one would be hurt since they weren't selling it and no one would be the wiser. Heinz quickly agreed as he pictured what it would be like to be rich. He had no savings and squandered his income between this tavern and another down the street from his apartment.

This letter of credit would simply allow Normal access to a trading account at one of the large firms in London's financial district. With Alfred's inside knowledge of oil companies, his trades would be one hundred percent. He would make millions. And with a devilish look, Normal quietly told Heinz that if he wanted in that he would be rich, too.

Once Normal was established and successful, they would dispose of this play letter with no harm done, he had said. Normal and Heinz would both be very wealthy by then. Heinz's conscience kicked in, and he started to hem and haw and balk at the deal until Normal offered him a ten-thousand-dollar signing bonus on top of his two-million-dollar cut. A signing bonus was something none of Heinz's many jobs had offered and sounded so important.

Normal convinced Heinz to answer the telephone and

pretend to be the bank president, Zietzer. Once Heinz answered the British investor Bedford's questions, they would be home free. No one could possibly ever know it was Heinz on the phone. "Besides," Normal said, "as smooth as I am, Bedford might not even call to confirm."

I ran up to the Marshal Services office in the Federal Building to check my desk for any case updates or new files. I picked up the yellow sticky note and studied the scribbled mess. "See me ref Rolla MO from The Lithuanian Adonis TLA." I gathered the note was from our warrant coordinator, and I had a good laugh. A warrant coordinator with a sense of humor; who knew? I had investigated some bandit activity around Rolla, Missouri, recently, so I figured it was about one of them. Rolla is a college town located just about halfway between St. Louis and Springfield, Missouri. The University of Science and Technology at Rolla is well known for graduating great engineers and scientists.

"Hey there, Lithuanian Adonis, what's up?" I asked, laughing as I sat in an empty chair opposite his desk in his office.

"Don't you know the sheriff in Rolla?" TLA asked.

"I do," I said. "Dan Bancroft. He's a good man, and so are his people."

"Fine. That's what I needed to know. Washington DC is sending us a warrant for some jerk wanted in Sweden that they have come up empty on." As TLA handed me a file he said, "The guy's ex-wife is a professor at the University of Missouri engineering school in Rolla. They can't seem to locate the guy, so poke around and see what you can find. The Swedish authorities want this guy real bad, and I might get to fly to Sweden before I retire." TLA laughed.

"Color it done, mister!" I said, leaving his office.

I began poking around on one Alfred Bartholomew Normal, PhD, a fifty-six-year-old white male who didn't leave much of a trail to follow. Not that anything like a cold trail will stop me, so I started tracking what I could. We had the lead on where he might be now, but we also needed to build a file on him and find out where he had been.

About thirty years before, Normal had married a gal who was also a PhD in a related field to chemical engineering. They both had taught in the university circuit down in Texas for some time. Mrs. PhD also did some consulting work for the oil companies there.

From what I could see, she had left a much larger impact on their community than he did. Her PhD appeared to be the genuine deal.

Alfred Normal, on the other hand, liked to hang out in campus coffee houses, pubs, and sorority houses. He was a busy little bee with the young women. He and Mrs. PhD had been divorced twice, yet they got back together each time. I figured she must have been a liberal in her youth, because they married decades ago and she never took his name. She also tolerated his affairs.

I noticed that about six years ago, a university in the United Kingdom hired her as an adjunct professor. Mrs. PhD lived in the UK for about three years. Her address was on the Isle of Man. Sounds very 007-ish. Where in the United Kingdom is that? I laughed to myself.

Mrs. PhD had lived in Texas again briefly when she returned to the United States from Europe. She then moved to Rolla, Missouri, about two years ago and began teaching at the University of Missouri's engineering school. There ended her trail.

I sat down at the computer and began to hunt for Alfred. Straight away I found Mrs. PhD again. She had a Missouri driver's license and owned a Volvo sedan. Mrs. PhD's address showed up as an apartment in Rolla, and she also had a rural route number in Phelps County.

Alfred Normal, on the other hand, was nowhere to be found.

I wondered how he was getting around without a driver's license. His Texas license had long since expired. I found out they had a son together. The boy was Alfred Normal with a different middle name, so he was not "Junior." He lived in Texas where he was teaching and was enrolled in a doctoral program.

The kid had three vehicles registered to his urban address in Texas. That seemed very odd to me. The Ford Mustang I understood. The Ford F-150 pickup truck? Maybe. But a new Range Rover? I strongly doubted that. The Range Rover alone would have cost twice the kid's annual salary. Paying for his new Mustang and school would have been a huge financial burden.

I ran the Vehicle Identification Number (VIN) from the Range Rover and found a recent ticket in Phelps County. A Missouri Highway Patrolman had issued the ticket to Alfred Normal at a rural route address in Phelps County—the same rural route address that Mrs. PhD was connected with.

I called my friend at the Phelps County Sheriff's Department. "Good morning, Dan Bancroft, Phelps County Sheriff's Department, may I help you?"

"What are you doing and why not more?" I asked.

"Hey, now, the county tax dollars are hard at work here, son," he shot back.

"That's my line, mister!" I laughed.

"Did you federal fellows lose another bandit?" he asked.

"Not so much as I know, Dan. Why? Did you fellows find one?" I joked back. "That's actually why I'm calling."

I filled Sheriff Bancroft in about Alfred Normal, Mrs. PhD, and their son Alfred "Not Junior" Normal.

"I knew that fella was up to no good," Bancroft said when I finished briefing him. "We got a call about him several months ago. Not so much about him as a complaint about helicopters landing at his place and men in suits. We thought for a minute that the DEA had landed. It wasn't them though; we checked." Bancroft paused. "I'm still not sure who those folks were, maybe organized crime types."

Bancroft went on to tell me about several complaints the Phelps County Sheriff's Department had received on this guy. So many that they began calling him "Ab-Normal."

"He's a strange duck, Luke," Bancroft said.

"How come you guys haven't locked him up yet?" I inquired.

"He's a slippery fish. A real slick one," Bancroft said. "The complaints have all been civil in nature. He doesn't pay his bills on time if he does at all. He didn't honor contracts, stuff like that."

Bancroft explained that Alfred and Mrs. PhD had shown up in Phelps County a couple of years ago. She had an apartment in Rolla where she stayed half the time. Mr. "Ab-Normal" was building a fancy house—more accurately, a compound—out in a rural part of the county. On two occasions neighbors had called to complain about helicopters landing at the place. A sheriff's deputy had been dispatched both times, but Alfred wouldn't let them near his place without a search warrant.

The most recent time, after being called out to the rural address, the deputy had asked Alfred for some identification. He produced an international driver's license. The license was issued to A. Bart Normal, PhD, in the United Kingdom, Isle of Man.

"Do you want me to go grab him for you, Luke?" Bancroft asked.

"No, sir, not yet. I've got some more hoops to jump through first," I said.

I explained to Dan that I was simply trying to get a solid location on Alfred Bartholomew Normal. I would send the information back to Sweden via our Washington DC headquarters and Main Justice.

The Justice Department is made up of many agencies and bureaus. To name a few: the Federal Bureau of Investigation (FBI), the Drug Enforcement Agency (DEA), the Bureau of Prisons (USBOP), the U.S. Marshals Service, the Bureau of

Alcohol Tobacco and Firearms (ATF), etc. However, the area in DC where the Attorney General's staff resides is referred to as Main Justice.

The United States Marshals Service is responsible for locating and arresting foreign fugitives who are present in the United States if a treaty exists between the two countries. Sweden had requested that the United States of America see if Normal was here. Now that we had located him, we notified the country that we had located their bandit. Then, in this case, the Swedes requested a provisional warrant.

A provisional warrant is nothing more than a federal arrest warrant for the person named in an indictment and arrest warrant from another country. The U.S. Department of Justice component, the Main Justice, provides proof to the federal district court that a treaty exists between the countries and probable cause exists to believe the person named in their warrant is present in our jurisdiction.

Then, our district court issues an arrest warrant for that person and says, "Hey, U.S. Marshal, go get this person and bring him here."

A federal arrest warrant reads: "To the United States Marshal or his authorized representative, you are hereby commanded to go forth and arrest so-and-so and bring him or her before this court forthwith." To me that language means serious business. This isn't a request or an option; it is a command.

The process can be time-consuming, and all of the high-profile muckety-mucks come out of the woodwork to get involved if it is high profile enough to get media coverage. Truth is, if it was just law enforcement and the police in the originating country, things would be much easier.

Apparently the Swedes had all of their political and law enforcement ducks in a row, because the process on this case proceeded rapidly. I passed the information up the ladder and across the ocean. Two weeks later I was handed the provisional warrant for the arrest of one Alfred B. Normal.

The next day I headed south to Phelps County, Missouri, and met up with Sheriff Bancroft and his posse. I brought along two other deputies from my office, so in total we had five folks that morning heading out to the rural address.

As I drove down the long driveway leading to Normal's home, I realized Bancroft was correct in his description of the place as a compound. A large log-cabin-type lodge was sitting atop a knoll in the center of the property.

Surrounding the lodge were several out buildings. The buildings were all log-cabin-style garages and storage barns. These buildings were a good sixty yards away from the lodge and sat lower, not obscuring the view from the lodge. Nice lines of fire.

Fifty yards beyond them was a wrought iron fence. A hundred yards beyond the fence was a row of evergreens. All of the trees reached twenty feet into the air. I could see a pad where helicopters might land. The windsock told me the wind was coming out of the north.

Bancroft had a contact telephone number for Normal, so as we approached the front door, I called him.

"Hello?" came the greeting from a very effeminate male voice.

"Yeah, Alfred, this is Luke Adler. I'm from the United States Department of Justice, the Marshals Service. Can you come to your front door to talk to me about these helicopters?" I said as I climbed the stairs to the front door.

"I'll be right there," he said in a sing-song voice.

A man actually answered the door, but I was surprised. Alfred Normal looked nothing like I had imagined the guy who wooed college girls and investment bankers. He stood six feet three inches tall and weighed maybe one hundred seventy pounds. He looked almost like a skeleton in his T-shirt, surgical pants, and the orange bikini briefs I could see through the thin material. His salt-and-pepper colored hair was disheveled and his mustache needed a trim. He quickly stepped outside the door and pulled the door closed behind him.

I placed my foot in the threshold, stopping the door from shutting, and told him to stop.

"You are under arrest, Alfred. Is anyone else here with you?" I asked.

"No, I'm alone. Wait, arrest for what? What did I do? Arrested for what?" He asked in a shrill voice.

I opened the door. The other Deputy Marshals detained Alfred while Dan and I conducted a protective sweep of the residence. A protective sweep is standard protocol to make sure no one else is present who might do us harm. Immediately Dan and I observed loaded rifles placed near windows on all sides of the house. We unloaded the weapons and made them safe.

The entire time of the protective sweep, Alfred protested. "You can't be in here. Show me a warrant."

"I'll get to that in a moment, Alfred," I assured him. "But before we go any further, let me read you your rights." Then I read the Miranda Rights straight off my card.

"Now then, Alfred. You are under arrest for the Country of Sweden," I said.

"Is this about that letter of credit?" he asked in a flat voice.

"Why, yes, I think it is," I replied.

"Take these handcuffs off, please. I need to turn my computers off and change clothes," he ordered with an air of authority, putting his chin in the air.

"Here's the deal, Alfred. You're under arrest, and Uncle Sam says I get to be in charge today," I said. "So the handcuffs stay on, and I'll turn off your computers if you would like."

Normal clearly wasn't accustomed to taking orders from anyone. However, he got the hang of it in short order. He gave me very specific instructions on how to turn his computers off, all three of them.

"Why so many computers, Alfred?" I asked conversationally.

"Oh, those two are hooked into the Chicago Board of Trade. I trade on them daily," he said, nodding to the hardware sitting on a heavy-looking walnut desk. His voice had changed, deepened, and now his words were thick with superiority, almost like he was bored explaining it to the likes of us.

The third computer was located in a room near some files. The three files were labeled Sveriges Riksbank, Letters of Credit, and Kingsford, Holmes and Bedford. Gee, a clue maybe? I laughed out loud.

As I followed the instructions for shutting down the computer, I watched the screen and noticed some of the same names on files in the computer. There were also spread sheets with figures that added into hundreds of millions of dollars.

After shutting everything down as promised and locking up, we headed back to St. Louis, but first we made a stop at the Franklin County Jail in Union, Missouri. That is where Normal spent his first night incarcerated on behalf of Sweden.

"I won't be locked up with those animals!" he protested wildly, shaking his head. "I demand to be in a cell by myself."

"Hey, Alfred, whatever you can work out with these folks is fine by me. Knock yourself out."

I gave the Assistant United States Attorney (AUSA) the information regarding the arrest, including what I had seen on the computers. The attorney had been coordinating with Main Justice and the Swedish authorities all day and into the evening. They wanted to seize and search the computers in Alfred's house.

When I answered my telephone that evening, the Assistant United States Attorney sounded like a kid going to the circus. "Hey, Luke, can you come back down to our office tonight? We are preparing a search warrant for you to execute tomorrow and we need you to go over the affidavit."

"Do you mind if I bring my daughter with me? She just got accepted to law school, and she is interested," I said.

"Tell her to come on down," he exclaimed and we disconnected.

"Hey, Kiddo. You want to go with your pops to swear out a search warrant?" I asked my daughter, Danielle. At the time she was in her early twenties and had just been accepted to the St. Louis University School of Law.

"Sure, Pops," she eagerly replied and literally ran down the hall to her room to get ready.

"How about you, Biggie?" I asked my thirteen-year-old son, Ethan.

"Are you going to execute the bandit tonight, Dad?" he asked quietly.

"No, son, it's a search warrant that we're going to execute, not the bandit," I said. "Tonight we're just going to talk with lawyers and judges."

"No, thanks," he said and returned his attention to his favorite movie, Tommy Boy.

"All right then, Kiddo, it's just you and me," I called down the hallway in the direction of Danielle's room.

Danielle hung in there with me until late that night. We made it to Judge Terrance Alderman's house just before midnight. What a class act he is. He was a great federal prosecutor and he was even better as a judge. As he went over the warrant, he read out loud and stopped to explain everything to Danielle.

He signed the warrant and wished us good luck. "I expect to see you in my court someday, young lady."

Danielle smiled and blushed crimson. I thanked the judge and we headed home. Secretly I hoped she'd be a federal prosecutor.

I returned to Normal's home in rural Phelps County, Missouri, the next day and brought several more law enforcement officers with me. We executed the search warrant, seizing Alfred's computers and pertinent files.

As is turned out, Normal had swindled some Americans out of their hard-earned cash, too. He made off with well over a million dollars from an investment firm in Florida. Normal also successfully gained control of about ten million dollars to trade within the stock market. He didn't let it all ride in the market; he had immediately transferred 1.4 million dollars to his personal accounts and spent it. When we went through his computers, we found he was in the process of "laundering" and transferring another ten million dollars to personal accounts.

So, we deduced, the guys in the suits flying around in choppers must have been the money-laundering firm.

The biggest problem with Normal getting caught was that a lot of guys in the drug trade used that firm to launder their money. That must have been the reason for the helicopter visits and all of the loaded rifles strategically placed around his house. They were all good weapons, .223 and .308-caliber semiautomatic rifles.

In the end, Normal's arrest was really a rescue mission. I suppose, once we got involved, the "helicopter guys" were afraid to come back and whack him.

The Internal Revenue Service volunteered to search the computer for Uncle Sam in this investigation. And as luck would have it, they found numerous violations of the IRS code.

Normal, in true "I'm-better-than-all-of-this" form, fought the extradition to Sweden. He lost that fight. However, he did beat the charges in Sweden. The court there found him not guilty.

Normal wasn't so fortunate back here in the United States.

Like most bandits, Normal didn't pay taxes on his illicit income. Also, as so often happens, he used the mail in his scheme, and some of the stolen funds were transferred by wire— both federal offenses. He was found guilty on several charges as a result of the search of his computers. Altogether, Normal was sentenced to nine years in federal prison.

To the best of my knowledge, Normal has served his time and should be out of prison by now.

As a side note, Danielle graduated law school, passed the bar, and became an attorney. Now, adding to her list of nicknames, I often refer to her as "the counselor." She's the total package. She inherited her mom's beauty, charm, wit, and brains.

Our "Biggie" son, Ethan, still loves to watch Tommy Boy. And occasionally, when he isn't out with his friends and there is nothing special on television, he will seek me out and ask about the bandits I've been chasing.

Heinz was arrested and prosecuted before the warrant went out on Normal. Heinz rolled over on Normal from the get-go. Apparently the Europeans (Swedes) don't like anyone messing around with their banking system. They went after Normal straight away.

Mrs. PhD was not found to be involved in the crimes, but I can't imagine she didn't know about the schemes of the man she married three times.

Whenever I see a European-American spy movie, I wonder about "Ab-Normal." I don't know how he made it in federal prison with all of those "animals," as he called them.

And I always ask Sheriff Bancroft if Phelps County had any helicopter sightings every time I get a chance to speak with him.

About the Author

A St. Louis, Missouri native, Luke Adler was the product of a dysfunctional home environment, eventually becoming a ward of the state and living in foster care under the purview of the juvenile justice system.

He left home at the age of fourteen and traveled two seasons with the carnival from the Gulf of Mexico to the Canadian border. After returning to St. Louis, Luke hit the road again at age sixteen and hitchhiked from St. Louis to Key West FL, Boston MA, back to Key West, then on to NY City NY, and back to St. Louis prior to enlisting in the United States Marine Corps (USMC) in 1975 at the age of seventeen.

While in the Marines, Luke attended the US Navy Dive School in San Diego California (1976) and the US Army Airborne School in Fort Benning Georgia. He was awarded Navy/Marine Gold Parachute wings in 1977.

He was honorably discharged from the USMC in 1979 and began working as a professional diver on inland river ways such as the Mississippi, Tennessee and Ohio Rivers while attending college in St. Louis.

Luke started his federal civilian service in 1982 and transferred to the United States Marshals Service (USMS) in 1984. He graduated with Top honors at USMS Basic Training; awarded Distinguished Honor Graduate; Top Shooter, the 500

Club (Physical Fitness Award); Academic Excellence; earned the highest combined score in the history of the USMS academy at that time. During his career, Luke has been involved in the apprehension of several USMS Top 15 Most Wanted fugitives and major cases. Luke has made over 3000 felony arrests.

Luke was also a member of the USMS Special Operations Group "swat team" for seven years, participating in numerous high profile national/international events such as 'Operation Just Cause' the Panama raids to seize military dictator Manuel Noriega, the prison riots at USP Atlanta Georgia, Los Angeles City riots, Ruby Ridge militant stand-off, special detail in Puerto Rico involving the "Los Macheteros" terrorist organization, supervised a dive operation involving an international drug cartel. He has supervised, organized and provided protection for federal judges and international dignitaries.

From July 2002 until his retirement in 2011, Luke was a member of the FBI Joint Terrorism Task Force (JTTF) in St. Louis specializing in Balkans terrorist and organized crime groups and intelligence operations in other high-risk communities.

Luke currently lives in St. Louis MO with his wife of thirty-four years, Tracy, whom he met in third grade.

REMEMBER

Also by Abby Rosser

Believe
Hope

Published by WordCrafts Press
Cody, Wyoming 82834
www.wordcrafts.net

Remember

Abby Rosser

WordCrafts Press

Contents

For Nathan and Slade

"It is only with the heart that one can see rightly;
what is essential is invisible to the eye."

The Little Prince

Chapter 1

DANCING SHAGAMAW BOARS

Dooley lay on his side, staring at his alarm clock while trying to ignore the sick feeling in his stomach. It was still hours until he needed to wake up, but he just couldn't go back to sleep. He switched on the little lamp by his bed and opened the top drawer of his bedside table. After pulling out a letter from his friend Leo, Dooley sat up and read it again—the third time since he had found it in his mailbox, the envelope taped to a small package.

Dear Dooley,

Thanks for your letter. Sorry it's taken me so long to write back. My mom signed me up for a pottery class, and it's keeping me pretty busy. I sure miss everybody from Camp Pukwudgee. (Well, mostly everybody—you won't catch me crying into my pillow because I don't get to see Tristen!) Beryl has written me twice. She's crazy about me, obviously, but can you blame her?

You're lucky you live next door to Cyrano. I'd give anything to be around other kids like us (magically gifted superstars) more than just that one week at summer camp. I am definitely NOT looking forward to going back to school. My mom keeps telling me that 7th grade will be great because we finally get lockers. I told her that it's a bad sign that lockers are the only good thing she can come up with about this year. I am planning to spend most of my free time in the art room.

Write me back when you start school. It will be interesting to see if schools here in Illinois are much different from your school in Minnesota. See you in 10 months!

Your friend,

Leonardo Rembrandt Johnson

P.S. I hope you like the bowl I made you. I call it "Dancing Shagamaw Boars." I have no idea what you should use it for— maybe loose change? Just make sure you take everything out of it before you give it a spin.

Dooley picked up the empty ceramic bowl from his bedside table. It easily fit in the palm of his hand. He held it under the lampshade, close to the light so that he could study the bowl's fine details. The inside of the bowl was black, and the outside was painted in an ombre pattern of pinks and reds and oranges and yellows, like the progression of a sunrise. On the outside of the bowl, near the rim, Dooley saw a dozen brownish-black creatures standing on hind legs in a line. He could just make out their tiny ears, stubby tusks, and black snouts. Each of their black eyes was as small as a pinhead. They seemed to form a chorus line with their arms and legs all akimbo, every animal configured in a unique way.

Dooley set the bowl back and carefully removed a small, blue button—the only item he'd found which he deemed special enough to keep there. After placing the button on the edge of the table, he positioned a hand on either side of the bowl. He spun it clockwise and bent down to observe the creatures. The spinning motion made the animals seem to come alive, animated dancing on the fiery background like a scene from a cartoon. For a moment Dooley forgot about what was awaiting him that morning—his first day at J.J. Lawrence Middle School. Suddenly, a memory rose to the surface of his sleepy thoughts: a brilliant dawn standing with his friends around a flagpole as they watched a girl and a dog disappear in the rising sun's rays.

Chapter 2

FIRST DAY JITTERS

"**F**inish your breakfast, Dooley." Rose, Dooley's mom, was writing something on a paper towel with a permanent marker. "You've got plenty of time to eat. You don't have to ride the bus this morning because I'll be taking you to school." Rose folded the paper towel twice and slid it into a brown sack with the peanut butter sandwich, chips, and banana Dooley would eat for lunch.

Dooley knew she had just put a note in his lunch, something she had been doing since his first day of kindergarten. That first one had just been a smiley face with hearts for eyes because he couldn't read yet. Who knows what this note—this embarrassing display of motherly affection scribbled on a paper towel—would say? Dooley vowed to quietly dispose of the note without his mother knowing and before any new classmates could read it.

"Can't I just ride the bus?" he asked. "I don't want to be known as the kid whose mom walked him in on the first day of 7th grade."

Rose half smiled and narrowed her eyes at her only child. "Okay, fine. How about this—I'll park the car and let you go inside before me. Then I'll count to 100 before I go in the office to turn in your papers from St. Bertha's. If we see each other in the hall, we'll just act like we're total strangers."

"All right." Dooley stirred his now-mushy cereal with a spoon showing no desire to eat it.

"Isn't it nice not wearing a uniform anymore?" Rose asked without looking at Dooley as she flipped through a stack of school enrollment papers.

He looked down at his green Boston Celtics t-shirt and khaki shorts. "I guess." Dooley had never really minded the white polos and navy pants from his last school in Boston—Saint Bertha Academy. As long as his friends wore the same thing, what did it matter?

Rose was attempting to sign the bottom of one of the papers, but she was having a hard time getting any ink to come out of the pen she had grabbed from the counter. "What's the matter with this thing?" she said while shaking the heavy pen vigorously. Dooley watched as drops of blue-black ink splattered across the kitchen cabinets.

"Wait, mom!" Dooley rushed over to stop her. "That's my pen. You know, the one I found in the burned spot in the field."

Rose looked at the pen in her hand and let out a short huff. "Of course it is." She gave him the pen. "Why don't you keep your things in your room?"

"I forgot. Cyrano and I were using it in here." Dooley looked at the old-fashioned ink pen, formerly a shiny silver now dull, rough and blackened. "Sorry."

"Is it really empty, or did I just put invisible polka dots all over the kitchen?"

"If they're invisible to you, do you really want to know?" asked Dooley.

"So I take that as a *yes*." Rose dug inside her purse, looking for something else to sign the papers. "Dooley, I'm glad you found that pen. I know you thought it was lost when the ash tree burned down, but you've got to do a better job of taking care of your things. You're not in elementary school anymore."

"Okay. I'll run upstairs and put it away."

Rose looked up from searching through her purse. "Or maybe you can take it with you and show it to the kids you'll meet at school today?" she said, hopefully. "That would be an interesting way to make new friends—with stories about your adventures this summer."

"I know it's been a *long time* since you were in 7th grade, but I'm pretty sure that bringing a crusty, old ink pen to school isn't going to help me make new friends. The last thing I need is to be different from everybody else."

Before Dooley could go up to his room, his mom stopped him, resting a hand on each of his shoulders. "I'm going to ignore that you just called me old because it's your first day of school and you're nervous, but I want you to promise me something."

"What's that?"

"Promise me that you'll remember how special you are. You are kind and smart and brave. And did I mention that you can see things that are invisible to other people?" Rose brushed away a stray hair from Dooley's eyes. "Sometimes being different from everybody else is its own magical power."

Dooley cleared his throat and blinked a few tears caught in his eyelashes. "Okay, mom. I promise."

Chapter 3

SKEETER

Dooley had been told to report to first period in Room 302, but J.J. Lawrence Middle School was a lot bigger than his old school in Boston, and he was having a hard time finding his way. Avoiding the areas with smaller students he assumed were 5th and 6th graders, he had walked the length of an entire corridor before realizing he was in the 8th grade hallway filled with bigger kids opening and closing lockers as they confidently greeted each other in the way that only the oldest students at a school can do with ease. He hustled to a busy intersection of hallways and started down another one, hoping he was back on track.

"Hey," came a voice from behind him, "are you new?"

Dooley turned to see a boy a few inches shorter than him with curly blond hair and freckles.

"Yeah," answered Dooley.

"Oh, cool. Do you like riddles?" he said in a quick, high-pitched voice.

"Huh?"

"Riddles. Like this one: My first name is the sound you make when you're tired plus what I am. What do you think? Can you guess it?"

"I don't know—yawn boy?"

"No! Simon. Get it? Sigh Man?" Simon giggled.

"Oh, yeah."

"Here's another one for my last name: My family is a real *gem* under pressure."

Dooley just looked at Simon blankly.

"A gem under pressure?" Simon repeated helpfully. "A diamond!"

"Your name is Simon Diamond?"

"Yes! Isn't it an awesome name?"

"Sure. It's really something." Dooley looked at the bustle of kids around them, wondering if Simon's enthusiasm was sincere. "I'm Dooley."

"Cool name! What grade are you in?"

"Seventh."

"Super cool! Me too! What homeroom?"

"Room 302."

"Super-duper cool! That's *my* homeroom! Hammond the Horrible, am I right?"

"Who?" Dooley asked.

"Mrs. Hammond, the Language Arts teacher. She's supposed to be the meanest teacher in J.J. Lawrence Middle School. Come on, I'll show you the way!"

Dooley followed Simon as he maneuvered his way through the crowded hallway.

"Hey, Skeeter!" a tall boy with floppy, brown hair called

to Simon. "How was your summer? Were you *itching* to get back to school?" The boy laughed at his own joke and walked away before Simon could respond.

"Did he just call you *Skeeter*?" Dooley asked.

"Yeah. That's my nickname. I have an allergy to mosquito bites. In first grade, I had a bad reaction after a weekend at Lake Superior—I was covered with bites—so some kids have called me Skeeter ever since." Simon smiled as if his nickname didn't bother him. Then his tone became serious, and he added, "I'm also allergic to shrimp and chickpeas and most melons."

Dooley nodded, absorbing the information.

"Did everybody from this school mainly go to the same elementary school?" asked Dooley.

"Yes. Most of us were at Beck Valley Elementary, home of the Mighty Loons! *A-whoo-ooo!*" Simon called loudly, howling like a wolf underneath a full moon. "Do I sound like a loon?" he asked.

"Yes. Definitely," answered Dooley.

"The Common Loon is the state bird of Minnesota. Fun fact: we're also called the Gopher State. Did you know our state muffin is the blueberry muffin?"

"Uh… no."

"Well, it is. Sometimes they have blueberry muffins in the cafeteria for breakfast. I'm so glad I'm not allergic to blueberries!"

In a moment, Dooley saw a square sign posted by a door reading *302 – Hammond*. "Here we are!" said Simon, triumphantly. The boys walked in. Dooley found an empty desk at the front of the room and quickly sat down just as the bell rang.

A woman in her mid-thirties with an oval-shaped face framed by her chin-length black hair stood up from behind her desk. She wore a dark gray shirt accessorized with a short string of pearls and black pants with a sharp crease ironed down the center. Her eyes were heavily-lidded and her thin lips were curved into a disappointed frown as she surveyed the hum of the excited classroom.

"Quiet, boys and girls." Her low voice was firm, not pleading. "In a moment, Mr. Ramsey will read the announcements. There will be no talking whatsoever."

The class was silent, responding to the no-nonsense of Mrs. Hammond.

"Good morning, J.J. Lawrence Middle School!" a voice shouted brightly over the intercom. "This is your principal, Mr. Ramsey, wishing you all a rootin' tootin' start to a new year! You know, when you spell the word principal, it ends with P-A-L—pal! And that's what I want to be for you—your pal! We'll have the best year in the history of our school if we can treat one another like we're all pardners ropin' cattle out on the range. It's like J.J. Lawrence used to say, 'Love your fellow man like a cowboy loves his horse—unconditionally, even if he bucks you or smells to high heaven!'" Mr. Ramsey ended his address with a brief yodeling demonstration.

Dooley looked around the room, reading the expressions on his classmates' faces. With the exception of Simon's broad smile and double thumbs-up, they all looked stony and disinterested. Dooley assumed this was a normal First Day announcement.

As she passed out a piece of paper to each student, Mrs. Hammond said, "This is 7th grade Language Arts, and I am Mrs. Hammond. On this paper you will find a list of books we will read this year. We will also practice diagramming sentences and essay writing. I expect you to be prepared for class, on time, and respectful. Take out your textbooks, and we'll begin our poetry unit with a look at Edgar Allan Poe."

Everyone took a collective deep breath, as if they were about to jump in a cold, bottomless lake.

Chapter 4

CHOW WAGON

Since they were all on the same hall, Dooley managed to make it to his next three classes without much difficulty. Sitting in class wasn't too bad, at least no one expected him to talk. Now it was time for him to face the cafeteria—the room where chaos and commotion meets lunch trays and potentially slippery linoleum floors.

Dooley felt the weight of the importance of first impressions as he entered the cafeteria, fiercely clutching and crumpling his brown paper sack. No one seemed to notice him in all the lunchtime ruckus, so he decided to walk to the empty end of a long table and just sit down alone. He reasoned that sitting by himself was less embarrassing than being rejected if he were to ask to sit with others.

But he wasn't alone for long.

"Dooley!" Simon exclaimed. "I've been looking everywhere for you!" He dumped his tray on the table next to Dooley and sat down. A boy and two girls followed Simon and sat across from them. "Guys, this is the new student I was telling you about. Dooley, this is Nathan, Lark, and Fiona."

"Oh… hey," said Dooley.

"So where are you from?" Lark asked as she took a bite from an apple. Her face was all sharp angles, and her hair was parted down the middle and pulled into two, low pigtails spilling out below each ear.

"Boston."

"I've never been to Boston," said Lark. "Do you miss it?"

"Yeah. Sometimes," Dooley answered.

"Do you mean Boston, *Massachusetts*?" Simon asked.

"Of course he means Boston, Massachusetts," said Nathan. He removed the top bun from his cheeseburger and added a layer of BBQ potato chips to the patty.

"Fun fact: There is also a Boston in Indiana," said Simon. "Due to a cholera outbreak in 1849, nearly half of the town's population of 120 people died in just over a month."

"Where do you come up with this stuff?" Nathan asked as he smeared applesauce on the underside of his top bun. He crushed animal-shaped cinnamon cookies still inside the package, opened it and sprinkled the crumbs on the applesauce.

"Nate, that looks disgusting," Fiona said, wrinkling her nose. The thin, metallic bracelets on her wrists clinked together as she shook up her bottle of juice.

Now that he was sitting down and half-listening to his tablemates' conversation, Dooley felt a little relief from his new school anxiety. For the first time since he had entered the cafeteria, he looked around the large room and noticed a theme. Above the two lunch lines, there was a sign which read:

JASPER'S CHOW WAGON. Wagon wheels were propped up against hay bales in every corner. The refrigerated cooler that held the milk cartons was shaped like a life-sized dairy cow, and the lunch ladies serving the food and taking up money all wore cowboy hats and hot pink bandanas tied around their necks.

"Is the cafeteria always decorated like a cowboy birthday party?" Dooley asked, interrupting Nathan's review of his newest culinary creation, *the cinnamon apple cheeseburger.*

"I heard the design motif was in J.J. Lawrence's will," Fiona answered, gathering all of her long, black braids into a loose ponytail. "But that may just be a school myth."

"Who was J.J. Lawrence?" asked Dooley. "Was he famous?"

"You haven't heard of J.J. Lawrence?" Simon asked, slamming his milk carton on his tray so hard that a drop of milk bounced up and landed on his cheek with a splat.

"No," Dooley answered, slightly embarrassed.

"Dial it back, Simon," said Nathan. "Dooley is new here. He isn't supposed to know everything about the school yet." He turned to Dooley. "J.J. was in cowboy movies a long time ago, like in the 1950's I think. You may know his other name, Jasper Lawrence. Anyway, he was born in Peacock Valley, and his family gave a bunch of money to build this school so they named it after him."

"Fun fact," Simon added, "J.J. Lawrence, a.k.a Jasper Jericho Lawrence, was famous for his lasso tricks and his expert yodeling. In the movie *Casa Grande Serenade*, J.J. Lawrence performed the fastest yodeling ever recorded and held the record until he was beaten by Donn Reynolds in 1984."

"So anyway..." Nathan continued. "That's why the school

is named after him and why it looks like a cheesy Wild West movie."

"Got it," answered Dooley. He finally opened his lunch sack and dumped everything out, forgetting all about his mom's paper towel note.

Lark saw the writing and asked, "What's that?"

Dooley quickly grabbed it and stuffed it in his pocket. "Just something my mom wrote. It's a stupid thing she's done since I was little."

"Awww! That's sweet!" Lark said.

"Yeah," said Fiona. "Your mom sounds super nice, but you're smart to hide that note. See those guys over there?" She pointed to a pack of boys laughing and throwing tater tots at each other. Sitting in the middle of the loud group, Dooley recognized the boy with the floppy hair who had called Simon "Skeeter" in the hallway that morning. "That's Jake Fossberg and his gang. They're always looking for some reason to make fun of people."

"Then Jake gives everybody a nickname," said Nathan. "Before I got braces to fix my two front teeth, Jake started calling me Bucky."

"And I've been Birdy since kindergarten," added Lark. "I don't know if it's my name or my nose." She ran her finger down the bridge of her long nose and grimaced.

"Last year, when we studied Greek mythology, Jake gave me the nickname Medusa—you know, that crazy lady with the snake hair—because of my braids," said Fiona.

"Fun fact: When Perseus cut off Medusa's head, Pegasus jumped out of her body," said Simon. "Pretty cool, huh?"

"Simon, I'm surprised your nickname isn't *Fun Fact*, instead of *Skeeter*," said Nathan. "Dooley, just keep your distance from Jake. His family is rich because they own the Fossberg Cracker factory, and he thinks he runs this place. If he knows about your paper towel note, you'll have a nickname for sure, like maybe *Bounty* or *Brawny*. Those are brands of paper towels, aren't they? I don't know... I'm not good at making up mean nicknames."

One of the lunch ladies held a loop of leather string tied to the top of a large metal triangle and began clanging all around the inside of it. "7th grade lunch is over," she shouted, in a monotone voice. "All you buckaroos dump your trash and stack your trays over yonder."

Chapter 5

NOTHING TO SEE HERE

When Dooley got off the bus and made it down the long driveway to his house, his mom was waiting for him on the front porch. She was sitting in the porch swing Dooley's father had hung for her at the beginning of the summer. She had a glass of iced tea in one hand, and with the other hand she turned the pages of the magazine resting in her lap.

"Dooley!" she exclaimed when she saw him still in the yard. "How was your first day?"

"Fine," Dooley answered.

"Did you make some new friends?"

"Yeah."

"That's great! What are they like?"

"Just like your average kids, I guess." Dooley mounted the porch steps.

"How were your teachers? Do you think you'll like your classes?"

"Fine, I guess." He reached for the handle on the screen door.

"Come on, son," she groaned. "You've got to give me more than just 'fine' and 'I guess.'"

"Sorry. I'm tired."

"Well, Cyrano was over here a little while ago asking when you'd be home, so why don't you go over to his house? At least that way you'd be telling *someone* about your day." She looked back down at her magazine, pretending not to care if Dooley ever discussed his experiences of starting 7th grade with her or not.

Dooley dumped his backpack just inside the door and went to give his mom a hug. "I'll talk to you about my day, mom. I promise." He started down the steps to walk to his neighbor's house. "Remind me to tell you about the principal yodeling on the announcements!" he said over his shoulder.

Dooley found Cyrano and his older sister Calix kneeling beside the red brick border which ran alongside an oval flower bed close to their house, yanking out weeds and placing them in a bucket.

"Finally!" Cyrano called to his friend. "I thought your school was never going to be over! This is why you should be homeschooled like us."

"What are you doing?" asked Dooley.

"We're clearing out this bed so Calix can use it," Cyrano answered.

"Indeed," Calix agreed. "This shady spot is a wonderful place to plant a Summersweet shrub, and the butterflies will love it!"

Dooley bent down to help.

"Tell him about the seeds, Calix," said Cyrano.

"Oh, yes! I was fascinated by dear Cyrano's description of the Vision Bush you learned of at camp this year. I combed through a rather obscure catalog and sent off for seeds. They arrived last week from a company in Romania. I hope to have berries for you very soon."

"If you just got the seeds, won't it take a while to grow berries?" Dooley asked.

"You're forgetting who you're dealing with, Dooley," said Cyrano, proudly. "Calix is about the best Greenie there is. Counselor Busby always said she was the most talented agricultural camper he'd ever seen."

"Such a sweet brother!" Calix patted Cyrano's arm. She picked up the bucket of weeds to add them to her compost heap. "Come by the greenhouse anytime and see how much they've already grown, Dooley. I hope you'll be able to make your special Visus ink in a week or so!"

As they watched her leave, Dooley asked his friend, "What do you think I should do with the ink we make from the berries? It seems like kind of a waste of time for Calix. I mean, if I'm the only one who can see it, what's the point?"

"I don't know. She's always up for a challenge. Maybe she can grow it, and then we can decide what to do with it later."

The boys went inside Cyrano's house and up to his attic bedroom. Dooley sat down on one of the plush rugs Cyrano's grandmother had made for him. This one was covered with stitches made to look like brown branches, green leaves, and a blue sky. It matched the tree that—up until a few months ago—had stood in Dooley's front field for centuries. Dooley sighed as he remembered the now-vanished tree, reduced to a pile of ashes.

"I've been meaning to ask you," said Cyrano, "Have you had any luck with that button you found in Busby's cabin?"

"No," Dooley replied. "I know it's supposed to make the person who's holding it remember something from their past, but it hasn't worked for me. And now that I started back to school, I won't have as much time to practice with it."

"So what was J.J. Lawrence Middle School like?"

"Boring." Dooley lay down with his hands behind his head and stared at the attic ceiling. "After hanging out with your family and going to camp with magically gifted kids, normal people are just so blah."

"My mom would say that you sound like a snob, Dooley. She says each person actually has some sort of gift. And, anyway, you can't tell me that everyone at your school is completely normal."

"Well, there is this guy who's allergic to chickpeas…"

"Come on. You're a Visus, right? Someone who's supposed to be able to see things other people can't."

"Yeah. So what?"

"So start looking around your school. I bet there's something crazy happening there, but you just haven't seen it yet because you think there's nothing to see."

Chapter 6

OMINOUS

On his second day of school, Dooley tried to remember Cyrano's words. He looked at the faces of the kids passing by him as he stood in front of his open locker. He read their expressions—sleepy, amused, irritated, glum. Nothing seemed out of the ordinary.

Before he made his way to his homeroom class, Dooley saw a squat, elderly man standing in front of a door and leaning on a broom. His sparse, gray hair was parted by his left ear and combed to cover his balding head. His face was framed by oversized ears on each side and a sizable forehead and chin on the top and bottom. He had a bulging nose with three or four gray hairs growing from each nostril and a scraggy, gray beard to match. Dooley read his embroidered nametag: GUS. Gus surveyed the hallway, shaking his head at the antics of some of the rowdier kids.

As Dooley concentrated on the man, a prickly feeling spread up his neck. Something flickered across Gus' face. The lines and wrinkles on his forehead and around his eyes disappeared, and his skin smoothed but only for a second. It was as if, in a brief flash, Dooley saw Gus as a younger man, and then, just as quickly as it had appeared, the youthfulness was gone.

"Mosey on to class, buckaroos," Principal Ramsey called to the students, cheerfully.

Dooley closed his locker and looked back at Gus. Mr. Ramsey was talking to the old man, and Gus was responding, "Yes sir. I'd be happy to oblige."

Dooley walked into his homeroom class and saw Simon waving to him. "I saved you a seat!" Simon said. "Over here!"

Dooley sat down and dropped a thick textbook on the desk.

"Did you read the assignment for today?" Simon asked.

"'The Raven?' Yeah, I read it."

"Edgar Allan Poe was one creepy dude," said Simon. "'Quoth the Raven: Nevermore!' *Squawk*! *Squawk*! Fun fact: a group of ravens isn't called a flock. They're called *an unkindness* or *a conspiracy*."

"Huh," Dooley responded vaguely. "That's interesting."

Mrs. Hammond straightened the items on her desk, meticulously lining up a row of red pens next to a neat stack of papers. Just after the bell had rung, she said, "Quickly and quietly find your seats, students. I have seen altogether too much horseplay this morning. I will tolerate no roughhousing in this classroom *whatsoever*. Mr. Ramsey will begin his daily announcements in a moment."

"Good morning, J.J. Lawrence Middle School!" came the principal's voice over the intercom. "Just a reminder that tickets go on sale today for the Fall Dance. Ms. Stearns tells me that the theme is 'The Sherwood Forest.' So I expect to see all of you Robin Hoods and Maid Marians in attendance! The money collected from ticket sales goes to the purchase of a new popcorn machine." Mr. Ramsey continued with information about auditions for the school play and tryouts for the swim team. He closed out his announcements with another display of his yodeling talent.

"I'm passing out a list of 35 vocabulary words from 'The Raven' which is the poem you were *supposed* to have read for homework last night," Mrs. Hammond said as she walked up and down the rows, distributing papers. "You'll find a dictionary under your seat. Look up each word and write the definition on this sheet. This is not a partner assignment, nor is it a verbal activity, so there should be no talking *whatsoever*."

Dooley looked up the first word—*ponder*—and wrote down the definition. He tried to focus on his work, but his mind was regularly pulled back to Gus, the custodian, and the brief change in his appearance. Dooley flipped the pages of the dictionary to find his next word—*countenance*. Next to the word, he wrote: "Face, look, physical appearance." Dooley remembered again how Gus' aged face seemed younger while he watched the kids in the hallway.

Dooley continued to work through the list until he came to the last word—*ominous*. When he found the definition, he experienced that same prickly feeling he had felt in the hallway before class. "Threatening evil," he copied, "or tragic events."

Chapter 7

WHATSOEVER

After Language Arts, Dooley went down the hall to a large classroom by the gymnasium for his General Music class. The room was also used for band practice, so there was a jumble of music stands and a big kettle drum in one corner. Dooley saw a large marimba standing in another corner with two mallets lying across the long wooden bars, and a line of ukuleles hung on the front wall. He sat in a metal chair in the second row and observed his classmates as they entered the room.

Jake Fossberg and a few of his friends swaggered in and sat down just in front Dooley. "So anyway, my dad said we'll make it to all the Vikings' home games this year," Jake told them.

"Seriously?" one of the boys responded. "Jake, you're so lucky!"

"There's nobody in town who's a bigger Vikings fan than my dad. In fact, for the past five Christmases he's given each of his employees Vikings merchandise—hats, shirts, stuff like that. He says it's better than a bonus. That first year it was Minnesota Vikings flip-flops." Jake moved his head in one swift motion to flip his hair out of his eyes. "And anyway, the Fossberg Cracker factory has to show up to big events like professional games. It's all about publicity, man. My mom just bought a new fur coat to wear to some ball coming up. I wouldn't be surprised if she and my dad hung out with the Governor all night. That's what important people do—scrub elbows with other important people."

Pfft! Dooley hadn't noticed that Fiona, one of Simon's friends from lunch, had sat down next to him. She was shaking her head and smiling.

Jake turned around and looked at Fiona. "What's so funny, Medusa?" he asked.

"It's *rub* elbows, Jake. Not *scrub* elbows."

"Whatever. Who cares." Jake noticed Dooley for the first time. "It looks like Medusa found herself a boyfriend. Hey, New Kid, don't look at her in the eyes or she'll breathe fire on you!" Jake and his friends laughed while pretending to shield their eyes.

"Medusa didn't breathe fire. She turned people into stone," Fiona corrected. "You're thinking of the Chimera."

Jake moved on without answering her. "So what's your name, New Kid?"

"Dooley," he answered timidly, hoping Jake wasn't formulating an embarrassing nickname for him.

"I like your shirt." Jake pointed to Dooley's purple and gold Minnesota Vikings t-shirt. His mom had bought it for him just before they had moved to Peacock Valley. Not really caring much for football, Dooley had only started wearing it the last few weeks. His appreciation for it had grown since he had seen a real life Viking.

"Thanks," Dooley responded. "I heard you're going to a bunch of games this year. That sounds amazing."

"Totally amazing. So when did you move here?"

"At the beginning of the summer. My dad got a new job at the Peacock Valley Jelly company."

"Oh yeah? I've heard my dad talk about the jelly people before. He said that years ago the jelly company thought about getting into the cracker business, but they learned pretty quickly that there isn't room for two cracker factories in this town. But that would've been before your time in Peacock Valley. Maybe my dad could get with your dad about a possible product merger—maybe a hot pepper jelly/multigrain cracker combo?"

Dooley realized that Jake knew a lot more about crackers than Dooley did about jelly.

Before he could respond, Ms. Stearns, the short, round music teacher, fluttered into the room twittering inarticulately. "I must put that on my list… perhaps he will help… never know unless you ask…" She looked up and noticed she had a classroom full of waiting students. "Oh, dear. I've been so preoccupied with the dance I nearly forgot I had a class…"

"Ms. Stearns is really nice," Fiona whispered to Dooley. "She just gets flustered easily."

Ms. Stearns pulled down a chart, covering the markerboard. "Eyes up here, boys and girls." She removed one of the many pencils she kept behind her ears or tucked into her hair and pointed to the chart. "We're learning about musical rhythm. These are music notes and their values. A whole note, half note, quarter note—"

"Pardon the interruption, Ms. Stearns," came a voice over the intercom. "You have a phone call in the office. Something about the school dance and some jousting equipment?"

"Oh, yes!" she squealed excitedly. "I'll be right there!" The jolly, little teacher told the class, "I need to run to the office, but I will only be gone for a few minutes. Copy the information from this chart into your notebooks." As she bustled out of the room, she muttered, "The jousters could be in the courtyard... but where to put the archers..."

Once she was gone, Jake hopped up and tucked pencils behind both ears. He paced briskly in front of the class, saying, "Oh my! Oh my! What to do about the jousters? And the archers need bows and arrows!"

Most of the class laughed at his imitation. One of his friends called out, "Do another one, Jake!"

Jake said, "Howdy pardners! This is your pal, Mr. Ramsey telling you cow pokes to rustle up some grub. Yodel-ay-hee-hoo!"

Clapping and laughing followed his imitation, along with cheering for more. Jake motioned to Dooley and said, "Let's hear one from the new kid!"

Dooley looked at Fiona for help, but she only shrugged her shoulders. Dooley rose from his seat slowly and stood in front of the class, watching as Jake sat back down.

"Okay... um," Dooley stammered as he was thinking.

Then he stood as tall as he could and frowned. "Turn to 'The Raven' in your textbooks. There will be no talking *whatsoever!*" Dooley paused, waiting for a reaction. "And no roughhousing *whatsoever!*"

"Ha! You're Hammond the Horrible!" Jake said. "Keep going!"

"My name is Mrs. Hammond. I have no friends *whatsoever* because I have no sense of humor *whatsoever*," Dooley continued without noticing Fiona waving her hand to get his attention. "I'm married, but I have no idea *whatsoever* why anyone would marry anyone as grouchy as me. Probably my husband would rather just die than live in the same house with someone boring like me."

"Dooley Creed." He spun around to see Mrs. Hammond's imposing presence in the doorway. "As soon as Ms. Sterns returns, you will accompany me to Principal Ramsey's office."

Dooley slumped his shoulders and bowed his head. "Yes ma'am," he muttered. He wanted to say something else to defend himself, but all he could think of was Poe's Raven: *This grim and ominous bird of yore croaking "Nevermore."*

Chapter 8

THE PRINCIPAL'S OFFICE

"This is very disappointing," Mr. Ramsey said. He was sitting in a large desk chair upholstered in black-and-white cow print. Unsurprisingly, the principal's office was filled with western-themed paraphernalia. The walls were covered with autographed pictures of actors sporting 10-gallon hats and standing by horses. A cat bed shaped like a cactus sat in the corner. "Showing disrespect to a teacher is never allowed at J.J. Lawrence Middle School. It's not in the spirit of Jasper Lawrence."

"I'm sorry," Dooley said for the fourth time since he'd left music class. He watched as a fat, orange cat stepped out of the domed opening of its plush cactus-shaped home. It stretched lazily before slinking over to rub against Mr. Ramsey's legs. "I never meant to be disrespectful. Anyway, I wasn't the only one saying stuff—"

"There's an old cowboy saying," Mr. Ramsey said. "'The biggest troublemaker you'll probably ever have to deal with watches you shave in the mirror every morning.'"

"Sir?"

"Mr. Ramsey means that blaming other students for your own actions is cowardly. What you did was unkind and rude," said Mrs. Hammond. "This is a shameful start for a new student."

"I will call your parents and let them know that you'll be staying after school the rest of the week and all of next week to assist with preparations for the school dance. I hope that eight days of hard labor will give you adequate time to learn from your mistake." Mr. Ramsey explained. "Gus, our school custodian, needs help painting and building and moving items, and you will be his assistant." As if on cue, Gus knocked on the closed door. "A-ha. Here he is. Come in, Gus!"

The older man stepped just inside the office and folded his arms across his chest. "They said you was looking for me?" Gus asked.

"Yes. This is Dooley Creed. Due to some misbehavior in Mrs. Hammond's class, he will be helping you set up for the dance."

Dooley stared at the pattern in the brown and blue carpet, too embarrassed to observe the faces of the adults in the room.

"I reckon that'll be all right with me," Gus responded without emotion. "Ought to be able to find something for him to do."

"Excellent," Mr. Ramsey exclaimed. "And Dooley, I don't want to hear any more about you getting into trouble."

"Yes sir," said Dooley.

"It's nearly time for lunch. Go and finish your day then

come directly to the office right after dismissal. Gus will explain your assignment." Mr. Ramsey waved him out of his office. Dooley could only look at Mrs. Hammond's sensible black shoes, but as he walked past Gus, Dooley quickly glanced at the elderly custodian. Something flickered across Gus' eyes, his pupils seemed to expand and shrink in an instant. At the same time, Dooley felt as if someone had zapped the back of his neck with a jolt of static electricity.

Simon was waiting for him in the hall outside the office. "Hey, Dooley! I heard what happened in your music class."

"So everyone knows?" asked Dooley miserably. Even though he wasn't hungry, he walked briskly to get his lunch from his locker.

"I don't know. Fiona told me, but word moves around this school pretty fast."

"Great." Dooley took out his sack lunch and slammed his locker shut. "Stupid first week of school," he mumbled.

"It is interesting how information can be transmitting so quickly. Fun fact: During the Han dynasty, people stationed in towers along the Great Wall of China would signal news to each other using colored flags." Simon hurried to keep up with Dooley's pace.

"Well, that's really helpful for me right now, Simon," Dooley said, sarcastically. "I'll remember that the next time I get sent to the principal's office in China."

Chapter 9

DEFINITELY DISAPPOINTED

Just as he was instructed, Dooley went to the office after the final dismissal bell. His last class was P.E. so he was still wearing his gym clothes as he sat on a hard, wooden bench trying to avoid the scowling gaze of Ms. Cato, the school secretary, as she answered phone calls and typed on her keyboard. In spite of his original apprehensions about Gus, Dooley felt relief when the custodian finally appeared.

"Might as well get started," Gus said. "Come on."

Dooley followed him to the gymnasium where Gus had a spacious work room next to the concessions area. There was a table saw and a tall shelf lined with paint cans. Various tools hung from a pegboard over a long, sawdust-covered work bench. The faucet steadily dripped into a deep sink in the back of the room, making a gulping sound as each drop was swallowed by a coffee can full of soaking paintbrushes.

Gus dragged a bundle of chicken wire to the center of the room and tossed work gloves at Dooley's feet. "Put these on," he said. "We're gonna fashion this wire into a big tree shape best we can. Then we'll covered it with paper mash and paint it after it's dry. The tree will go in the middle of the gym." He pointed to stacks of plywood leaning against a wall. "Then we'll have to cut them boards into more trees to put all around the walls. Wilhelmina—er, Ms. Stearns—wants it to look like a forest." Gus showed Dooley the drawings tacked to a bulletin board. "How are you at painting?" Gus asked.

"Okay, I guess. I'm not an artist or anything."

"Well, this job will involve a lot of painting, so you might want to bring a change of clothes to school tomorrow."

Dooley and Gus put on gloves and began unrolling the wire. At first, Dooley had a hard time visualizing what their end product would look like. Gus had already built an 8-foot tall wooden stand with arms extended from it on all sides to serve as a frame for the tree, and they started by wrapping it with the wire. After a while, the mass began to take shape. Dooley held the ladder as Gus climbed to the top to cover the upper "branches" with the wire.

"That'll do for today," Gus said as he climbed down the ladder. "I expect your mom is here to fetch you." Dooley took off the gloves and laid them on the work bench. "Just come straight down here after school is out tomorrow."

"Yes, sir."

"And son, don't look so gloomy. Things aren't always as bad as they seem at first sight."

Dooley nodded then bent down to grab his backpack before leaving.

Even before Dooley could buckle his seat belt in his mom's minivan, she began interrogating him. "I can't believe you got sent to the principal's office! And being disrespectful to a teacher? What were you thinking? No, I'll answer for you—you weren't thinking! Because if you had been thinking, you would've thought about all of the things your parents have taught you!"

"Mom, I'm sorry."

"Well, you should be! I've never been so embarrassed in my life!"

"You're embarrassed? Imagine how I feel? The whole school knows what happened."

Rose inhaled a deep breath and took a long look at her son. After a few seconds, she reached over and patted his hand. "All right. You made a mistake, and now you're paying for it. Lesson learned."

"Have you told Dad yet?"

"Yes."

"Is he pretty mad?"

"He's definitely disappointed."

Dooley leaned his head back against the headrest and closed his eyes. "I think I'd rather he be mad."

"He knows about you helping the custodian after school, but he's also planning for some extra punishment for you on Saturday."

"But Mom… Cyrano and I were going to hang out on Saturday!"

"You should've thought of that before you made fun of a teacher, Dooley." He slumped down in his seat. "Why would you ever think it was okay to mock a teacher, especially making fun of the fact that she lost her husband? I thought you were more compassionate than that."

"I—I didn't know her husband died. Honest." Dooley felt sick to his stomach. Just then he wished he had the power of a Skrito, so he could make himself invisible.

Chapter 10

BELOW THE SURFACE

After a few more afternoons with Gus, it was time for his weekend punishment. Early Saturday morning, Dooley found himself sitting cross-legged on the floor of his dad's office, sorting jelly jar labels into piles.

"Make sure you separate the boysenberry labels from the blackberry ones," Paul, Dooley's father, told him. "They look very similar."

The printing company had shipped the labels to the Peacock Valley Jelly company in a big box leaving the 52 varieties in a jumble. Paul had decided the tedious task was an appropriate punishment for Dooley's misbehavior at school.

"So your mom told me what happened," Paul started, "but I'm ready to hear it from you."

Dooley hadn't wanted to talk about getting in trouble at school to anyone—not Simon or the other kids at the lunch table, not his parents, not even Cyrano. Now that the initial sting had worn off a little, he felt like he could discuss it.

He told his dad all about Jake and his fondness for teasing people. He described the events leading up to his unkind impersonation of Mrs. Hammond. Before he realized what had happened, Dooley had laid down all his anxiety about starting a new school, including his indifference when it came to spending time with non-magical people.

"Does that include your mom and me? We don't have any magical powers."

"No. I don't mean to sound snobby. It's just that—"

"I know what you mean," Paul stopped him. "You know, when I was about your age I had a friend who was a master violinist. He was the best around, eventually even better than his teachers or the adults he played with. He said that whenever his mom thought he was getting an oversized ego about his talent, she would send him outside to shoot baskets on the basketball hoop over their garage door."

"Why'd she do that?"

"Well, he was pretty awful at basketball. She said he needed to be reminded that he wasn't the best at everything. She wanted him to appreciate his talent but also understand that we're all good at different things."

Dooley had finished sorting the labels, so he wrapped each bundle with a rubber band. "Are you saying you want me to go shoot baskets or do math or something else I'm bad at so that I won't act like a bully?"

Paul smiled. "Maybe. It might help."

"One thing I know for sure is that I'm definitely not going to try to make friends with Jake Fossberg. I don't care if he is the heir to the Fossberg Cracker empire and his family's rich." Dooley stood up and stretched his back. "He's a jerk."

"Don't be too quick to judge him. You never know what's going on just below the surface. Take Mrs. Hammond, for example. Mr. Ramsey told your mom that since Mrs. Hammond's husband died five years ago, she just hasn't been the same."

Dooley felt the shame of his hurtful words burning his cheeks and the tops of his ears. "I feel really bad about that."

"There was some mystery about how he died—a lot of unanswered questions and people blaming each other."

"Really? What happened?"

"I don't know all of the details. None of the employees who were around when he worked here will talk much about it."

"He worked here at the jelly factory?" asked Dooley, surprised.

"Apparently so. They say he was in an accident on the factory floor and died from his injuries, but I can't seem to get much more information than that."

Dooley and his dad went home for lunch. Considering how penitent he was, Paul decided he had been punished enough and relented to let Dooley spend the rest of his Saturday with Cyrano.

Up in his attic bedroom, Cyrano asked Dooley if he'd tried to use the charmed button again. "No," Dooley responded. "I've been so busy with school stuff I haven't even picked it up in days. Honestly, I don't even know where to start."

"I was talking to my mom about the button, and she suggested that you write to Elenore."

"The craft shack teacher from camp? Why her?"

"Mom said she's the N.A.M.E.S. coordinator for the Great Lakes region."

"Names?"

"Oh, sorry. North American Magical Enthusiasts Society. She knows all sorts of people, so she might be able to direct you to someone who could explain how to use the button." Cyrano found a piece of paper on top of his bookshelf. "Here's Elenore's address. It's worth a try."

Chapter 11

JUNEBERRY MEADOWS

As Dooley slathered green paint on the now dried papier-mâché tree branches Monday afternoon, he noticed he didn't mind working with Gus anymore. The time he spent with the elderly custodian had actually been fun. It was a rewarding feeling to be a part of creating something for his new school.

The mostly taciturn Gus spoke up a little more each time they met. He shared about his duties at the school and his love of fishing. Dooley told Gus about living in Boston. He didn't reveal anything exceptionally personal, such as how he was a Visus with supernatural eyesight, just minor details like hobbies and places his family had visited.

Dooley nearly mentioned his Visus power on Friday when he saw that same flash of transformation in Gus' appearance again. It was so sudden that Dooley had fumbled the hammer he was holding, dropping it on his own foot. When Gus asked what had happened, Dooley had stopped himself before telling the old man what he had seen.

With their afternoon tasks completed, Dooley walked out to the empty parking lot to find his mom. Carrying a tan canvas rucksack over one shoulder, Gus walked with him, stopping at his rusted pickup truck.

"See you tomorrow, Dooley," Gus grunted as he climbed into his seat.

"Yeah, see ya," replied Dooley.

Dooley watched as Gus tried to start his truck, the engine revving pathetically before sputtering out each time. When his mom arrived, Dooley told her, "Can we see if Gus needs a ride? I think he's having trouble with his truck."

After they had convinced him that it was no trouble to drive him home, Gus buckled into the backseat of the minivan. Dooley's mom asked, "What's your address, Mister…"

"You can call me Gus."

"Okay, Gus, where do you live?"

"3225 Juneberry Meadows Lane."

When they arrived at the address, Rose asked, "Is this right? It looks like a nursing home."

"Yep," Gus answered as he slid open the van door, "this is it. I live here with my brother Theo in this old folks' home. He weren't doing too good living here without me, so they said we could both stay. Being handy and all, I fix things for them when it's needed, and we call it even." Gus got out of the van and stood by Dooley's open window. "Thanks for the ride, ma'am."

"You're welcome," said Rose.

"What are you going to do about your truck?" Dooley asked.

"I'll grab a few things and ask one of the nurses to run

me back to the school after dinner. I reckon it's needing a new battery."

After they said good-bye, Dooley noticed Gus' canvas bag in the backseat. "Hang on, mom. Let me run this inside."

Dooley hopped out and walked to the front door of the gray brick, one-story building. Wooden benches flanked the covered entryway. Glass double doors painted with the greeting, *Welcome to Juneberry Meadows Nursing Home*, opened automatically when he stepped on the mat.

A woman sat behind a desk just inside the door. "May I help you?" she asked.

"A man who lives here left his bag in our car. His name is Gus."

"Oh yes. To get to Gus's room you go to that sitting area there, then turn left and it's down the hall, on the left. Room 117."

"Thank you."

Dooley walked through a spacious living room, passing three elderly women sitting side-by-side on a green plaid sofa. They each had loose gray buns perched atop their heart-shaped faces and matching bright blue cardigans. They were all knitting but without looking at their hands. Instead they glanced around the room, smiling toothlessly. A ball of yellow yarn dropped from the lap of the third woman and rolled until it bumped into Dooley's foot.

Dooley picked up the yarn and handed it to the woman.

"What a nice boy!" Woman #3 said. She was the only one of the three wearing eyeglasses. She turned to Woman #2 and asked, "Isn't he a nice boy, Jessamine?"

Woman #2 took the glasses from the first woman's face and put them on before replying, "Why, yes! Such a nice boy! Wouldn't you agree, Delphinium?"

"I can't remember when I've seen a nicer boy! And he arrived at just the right moment!" exclaimed Woman #1, after she had taken the glasses and placed them on herself. "Marigold is forever dropping and losing things, aren't you, dear sister?"

Woman #3 responded, "That is true! I can be a bit of a Forgetful Franny, but it's you, dear Delphinium, who forgot to bring the teeth out to the parlor today. You were wearing them last!"

"We sisters share everything," Woman #2 commented, happily, "even our dentures!"

"Oh… Well, it was no problem," said Dooley. "I've got to go—"

"If I tell you our names, will you tell us yours?" asked Woman #1. Without waiting for Dooley to respond she continued, "We are the DuBois sisters. I am Delphinium, the eldest sister." Delphinium pressed a frail hand with four beringed fingers to her chest. "Next is Jessamine, second-born." Jessamine waved to Dooley. "Last is Marigold, the baby of the family." Marigold sat up straighter and nodded. "And you are?"

"Dooley Creed. I'm here to drop off—"

"Creed, you say? There was a Creed here at Juneberry Meadows, wasn't there, Jessamine?" asked Delphinium.

"I believe you're right, sister," Jessamine answered. "A Jonathan Creed, if I'm not mistaken. Delightful dancer! Always wore that rather striking purple necktie."

"No, dears, that was Jonathan *Reed*," Marigold corrected. "*Reed*, not Creed."

"Ah, yes!" said Jessamine. "Of course, you're right! He had that horrid cat when he first moved here—Oscar was its name. Nasty thing." She wrinkled her nose in disgust.

"Cats are often a knitter's nemesis, always unraveling and unwinding things," said Delphinium. "We reported that cat to the management, and it was gone soon enough."

"All three of us are highly allergic to cats," Marigold added. "We can hardly breathe when one of those vile animals are nearby. I'm afraid we've developed a rather paralyzing fear of them!" She removed a lacy handkerchief from her sleeve and blew her nose. "You don't have a cat in that bag, do you, dear?"

"Oh, no. I don't have a cat. Actually, I've got to take this bag to a friend. He left it in my car." Dooley began to back away.

"Dooley to the rescue again!" Jessamine cried. "What a nice boy!"

"Well, I've really got to go," called Dooley over his shoulder as he hurried out of the waiting room. "Good bye!"

He continued to follow the directions he was given to Gus' room, glancing at the numbered doors as he walked. Each one had a small black placard with white numbers, and below the numbers was a clear sign holder with a paper displaying the name of the room's occupants. When he saw *117*, Dooley knocked on the door. Then he looked down and noticed his undone shoestrings. He bent to tie them. Standing up, he jostled the bag causing the contents to jumble out.

Just as the door opened, Dooley reached to pick up an opened composition notebook. He had just read the phrase *to find a way to get Slade back,* before closing the book and stuffing it back in the bag. Gus was standing in the doorway. "You left this in our car," Dooley said. He handed the bag to Gus. "See you tomorrow."

"All right," said Gus. "Thanks again."

After he had shut the door, Dooley read the paper in the sign holder: *Theodore Hammond and Augustus Hammond.*

Chapter 12

LIKE DIGGING A WELL

Even though the school gossip about his impersonation of Mrs. Hammond had faded and the J.J. Lawrence Middle School student body had moved on to other news, Dooley still dreaded going to homeroom every day. He just knew his teacher despised him. He could barely look at her while she was talking. If they did make eye contact, he would always look away, imagining what he first assumed was the characteristics of a strict teacher, he now saw as her complete abhorrence of his very existence.

On Tuesday, he discussed his feelings with Simon by his locker after first period. "I don't know how to make it better," Dooley said. "I mean, should I apologize again? Should I write a note? I just know she hates me."

"Maybe you could find out what her favorite kind of cookie is and make her some," offered Simon. "Or maybe a fruit basket or a potted plant? Fun fact: The Purple Hyacinth is the flower which symbolizes regret."

"Yeah. Maybe."

"You know, it's like that quote from J.J. Lawrence that's painted above the water fountains in the 6th grade hallway," Simon offered. "'Saying you're sorry is like digging a well for your livestock. It can be hard, and you may hit a few rocks along the way, but it's as much for you as it is for them.'"

Fiona met up with them in the hallway. "Ask Fiona," Simon suggested before heading off to his math class. "I've found that girls are better at thinking up stuff like that."

"Ask me what?" asked Fiona. They began walking together to music class.

"It's nothing," Dooley blushed. "I was just asking Simon what I should do about Mrs. Hammond and the fact that she hates me."

"Oh, you're one of those people," she said.

"What do you mean?"

"One of those people who can't stand to have other people mad at them. It's a disorder, you know."

"I don't have a disorder," said Dooley.

"I don't know about that. I've been watching you, and you do some strange things. For instance, you stare really hard at people, almost like you're trying to see through them." Fiona opened her eyes wide and leaned toward Dooley until they were nearly nose to nose.

"I just like to people watch, I guess."

They had made it to the music classroom and sat down in the metal chairs.

"I like to study people too, and I know a bit about disorders," Fiona continued. "I have an uncle who won't open a door until he taps the door knobs three times. That's a disorder."

"Well, I don't tap doorknobs, and I don't feel like every-body has to like me. I just don't want to go through this schoolyear spending the first hour of every day with a teacher who thinks I'm a complete jerk."

Fiona gave Dooley a friendly punch on the shoulder. "You're not a complete jerk, so I'm sure you'll think of something."

For the remainder of the day, Dooley wrestled with the idea of truly showing how sorry he was for upsetting Mrs. Hammond without settling on what he should do.

While he was helping cut out leaf shapes from green construction paper after school, Dooley thought about Gus' room in the nursing home. "So do you like living at Juneberry Meadows?" Dooley asked.

"I reckon. The food ain't great, but I can rest easy knowing Theo is taken care of when I'm working."

"The sign on your door said your last name is Hammond." Dooley paused. "Are you related to Mrs. Hammond, the teacher?"

"I am. Clara's my kin by marriage."

Dooley felt sick. He had come to think of Gus as an ally at school—perhaps one of the few adults who didn't think he was unkind and insensitive. He swallowed past a lump in his throat and asked, "Why didn't you tell me that before?"

"You never asked." As soon as Dooley cut them out, Gus punched holes in the top of each leaf, scattering tiny green dots all over the floor. "Don't fret, son. I don't hold nothing against you."

"I just feel so bad about everything. I never meant to hurt her feelings. And anyway, I had no idea her husband died."

"Clara may seem tough on the outside, but she's actually real tender. Her heart's been forever marked by death. It can be mighty hard for some folks to get over losing someone."

Gus stood to hang a few of the leaves on the nails he had added to the upper branches of the wooden trees they had cut. Dooley collected his scraps and carried them to a nearby trashcan.

"Since Mrs. Hammond's your relative, maybe you can help me think of something I can do to show her how sorry I am."

"What did you have in mind?"

"I don't know. Should I write her a letter? Simon thought I should bake her cookies. Or maybe I should just leave it alone and focus on surviving 7th grade."

"I'll think on it and let you know," Gus replied.

Dooley frowned as he grabbed a broom and began sweeping up the green dots. He wasn't very confident that Gus would come up with an idea. Why would this old man want to help the kid who had insulted his relative?

"So how are you related to Mrs. Hammond anyway?" Dooley asked as he swept the mound of green dots into the dustpan.

"She was married to Slade, my older brother."

Chapter 13

I'LL SEE YOU IN MY DREAMS

W hen Dooley's mom picked him up after school on Tuesday, he noticed a stack of mail in the front passenger seat. The letter on top was addressed to him in an expressive, curly cursive script. He hastily ripped opened the envelope and pulled out a pale pink sheet of paper.

Dear Dooley,

It's always a pleasure to receive correspondence from my Puk-wudgee campers, especially ones who are so interested in the camp's history and their own continuing education in magical concepts and practices!

I contacted several of my colleagues from N.A.M.E.S. to ask them about the button you found. Best I can tell, your button is asleep. I was told that a charmed object can convert itself into a dormant state after decades of non-use. It needs to be jump-started back to its magical state. Once you've achieved this, you need only to hold the button tightly in your right hand, briefly focus on an object that might stir a memory, and close your eyes. Then say a few lines of a sentimental song from the era of the button's creation. I'd suggest something such as, "I'll see you in my dreams, and then I'll hold you in my dreams. Someone took you out of my arms, still I feel the thrill of your charms." Lovely, isn't it?

I'm unsure of what will happen next. For most people, the button will work according to its original design in that it will evoke old memories from their past, making them seem so authentic and detailed that they feel like they've just happened. Considering that you are such an exceptional young man, you may have a completely different experience. How exciting!

As far as how to wake up the button, I recommend using the Visus Encyclopedia which I leant you this summer. It should have the answers you require. If you encounter any issues, do not hesitate to write again!

Warmly,

Elenore Larkspur

"Who's the letter from?" Rose asked.

"It's from the camp arts-and-crafts teacher. We called her Sensei Elenore. I wrote to her and asked her a question, and she wrote me back."

Dooley felt his chest fill with a happy contentment as he remembered his week at Camp Pukwudgee. He was already counting down the days until he could go back. Glancing down at his open backpack and seeing his language arts textbook Dooley's present reality came rushing back to him.

When they pulled into the garage Dooley was surprised to see his dad's car already there.

"Hey, buddy!" Paul called. He was standing by the kitchen counter, reading the newspaper.

"Why are you home so early?" asked Dooley as he dropped his backpack on the table and opened the refrigerator.

"I had a dentist appointment this afternoon. How was school?"

"Good." Dooley took out an apple and washed it in the sink.

"How's Sherwood Forest?" Paul asked.

"Almost finished. It looks pretty cool." Dooley took a bite of his apple and chewed slowly. "Okay. Random question," he began, "You're older than mom, right?"

"Yes. I'm three years older. Why do you ask?"

"I was just thinking—is it weird for people who have a big difference in their ages to get married?"

Suddenly, Rose sprung from the sofa in the living room and bolted into the kitchen. "Why are you asking that? Do you like an 8th grader? Is this about the Fall Dance?" she sputtered.

Dooley rolled his eyes. "No! This isn't about me!"

"Oh," said Rose a little sadly as she sat down in one of the kitchen chairs.

"Then why are you asking about people getting married who are different ages?" Paul asked.

"Yesterday, Gus told me that Mrs. Hammond used to be married to his brother. His *older* brother."

"That *is* strange," said Rose. "Gus must be in his late seventies and I would guess Mrs. Hammond is maybe 35?"

"But Slade Hammond wasn't that old when he died five years ago." Paul walked to the coat closet and took out his briefcase. "I was concerned that the senior supervisors were covering up information about accidents and safety protocol at the jelly factory, so I did a little digging." He found a piece of paper and laid it on the table. "This is the obituary for Slade Hammond. I found it at the library and made a copy."

Dooley picked up the paper. He looked at the tiny black-and-white headshot and skimmed the short paragraph. *Slade Hammond, 31, of Peacock Valley... He leaves behind his beloved wife Clara (Bedford) Hammond and various Hammond relatives... died too soon doing what he loved best—making jelly.*

"It doesn't explain much about how he died, does it?" Paul asked.

"No. It sure doesn't, but it does tell me one thing," said Dooley. "There's no way Slade Hammond could be Gus' *older* brother."

Chapter 14

REBOOT

Dooley felt foolish that he hadn't already thought of using his *Cantata Liber*, the reference book for Visus which Elenore had suggested in her letter. After supper, he ran up to his room and found the massive, ordinary-looking textbook on the floor of his closet. The book was charmed so that if any non-Visus person tried to read it, it would appear to be a mind-numbing book about mathematics. But being a Visus with supernatural vision, when Dooley opened the book it presented him with answers to whatever questions he had at that moment.

Dooley closed his eyes and concentrated on his question—*How do you wake up a bewitched button?* Then he opened his eyes and turned to the title page.

REBOOT: The Art of Resuscitating Charmed Objects in a Resting State, By Karen Keepe

He flipped to the next page and scanned the introduction,

then he moved on to the Table of Contents. Dooley ran his finger down the list of chapters, reading the names of various inanimate objects one might charm. "Household appliances, writing utensils, automobiles, photographs, clothing… hmmm… page 53…" Dooley flipped through the book, trying not to let himself get distracted by the pictures and diagrams on the preceding pages.

Finding the chapter about magical clothing, Dooley read about a French magician who originated the "pull a rabbit out of a hat" trick in the 19th century. "After the magician's death," he read aloud from the book, "the silk top hat sat unused for more than a century. The hat embarked on a journey made up of a series of estate sales and consignment shops, which eventually led the worn and tattered hat to a table at a yard sale in Yeehaw Junction, Florida. The hat was spotted by a shopper who recognized the hat's significance, purchased it, and set about trying to awaken its dormant magical powers which lay beneath the thin silk fabric."

"Dooley," Rose called from the bottom of the stairs, "Cyrano is here."

Cyrano opened the door and sat next to Dooley on the floor. "Whatcha doing?"

"Oh, hey," Dooley said, barely looking up from his book, "I'm reading about how to wake up magical clothing."

Cyrano glanced down at the page, trying to see what Dooley saw. He had to take off his glasses and rub his eyes instead. "Looks like Cicely's geometry homework to me. What does it say?"

"Well, this guy found an old top hat that belonged to

a magician. He worked for years to get the hat to be magical again."

"Did he get it to work?" asked Cyrano.

"Yes, for the most part." Dooley turned a page. "But he could never pull a regular white rabbit out of it. All of them had extra-long ears or purple stripes or something weird like that."

"Does it say anything about buttons?"

"Not really. There's a chapter at the end of the book about miscellaneous objects that are small and really ordinary—it's called 'Tiny not Shiny.' I think I might find what I'm looking for in that one."

"Oh, I almost forgot," said Cyrano. "My mom said I could invite you to go to Eddie's with us to get some ice cream. Cicely's working tonight, and she said it's pretty empty."

"My mom won't usually let me go out on a school night, but it's worth a try."

After Rose's initial hesitation, she said it was okay as long he had finished all his homework. Dooley tossed the book back in his closet and rushed over to Cyrano's house.

"All aboard the Mulligan Express," Cyrano's dad called as Dooley hopped into an orange and white Volkswagen bus and found an empty back seat.

Chapter 15

EDDIE'S

With Cicely working behind the counter, Cyrano's parents and his five other brothers and sisters sat at the two larger tables in the ice cream parlor. Dooley and Cyrano sat together at one of the smaller tables, quietly discussing the information about Gus' brother Slade and what kind of accidents could happen at a jelly factory.

"I bet that jelly gets pretty hot," Dooley offered. "Maybe he got burned really bad."

"Or maybe there was a fire," said Cyrano, "or the machinery exploded."

The door opened, making a metallic, tinkling noise. Simon and Nathan walked in. When they saw Dooley, they waved and walked over.

"Hey, Dooley!" said Simon.

"Hey," said Dooley. "This is my friend Cyrano."

"Cool! I'm Simon, and this is Nathan. We go to school with Dooley. We eat lunch together!" Simon said happily.

"My mom gave us a ride to the book store a few doors

down, and then she's picking us up here later," Nathan
explained with only a fraction of Simon's trademark enthusiasm. "Let's go order. I'm starving."

The boys paid for their cones—one scoop of fudge ripple
for Simon and one scoop each of licorice and lime sherbet for
Nathan—and they joined Dooley and Cyrano at their table.

"We were just talking about how Mrs. Hammond's husband died," said Dooley. "Do you know anything about it?"

Simon and Nathan looked at each other warily. "Are
you sure you want to get into that?" Simon asked quietly.

"Yeah, seems like you got into enough trouble already,"
said Nathan. "Maybe you should just let sleeping dogs lie."

"Which reminds me," Simon replied, "Fun fact: Pekingese
are one of the oldest known dog breeds. They were once
owned by Chinese royalty." Simon looked at his tablemates
expectantly but was met instead with blank expressions.
"What? I've been learning Mandarin Chinese. I find the
Chinese culture really fascinating!"

"I'm not trying to start any trouble or anything," Dooley
declared. "I just feel like there's something strange going on
at J.J. Lawrence Middle School. People are keeping secrets."

"So you think there's some kind of a conspiracy?" said
Nathan.

"I don't know. All I know is that after being there a few
weeks, I think stuff is happening that we aren't supposed
to see, and it has to do with Mrs. Hammond and Gus. Did
you know they're related?"

"Gus, the custodian?" Nathan asked. "They don't even act
like they know each other."

"Right? Gus' brother was married to her. His name was Slade, and he's the one who died at the jelly factory," said Dooley.

Simon sighed. "Okay. So I asked my older brother Jason about her. He was in Mrs. Hammond's class when her husband... you know..."

"Died," Nathan offered.

"Right. So Jason said she was all smiles and games and candy prizes one day and then... well, everything changed. After the accident, they had a substitute teacher for a couple of weeks. One day Ms. Stearns came in and cleaned off the top of Mrs. Hammond's desk, put framed pictures and her collection of little stuffed lambs in a box. Jason asked her if Mrs. Hammond had quit. Ms. Stearns said that she was coming back, but she didn't want personal stuff sitting out to remind her of what had happened to her husband. She said some memories just hurt too much to remember."

The boys sat, silently licking the sides of their ice cream cones. As Dooley watched Nathan's strange flavor combination turn an unappetizing gray-green color where the scoops touched, he wondered what memories he would rather erase if given the chance. But who would he be without them?

"Alright, boys," Cyrano's dad said, "time to go. Let's get Dooley back home."

Chapter 16

THEO

After school on Wednesday, Dooley went as usual to Gus' workroom by the concession stand in the gymnasium. The lights were off, and the room was empty. The branches of the giant tree they had made cast inky shadows in the back corner.

"Gus?" Dooley called. No one answered.

Dooley headed back to the office to ask the school secretary if Gus had left.

"Ah, yes. I was supposed to leave a note in the workroom for you," Ms. Cato said. "As if I didn't have enough to do already—delivering notes across the school, finding recipes for cakes shaped liked medieval castles, babysitting that lazy cat just because he likes my desk better—but no one cares about my to-do list. It would serve him right if Pumpkin escapes." She looked up at Dooley with tired eyes.

"Pumpkin?" he asked.

"Principal Ramsey's cat."

"Oh."

Ms. Cato sighed. "Gus called this morning to say he wasn't able to come to school today."

"Is he sick?" asked Dooley.

"I don't know. Possibly." She squinted at her computer screen. "I'm not a doctor, so I couldn't say for sure."

Dooley realized he wasn't going to get any more information from her. "May I use this phone?"

She nodded indifferently as she continued to type.

"Mom?" Dooley said as soon as his mom answered. "Yeah, everything's okay. Gus isn't here today, so can you come pick me up now?"

Rose arrived, and he jumped in their minivan.

"I'm heading to my haircut appointment," she said. "You'll have to come with me, or I'll be late."

Dooley recognized the neighborhood where they were driving. "Do you get your haircut near the nursing home?" he asked.

"Actually, we'll drive really close to it. Why?"

"I'm worried about Gus. Could you drop me off there, then come back and get me after your appointment? I want to check on him."

"Sure, as long as you don't think he'll mind you dropping in unannounced."

"I think he'll be okay. If he's asleep or not feeling good, I'll just sit outside on one of those benches and wait for you."

When Dooley arrived at the nursing home, the receptionist told him that Gus and his brother were in the solarium, a sunny room where the residents with the most severe memory loss often congregated in the afternoon.

Moments later Dooley was standing in the doorway of the solarium and looking at a room full of windows and comfortable recliners. Residents filled half of the seats and most seemed to be napping. He was surprised to see that a few of the adults were younger than he had expected, maybe in their early sixties. A nurse was sitting by a woman who was trying to recall a detail from a story about one of her children. The nurse listened patiently.

By the far wall of windows, Dooley noticed a man sitting in a rust-colored recliner. The window panes were covered with suction cups holding stained glass ornaments of hummingbirds made from tiny pieces of green and red and blue glass. The late afternoon sun streamed through the suncatchers, casting colored light on the man's face, making his nose appear green and his right eyelid red with a patch of blue on his cheek.

Dooley assumed the man must be Theo, Gus' brother. He recognized a similar balding head and prominent ears, forehead and chin. Missing was Gus' scraggly beard. This man was clean shaven. Dooley approached the man, but seeing that his eyes were closed, he started to back out of the room quietly.

"No need to hurry off," Theo said, groggily.

"Oh, I'm sorry."

"Sorry for what?"

"I didn't mean to wake you up. I was looking for your brother Gus."

"He's probably gone to the flagpole," Theo suggested. "It must be past time for morning announcements."

"The flagpole?"

"Sure, that's where we get our chore for the day. Yesterday I had to clean the boys' toilets."

Dooley looked confused. "They make you clean the bathrooms here?"

"Yeah, but it's not too bad. As long as we do it every day, it stays pretty clean."

"I guess that's true."

"The worst chore I ever had was cleaning up after the Shagamaw. Who would've thought a boar could make such a mess? The cooks should know better than to leave out the cake frosting."

"You know about the Shagamaw Boar?" Dooley asked.

"Slade always says you can get a Shagamaw Boar to do anything if you give him something sweet," Theo continued, ignoring Dooley's question. "O' course, Slade also likes to give sweets to girls, too. Ever since he turned 15, girls are all he talks about. I reckon he'll find a pretty one this summer."

"This summer?" Dooley repeated, without knowing what else to say.

"Sure. Me and my brothers are here year round, but there's always new kids coming for the summer to Camp Pukwudgee."

Chapter 17

SPECKS & MITTS

"**D**ooley?" Gus was standing just behind Dooley, holding a plate of cookies in one hand and a glass of milk in the other. "What're you doing here?"

"You weren't at school today, so I came to check on you," Dooley stammered, a little flustered by Gus' sudden appearance.

"That was kind of you," Gus answered as he laid the glass and plate on the end table by Theo's chair. "My brother wasn't feeling too good this morning." Gus patted Theo's shoulder. "But he's better now, aren't you, Specks?"

"I'm as right as rain, Mitts." Theo looked down at the plate and asked, "Vanilla wafers? Didn't they have any chocolate chippers?"

"Sorry. That's the best I could do." Gus rolled a wheelchair next to Theo's recliner. "Hop in and let's get you back to our room so you can watch your programs." Theo held the plate of cookies in his lap, and Dooley carried his glass of milk while Gus wheeled him to their shared room. Then he switched on the television. "Your game show is on. Me and Dooley will visit in the other room while you watch and eat your snack. How's that sound?"

"206!" Theo shouted at the television. "Everyone knows the human adult body has 206 bones. Gimme a hard one!"

"Come on, Dooley," Gus said. "He'll be happy for a while. He loves them trivia game shows. Theo is just full of worthless facts."

"I should bring Simon over to meet him. He's always telling people his random fun facts."

Dooley followed Gus to two green plaid armchairs situated on either side of a cold fireplace. Gus sat down with a tired sigh and hunched forward.

"Theo hasn't had a morning this bad in months," Gus said as he stared down at his hands. "His poor memory keeps him in a kind of a fog most days, but today it made him angry. None of the nurses could get him calmed down. They was afraid he'd hurt hisself. Only thing that made him happy was if I promised to stay with him."

"If he has a memory problem, how is he able to remember the answers to the questions on that show?"

"From what I been told, memory loss and dementia don't always follow the rules. Some folks can remember what happened 50 years ago, but not what happened yesterday. They've tried all kinds of things with Theo—medicines, vitamins, music therapy. He seemed like he liked art therapy. That's when they give the patients art projects to do. They say it's good for them to express themselves, how they're feeling and such. That's when he made those hummingbird sun-catchers I hung on the window in the solarium. It helped put him in a better mood for a while, but it didn't bring him back to his old self."

Dooley didn't speak for a moment as he tried to decide how to bring up the things Theo had revealed to him about Camp Pukwudgee. "Does he always think he's still a young boy?"

"Yep. His memory is stuck in a stretch of time that happened years ago. I reckon it was when he was his happiest."

"At summer camp?" asked Dooley quietly.

"That's the one."

"I don't blame him for feeling that way," said Dooley. "My week at Camp Pukwudgee was the best time of my life, too."

Gus swiveled his head quickly to look at Dooley. "You went to Camp Pukwudgee?" he whispered.

"Last summer. I can't wait to go back."

"Will wonders never cease," said Gus, leaning back in his chair and smiling. "How is the old place?"

"Really great. The craft shack looked like a Chinese pagoda this year."

"I've thought about taking Theo back there, but I don't know if it would just confuse him more."

"I heard you call him *Specks*," said Dooley. "What was that about?"

"Oh, all of us had nicknames for each other growing up. Theo was Specks, short for spectacles because he could see things other people couldn't…"

"He was a Visus?" Dooley exclaimed.

"Shhhh," Gus warned. "Not so loud, son. Yep, Theo was a Visus."

"What about you?" Dooley whispered. "Why did he call you *Mitts*?"

"Oh, that's an old story," Gus chuckled. "I once caught a wapaloosie."

"Wapaloosie? I don't remember that one from the field guide."

"I reckon that's because I caught the last one ever seen in the Bloodstone Forest. It was furry, about the size of a wiener dog with a spiky tail. It could climb better than any creature I ever seen. Well, I caught it and killed it and skinned it. I made a pair of mittens out of the fur. When I wore them mittens, I could climb just as well as a wapaloosie. And that's how I got the nickname, Mitts." As Gus spoke, Dooley saw his face change into a younger version of the old man. The change ironed out his wrinkles and erased his age spots until he looked like a teenager.

"Gus, how do you do that?" Dooley asked.

"Do what?"

"Change your face to look young." Dooley dropped his voice to a whisper. "Is that your power?"

"Oh." Dooley watched as Gus' face suddenly changed back to his older self. "That's just the leftovers from what I used to be able to do." He looked back down at his hands again. "You must also be a Visus, if you can see that."

"Then what was your power?" asked Dooley.

The three DuBois sisters walked into the sitting room, each carrying a cloth bag and wearing their matching peacock blue cardigans. Gus frowned as he watched them sit down on the sofa and take out their balls of yarn and knitting needles.

"Let's go sit outside," said Gus. "It's not too hot this afternoon, and I could use a bit of fresh air."

Chapter 18

JINXY

Once they were situated on the bench, Gus began, "Me and my brothers were different right from the start, but that didn't make things easy for us. Both our parents had died. We were living with an old aunt who didn't really want anything to do with us. It was 1939, and the war was in full swing over in Europe. Most of the folks here in the States looked at it as none of our business. 'Let the Frenchies figure it out,' they'd say. But there was a man—everybody just called him Mr. G—whose job it was to find people, kids mainly, with special abilities. Unique talents, you might say. Us kids had special abilities that Mr. G could use if America were to join in the fighting."

"So he found out about you and your brothers?" asked Dooley.

"Yep. When news gets out that you're a Binoc, it's not too hard for people to find you."

"What's a Binoc?"

"That's what we call someone who can see things very

far away, like binoculars. My chart at the Institute called it *Remote Viewing*. But we never really called it that."

"What about Slade? What was his power?"

"He was a Jumper," Gus answered. "He could travel through time." Gus stopped speaking to intently watch a robin pecking in the ground. Each time Gus took a breath, his shoulders would rise up, and with each exhale he would slump forward a little. Dooley thought he looked older than he had just the day before. After a few seconds, Gus continued. "A tricky thing, time travel. More often than not, Slade bungled his jumps. That's how he got the nickname, *Jinxy*. It was like he was jinxed, cursed with bad luck."

"I don't know anyone who can time travel. That must be really difficult."

"It's unusual, that's for sure. I was able to do a bit of jumping myself. Short jumps, mind you, not like Slade's long ones. I was more of a hopper, I reckon. That's why my face can sometimes looked younger. It's the effects of fooling with time."

"Would you jump to the future or to the past?" asked Dooley.

"Both of us could only jump forward and then back to present time. With me, it was a little hop—maybe half an hour at the most. But Slade got to where he could go days and then months and eventually years into the future. Most times when he'd get back to us, he'd have to take to his bed, sick as a dog. He'd run a fever, and he wouldn't be able to keep anything in his stomach. Almost like having a bad case of the flu. Me and Theo begged him to stop jumping, but Slade wasn't one to shy away from a challenge."

As if suddenly solving a complex puzzle, Dooley cried out, "Of course!"

"What is it?" a startled Gus asked.

"That's how Slade was married to Mrs. Hammond. He jumped into the future!"

"Keep your voice down," Gus hissed. "Do you want all of Juneberry Meadows to know?"

"Sorry."

"We were young kids when Mr. G found us and brought us to the Institute. I was just five years old. But there was a different man, a kind man who understood what it was like to have these powers. After two years at that awful place, he took us to live full time out in the woods at Camp Pukwudgee. His name was—"

"Peter Johansson," Dooley said, finishing Gus' sentence.

"That was him. As much as the Institute was miserable and cold, Camp Pukwudgee was wonderful—the best home us boys had ever had. Peter took us away from that awful place, then after his mom died, he moved away. Maybe if he had still been there Slade wouldn't have done what he did…"

"What happened?"

"When he was 18 years old, Slade jumped so far to the future—me and Theo thought he'd be gone forever. We was only kids, Theo 15 and me just turned 12. We wouldn't see him again for 55 years."

"Slade jumped 55 years into the future?"

"Yep. That was the only jump he made when he couldn't get back to the present. We were old men when Slade showed up back at Pukwudgee. We had stayed on as caretakers at the camp. I was head of forestry and bee-keeping, and Theo ran the craft shack. In fact, they fixed up the craft shack—put in a bedroom and a kitchen—so that we could live there. Then one day, Slade just appeared at our back door, nearly dead. After a few days, we decided to leave camp to take care of Slade. Too many people might recognize him and start trouble for us. We moved to Peacock Valley to start fresh and called Slade our nephew."

"And that's when Slade met Mrs. Hammond," Dooley concluded. "Because they at least looked like they were the same age."

"As far as Slade was concerned, they were the same age. You couldn't hardly count the years he was mid-jump between places."

They stopped talking as a couple walked by them, carrying flowers and chatting happily. The automatic doors opened, and they walked inside. Dooley assumed they were coming to visit a resident at the nursing home, such ordinary moments happening just down the hall from such extraordinary men.

"You know," Gus said, "since you're a Visus and all, I have a favor."

"What is it?"

"I carry a book with me wherever I go. It's an old note-book that Theo kept notes in—Visus notes, mind you—and I can't read it."

"If you can't read it, why do you carry it around?"

"I don't know if it's from our time at the Institute or just an old man's nervousness, but I don't feel like it's safe unless it's with me."

"Was it in that bag you left in our car?"

"That's the one," answered Gus. "Do you mind giving it a look? Theo hasn't been in a state of mind to read it for years, and I've always wondered if it had something written in there that I should know."

"I'd be happy to look at it. Anything to help."

Chapter 19

THE LONG JUMP

As soon as Dooley got home, he went straight to his room to study Theo's notebook. It looked like any regular composition notebook with its black and white marbled cover. This one was obviously old, the cover had a brown ring near the center, as if someone had rested an over-filled cup of coffee on it, and the upper right corner looked like it had been chewed by a dog. Dooley opened it to the first page and saw a date at the top—January 1, 1945. Below the date, it read:

Slade has decided to jump to learn how this war will end. He has tried in the past, but each jump takes him to a time when the world is still fighting. We tried to tell him to stop, but I think he feels guilty because he cannot enlist. He tried when he turned 18, but the army doctor said he has a bad ticker. All of his jumping has weakened his heart, so the army will not take him. I reckon he is looking for any way he can be of help to his country. He asked me to keep this journal as a log of what happens. He said that is what scientists do.

Dooley continued reading to the days after Slade's jump.

We must find a way to get Slade back. He has never been gone this long. I worry that he got back but missed his mark and landed outside of Pukwudgee. I know he would want us to be brave, and I am trying. Mitts is only 12. He wants to jump and find him, but I do not think that will work. I wish Peter was here.

Flipping through the notebook, Dooley saw pages of notes in blue-black ink, words pressed down with a heavy hand at times so that the ink flowed too freely, making the letters thick and jumbled. Aware that Gus had charged him with reading all of the journal, Dooley realized he would have to read the entries dated 1945, 1946, 1947 and on, but knowing how the story ended made the thought of reading Theo's words of anguish and worry too difficult for him to absorb just then. He wanted to get to the end, to the part when Slade returned.

Dooley saw that there was a wide space of time when Theo had stopped writing. Somewhere in the early 1960's he must've given up on ever seeing his older brother again. Then, as if he'd dug up the forgotten journal after nearly 40 years, Theo wrote another entry. It was dated January 1, 2000. He had written just three words: *Slade came home.*

The following day, Theo wrote:

January 2, 2000. Slade was lying on the ground by the back door. He was as white as a ghost and so thin. Me and Gus dragged him inside and bundled him up in quilts in front of the stove. He was shaking so bad he could not say a word, though he tried to speak. Gus warmed some broth and ladled it to him like he was a baby. When his color finally came back, he asked us who we were. He did not know us. When he left all those years ago, we was his younger brothers, just 15 and 12 years old. Now we are old men past 60. He shook his head because he did not believe me. When I called him Jinxy and explained that he had jumped to the year 2000, Slade passed out cold.

Dooley turned the page of the journal and read on.

January 3, 2000. Me and Gus have decided to leave Pukwudgee. People are starting to ask questions about Slade, and we do not want any trouble. We will look for some quiet place with a lot of trees and birds where Gus can find work as a handyman or a janitor, and I will tend to Slade. A change in scenery and new faces are just what he needs.

Just before his dad called him down to eat supper, Dooley read an entry dated about four years after the brothers had moved to Peacock Valley.

Slade came home from work at the jelly factory as happy as a lark today. I asked him if he got a raise, but he said he met a girl. After the summer break, she is to be a teacher at the new middle school they are naming after that cowboy star. Slade said her name is Clara, but he kept calling her Lamb. He said she is as gentle and sweet as a little lamb. Sounds like Jinxy found himself a girlfriend. Maybe it will be just the thing to keep him from ever jumping again.

Chapter 20

TINY NOT SHINY

Dooley hurried back up to his room after eating supper with his parents. Just as he picked up Theo's journal to continue reading it, he spied the blue button sitting alone in the Dancing Shagamaw Boars bowl. His curiosity had been piqued by Theo's description of Clara Hammond, his seemingly unfriendly and unforgiving teacher, but Dooley knew he needed to finish solving the riddle of waking up the magical object.

He set the notebook back on his bed and pulled out his *Cantata Liber*, searching for the place where he had stopped reading. "Chapter twenty-two, tiny not shiny," Dooley read aloud.

Commonplace items which can be held in the palm of one's hand are most easily charmed and then hidden in plain sight. It was originally assumed that the smaller the item, the less magic it could absorb. This hypothesis was famously tested by Professor Samson Hubert's Toothpick Experiment which ultimately lead to the extinction of a once-plentiful species of Australian butterfly, but that story is for another time. The lesson Professor Hubert learned was that size often doesn't matter. What does matter is the method you use to awaken something small and possibly delicate. In this chapter, the reader will find a variety of options, but the basic rule of thumb is always begin with the simplest method. In this case, it is the following: hold the object in your hand, stroke it gently and whisper, "Wake up, sleepyhead." To test its alertness, attempt to use the object for its intended purpose.

Dooley chuckled quietly at the idea of whispering to a tiny button, but he decided it was worth a try. Leaving the book open in his lap, he picked up the button and placed it directly in the center of his hand. He rubbed it with his finger and brought his hand to his mouth. Then he whispered, "Wake up, sleepyhead." Dooley waited, watching the button for any changes in appearance, but nothing happened. He opened his bedside table drawer and pulled out Elenore's letter to remind himself what to do next.

Dooley read her words aloud, "…hold the button tightly in your right hand, briefly focus on an object that might stir a memory, and close your eyes. Then say a few lines of a sentimental song from the era of the button's creation. I'd suggest something such as, "I'll see you in my dreams, and then I'll hold you in my dreams. Someone took you out of my arms, still I feel the thrill of your charms.'"

Following Elenore's instructions, Dooley firmly grasped the button so that he could feel it making a round impression in his palm. He reread the song lyrics a few times to commit them to memory. Then, before closing his eyes, he glanced around his room for something to focus on. His eyes lit on a red pencil he was given on his first day of 7th grade. J.J. LAWRENCE MIDDLE SCHOOL was printed on the side in gold letters. Dooley closed his eyes and repeated the sentence, "I'll see you in my dreams, and then I'll hold you in my dreams. Someone took you out of my arms, still I feel the thrill of your charms."

When Dooley opened his eyes, he saw a thin, long-legged man standing in front of him wearing a black shirt accentuated with white piping along the collar and front pockets. A yellow bandana was tied around his neck and pulled to one side. When the man noticed Dooley sitting on his bed, he took off his tall, white Stetson and held it to his chest. He took a step toward Dooley, the spurs on his boots clanking together.

"Howdy," said the man with a soft, Southern accent.

Dooley shrieked and crawled backwards over his bed, grasping for his covers.

"Awww, I didn't mean to frighten the little fella." The cowboy returned his hat to his head and bent down toward Dooley with a big hand on each knee. "I ain't gonna hurt you none, I promise. And a promise of mine is something you can count on. It's just as sure as the Rio Grande will keep a-flowing into the Gulf of Mexico." The man displayed a friendly gap-tooth smile and thrust out his hand.

"Who are… How did…" Dooley stuttered as he shook the man's hand limply. "Are you from my memory?"

"I couldn't rightly say."

"How did you get here?"

"I couldn't rightly say that neither."

Dooley's mind was spinning. "Are you… real?"

"I reckon you're plumb full of questions, aren't you, little fella?" The man unsnapped a coil of rope from his belt and weighed it in his hand. "All's I can say is that it feels mighty nice to be standing here. Makes me wanna sing. *Yodel-lay-yodel-lay-yodel-lay-eee!*"

"Are you Jasper Lawrence?" Dooley gasped.

Suddenly, there was a knock on the door. "Dooley," his mom called from the hall, "time to get ready for bed."

Dooley fumbled the button and dropped it on the floor. The cowboy vanished.

Chapter 21

JASPER

Early the next morning, Dooley lay on his side and stared at the button sitting in the bowl on his bedside table. After dropping it the night before when his mother knocked on his door, he had retrieved the button from the floor and placed it in the bowl, deciding that he'd wait to make another attempt at using it. Seeing the late J.J. Lawrence standing in his bedroom—spurs, boots, hat, and all—had unsettled Dooley more than he'd wanted to admit, even to himself.

He glanced at his clock. He still had time before school to try the button again. Dooley slid out of bed and stood barefoot next to his bedside table. Repeating his actions from the night before, he held the button tightly in his hand, closed his eyes and said, "I'll see you in my dreams, and then I'll hold you in my dreams. Someone took you out of my arms, still I feel the thrill of your charms."

Once again, the same skinny cowboy was standing before him.

"Jasper?" Dooley asked.

"That's me!" Jasper responded, cheerfully. "Jasper Jericho Lawrence, at your service!"

"I don't understand," Dooley said, as much to himself as to Jasper. "I have this button and, well—it's supposed to bring back memories, *my* memories."

"And you're wondering how's come I'm standing here when we never met before, so I can't be from your memory."

"Right!" agreed Dooley.

"Well, here's the thing—I'm not really here."

"Oh."

"When you were pulling from the air to bring out a memory, you must've breathed in one of the memory puffs I left here." Jasper walked over to a window and pulled back Dooley's curtain. "Where are we anyway?"

"Peacock Valley, Minnesota."

"Is that so?" Jasper responded cheerfully, slapping his knee. "Well, I'll be hornswoggled! This is where I was born and raised!"

"I know," said Dooley. "They named the middle school after you. You're pretty famous."

"That is something, isn't it, little fella? I left memory puffs all over the place—in France when I was fighting in the war and in Hollywood when I was making movies, but it's like they always say, *There's no place like home.*"

"What's a memory puff?" Dooley asked.

"It was a little piece of magic of my own invention." Jasper smiled proudly. "I made up a cloud with tiny drops of myself in it, then with a *yodel-lay-yodel-lay-hee-who* I could set that cloud to roost wherever I wanted it to."

"I've never heard of anything like that before," said Dooley with admiration in his voice. "Is your yodeling kind of like casting a spell?"

"I reckon you could call it that." Jasper unholstered his pistol, spun it around his trigger finger and re-holstered it with lightning speed. "I was real particular where I hung those clouds. I wanted them to be in places where my memory could serve the people who were living there, places where I encountered some kind of evil."

"Evil? Here in Peacock Valley?"

"You'd be surprised, little fella."

Dooley instantly summoned a mental picture of Birna, the Valkyrie on the flying horse he had defeated right in his front yard. On second thought, maybe he could imagine forces of evil in Peacock Valley.

"I've got to get ready for school now, so I guess I'll talk to you later, Jasper."

"It's been real nice visiting with you. I didn't catch your name."

"Dooley."

Jasper tipped his hat. "Well, Dooley, you feel free to pull up this memory again, if you're so inclined. I should tell you, though—there's a limit on how many times a memory puff can be opened. The tiny drops start to break away from each other every time you breathe in this memory."

"How many times will I be able to find you?"

"Hard to say, but you'll know when it's nearly spent."

Dooley nodded his head, creases of concern etched on his forehead. "Thanks for the advice. I'll talk to you soon."

"Farewell, partner and remember: Keep your hat handy, your socks dry, and your friends close."

Dooley dropped the button in the bowl and watched Jasper disappear in a blue mist.

Chapter 22

UNTYING A DIFFICULT KNOT

As Dooley carried his lunch sack and sat down at the table he shared with Simon, Nathan, Lark, and Fiona, he looked at the cafeteria's cowboy decorations in a new light. He could imagine Jasper standing in the middle of the chaos, tipping his white hat and yodeling until a blue cloud was suspended above them. He was so engrossed in his imagination, Dooley didn't realize that Nathan was talking to him.

"Earth to Dooley," said Nathan. "Hello…"

"Oh, sorry."

"What are you thinking about?" Lark asked. "You look like you're about a million miles away."

"I was just thinking about Jasper Lawrence," Dooley said. "He must've been a pretty interesting guy."

"That's for sure!" Simon chimed in. "Seems like he was great at everything he did! He held records in yodeling, sharp-shooting, and knot-tying. Fun fact: J.J. Lawrence held the record for being the fastest to untie one of the most difficult knots—the Double Fishermen's Bend." Simon took a bite of his sandwich and chewed thoughtfully. "What a guy! I wish I could've met J.J.!"

"Yeah, he sounds amazing," Dooley said, smiling. "Sorry, Nathan. What were you saying before?"

"I was asking you if everything is ready for the dance on Saturday," said Nathan. "It's only two days away."

"I bet Ms. Stearns is going crazy with all those last minute details," Fiona said. "She came to choir practice yesterday wearing two different shoes."

"As far decorating the gym, everything should be finished in time. I think we're almost done. We didn't do anything yesterday because Gus had to stay home. His brother was sick."

On the other side of the cafeteria, a girl with long black hair suddenly dropped her lunch tray, dumping taco meat, tortilla chips, and nacho cheese all over the lunchroom floor. Jake Fossberg and his friends cheered and began chanting, "Butterfinger! Butterfinger! Butterfinger!"

Two lunch ladies came to the girl's aid, sweeping up the chips and meat. Lark frowned and grabbed a wad of napkins from their table. She went to help the girl wipe the gooey cheese from her socks and sneakers.

"I heard Jake and his gang all asked girls to be their dates to the dance," said Fiona, frowning as she watched the boys still pointing and laughing hysterically.

"Do most people take dates to the dance?" asked Dooley, a wave of panic rising inside him, threatening the bite of peanut butter sandwich he was attempting to swallow.

"No," Nathan answered. "Jake just feels like he has to

outdo everybody, and his knuckle-dragging friends just go along with whatever he does."

"I brought cupcakes for my birthday when we were in the third grade. The next day, Jake brought cupcakes *and* ice cream, and it wasn't even his birthday," said Fiona. "He's never happy unless he can prove he's better than you."

Lark rejoined them, wiping her hands on a napkin. "So, Dooley, can you meet tonight to work on our science project?" she asked.

"Oh, yeah. I almost forgot," said Dooley. "What time?"

"Simon can't be there until after band practice, so we're thinking 7:00 at Eddie's, the ice cream place on the square," Fiona said.

"I wish I had science 3rd period with you guys instead of 5th period, so I could be in your group for the project," said Nathan. "My group wants to grow mold. It's so boring."

"That really stinks, Nate, but it's partly your fault if you don't say anything when they make dumb suggestions for the project. Stand up to your group and tell them what you want to do," instructed Fiona. "Let's all come tonight with a list of possible project ideas and pick which one sounds best."

Simon and Dooley agreed with Fiona's plan while Lark sympathetically patted Nathan on the back.

Chapter 23

VISUS BERRIES

Dooley and Gus worked all afternoon, cutting long pieces of black fabric which they planned to drape across the gym ceiling for the dance. "We can't hang these yet on account of basketball practice, but we can get 'em all cut," Gus said.

When they had finished with the fabric, they began twisting wire on the top of open glass jars, then placing a small battery-powered candle in each one. "These jars'll hang from them tree branches we made. Wilhelmina said she wants the forest to look like it's got a host of pixies living in it. We'll string up some white twinkle lights with the black fabric in the ceiling, too."

On his ride home from working with Gus, Dooley found that he was actually excited to see how all of the dance decorations came out. He realized he was finally beginning to think of J.J. Lawrence as *his* school, and the people he sat with at lunch as *his* friends. He was also relieved to notice that the panic he had felt at lunch about asking a girl to the dance had faded.

When his mom pulled up to their house, Cyrano was waiting for him on the front porch.

"Hello, Cyrano," Rose called.

"Hey, Mrs. Creed," said Cyrano. "Is it okay if Dooley comes over to my house for a little bit? My sister Calix has something to show him."

"That's fine as long as he's home for supper."

Dooley and Cyrano hurried next door.

"Is it ready?" Dooley asked, panting as he struggled to keep up with Cyrano's long legs.

"Yep," said Cyrano. "Calix saw the berries on the plants this morning."

"That was fast!"

When the boys got to the backyard and entered the greenhouse, Dooley saw Cyrano's older sister Calix wearing a short gardening apron and work gloves. He could hear a voice speaking, but it wasn't hers.

"Dorești să dansezi cu mine? Would you like to dance with me?"

"Where's that voice coming from?" asked Dooley.

"Unde este toaleta? Where is the bathroom?"

"Calix thought the plants would feel more comfortable hearing this since the seeds came from Romania," Cyrano answered. "That's one of those tapes people listen to when they want to learn a new language. This one has some guy speaking Romanian."

"Poți vorbi mai rar? Can you speak slowly?"

Cyrano turned off the tape recorder. "Hey, Calix. I brought Dooley over to see the berries."

"Thank you, dear brother! I was so eager to show them

to you!" Calix held a plastic margarine bowl full of plump, yellow berries. "Aren't they just beautiful? The berries are similar to the *Celastrus scandens*, commonly known as the American Bittersweet which are poisonous, but these non-poisonous berries are distinguished by these lovely green and blue spots. Adorable!"

"So what are these called?" Dooley asked.

"The seed packet just said: *bacă galben pătat* which I think means 'yellow spotted berry,' but all indications lead me to believe that it's the same plant used to make Visus ink." Calix took out a paintbrush from her apron, dabbed it in a small pot of silvery powder, and painted it on one of the berries still on the plant. Right before his eyes, Dooley saw the berry swell slightly as spots appeared all over the yellow fruit. Calix plucked the berry and added it to the bowl. "Hopefully, this will be enough berries for what you need."

"Yes," Dooley said, still unsure of what to use the ink for, "I'm sure it will be more than enough. Thanks, Calix."

"You're welcome! It's been such a pleasure to learn about this interesting plant!"

Dooley picked up the bowl. "I'd better get home for supper. Bye!"

"*La revedere!*" Calix called.

"What does that mean?" Dooley asked Cyrano as they left the greenhouse.

"I think it means *goodbye* in Romanian."

"Oh." Dooley nodded. "Bye, Calix!" he called.

"I don't think she was talking to you," said Cyrano. "She was saying goodbye to the berries."

Chapter 24

INVISIBLE INK

"Lasagna will be done in twenty minutes," Rose told Dooley as soon as he had walked in the front door.

Dooley went upstairs to his room and set the plastic bowl of berries on his desk. He found the *Cantata Liber*, the giant charmed encyclopedia he kept tucked away in his closet, to look up how to make Visus ink.

He opened the book and read the title page, "Invisible Ink: A Thorough Examination of Visus Supplies, by A. T. Ramentum." Fighting the urge to read about other tools a Visus might use, such as the chapter devoted to erasing someone's visual memory and another one about improving night vision, Dooley flipped to the back of the book to look for an index. Once there, he found the heading RECIPES. He slid his finger halfway down the list, reading, "glass cleaner, horseradish ointment, ice cream syrups, ink—page 719."

Dooley turned several pages until he came to the recipe for making Visus ink. Above the list of ingredients and numbered directions, he saw a section at the top of the page with the heading: BEFORE YOU BEGIN in big, bold letters.

In most cases, the following recipe would be made and dispensed into the reservoir of a standard ink pen. The ink can also be poured in an inkwell and used with a dip pen. (For an old-fashioned twist, a feather can be used as a writing utensil, but only the feather of a blue-throated hummingbird can be dipped in Visus ink without inviting serious injury.) The reader should know that a properly concocted batch of Visus ink can be ingested. The potion will either temporarily enhance a person's powers or induce vomiting. Proceed with caution.

Just as he began to read how to make the ink, his dad appeared in the doorway. "What's in the bowl?" Paul asked.

"What?" Dooley muttered, barely looking up from his reading. "Oh, it's some berries Calix grew for me. I'm going to use them to make ink."

Paul picked up one of the yellow, spotted berries and examined it closely. "This is an unusual fruit. It's not poisonous, is it?"

"No. I don't think so. Calix said it just looks like a poisonous berry called an American bittersweet."

"Well, you need to be careful with these things." Paul returned the berry to the bowl. Dooley noticed a look of concern on his face as his dad said, "Wash up and come down to the kitchen."

Dooley reluctantly closed his book and headed to the kitchen. Just as he reached the bottom of the stairs, Dooley's dad called to him from the living room. "Hey, come in here for a minute." Paul was sitting on the sofa, looking through a stack of photographs spread out on the coffee table. "I knew I had seen that berry somewhere before."

"What is all this?" asked Dooley, sitting next to him on the sofa.

"These are the pictures taken at the jelly factory the night that Slade Hammond died." Paul stood up and walked to the roll-top desk standing in the corner of the room. He found a magnifying glass in one of the drawers.

"Like crime scene photos?"

"Kind of. I finally got the factory safety manager to give me a little more information about the accident. I guess they took these to have a record of what happened that night." Paul pointed to one of the pictures. "See what's in that bucket? Berries that look just like the ones you have upstairs."

Paul handed the magnifying glass to Dooley. His dad was right—the berries in the photos were yellow with green and blue spots. "Weird," said Dooley, quietly.

"Yes and also a reason to be very careful." Paul still wore a concerned expression.

Rose entered the living room and placed her hands on her hips. "I didn't work all afternoon on this lasagna just so it could get cold and gummy," she said with a hint of frustration in her voice. "And besides, Dooley, you need to get in here and eat if you're going to make it to your science project meeting by 7:00."

Chapter 25

SCIENCE PROJECT GROUP

Dooley was the last person in his science project group to arrive at the ice cream parlor. Lark, Simon, and Fiona were already sitting together, chatting intently. Before approaching their table, he observed the group's dynamics from the doorway. Using his past experiences from being part of groups like this one, Dooley knew it was always best to have one person step up and be the leader, preferably someone who kept everyone on track, followed the directions, and made sure they met all of the deadlines. Fiona was definitely that person. She was smart, organized, and unafraid to have an opinion. Luckily, the other members of the group were happy to let her hold that title.

"It's about time," Fiona said, checking her watch. "We've already started discussing the project."

"I'm only 10 minutes late," said Dooley.

"Eleven minutes by my watch and now we've wasted another minute talking about it." She tapped her pen on an open spiral notebook.

"Sorry." Dooley sat down in his chair, slightly abashed but mostly happy to be in a group with his friends.

"Unless you have a better idea, Dooley, we narrowed down our choices to these two," Fiona said, pointing to her notes, "a homemade battery or a Rube Goldberg machine."

"What's a Rube Goldberg machine?" asked Dooley.

"You see them a lot in cartoons," Lark explained. "A ball hits something that knocks over something else that rolls down a slide and it keeps going, kind of like dominoes, until it completes a simple task."

"Fun Fact," said Simon. "Rube Goldberg was a cartoonist and inventor. One of his famous cartoons was called *Professor Butts and the Self-Operating Napkin*."

"So what do you think?" Fiona asked. "Do you like one of those, or did you bring a different idea? We're brainstorming here, so there's no such thing as a bad idea at this point."

Dooley thought for a few seconds. "I like the battery idea better. I think the other one would be too hard to bring to school. Sounds like a lot of pieces to set up."

Fiona and Lark looked at each other and smiled, while Simon slumped in disappointment. Lark noticed Simon's sad expression and said, "The Rube Goldberg machine still sounds really cool, Simon. Maybe we can just make one for fun. Right, guys?"

"Really?" Simon brightened.

"Sure," said Dooley. "Why don't you sketch out a plan and decide what things you'll need for it, then we can make one later."

The bell above the door jingled as another customer

entered the ice cream parlor. Dooley turned to see Cyrano.

"Sorry to bug you," said Cyrano, "but can I talk to you for a minute, Dooley?"

"How did you know I was here?" asked Dooley as he stepped over to the row of trash cans by the door.

"I went to your house, and your dad told me. Calix sent me over to tell you something about the Vision Bush."

"What's the matter?"

"When she went in the greenhouse to tell her plants good-night—yeah, she does that—she saw that the Vision Bush was just a heap of gray dust. She thinks that when she picked all of the berries, the bush died. She wanted to make sure you knew, because she doesn't think she'll be able to get more seeds."

"Oh, okay."

"She called the company from the seed catalog the other day, and—using some of the phrases she learned from those language tapes—she asked them about the seeds. They couldn't find any more. I guess they're pretty rare. She was afraid you might just forget about the berries and maybe they'd go bad or something. Anyway, message delivered." Cyrano stood awkwardly when he had finished speaking.

"Do you want to come over and sit with my group for a while?" Dooley asked.

"Well, I have to hang out here until Cicely finishes her shift to get a ride back home, so I was planning to stay around until she's done."

"We're just working on a science project. It's no big deal, really."

"I guess so. I'll come over, unless you think that would be weird."

"It won't be weird," said Dooley. "Maybe you can help. Have you ever made a battery?"

Cyrano joined the group and listened in as they listed what materials they would need—pennies, aluminum foil, paper towels, vinegar, electrical tape, alligator clips, voltmeter, a small LED light—and who would bring them. Each time Simon would share a Fun Fact, like, "The U.S. penny has had the profile of President Lincoln on it since 1909, which would've been Lincoln's 100th birthday," Fiona would encourage him to stay focused on their project. She made a separate list for each of them with items to find and concepts to research.

As Dooley was reviewing his list, he overheard Lark and Cyrano talking. "You went to puppet camp?" Cyrano asked. "That sounds awesome."

"It really was! This year I got to make my own... dummy." Lark whispered the last word as if it was an insult to all puppets. "I named her Polly. She looks just like me. I even gave her a big nose." She smiled shyly.

"You think your nose is big? Come on! Your nose is great!"

"What is going on over here?" Dooley whispered to Cyrano. "I've never heard you talk about puppets before."

Cyrano blushed and began to speak, but Cicely appeared by their table before he could form a reply. "Ready to go, Cy?" his older sister asked.

"Yep," Cyrano said quickly. "See you guys around."

Dooley noticed his friend was only looking at Lark.

Chapter 26

THEO'S NOTEBOOK

Before he went to bed, Dooley took out Theo's notebook to read more about the events leading up to Slade's death. He wondered if the picture with the bucket of spotted yellow berries was connected to the accident or if it was just a coincidence. He was nearing the end of the entries, which—even though he knew what had happened—somehow made him feel nervous as he was getting closer to Slade's death. Dooley settled into his bed and leaned toward the yellow circle of light from his lamp.

Having a baby is all Clara ever talks about. They been married for nearly ten years, and most of that time she has been set on becoming a mother. It has been worrying Jinxy quite a bit here lately. Me and Mitts are getting afraid he might do something reckless. He has been ever so stable and reliable since he and Clara got hitched, but now I am starting to wonder.

Dooley turned the page and read the next entry dated a few weeks later.

I found Jinxy out in the woods trying to jump again. I knew right away what he was doing. He was standing in that way he used to do, with his knees bent and his eyes closed and his hands in hard fists. I gave him quite a scolding. I asked him what in heaven's name he was thinking trying something so dangerous and foolish. He fell to the ground and began to cry. He said he could not watch Clara—Lamb, he calls her—so down and desperate. He wanted to jump and see what would happen. Would they have a baby? Would she always be so sad? He said he is at the end of his rope.

Dooley had to pause and try to imagine his teacher, the intimidating and emotionless Mrs. Hammond, despondent because she couldn't have a child. It seemed doubtful to him. In the classroom, she didn't appear to like kids at all. Baffled but engrossed in the story, he turned another page and continued reading.

Jinxy says he remembers something about a bush Peter would grow back at Pukwudgee that he would use to make the ink. I told him that my pen has got the last of what Peter made and what good would it do him anyhow seeing as I am the only Visus in this family. But he says he once heard Peter telling another counselor that you can drink the ink. He said it is supposed to make your power stronger. I cautioned him against anything so foolhardy as drinking something like that, but Jinxy can be as hard-headed as they come. He says he is heading out to Puk-wudgee this afternoon to see if he can find that bush and pick the berries. I told him that if I was a betting man, I would lay dollars to donuts he will have no luck finding one of them bushes. If you pick every berry, the bush dies, and surely every berry has been plucked from anything Peter grew all those years ago.

Dooley noticed that the following page was the last one with Theo's writing. The final sheets in the notebook were blank. He felt his heart begin to race at the thought of what he would read next.

Me and Mitts always said he was jinxed, but we never expected him to live up to his name in this way. As I sit next to Jinxy in this hospital room with the beeping machines all around us and nurses shuffling in and out, I can hardly believe what the doctors just told me. They said he will not likely make it through the night. To think of all those years we wasted looking for him. We had thought that jumping would kill him, but it turns out his undoing would be his bad luck. When I first got to the hospital, Jinxy kept saying it wasn't his fault, but he tried to put out the fire anyway. He kept on asking if the others are alright. I couldn't make heads or tails of what he was saying because they said he was the only one at the factory.

Mitts has gone to fetch Clara, so I hope Jinxy won't pass on until she gets here. Waiting on her gives me a chance to do some figuring. Just before he fell into a coma, Jinxy begged me to take away all of Clara's memories of him. I am an old man now, so I do not know if I can swing it, but I used to be able to cast a pretty good forget-me charm. It was my brother's last wish to erase him from her, but it will not be easy. It has been years since they met. I am bound to leave a few traces of him inside her head. But what else can I do? He made me promise. Even though he was burned up pretty bad and barely alive, he would not let go of my hand unless I said I would do it.

Chapter 27

HAPPY FRIDAY

"Happy Friday, J.J. Lawrence Middle School! Well, bucka-roos, I hope everyone of you will ride into the sunset tomorrow night for the big barn raising in the gymnasium," Principal Ramsey announced over the school intercom. "Ms. Stearns told me we have already sold enough tickets to get that new popcorn machine, so that calls for a real *yee-haw-howdy!*"

After the morning announcements were finished, Mrs. Hammond passed out graded quizzes to all of the students. "I am disappointed by the general performance of this class. You had plenty of time to prepare for this quiz, matching various Edgar Allan Poe quotes with the appropriate title from which the quotes came." She continued walking up and down the aisles of desks after she had passed out all of the papers. "For instance, many of you missed number seven. Lydia, read it aloud."

A girl with curly red hair sat up straight in her seat and delivered her answer in a nervous voice, "We loved with a love that was more than love."

"And where would one find that quote?" Mrs. Hammond asked.

"*Annabel Lee*," the girl answered.

"That's correct," said Mrs. Hammond, stopping next to Simon and Dooley's desks. "Simon, read your answer for number 12."

"I was never kinder to the old man than during the whole week before I killed him," read Simon. "*The Tell-Tale Heart?*"

"That's correct," Mrs. Hammond replied. "Dooley, I believe you are the only one who answered number 15 correctly, whether it was from studying or a lucky guess I can only imagine. Please read the quote and your response."

"In our endeavors to recall to memory something long forgotten, we often find ourselves upon the very verge of remembrance, without being able, in the end, to remember," Dooley read softly, feeling the invisible weight of his knowledge of this teacher's lost memories pressing down on him. "It's from a short story called, *Ligeia*."

"Correct," Mrs. Hammond answered with a hushed hesitancy strangely unlike her usually-commanding teacher voice.

Throughout the day and all around the school, Dooley sensed a certain buzzing chatter about the dance. The excitement was most noticeable at lunch.

As Dooley sat at his usual table, Jake Fossberg approached their group, holding his orange plastic lunch tray. "What's up Birdy, Bucky, Skeeter, Medusa… Dooley?"

"Nothing much, Jake," Fiona answered. "Just eating our chicken sandwiches. You should try it—over there." She pointed to a table across the room.

"So which of you lunch buddies are going to the dance together? Since there's five of you, somebody will have to go alone. Who's going to be the loser—I mean single dude?" Jake let out a mean laugh and strutted over to his friends.

"I can't believe how many people are going with dates to this thing tomorrow night," Nathan said as he carefully arranged mandarin orange segments in a neat circle on top of his chicken patty.

"Yeah, we're in the 7th grade, for Pete's sake! We're just kids!" said Fiona. "It's just an excuse to hang out at school on a Saturday and a way to pay for concessions equipment. Not a big deal."

"It might be fun to bring someone who's not from J.J. Lawrence Middle," Lark said, smiling dreamily. "You know, to mix things up a bit."

"Were you thinking of anyone in particular? Maybe a certain homeschooled kid?" Fiona asked.

Lark blushed. "No, I was just thinking of how it's nice to bring people together from different places, like how we learned in history class that people coming to America make it like a melting pot because they come here from other countries."

"Yeah. Right," Fiona replied. "Give me your tired, your poor, your huddled masses yearning to go to a middle school dance."

"Fun fact," Simon began, "The Statue of Liberty's shoe size would be a size 879."

"That *is* a fun fact, Simon," said Nathan as he gleefully added a layer of onion rings to his chicken patty and orange slices. "And this will be a fun lunch!" He sprinkled it with a tiny packet of soy sauce he took out of his pocket and topped it with the bun lid. Looking pleased with his creation, Nathan exclaimed, "Voila! Chicken l'orange sandwich!" He took a giant bite and chewed meditatively.

"I don't know how you come up with these recipes, Nathan," Lark said. "Is it any good?"

"Not bad. Maybe a little too salty." Nathan pulled out a small spiral memo pad and wrote a few notes about his chicken sandwich recipe.

"Someday," said Dooley, "when you open your restaurant, you'll have to let all of us eat for free to pay us back for all of the times we had to watch you eat this stuff."

Chapter 28

THE ACCIDENT

Dooley kept Theo's notebook in his backpack all day so he could return it to Gus after school. As he entered the gym where Gus had already begun to set up the scenery and decorations for the dance, he felt a sudden twinge of sadness that his eight-day punishment was coming to an end. Though he regretted making fun of Mrs. Hammond and getting sent to the principal's office, Dooley was glad for the time he had spent with the elderly custodian. Gus had never treated him like he was a bad kid. Instead, he had given Dooley something useful to do while he worked through feeling guilty about his mistake.

"Set your satchel down, Dooley, and let's get to work," said Gus. "We got plenty to do this afternoon." Gus was finishing taping down black butcher paper to protect the gym floor.

They set out the wooden tree-shaped cut-outs, blocking two of the long walls and leaving open the main door to the gym and the opposite end where the concession stand could be accessible. Then they wrapped lights around the trunks of the cut-out trees and hung the glass jar lanterns from the branches.

"Let's take a break for a minute before we hang the fabric from the ceiling," said Gus. "I'm no spring chicken, and this is getting me pretty well tuckered out." They sat down in two metal folding chairs near the concession stand. "I already got the wire tied to them eye bolts way up there in the walls, so all we have to do is climb the ladder and drape all that black fabric over the wires. After that we just got to put up the big tree in the middle. It's a good thing I set it on caster wheels. It's a giant!" Gus took a drink from his thermos and wiped his forehead with a handkerchief.

"I brought Theo's notebook," said Dooley. "I finished reading it last night."

Gus took a breath. "Is there anything in there I oughta know?"

Dooley swallowed past the lump in his throat, summoning the right words to explain what he had read. "I don't know. What do you remember from the night Slade had his accident?"

"Well, he went to the jelly factory—something about making a juice with berries he got from Pukwudgee. He had heard the juice might bring back his power to jump into the future. It was late. He stopped by our house first. I remember Theo tried to talk him out of it, but Slade could be so stubborn when he was in a dark mood. He said he was gonna sneak in to mash and boil up the berries. Said it was easier to do it with all the equipment they had over there at the factory. Plus, I don't think he wanted Clara to know what he was up to. Maybe he didn't want to get her hopes up, or maybe he didn't think she'd approve. I couldn't say."

"Then there was some kind of explosion?" Dooley asked.

"I reckon so. They never said for sure what made the machines catch fire. The fire department said it started on the other side of the factory from where the boiling happens. They said it started over at the capping machines, which was strange seeing as how Slade wouldn't have needed to be in that area, so he wouldn't have turned any of them machines on. They was clear across from the juice vats. I guess we'll never know…" Gus' voice trailed off as he absentmindedly picked at a splinter on his thumb.

"Did the police call you to let you know what had happened?"

"Slade called us. It was quite a piece past midnight, but me and Theo was still awake. We both felt scared that he was going to have one of his bouts of bad luck. His voice was faint on the phone. I could barely make out what he was saying, but I could tell he was in a lot of pain. We called an ambulance to go and pick him up. Then Theo went to the hospital, and I went to their house to get Clara."

"Did Theo tell you what happened at the hospital? Did he say what Slade asked him to do?"

Gus' eyes began to fill with tears causing Dooley to regret beginning the conversation. He could see that these were painful memories for this old man who had already suffered so much. Gus blew his nose on his handkerchief and spoke with a gravelly voice. "Theo left the hospital a different man after that night. At first I thought he was just so sad at Slade's passing that he couldn't speak of what had happened, but I soon saw that our brother's tragedy was the start of Theo losing hisself. Just a year later, I had to move him into the old folks' home."

Dooley retrieved the notebook from his backpack and returned to his seat next to Gus. He flipped through the pages until he came to Theo's final entry. Though Gus couldn't see any of the writing on the pages, Dooley held the notebook open so that he could point to the section he wanted to share.

He read aloud, "'Just before he fell into a coma, Jinxy begged me to take away all of Clara's memories of him. I am an old man now, so I do not know if I can swing it, but I used to be able to cast a pretty good forget-me charm. It was my brother's last wish to erase him from her, but it will not be easy. It has been years since they met. I am bound to leave a few traces of him inside her head. But what else can I do? He made me promise.'"

Expecting Gus to begin crying again, Dooley braced for the old man's tears. Instead, Gus stood up and wiped his nose on his sleeve. Then he walked over to where his tallest A-frame ladder stood. "Go fetch me one of them pieces of black fabric," Gus barked, gruffly.

Dooley jumped up and hurried over to the workroom. He came back to the gym to see Gus already halfway up the ladder. "Haven't got all day. Toss up one of them ends."

Dooley did as he was told. When Gus reached out to catch the fabric, he caused the ladder to wobble, making everything—ladder, fabric and Gus all come crashing down to the gym floor.

"Gus! Are you okay?" Dooley asked as he dashed to his side.

Wrapped up in the fabric and lying on his back, Gus answered, "I'm alright, but you better go get Ms. Stearns. Seems I've hurt my ankle pretty bad."

Chapter 29

SERENADE

Fortunately, the school nurse was still in the building when Gus fell, so she was able to rush to the gym and examine his ankle to determine the extent of his injury. The nurse said it was just sprained, and Gus should thank his lucky stars that it wasn't worse. "A man of your age climbing a ladder!" she repeated several times.

Ms. Stearns offered to give him a ride home, assuring him that she could find a few parents to help her hang the fabric and set up the giant tree Saturday morning. Dooley stayed in the gym, finishing last minute details and sweeping up until his mom arrived to get him.

After supper, Dooley asked Rose if he could bake a batch of cookies. "I'd like to bring some over to the nursing home tomorrow," he told his mom. "Chocolate chip is Theo's favorite."

Rose agreed and set out ingredients for the cookies. She unwrapped two sticks of butter, dropped them in a bowl, and beat them with the mixer. "Did Gus say how Theo is doing? Is he better from the other day when Gus had to stay home with him?" she asked as she measured two teaspoons of vanilla extract.

"I think so." Dooley cracked the eggs to add to the bowl. "It would be so hard to live with someone who can't remember anything."

"It can definitely be frustrating, but it's even worse for the person with the memory loss," Rose said. She ran the mixer again until the butter, sugar, eggs, and vanilla turned a creamy golden color. "My grandfather was diagnosed with Alzheimer's disease when I was about your age. They had to put him in a nursing home a lot like Juneberry Meadows. I used to hate going to visit that place. It just made me so sad to see my grandfather looking and acting so different than how he used to be."

"Did your parents make you go anyway?" asked Dooley, stirring the batter as Rose added the flour.

"Yes," she answered. "And I'm glad they did. My mom sat me down and told me that it was okay to be sad about Grandpa. She told me that it made her sad too, and sometimes a little scared when he got angry or frustrated. She said that when he thought he was living in the past—in a happier place and a time—that sometimes it was like he was on vacation, a break from feeling so confused. And anyway, he was at the end of his life, so if he wanted to believe he was 10 years old and living on a farm, we should just let him."

After they had three dozen cookies laid out on cooling racks, Dooley went in to the cozy den where his dad liked to watch TV at night.

"I was just about to get you," Paul said. "Look at what's coming on."

Dooley glanced at the black and white screen and saw a bare landscape that looked to be somewhere out west. There was mostly light gray sand dotted with scrubby, low bushes and dark gray mountains in the distance. Just as he was about to ask his dad what it was, a thin man with a tall white cowboy hat and a bandana tied around his neck came galloping onto the screen riding a speckled horse. Across the top in bold, curving letters, he read the movie's title—*Casa Grande Serenade*.

"That's Jasper Lawrence," Dooley gasped as he slid into a bean bag chair on the floor.

"That's right," said Paul. "He's the guy your school is named after, isn't he?"

Dooley could only nod his head. He had the weirdest feeling watching this black, white, and gray Jasper on the screen. Even though it was only on TV, he felt as if this version of the same skinny cowboy he'd seen in his room would step out of the screen, look right at Dooley, and start yodeling as he smiled his gap-tooth grin.

Rose brought a bowl of popcorn in the den, but Dooley waved her off. "No, thanks," he muttered without taking his eyes off the screen. He was riveted by the story.

Jasper played Sheriff Matt Wainwright, the only lawman in a sleepy desert town which was mostly made up of the owners and employees of two competing silver mines— *Lucky Pete* and *The Poker Chip*. The owner of *The Poker Chip* mine sent some of his thugs to sabotage the *Lucky Pete* by setting dynamite in one of the tunnels where they had just found a vein of silver deep in the mountain. Little did they know, Young Tom, newly married to the daughter of the man who ran the general store, was in a nearby tunnel when the dynamite exploded, trapping him inside.

By the end of the movie, Sheriff Wainwright had rescued Tom, solved the mystery of who had destroyed the *Lucky Pete* mine and arrested the guilty men. Interspersed throughout the story, the sheriff would find opportunities on moonlit nights to stand in dusty streets and play his guitar and sing to pretty women watching him from second floor windows. The women seemed to be especially impressed by his high speed yodeling. The final scene showed Jasper saying goodbye to one of those women before mounting his trusty speckled horse and riding slowly into the setting sun.

"Well, what did you think, Dooley?" Paul asked.

"It was great," said Dooley. "I really liked the yodeling."

"Yeah, you can tell why they call it *Casa Grande Serenade*," Rose said as she picked up the empty popcorn bowl. "Sheriff Wainwright sure did a lot of serenading."

As he walked through the living room to go up to his bedroom, Dooley glanced over his shoulder at the coffee table. The room was dark apart from one floor lamp which cast a glow on the photographs of the jelly factory accident still spread across the table. He stepped into the room and bent to examine the photographs again. On one of them, he saw what he assumed must be the capping machine Gus mentioned. There were the remains of a conveyer belt with mostly melted jars in a row. In the area above the jars, there was a kind of chute. Dooley wondered if the lids were supposed to slide down there and get tightened onto the jars by some missing mechanism. So much of the metal was melted and twisted, making it difficult to know exactly what he was looking at.

The magnifying glass was resting on one of the pictures, enlarging something purple under a pile of burned debris. He picked up the magnifying glass and examined the purple object closer. He could just make out a yellow strip along the top and the profile of a man with a long, yellow moustache.

Dooley held his hand to his mouth and whispered, "It's a Minnesota Vikings flip-flop."

Chapter 30

CHOCOLATE CHIPPERS

"**D**ooley! Let's go," his mom called from downstairs. "I've got some shopping to do after I drop you off at the nursing home."

"Coming." Dooley was pulling on his socks and thinking about the movie he had watched with his parents the night before. In his mind, he was replaying the final scene from *Casa Grande Serenade* when Sheriff Wainwright had said goodbye to the town's new schoolteacher, one of his many female admirers. She had asked him if he'd ever come back to their town. The sheriff had answered, "Yes, I promise to return. And a promise of mine is something you can count on. It's just as sure as the Rio Grande will keep a-flowing into the Gulf of Mexico."

Dooley smiled, thinking of Jasper saying the same thing to him when he had conjured his memory cloud using the charmed button. He picked up the button and considered for a moment if he should bring Jasper back again. Deciding he'd save it for later, Dooley slipped the button in his pocket and hurried downstairs.

Sitting in his wheelchair and watching a TV show about animals that live on the tundra, Theo happily took the box of cookies Dooley offered him. "Chocolate chippers? My favorite!" Theo cried, smiling broadly. "Mitts, look what he brought me!"

Gus was sitting in his bed, his bandaged ankle resting on pillows. A dripping bag of ice was forming a dark, wet spot on his bedcover. "Hmmph," responded Gus, his arms folded across his chest. "Like that old fool deserves any cookies! Dooley, help me up so I can talk to you out in the sitting room. Specks, don't you eat all them cookies! You'll get indigestion!"

Gus leaned on Dooley as they hobbled out to the large lobby area with the green plaid furniture. Once the old man was situated in a chair and his foot was elevated on a stool, he began to apologize. "I'm sorry I got so mad yesterday after you told me what was in Theo's notebook. I never should've behaved that way. Eighty-four years old, and I still carry on like the baby of the family. Falling off that ladder was my punishment for acting so childish."

"You're 84?" Dooley asked, surprised.

"Yeah." Gus looked around the room to see who might be listening before whispering, "But the school thinks I'm 64, so let's keep that between us."

Dooley nodded.

"Anyhow, hearing that Theo cast a memory erase spell on Clara just made my blood boil. I don't care if Slade asked him to do it, nobody should tamper with another person's memory."

"Have you ever tried to talk to Mrs. Hammond about what happened?"

"Oh, I tried, but she just got mad. She remembers that she was married, but I reckon on account of what Theo done, she's got so many holes in her memories of Slade that it's like her brain is a piece of Swiss cheese." Gus reached forward and massaged his hurt ankle. "And now that I know Theo is to blame—well, it just breaks my heart. To top it all off, I reckon that Theo's spell bounced off Clara and hit him square in the face."

"And that's why he lost so many of his memories from that night," Dooley exclaimed.

"Makes sense to me—the old fool."

"I have an idea." Dooley told Gus about the button he'd found at Camp Pukwudgee and how it was supposed to give the person using it the ability to revisit a special memory. "Maybe we should try it on Theo," Dooley continued. "It might give us a little more information about that night."

They went back into Gus and Theo's room. Theo was looking out the window, cookie crumbs covering his shirt.

"Whatcha looking at, Specks?" Gus asked as soon as he was sitting on his bed again, propped up with pillows.

"There's a bird sitting on the window sill, but I can't remember what it's called." Theo's voice sounded vague, almost dreamy, as he spoke. "It's white and gray; chubby, little thing just looking for seeds, I reckon."

Gus strained to peer out the window. "Why that's a

white-breasted nuthatch, Specks. One of your favorites.
You always say its call sounds like it's laughing."

"Do I?"

"Sure, you do." Dooley could see Gus was softening
toward his brother as he watched him struggle to remember. "Specks, Dooley wants you to try something."

"More cookies?" Theo asked, still a little dazed.

"No," answered Gus. "Magic."

Chapter 31

A MAGIC BUTTON

"What kind of magic?" Theo asked.

"Well, as it turns out, Dooley has got a magic button that may help you get back a memory or two," said Gus.

"I'm not sure exactly how it will work for you—what will happen and how long it will last," Dooley added. "When I used it, it had a completely different effect on me than what I expected."

"I'm game," said Theo, his eyes clearing as the fog lifted a bit from his mind. "What do I do?"

"You're supposed to hold this button in your hand real tight," Dooley instructed. "Then you think of something that'll bring on the memory you want."

"I've got something he can use for that." Gus pointed to the brothers' shared dresser which sat by the open door to their room. "Dooley, look in that bureau. Yeah, that one, top drawer. There's a picture frame in there that I want you to bring to me." Dooley did as he was told, taking out a framed photograph from the top drawer of the dresser. He saw a smiling bride and groom in front of a tall wedding cake. Dooley instantly recognized his teacher and the man from the newspaper obituary picture—Clara and Slade Hammond.

"Yes," Dooley said, softly. "That should work." He handed the button to Theo and laid the frame in his lap. "After you've concentrated on this picture and you have it in your mind, close your eyes and say the words of a song, like this: 'I'll see you in my dreams, and then I'll hold you in my dreams. Someone took you out of my arms, still I feel the thrill of your charms.'"

"What do you think, Specks? You ready to try it?" asked Gus.

Theo nodded. Grasping the button in his hand, he cocked his head to one side as he looked at the photograph, a mixed expression written on his face. His mouth was turned up into a smile, but his eyes were all questions.

Theo closed his eyes and said, "I'll see you in my dreams…" He stopped without finishing the line. Just as Dooley was about to repeat it for him, Theo began again, but this time he sang it in a deep, throaty baritone. "I'll see you in my dreams, and then I'll hold you in my dreams. Someone took you out of my arms, still I feel the thrill of your charms. Tho' the days are long, twilight sings a song of the happiness that used to be; Soon my eyes will close, soon I'll find repose, and in dreams you're always near to me."

When he opened his eyes, Theo looked at Gus. As his face changed from dreamy contentedness to despair, Theo said, "Oh, Mitts! I'm so sorry for what I done. It was wrong of me, but I was beside myself with grief that night. I thought it would help to do what Jinxy asked me to do, but it only made matters worse."

"I understand. It was a dark night whichever way you look at it," Gus replied.

"While you was out in the hall, talking to the hospital doctors, Clara came in to say goodbye to him. She looked so sad—sadder then I'd ever seen anybody look in all my life. That's when I done it. I thought it would take away her sadness. I reckon it did, but it also took away her good memories of him, too. I made a mess of everything." Theo began to cry. It began as a loud wailing, then his tears were accompanied by low moans. The sound made Dooley ache from the tips of his ears and deep inside his head, spreading to his shoulders, arms, and fingertips.

"Go and take the button from him, Dooley," said Gus. "This was a mistake. I never should've made him remember that night. What kind of man picks a memory from the worst moment of his life to have his brother remember?"

Dooley gently took the button from Theo's worn hand and pulled the photograph from his lap. He laid both of them on top of the dresser and went back to try to comfort the old man. "It's okay," Dooley said. "It'll be okay."

"Help me get over to him," Gus said to Dooley. Gus leaned in as Dooley supported him and helped him sit down in a wooden chair next to Theo's wheelchair. "Don't fret, Specks. You're alright now." Gus held his brother's hand.

Dooley noticed some movement out of the corner of his eye by the doorway, a flash of peacock blue. He didn't think much of it, since the hallways of Juneberry Meadows were often busy with residents and visitors.

Theo eventually stopped crying. He rested his head on Gus' shoulder, sniffing in between ragged breaths. Dooley went to put away the picture frame in the top drawer and pick up the button from the dresser. When he looked down at the spot where he had set them, the only thing he saw was the wedding picture of a happy couple. The button was gone.

Chapter 32

LOST FOREVER

"**W**hat are you doing, son?" Gus asked as he watched Dooley crawl on his hands and knees in the area near the bottom of the dresser.

"I can't find the button. I must've dropped it." Dooley scooted the dresser to check behind it and even walked out into the hall to be sure it hadn't rolled away, but he had no luck. The button had vanished.

He kept searching until it was time for his mom to pick him up. Gus promised that he'd keep looking, but Dooley felt like it was lost forever.

As his mom drove him back home, Dooley was miserable with feelings of regret that he had waited too long to summon up Jasper's memory cloud. Now he'd never see Jasper Lawrence again.

"Everything okay?" Rose asked. "You're awfully quiet."

"Yeah, I just lost something in Gus' room."

"Oh, that's too bad. Maybe it'll turn up."

"Maybe."

"Look on the bright side," offered Rose. "Simon is coming over this afternoon, and then you have the big dance tonight. You'll get to see all of your hard work finished."

"I almost forgot about Simon! I promised him we'd make one of those Rube Goldberg machines." Dooley sat thinking for a second, then he said, "And a promise of mine is something you can count on. It's just as sure as the Rio Grande will keep a-flowing into the Gulf of Mexico."

Rose smiled at Dooley. "Awww, sheriff," she said.

When they got home, Dooley found his dad making a sandwich in the kitchen. "Hey, Dad, I noticed something in one of those photographs you brought home, you know, the ones from the jelly factory accident."

Paul followed him into the living room, and Dooley showed him the magnified purple flip-flop. "I know this sounds crazy, but Jake Fossberg told me that his dad gave all his employees Minnesota Vikings flip-flops that year instead of a Christmas bonus."

"I'm sure there are lots of people with those flip-flops in Minnesota," said Paul. "That really isn't enough proof to connect Fossberg Crackers to the accident."

"Okay, but don't you think it's worth looking into? All this time, everybody has said it was Slade Hammond's fault, that he snuck in there at night to do something and then got careless. But if someone else came in and purposely sabotaged the jelly factory equipment…"

"Like in the movie last night?" Paul asked.

"Yeah, like in the movie, except this time it's jelly instead of a silver mine—then they should be punished for what they did."

"But why would anyone want to mess up jelly-making equipment?"

"Jake also told me that years ago, the Peacock Valley Jelly company was looking into getting in the cracker business. He said they learned that the Fossberg Cracker factory was the only company in town who should be allowed to make crackers."

Paul put a hand on each hip, pretending to hold imaginary pistols. "Looky-here, partner. There isn't room enough in this town for the both of us." He drew his imaginary guns and pretended to shoot at Dooley.

"I'm serious, Dad."

Paul stacked up the pictures and placed them in his briefcase. "All right. I'll check in to this and see if they ever investigated any other people who might've been involved, but I don't want you to get your hopes up." Paul snapped his briefcase closed and set it by the front door. "I can tell you care about these people, so I'm willing to help."

"Slade's brothers and Mrs. Hammond have been through a lot in the last few years. It would at least make them feel a little better if they knew that the accident didn't happen because of something stupid Slade did."

Chapter 33

RUBE GOLDBERG

Dooley stood at the kitchen sink, rinsing the yellow, spotted berries in a colander while glancing at the book lying open on the counter. He was skimming the instructions for the "Invisible Ink" recipe in the *Cantata Liber*.

When he had first read the steps to make the Visus ink before going to bed on Thursday night, Dooley had remembered Simon's description of a Rube Goldberg machine. In the instructions, the recipe described the process as a "slow drip of culinary mystery." It explained that the ink would develop its properties of invisibility through a series of tubes and progressing movements. Considering that a Rube Goldberg machine was made up of a sequence of actions, and Simon had been asking him when they could make one, Dooley felt like this was a way to both make the ink and make Simon happy simultaneously.

Dooley quickly jotted down the instructions on a skinny notepad his mom kept clipped on their refrigerator. He had decided he wasn't ready to tell his friends from school everything about his Visus powers, and if Simon saw him reading an enchanted book with words only visible to him, Dooley would have some explaining to do.

He scribbled the last line of the instructions just as the doorbell rang. He closed the book and set it on the coffee table as he went to the door. "Hey, Simon."

"Hey, Dooley!" Simon was holding a cardboard box full of plastic tubing, pieces from a metal building set, a box of dominoes and various other items. "This is so exciting!"

"I'm glad you could come over. I think it'll be fun."

Simon set his box on the kitchen floor and asked, "So, what do we do first?

The boys got right to work. They dumped the berries in a pot and added water. "We have to boil the fruit so it'll be easier to press out the juice," said Dooley.

The kitchen warmed, and the space above the stovetop was engulfed in steam as they cooked the berries until they were mushy, yellow blobs. While Dooley strained the cooked fruit into a bowl, leaving the skin and tiny purple seeds in the colander, Simon began setting up the contraption.

"The first thing that needs to happen is for this candle to be lit so it can heat up the bottom of the pot that'll be holding the juice." Simon was carefully lining up dominoes on the kitchen table. "My plan is for the dominoes to fall, and the last one will knock into this wheel with a bunch of matches attached to it. Then the match should strike against this piece of sandpaper, lighting the candle. Fun fact: The first match was made when an English pharmacist was stirring a bowl of chemicals and saw that there was a dried lump on the end of his stirring stick. When he tried to scratch the dried bit off, the stick caught fire."

"Huh," said Dooley. He was mostly used to Simon's fun facts, but he still wasn't sure of the best way to respond to them. "When the juice is heated over the flame," Dooley continued, "condensation will form." Dooley pointed to a curly plastic tube taped to the lid of the pot. "Since the lid will be taped on the pot tightly, drops of liquid will have to go somewhere, so they'll move up this tube as they come out of the pot. Then they'll drip down into the next pot." He pointed to a second pot with tubes coming out both sides—one for dripping in and one for going back out.

"The flame will burn until the candle melts all the way down," said Simon. "When the melted wax is heavy enough, it will weigh down the end of this popsicle stick like a seesaw. The other end will go up, striking another match to light this other candle."

"That's right," Dooley agreed. "Then it will heat up the liquid again and send it through another tube until it eventually ends up in this bowl."

Once everything was in place, the boys prepared to start the process, beginning with the line of dominoes. Simon thought it was too boring just to tap the first domino. Instead, he built a series of angled, wooden ledges which a small, rubber ball could roll down until it knocked into the domino row.

"Ready?" asked Simon, standing on his tiptoes to place the ball at the top of his structure.

"Ready!" Dooley replied.

The ball crisscrossed down until it came to the table and bumped the first domino. The line fell, one by one, and the first candle was lit.

"How long do you think it will take the candle to heat up the juice enough for it to go on to the next step?" asked Simon.

"I don't know."

The boys sat in the kitchen chairs, staring at the flame.

"I feel like we're scientists working in a laboratory!" Simon said excitedly. "What did you say this juice will be used for?"

"It's going to be ink."

"Really? That's cool! Then maybe you can write with one of those old-fashioned feather quill pens. Fun fact: the same inkstand—that's a little tray that holds an inkwell and other writing tools—was used during the signing of the Declaration of Independence and the U.S. Constitution."

"Oh yeah?" asked Dooley. He wanted to change the subject, so he stood up and walked to the refrigerator. "Are you hungry?"

"Nah," Simon answered and turned back to continue looking at the flame. "Wow! It's blue!"

Dooley shut the refrigerator door and hurried to watch the warm, wet drops of steam drip down the coiled, plastic tube. Though the juice began as a milky yellow liquid, now that it was visible through the plastic, he could see it was an intense sky blue. He hoped the color change meant that the "slow drip of culinary mystery" was actually happening.

Dooley's mom came in the kitchen. "How's it going?"

"I think it's working," Dooley answered.

"Well, it's after 3:00. You boys will need to get ready for the dance pretty soon."

"I guess I should call my mom to come and pick me up," said Simon, reluctantly.

"I'll keep an eye on it and let you know what happens," said Dooley, relieved that any other magical transformations could happen without him having to explain it to his unsuspecting friend.

Just before it was time to leave for the dance, Dooley checked the glass measuring cup where the finished liquid had collected. In the steps before it had accumulated into the cup, the juice had gone from yellow to blue to hot pink.

"It looks like it all evaporated," his dad said as he grabbed his car keys to drive Dooley to the school. "Sorry, buddy."

It was at that moment that Dooley knew the recipe was a success. Where his father saw nothing, Dooley saw a few tablespoons of a thick blue-black liquid ribboned with an oily sheen—invisible ink.

Chapter 34

WELCOME TO SHERWOOD FOREST

Dooley was grateful when he saw Nathan getting out of a car just ahead of him. He realized on the drive to school that he was nervous, and a friendly face chipped away a little of his feelings of uneasiness.

"You and Gus did a great job decorating," Nathan said as they walked into the school gymnasium together, both wearing khaki pants and short-sleeved polo shirts. "You'd never know this is where we play dodgeball."

"Thanks." Dooley was just as impressed as Nathan. He expected it to look good, but he was amazed at the final transformation. With yards of black fabric covering the gym ceiling, the only brightness in the spacious room came from the strings of twinkling lights zigzagging across the black cloth, the candles nestled inside glass lanterns hanging from the tree branches all along the walls and the hundreds of tiny white Christmas lights wrapped around the tree trunks.

Loud, cheery pop music played on the gym's sound

system as kids darted around the massive tree in the center, sloshing their plastic cups of lemonade.

"Small cheer and great welcome makes a merry feast," said Ms. Stearns, standing at the door and greeting the students as they entered. She was dressed like she had just been to a Renaissance Fair with her long-sleeved, floor-length, high-collared silk dress. "Welcome ever smiles, and Farewell goes out sighing."

"That's Shakespeare," said a rough voice behind the boys.

"Gus!" exclaimed Dooley. "How's your ankle? Should you even be here?" Dooley looked at the old man leaning on a crutch.

"You sound like Wilhelmina Shakespeare over there," he said, pointing his crutch at Ms. Stearns. "She's been hounding me about sitting down all afternoon."

"Well, maybe you should put your foot up," said Dooley. "Just to be on the safe side." He unfolded one of the metal chairs propped against the wall.

Gus rolled his eyes but gave in and wearily thumped down in the chair. Dooley unfolded another chair so he could rest his foot. "A couple of almost good-looking boys like you two must have brought girls to this silly dance— where are the lucky ladies?" he teased.

"We didn't ask anyone to the dance," said Nathan. "And as far as I'm concerned, anyone who did is a grade-A clown."

As soon as he had finished speaking, a man walking backwards while juggling bumped into Nathan, causing the juggler's three wooden pins to tumble to the floor. He was wearing a colorful costume with red and yellow striped pants and a long, green tunic. On his head was a green, yellow, and red hat with a tiny bell at the tip of each of the three points. A strap was slung across his chest holding a round, stringed instrument.

"Watch out, kid," grumbled the man as he picked up the juggling pins. Ms. Stearns approached him and cleared her throat loudly. "I mean…" He dropped the pins and strummed a cord on the stringed instrument he was carrying. "Tra-la-la! Welcome to Sherwood Forest," he said. "All ye are welcome unto this place. I am the Jester, the king's fool." He bowed then picked up the pins and began juggling again as he walked away from them.

"They hired all manner of people for this dance. I've never seen anything like it," said Gus. Dooley noticed the youthful change ripple across the old man's face as Gus tried to hide his enjoyment in the festivities. "Did you boys see the man swallowing fire in the parking lot? I don't know where Wilhelmina finds these peculiar folks."

Dooley and Nathan decided to go to the snack table, promising to bring a lemonade back to Gus.

"Out of curiosity," Nathan said as he examined the platter of cupcakes, decorated with circles of icing to look like a bullseye, complete with a plastic arrow in the center of each one. "If you were going to ask a girl to the dance, who would it be?"

After all of Nathan's disparaging remarks about Jake Fossberg's friends finding dates for the dance, Dooley hadn't expected this question. Just as he was about to answer, Dooley saw Fiona across the gym. She was wearing an orange dress covered in yellow butterflies and a matching orange headband with a yellow butterfly perched on top. Each of her black braids were curled on the ends, and they bounced as she swayed to the music. Fiona noticed Dooley and waved to him. He waved back. "I don't know," he answered softly, a strange pulsing in his throat. "Nobody, I guess."

Ms. Cato sliced two servings from the giant Rice Krispy treat shaped to look like a medieval castle and slid them onto dessert plates. The boys took their plates and made their way back to Gus.

"Dooley! Nathan!" Simon called to them once they'd reached where Gus was seated by the entrance. The boys instantly realized that Simon had fully embraced the theme for the dance. He wore a brown tunic with a wide, black belt around his waist. An emerald green felt hat with a red feather in the brim sat on his head and a pair of tall, brown suede riding boots on his feet. He grabbed the straps of a small brown backpack resting on his back. "This is so cool!" Simon exclaimed while gesturing around the room.

"Are you wearing tights?" Nathan asked, slightly shocked by his friend's costume.

"Yes," said Simon, apologetically. "It's not quite historically accurate, but it was the best my mom could come up with. Fun fact: Men in medieval times didn't wear tights. They wore hose, or very long socks that were tied onto their underwear."

"What's the backpack for?" asked Dooley.

"I had a bow and arrows, but Principal Ramsey confiscated

it at the door." Simon said, gloomily. "But I can't blame him! If I really were Robin Hood it could be a deadly weapon!" He mimed shooting arrows at an invisible target.

"Let's go find Fiona and Lark," Nathan whispered to Dooley. "I know they'll want to see this." He pointed his thumb in Simon's direction.

Just as they were about to step into the throng of lively middle schoolers, Gus grabbed Dooley's wrist. "Wait," he said. His eyes were big and round and full of fear.

"What is it?" asked Dooley, bending nearer to the old man so he could hear him above the loud music.

"Trouble is coming."

"What trouble?"

"I can see them, though they're still far off."

Dooley leaned closer, his shirt suddenly soaked with sweat and pasted to his back. "Who's far off?"

"It's just like in the old days, when I was a Binoc." Gus was staring up at the black ceiling lined with artificial stars.

Dooley laid his hands on each of the old man's bony shoulders and shook him. "Gus, who's coming?"

Gus turned to look at Dooley. "The three sisters."

Chapter 35

TOIL AND TROUBLE

"**G**ood evening, J.J. Lawrence Middle School!" said Mr. Ramsey into a microphone as the music abruptly stopped mid-song. He was standing on stage wearing a long brown bathrobe tied at the waist with a white cord. His mostly bald head was crowned with a ring of fake fur. "As you have probably guessed, I am dressed as Friar Tuck, one of Robin Hood's Merry Men. It was my understanding that *all* of the teachers would be in costume…" He glared at the Mr. Sanchez, the history teacher, who was comfortably wearing blue jeans and a button-down shirt. "But it is still my honor to participate in such a rootin' tootin' success! Let's take a moment to thank Ms. Stearns for all her hard work."

"I don't understand," Dooley whispered to Gus while they made their way over to the workroom on the other side of the gym so they could hear each other better, away from loud music and announcements. As the attendees applauded and Mr. Ramsey continued to thank people for their help, Dooley asked, "Who are the three sisters?"

"At first glance, they seem like flowers—fragile and sweet-smelling—but they're really pure poison," said Gus as they entered the dark, sawdust-filled room. "And they're here."

"And a special thanks to our beloved custodian, Gus Hammond," Mr. Ramsey continued. "And his assistant, Dooley Creed."

As soon as Mr. Ramsey said his name, the workroom door swiftly slammed shut. Dooley gasped and fumbled for a light switch.

"Dooley Creed?" a voice cackled from somewhere in the black room.

"I know Dooley Creed," crowed another voice.

"Such a nice boy!" a third voice screeched.

Dooley found the switch and turned it on.

There, in the center of the room stood Delphinium, Jessamine and Marigold DuBois. They were wearing their trademark peacock blue cardigans. They no longer appeared to be harmless, old ladies, knitting away the hours at the Juneberry Meadows Nursing Home. Their sweet smiles and stooped backs were replaced with mocking eyes and smug sneers; their heads thrown back in arrogant satisfaction.

"Look at his stupid face!" Jessamine jeered. She pointed a knitting needle at Dooley and Gus as if it were a weapon. "So scared." She pretended to cry, sticking out her lower lip.

"What do you want with the boy?" Gus growled.

"The boy? The boy means nothing to us!" said Delphinium, repeatedly tossing a small, compactly-wound ball of yarn in the air and catching it with one hand.

"Well, I wouldn't say *nothing*, Del," said Marigold. "After all, if it weren't for itty-bitty Dooley-kins we might still be sitting on that horrid sofa at that wretched place, day in and day out with nothing to do."

"So true, Mary," answered Delphinium.

"What did *I* do?" Dooley asked.

"Why, you gave us this." Marigold opened the canvas tote bag hanging from her arm and took out something small. In the palm of her tiny, wrinkled hand, Dooley saw an ordinary-looking blue button. "And you showed us how to use it." Her smile made Dooley shiver. "Now that we have our memory back, we won't be needing it anymore." Marigold threw the button at him, bouncing off his nose and falling to the floor.

"I should've known," Gus said. "I should've been more careful."

"Should've but didn't, Augustus, and now we're back," said Delphinium triumphantly. "You and your daft brother are the only ones who might've stopped us. Everyone else from The Institute is long gone."

"Did you know about them?" Dooley asked Gus as he picked up the button from the floor and grasped it tightly in his hand. "That they had powers?"

Gus's brow crinkled as he struggled to remember. "I was only 8-years old when we left for Pukwudgee, so I can't recall knowing them, though I've been wary of them for a while. Years ago, before Theo's memory got real bad, he had a clear day and told me of his suspicions. I don't know that he remembered them, but he reckoned something was off about these sisters."

"The old fool!" Marigold shrieked.

"He had no idea how powerful we are!" cried Jessamine.

"What are your powers?" Dooley asked, stalling for time and hoping Gus would think of a way to get them out of there.

"We're Knitters, of course, but we also like to dabble in other art forms," Delphinium explained, a mean smile on her face.

"That's right," Jessamine agreed. "I prepare a soup that's quite tasty. All of the children find it absolutely delicious. Eye of newt and toe of frog, wool of bat and tongue of dog. Isn't that right, sisters?" All three of the DuBois sisters cackled.

"And when they drink it, they help me with my collection," said Marigold as she opened her tote bag and pulled out a long measuring tape.

"What kind of collection?" Dooley asked.

"I collect statues of children." Marigold smiled, stepping closer to Dooley and measuring across his chest as if she were planning to knit him a sweater. She stepped back and dropped the measuring tape in her bag. "And Jessie's soup turns them into statues. It's a marvelous sight to see. Perhaps I'll start with a few of your friends in the other room and let you go last. That way, you can see how it works." She opened the tote bag and showed him an orange Tupperware container inside.

Dooley gulped and backed away from the sisters until he bumped against a work table. A coil of unused Christmas lights fell from the table and onto the floor.

Dooley squeezed the button in his hand and shut his eyes.

Chapter 36

CALL IN THE CAVALRY

"**L**ook at the little idiot," Jessamine taunted. "Shaking like a tiny, frightened mouse."

Dooley kept his eyes shut and spoke as clearly as his pounding heart would allow, "I'll see you in my dreams, and then I'll hold you in my dreams. Someone took you out of my arms, still I feel the thrill of your charms."

When he opened his eyes, Dooley saw Jasper Lawrence standing before him—every inch a real cowboy hero to the rescue.

"Howdy!" the skinny cowboy piped up, happily.

"Jasper! It's me, Dooley!"

"I recognize you." Jasper glanced around the large workroom full of tables and tools and shelves of paint cans. "Looks like you changed locales on me, though."

"Who is this tall drink of water?" Marigold asked, puckering her lips and winking at the cowboy.

Dooley tossed the wound coil of Christmas lights to Jasper and shouted, "Quick! Tie them up!"

Instantly reading the situation without requiring further explanation, Jasper lassoed the startled sisters together before they could make a move. With lightning quick motions, he tied an impossibly intricate knot, then he clapped his hands together as if removing dust from them. "That should do! Knots are one of my specialties."

"Let us go!" the sisters cried, struggling in their tight constraints.

"What seems to be the problem here, Dooley?" Jasper asked as he tipped up the front of his ten-gallon hat with one finger and coolly strolled around the enraged sisters.

"They used the button to get their memory back, and now they're going to turn kids into statues by making them drink some poisonous soup!" Dooley cried.

Jasper looked at an ashen-faced Gus leaning on his crutch and a scared, panting Dooley before saying, "Seems like you'll need yourself a bigger posse to take these scoundrels to the sheriff."

The muffled music continued in the gym.

"The dance should be over soon," said Dooley, ignoring the cries of the tangled sisters. He saw a phone mounted on the wall over the table saw. "I'm going to call some people who can help."

In less than 30 minutes, an orange and white Volkswagen bus arrived at the school, and half of the Mulligan family tumbled out. Dooey met them in the parking lot while Gus and Jasper kept watch over the ensnared prisoners.

As they weaved through the active swarm of middle

school students enjoying the tail end of the dance, Dooley filled in Cyrano and the Mulligan family about the events leading up to the DuBois sisters' capture.

"And you say you brought up the late Jasper Lawrence's memory which was a physical manifestation of himself?" Lloyd, Cyrano's dad asked. He was the only non-magical person in his family, but he was always eager to learn new things. "Fascinating!" He removed his glasses and wiped them with a cloth he withdrew from his shirt pocket.

"I'm so glad you're all right," said Callidora, Cyrano's mom. "These women sound very dangerous. It seems they have lived up to their names."

"What do you mean?" Cyrano asked. "Jessamine, Marigold, Delphinium. Aren't all of those kinds of flowers?"

"That's right, Cyrano!" beamed Calix, always proud when one of her siblings showed an interest in plants. "They are all flowers, but they're also poisonous, either to people or pets or both. Sometimes evil hides beneath beauty."

"That's the truth," Dooley replied as he opened the door to the workroom. "I thought they were just sweet, old ladies who shared dentures and reading glasses. Boy, was I wrong!" He found Gus sitting on a short stepladder, his hands tied to a table leg with the measuring tape from Marigold's bag. "Gus! What happened? Where are the DuBois Sisters? Where's Jasper?" Dooley quickly untied Gus' hands.

"He disappeared," said Gus, massaging a bump on his forehead.

"Disappeared?" Dooley asked, looking at the button he still grasped tightly in his hand.

"He just started fading, and then he was gone," grumbled Gus. "Before I knew it, one of them ladies pulled a pair of scissors out of that doggone bag. They cut the lights they was tied up with and attacked me."

"Some old ladies attacked you?" Crispin, one of Cyrano's brothers, asked.

"There was three of them and just one of me!" barked Gus. "They hit me with a knitting needle and tied me up."

"Dooley said you're a Binoc. Didn't you see them coming?" Crispin teased.

"No, I didn't see them coming! I was too focused on the cowboy who had just vanished into thin air!" Gus rubbed his sore wrists. "What's your power, anyway—that is, besides irritating old men?"

"I make shoes that can walk on the ceiling," said Crispin, proudly pointing to his loafers. "And my sister Calix is a Greenie, and Cicely is a Siren. Her voice can do crazy things, like heal people or hypnotize them."

"Well, this has been a real interesting conversation, and your family sounds like they're just amazing," Gus said, sarcastically. "But we need to find these sisters before someone else gets hurt."

Chapter 37

TWILIGHT SINGS A SONG

"Since the sisters plan to turn kids into statues by making them drink a potion, they may be out there poisoning the students right now!" said Callidora. "We've got to stop them!"

"I don't know if this would help, but they mentioned what's in the recipe—frog toes and eye of newt," Dooley listed. "Then there's bat something and dog tongue…"

"That's from the Witches in *Macbeth*," said Cyrano.

"Huh?"

"You know—Shakespeare? They're based on the Grey Sisters from Greek Mythology."

"Oh, well, I don't know what to look for then. They said it was soup, and they had it in a plastic container."

"I'll make an announcement from the stage for people not to eat or drink anything. I'll say that there's been a case of food poisoning or something," Cicely suggested. "Dooley gave us a good description of the sisters. Three elderly ladies should stand out in a room full of middle schoolers. You all spread out and find them."

Just as they were leaving the workroom, Cyrano asked, "Wait. What do we do with them if we find them?"

"First, we need to get them all in one place," said Callidora.

"How about the music room next door to the gym? It should be empty," Dooley offered.

"Good idea," Callidora replied, "We'll hold them there until someone from N.A.M.E.S. can get to the school. I called them before we left the house."

"I thought N.A.M.E.S. was just a club for people with magical powers," Dooley said. "What can they do?"

"There's a crime squad division," Callidora answered. "They investigate when magical things go wrong. They'll know what to do with the DuBois sisters."

Dooley and the Mulligans ran into the dark gymnasium. Though many of the students had been picked up by their parents, the music was still playing. Dooley saw Nathan, Simon, Lark, and Fiona standing together by the refreshments table. Nathan was holding a cup of lemonade.

"Nathan, don't drink it!" Dooley said as he ran to his friends. He slammed the cup out of Nathan's hand, showering them with sticky juice.

"Dooley!" Fiona cried. "What is your problem?"

He was already picking up the punchbowl and dumping it in a nearby trashcan. "There's too much to explain right now, but you have to listen to me," Dooley began. "We need to make sure no one drinks anything. Understand? Any drop of liquid in this room could be fatal." Their conversation was interrupted by a high-pitched microphone squeal.

"Hello," said Cicely in a clear voice from the stage. "I

have a quick announcement—please do not eat or drink anything in this room. Some students have been diagnosed with severe stomach pains." She looked out at the indifferent, unconcerned faces staring back at her. "Like acute diarrhea and projectile vomiting."

Mr. Ramsey hurried on stage. "Who are you?" he asked Cicely with a hand over the microphone. "Who gave you permission to use this? Only teachers and administrators are allowed to operate A/V equipment."

From her vantage point on stage, Cicely could see one of the sisters standing near a clump of students. "Dooley," she hissed. "Over there," nodding her head to the area near the concession stand.

Dooley looked in the direction where she was gesturing and saw Marigold with her tote bag hanging from the crook of her arm. He nodded to Cicely, deciding what to do next.

Cicely turned to face the principal. "I'm here to sing the final song for the dance," she told him. Mr. Ramsey scanned the group to find Ms. Stearns for confirmation in this change in the evening's schedule.

"Ms. Stearns is in the courtyard," said Ms. Cato from the refreshments table. "Some problem with the jousters."

Dooley asked Simon, "Do you think you could play that guitar thing the jester is holding?"

"It's actually a lute. Fun fact—"

"Simon!" Dooley interrupted. "Focus! Can you play it?"

"Sure."

"Go up on stage with Cyrano's sister and play that… whatever it is, while she sings," Dooley instructed. Simon quickly went to find the jester. Then Dooley told his friends, "Come with me."

After consulting with Cicely a few more minutes, Mr. Ramsey consented to give her permission to sing. Simon returned with the lute, and she conferred with him for a moment. He strummed a chord, then she began to sing, "I'll see you in my dreams, and then I'll hold you in my dreams. Someone took you out of my arms, still I feel the thrill of your charms. Lips that once were mine, tender eyes that shine, they will light my way tonight. I'll see you In my dreams."

Her voice washed over the room like a tidal wave of thick, sticky molasses. Everyone stood and listened intently. Dooley had to force himself to move and drag his friends with him. He knew Cicely's song was a great distraction, and he wanted to take full advantage of her musical powers. "Run to the school office and see if you can find Pumpkin," he told Nathan, Lark, and Fiona.

"Principal Ramsey's cat?" asked Fiona.

"Yes. Bring him back to the gym and hurry!" Dooley watched them sprint down the hall.

Cicely continued singing, "Tho' the days are long, twilight sings a song of the happiness that used to be; Soon my eyes will close, soon I'll find repose, and in dreams you're always near to me."

As Dooley motioned for her to keep singing, he spotted Jessamine and Delphinium. He was grateful that the sisters seemed to be under Cicely's spell, too.

Chapter 38

PUMPKIN

While Cicely continued to sing, Marigold joined Jessamine and Delphinium, and the three of them huddled together in a dreamlike state, hypnotized by the magical voice. Unbeknownst to the sisters, Dooley's group slowly encircled them—Callidora and Lloyd stood just behind them, Calix was on their left, and Cyrano was on their right. Dooley stood farthest back, near the gym door, ready in case one of them tried to escape.

Dooley glanced around the room, looking for Crispin. A movement overhead made him realize that Crispin was standing just above the sisters, upside down, his feet anchored to the ceiling by his enchanted loafers and mostly hidden by the strips of black fabric. He was holding a long piece of metal with a hook at one end. Dooley recognized it as the pole Gus used to raise the basketball goals in the gym. Crispin gradually lowered the pole until the hook end was inches away from Marigold's elbow. As Cicely was finishing her third delivery of the song, Dooley rushed up and attached the handles of the tote bag onto the hook. Crispin jerked the pole up, flinging the bag high in the air so that he could reach out and catch it.

"Why, you bothersome troublemaker!" Marigold shouted, shaking her fist at the ceiling. The spell cast by Cicely's singing was broken.

Jessamine unsheathed her knitting needle and grabbed a nearby student, dragging him past Dooley and into the deserted hallway. It wasn't until she turned him around, the needle pressed against his neck, that Dooley discovered the identity of the student.

"Jake!" Dooley exclaimed.

"Somebody help me!" Jake screamed. "Get her off of me!" Jake struggled against Jessamine's grasp, but she was stronger than Dooley expected. "I'll give you anything you want," Jake cried. "My family is rich—so rich!"

"Let him go!" Dooley ordered as the Mulligans closed in on the sisters.

"*Let him go*," Delphinium mocked. "No, thank you, dearie. We would rather keep this one. He'll make a lovely addition to our collection." She had Simon's bow tucked under her arm. In her hand, she held a ping-pong ball-sized ball of yarn which she attached to the sharp tip of an arrow. "Take one more step and you'll find out what a few old knitters can do!"

Cyrano sniffed the air. "Watch out!" Cyrano shouted. "They've got a stink bomb!"

"Masks!" Delphinium commanded. The sisters pulled the collars of their sweaters over their mouths. Then she shot

the arrow at the group crowded in the hallway. When the
ball hit the floor, it exploded into a cloud of acrid smoke.
Other than the sisters, everyone else began coughing and
choking.

As the sisters quickly dragged their hostage down the
hallway, Dooley was right behind them, his eyes stream-
ing with tears. A moment later, Fiona, Lark, and Nathan
returned from the opposite direction. Fiona was holding
Pumpkin, the giant, orange cat. "Dooley!" Fiona yelled.
"What's going on?"

Dooley grabbed Pumpkin and ran toward the sisters.
"Hey, ladies! I've got something for you!"

"A cat!" Marigold shrieked, tripping over Jake as she tried
to get away.

Dooley continued to shove the bored cat in their direction, pushing them toward the open door of the music
room. Jessamine eventually dropped her knitting needle,
and Jake managed to wriggle free.

"Get that awful creature away from us!" Delphinium
screeched.

As soon as all three of them were in the music room,
Dooley tossed the cat inside and shut the door. Callidora,
Lloyd, Calix, and Cyrano quickly joined him. They found a
bench in the hallway and pushed it against the door, barring
the sisters from leaving.

Simon and Cicely ran to group. "Did you catch them?"
Cicely asked.

"Yes," Dooley answered, his eyes still red and watery from
the smoke. "They're trapped in the music room."

"Who's watching the outside door?" asked Simon.

"Outside door?" Dooley gasped. "I didn't know there was an outside door."

"Sure," Simon replied. "It's a big double door. That's how we leave with our band instruments when we're getting on the bus."

Dooley shoved the bench out of the way and threw open the door. The only things he saw inside were the two open doors on the other side of the room and a big, orange cat curled up on a kettle drum, already asleep.

Chapter 39

HOW THE CRACKER CRUMBLES

On Monday morning, Dooley came downstairs for breakfast and found his father reading the newspaper at the kitchen table. "Well, it's all in here," Paul said, pointing to the front page.

Dooley sat down next to him and read the headline, *Cracker Tycoon Sees Company Crumble*. He read aloud from the article, "Police arrested William D. Fossberg at his home Sunday night on charges of his alleged connections to arson-related damages to the Peacock Valley Jelly Company and the subsequent death of Slade Hammond. Authorities cite recently uncovered evidence linking Fossberg and two of his employees to the incident."

Dooley looked up from the paper and sighed gloomily.

"What's the matter?" Paul asked. "I thought you'd be pleased."

"I *am* happy—Slade's name will be cleared and the real bad guys will finally be punished." Dooley put his elbows on the table and rested his chin on his hands. "I just wish the accident had never happened. I wish Slade was still alive. I know Gus does, too."

Paul stood up and patted Dooley on the back. "It's hard to lose someone you love, but that's the time to be grateful for all the memories, to remember the good times. I'm sure Gus treasures his memories of his brother."

"But what if someone can't remember?" asked Dooley.

Paul sighed. "They may need a reminder. It's like the old story about the people who crossed a rushing river to get to safety. Once they were on the other side and out of danger, their leader told them to pick up stones and stack them on top of each other to help them remember what had happened. He told them that their children would ask them what the stones were for, and that would give them a reason to tell the story." Paul rinsed his coffee cup and placed it upside down in the dishwasher. "It's okay if a person needs help to remember."

Paul left for work, and Dooley poured himself a bowl of cereal. While he was eating, he read the rest of the front page article and studied the photographs—Jake and his parents dressed up for some charity event; the front of the cracker factory; Mr. Fossberg at a Minnesota Vikings football game. The article continued on a different page. As Dooley was flipping to the back of the newspaper, he found a short article that caught his attention.

Several witnesses reported seeing three elderly women running from J.J. Lawrence Middle School on Saturday night. The principal, Lionel Ramsey, stated that students were participating in a school dance inside the gymnasium when the witnesses claimed to have seen the fleeing women. These women were allegedly tackled and detained in the parking lot by a squadron of officers who appeared to be unidentified law enforcement. "They were probably a branch of the FBI," said Jason Diamond, one of the witnesses who was at the scene picking up his younger brother, a J.J. Lawrence Middle School student, from the school function. "Watching them work, it's obvious these guys have gone through a lot of martial arts training, probably Krav Maga. Fun fact: In Krav Maga, instructors show you how to use anything as a weapon—a pencil, a twig, a popsicle stick."

Dooley smiled as he remembered running through the music room and out the outside door, followed by the Mulligans and his school friends. He was afraid the sisters had escaped and were on their way to put their evil plan into action. Instead, he had been relieved to see the sisters had been caught. The officers who had captured them approached Dooley's group after the sisters had been handcuffed and put into a van. They had shown them identification, badges with the N.A.M.E.S. logo printed across the top. They promised that they would follow-up with Callidora to inform her of the ultimate fate of the DuBois sisters.

Dooley was still reliving the details of the scene in the parking lot when the doorbell rang.

"Hey, Dooley," said Cyrano. "Have you got a minute before you leave for school?"

"Yep. Come upstairs while I get my backpack ready."

"My mom wanted me to tell you that N.A.M.E.S. called this morning. They said to tell you that they're really grateful for all you did to catch the DuBois sisters. They took the poisoned soup stuff that one of them made…"

"Jessamine," Dooley said.

"Right—the soup that Jessamine made. Anyway, they took it to the lab, and it's for sure poisonous. Crazy ingredients that they haven't seen in decades. They said your quick thinking may have saved a ton of lives."

Dooley blushed. "Well, it wasn't just me. I couldn't have done it without your family and Gus and Jasper."

"And your school friends," Cyrano offered. "Nathan and Simon and Fiona and Lark."

Dooley was digging through the books and papers on his desk, looking for his binder with his math homework from the weekend. Sitting on top of the *Cantata Liber,* he saw the dried seeds from the Visus berries spread over a paper towel now stained with a design of purple splotches. The measuring cup still held a few precious tablespoons of invisible ink. He picked up the cup and held it at eye level.

"Would it be crazy for me to drink this?" Dooley asked.

"Drink what? I don't see anything."

Dooley flipped through the huge, enchanted textbook until he found the recipe for Visus Ink. He read aloud, "The reader should know that a properly concocted batch of Visus ink can be ingested. The potion will either temporarily enhance a person's powers or induce vomiting. Proceed with caution."

"I don't know, Dooley. Are you sure you want to try it?"

"I'll just take a tiny sip while you're standing here with me. That way, if I start barfing or turning green or something, you can go get my mom."

Cyrano reluctantly agreed.

Dooley lifted the cup to his lips and took a drink. The ink tasted bitter and coated his tongue with a thick sliminess.

"So? How do you feel?" Cyrano asked.

Dooley swallowed. "I feel… fine."

Cyrano exhaled. "Oh, good. Do you feel like your Visus powers are working better?"

"Something is different. I'm not sure what it is though." Dooley took a hard look at his friend. "I feel like I can sort of see through you."

Cyrano grabbed a blanket from Dooley's bed and wrapped it around himself. "What?"

"No. Not like that. I can see what you're feeling, what you would most like to happen."

Cyrano dropped the blanket. "Okay… so what do you see?"

Dooley gave a little laugh. "I see that you really like Lark."

Blushing, Cyrano punched Dooley's arm. "Cut it out."

"No, really. That's what I see. You want to hang out with her and go to Puppet Camp with her."

"Dooley!" his mom called from the kitchen. "The bus will be here in a minute."

"I've got to go," said Dooley, "but we'll talk more this afternoon."

Cyrano slumped his shoulders, embarrassed and exposed.

"By the way, I also see that you worry about me a lot and that you're the best friend I've ever had. Lark is one lucky girl."

Chapter 40

I'LL HOLD YOU IN MY DREAMS

By the time Dooley got off the bus, he was emotionally exhausted by all that he was seeing. As he watched an 8th grade boy rummage through a 6th grader's lunchbox and steal the younger kid's bag of chips, Dooley began to realize what the Visus ink was giving him. The boy chomping on the bag of Doritos wasn't just a bully. He was also lonely and bullied at home. Seeing the 8th grader's motivation for his behavior fueled Dooley in a way he'd never felt before.

"Those aren't yours," Dooley had said to the bigger boy as he grabbed the bag out of his hands and gave it back to the surprised 6th grader.

"Hey!" the 8th grader yelled. "I was eating those."

"You know," Dooley began, "when your older brothers eat your breakfast in the morning, it makes you really cranky, but you don't want to be a jerk like them, do you?"

"No…" the boy said, disbelievingly. "But how did you know…"

"Try to get up earlier and eat before anyone else is up,

then you can go outside and sit with those nice twin sisters who live next door and wait for the bus with them. Remember that time when they shared their Pop Tart with you? Now didn't that feel good? In the end, sharing feels better than stealing."

Dooley had stepped off the bus before the 8th grader could respond.

Now that he was inside the building, Dooley was overwhelmed by all of the strong feelings and emotions around him. He decided to duck inside the office for a minute to collect his thoughts.

"Mr. Creed, there's no dawdling in the office," the school secretary declared, barely looking up from her computer monitor. "Get to your homeroom." Then Ms. Cato picked up the phone and said, "Yes, there is band practice this afternoon until 5:00." After she had hung up the receiver, she gave her attention to a classroom desk, upside-down with a leg in need of repairs. She tightened a screw and tested it by jiggling the leg, then flipped it upright.

Dooley watched her intently. "Ms. Cato, I think you're the most efficient person I've ever seen."

"What did you say?" she asked, surprised by his comment.

"You can do so many things at the same time," he answered. "It's pretty cool."

"Well, I've always been good at multi-tasking."

Dooley noticed a softening in her eyes. She was almost smiling. "I bet you could run your own company, if you wanted to," he said.

"As a matter of fact, I've always wanted to do just that,

maybe a bakery or a coffee shop." Ms. Cato's smile grew until it was complete. "Would you like a piece of candy?"

Dooley took the offered candy and thanked the normally irritable secretary. As he was leaving the office to get to his homeroom, he passed Mr. Ramsey.

"Everything alright there, buckaroo?" Mr. Ramsey asked.

Dooley looked at his principal as if he were seeing him for the first time. He was a towering man with broad shoulders and a wide, friendly face. From the top of his thinning hair to the tip of his pointed toe cowboy boots, Mr. Ramsey radiated responsibility and a desire to protect those under his care.

"I'm fine," Dooley answered. "I was just thinking—if you were living years ago, like in the Wild West, you'd definitely be a sheriff."

Mr. Ramsey puffed out his burly chest and hooked his thumbs in his beltloops. "Why, thank you!" he said, proudly.

"And I know that if you had been around when Jasper Lawrence was alive, he would've been one of your best friends," said Dooley.

"That's about the nicest thing anyone has ever told me." Just when Mr. Ramsey looked like he might tear up, he sniffed and cleared his throat. "I've been really pleased with how you've improved since the rocky start you had at the beginning of the school year, Dooley. You just promise me that you'll keep doing the right thing and head down the straight and narrow path."

"Oh, I promise," Dooley vowed. "And a promise of mine is something you can count on. It's just as sure as the Rio Grande will keep a-flowing into the Gulf of Mexico."

As Dooley made his way down the hallway, he saw Ms. Stearns standing on a short stepladder as she took down posters advertising the school dance.

"Hey, Ms. Stearns. Do you need any help?"

"Oh, hello, Dooley," she said. "I appreciate your offer, but this is the last one."

"The dance was really amazing the other night and super fun."

"I'm glad you had a good time," she answered as she gently peeled strips of tape from the wall.

Dooley studied her, trying to decide what her secret motivation might be: Professional party planner? Renaissance Fair fanatic? Then he saw it—as she flicked her hand to remove a wad of tape from her finger, Dooley had a vision. He could imagine her standing on a platform in front of an audience as she led an orchestra.

"Being the band teacher, you must really love music," he said. "I bet your favorite is... Chopin?"

"That's right," Ms. Stearns replied. She stepped down from the ladder. "Did you know that Frederic Chopin was writing his own compositions as young as seven years old? Remarkable!"

"J.J. Lawrence Middle School is lucky to have someone as talented as you teaching here. I hope that one day I can go and watch you lead a whole orchestra playing Chopin."

Her eyes grew large, and she laid a hand on his arm. "That is my greatest dream."

As he walked away from her, Dooley felt her happiness pulsing throughout the hall, bouncing off the metal lockers and the linoleum floors, propelling joyfulness into the ceiling tiles where it would echo back to him.

Dooley entered his homeroom class and sat down in his usual seat next to Simon. Students were chattering around him, cramming in as much talk as possible before the bell rang.

"Hey, Dooley!" Simon greeted him. He pointed to an open book on his desk. "I got this from the library. It's about hypnosis. After seeing what Cyrano's sister did at the dance, I just had to learn more!"

Dooley studied his friend, looking for the extra insight the Visus ink would give him. After a few seconds, he shook his head and chuckled.

"Simon, you are the most genuine person I know."

"What do you mean?" asked Simon.

"You're 100% Simon Diamond—you know, like, what you see is what you get. I think that's really awesome."

"Thanks, Dooley," said Simon. "Fun fact: when you're hypnotized you're not actually asleep. Did you know that?"

Simon went back to his book while Dooley glanced around the room, looking at his classmates.

"I heard his dad is going to prison," one student said.

"Well, I heard Jake and his mom are moving away just to escape the scandal," another student replied. Dooley recognized her as the girl who had dropped her lunch tray on Nacho Day.

"I hope he does come back to school, at least for one day," a third student added. "After all those years of him making fun of everybody, I think it's time for Jake to get a nickname!"

"How about Fake Fossberg!" said the first student. "Or Jake Jerkberg!"

"They could change their company from making crackers to training assassins. Instead of Fossberg Crackers, they could rename the company Fossberg Attackers!" said the second student.

The students laughed, but Dooley felt sorry for Jake. The Fossberg family didn't have to be standing in front of him for Dooley to imagine what they were feeling. When he had first discovered who was really to blame for the accident at the jelly factory, Dooley had experienced a profound satisfaction as he envisioned the Fossberg family's ruin. Now that he watched Mrs. Hammond frowning as she lined up the items on her desk, he only felt sadness for the way it had all turned out.

Mrs. Hammond instructed the class to stop talking just as Mr. Ramsey began the announcements with a "Howdy, J.J. Lawrence Middle School!"

Dooley settled into his seat and smiled. For the first time since school had started, he swelled with a newfound pride for his principal and his school.

After Language Arts class, Dooley held back, pretending to look for something in his folder. He wanted to speak to Mrs. Hammond without anyone else listening in. He almost changed his mind and left, but finally found the courage to approach her.

"Mrs. Hammond, can I talk to you for a minute?" he asked.

She was sitting at her desk, grading tests with a red pen. "Yes. What can I do for you?" she asked without looking up from her grading.

"I just wanted to say that I'm so sorry for what I said about your husband." She stopped writing but continued to look down at the paper. "Gus and Theo have a lot of regrets, too. I know they feel partly to blame for what happened, and they wish they had protected Slade so you two could still be together."

Mrs. Hammond met his gaze. "They never should've told you about him," she replied, barely bringing her voice above a whisper. "That subject is not up for discussion, not with you or with his family. I just can't talk about him."

"I know you can't, and I know why. I also know that you always wanted to be a mom and that your favorite quote is from Shakespeare: *Praising what is lost makes the remembrance dear.* You don't know why it's your favorite, but you think about it every morning before you leave the house when look at the little stuffed lamb you keep on your fireplace mantle. I know all of this, and I want to help. That's why I brought you this." Dooley reached into his pocket and pulled out a button.

Timidly, Mrs. Hammond picked up the button from Dooley's outstretched hand. She held it between two fingers and examined it, as if she were inspecting a butterfly.

"Hold on to the button really tight, concentrate on your husband—maybe think of a picture of you and Slade together, then close your eyes and repeat after me: 'I'll see you in my dreams, and then I'll hold you in my dreams. Someone took you out of my arms, still I feel the thrill of your charms.'"

Mrs. Hammond followed his directions. As soon as

she had finished speaking, Dooley saw tears trailing down both cheeks. Her eyes remained closed and she sighed. As Dooley walked out of the classroom, just before he shut the door, he heard her whisper, "Oh, Slade. I remember."

When he got to his locker, Dooley opened his backpack and pulled out a sandwich bag full of an assortment of plastic buttons in purple, yellow, green, red, and black—whatever he could find in his mother's sewing basket. After working late into the night and with the help of the *Cantata Liber* and its reference to a book titled *Making Memories: A DIY Guide to Crafting Memory Charms*, he had transformed the buttons. The last thing he had done before going to bed was to write three words on the bag he was planning to bring with him that afternoon. In permanent black ink, he had written: FOR JUNEBERRY MEADOWS.

CHAPTER QUESTIONS

PART ONE: (*Chapters 1-5*)

Creative Writing Prompt—You've just been assigned a pen pal from a different country. Write a letter to her/him describing your normal school day. Be sure to include a greeting and a closing line with signature.

1. ***Dancing Shagamaw Boars:*** In the first chapter we learn that Dooley is awake very early on the morning of his first day of school. He reads a letter from Leo, his friend from camp. The text says, "Dooley sat up and read it again—the third time since he had found it in his mailbox…" Why do you think he has read the letter three times? What is he feeling? Support your opinion with evidence from the text.

2. ***First Day Jitters:*** Just as she's been doing since he was in kindergarten, Dooley's mom writes a sweet message on a paper towel and puts it in his lunch bag. Have you ever been embarrassed by a family member's show of affection? Describe the situation and

how you dealt with it. If it happened again, would you respond differently? If so, how?

3. *Skeeter:* Dooley meets Simon, a fellow 7th grader with an enthusiastic personality. Simon tries to get Dooley to guess his name by answering a riddle. Think of some aspect of your personality—your pet's name, your favorite sports team, a place you like to visit, a hobby, etc.—and write a riddle about it. Show it to someone and see if they can guess it.

4. *Chow Wagon:* In the lunchroom, Dooley sits with Simon, Nathan, Fiona and Lark. Make "trading cards" for these first four new characters. Include a drawing, description and interests. (You'll be adding to these cards as you continue through the book.)

5. *Nothing to See Here:* Dooley begins the schoolyear still sad that his adventures from the summer have ended. He assumes something about his new class-mates. What does he assume and what does Cyrano advise him to do?

Think about it: Irony

Irony is a tool writers use to give their story layers and make it more interesting for the reader. Oftentimes, ironic characters and situations aren't immediately obvious. Sometimes you have to dig deeper to find them. Here are a few examples:

- Dooley's mom writes a note he won't want others to read, but Dooley has a pen with ink no one else can see.

- Simon has an unwanted nickname given to him by

another student, but Simon loves his actual name so much that he creates riddles about it.

PART TWO: *(Chapters 6-10)*

Creative Writing Prompt—You are a brave warrior. You were given an important mission, but you failed. Now you must meet with the king to tell him why you were unsuccessful. What was the mission? How did you fail? What will the king say?

6. ***Ominous:*** Make a prediction: What do you think is causing Dooley to see a change in the custodian's appearance? (Predictions can't be wrong! All guesses are welcome!)

7. ***Whatsoever:*** Add another character to your Remember "trading cards"—Jake Fossberg. Include a drawing, description and any other information.

8. ***The Principal's Office:*** Mr. Ramsey says, "The biggest troublemaker you'll probably ever have to deal with watches you shave in the mirror every morning." What does this mean to you?

9. ***Definitely Disappointed:*** Dooley's mom tells him that his dad is "definitely disappointed." Dooley says he'd rather have his dad mad at him instead. What's the difference? Why does Dooley feel this way? How does it feel to know you've disappointed someone?

10. ***Below the Surface:*** Have you ever heard the phrase "one-dimensional character"? This refers to characters who don't change throughout a story. They don't improve or fail. They just stay the same. Dooley sees

Jake this way—a rich jerk, plain and simple. Jake Fossberg is a fictional character, but what about real people? Can a person be just what you see on the outside? Is there always more going on below the surface?

Think about it: Conflict

- In most every story, there should be three basic elements—a beginning, a middle with tension and conflict, and an ending with some resolution to the conflict. This section of Remember establishes the central conflict for the main character. As a reader, how does it feel when you read Dooley's predicament? Does it evoke (bring out) any particular emotions or feelings of empathy?

PART THREE: *(Chapters 11-15)*

Creative Writing Prompt—Write a short story beginning with this sentence: I wasn't always able to make myself invisible, but ever since my birthday…

11. ***Juneberry Meadows:*** List three things you find unusual about the DuBois sisters.

12. ***Like Digging a Well:*** If you were giving Dooley advice about the best way to apologize, what would you suggest?

13. ***I'll See You In My Dreams:*** Imagine you have a button similar to the one Dooley found. Instead of being created in the 1940's, your button was made yesterday. What current song lyrics would you sing to cause the button to bring up a special memory?

14. *Reboot:* Fill in the rest of the story of the magician's hat. What do you think happened to the hat from the time the French magician died until it showed up at a yard sale in Florida?

15. *Eddie's:* As Dooley thinks about the death of Mrs. Hammond's husband, he ponders "what memories he would rather erase if given the chance." Then he wonders if he would be a different person without those struggles and negative memories. What do you think? Are there ever benefits to unpleasant memories?

Think about it: Metaphors/Similes

- Metaphors and similes are phrases used to make comparisons helping the reader better understand what's happening in the story. Metaphors directly compare two things: "A good conscience is a continual Christmas." (Benjamin Franklin) Similes use like or as to compare two things: "Forgotten, like the form of last year's clouds." (Also Benjamin Franklin) Look for examples of metaphors and similes as you read and try to use them in your own writing.

PART FOUR: *(Chapters 16–20)*

Creative Writing Prompt—If you had a time machine and you could travel to the past, when/where would you go?

16. *Theo:* In order to keep a reader engaged in a story, an author will often use elements of suspense and surprise. What's the difference between these two tools? Can you think of any examples from this text?

17. **Specks & Mitts:** What is the story behind Theo's and Gus' nicknames? If you had a nickname, what would it be?

18. **Jinxy:** Add three more "trading cards" to your collection: Gus, Theo and Slade. Include drawings, descriptions, nicknames and any other information.

19. **The Long Jump:** Make a "trading card" for Clara Hammond, aka "Lamb."

20. **Tiny Not Shiny:** Size often doesn't matter: True or False? Explain your answer.

Think about it: Flashbacks

• Flashbacks are defined as interruptions in the chronological sequence of events in a book or movie. For the most part, we assume interruptions to be inconvenient disruptions, but a flashback can offer important insight into the backstories of characters, giving reasons for their choices and actions. In your opinion, do you prefer a story to be set up strictly chronologically, or do you like it to bounce around in time with an out of order timeline? Why?

PART FIVE: *(Chapters 21–26)*

Creative Writing Prompt—Create a week's menu for your school lunchroom. What would you serve for those five days?

21. **Jasper:** Jasper's parting advice is: "Keep your hat handy, your socks dry and your friends close." These instructions seem especially important for a cowboy out on the range. Create your own three-part life

advice and tailor it to your day-to-day experiences.

22. *Untying a Difficult Knot:* Fiona says that Jake always feels like he needs to outdo everyone. Do you know anyone like this? Without naming names, describe how it feels to be around someone who always has to be first/best.

23. *Visus Berries:* Calix likes to talk to her plants. Some studies show that plants grow better when exposed to the human voice, or a sound coming in at about 70 decibels in volume. Other studies claim that talking to plants doesn't make a difference. What's your opinion? Do you think it helps to talk to plants? Why do you think Calix talks to her plants?

24. *Invisible Ink:* What's the connection between the berries Calix grew and the ones in the photo from the night of Slade's accident? What do you think will happen with Calix's berries?

25. *Science Project Group:* Standing in the doorway of the ice creams hop, Dooley analyzes the different personalities of his science project group. Have you ever had to work in a group for school? Did you like it? List the pros and cons to this kind of collaboration (partnership).

26. *Theo's Notebook:* Theo is faced with a difficult dilemma (problem) while sitting by Slade's hospital bed. What does he have to decide? Do you think he made the right choice?

Think about it: Dialogue

- Dialogue is the conversation between characters in a

book, play or movie. The way these characters speak, as much as the words that they actually say, shapes who they are. Whenever possible, the writer needs to use dialogue and action to convey how a character feels.

Which is better? Why?

- Sam was sad. He didn't want to go home.
- "I don't want to go home!" said Sam as a fat tear rolled down his cheek.
- Even though the words may only be read silently, as you write dialogue, consider how it falls on the ear. Author John Steinbeck said, "If you are using dialogue—say it aloud as you write. Only then will it have the sound of speech."

PART SIX: *(Chapters 27-32)*

Creative Writing Prompt—You are a reporter for your local newspaper, and you've been called to investigate a recent burglary. Include a headline (title), byline (author), lead (the most important facts—the who, what, when, where in the first few sentences), body (more facts), and quotations.

27. **Happy Friday:** "Dooley sensed a certain buzzing chatter about the dance." The word buzzing is an example of an onomatopoeia. These are words which either make the sound they name or are closely associated with a sound. What's the advantage of using an onomatopoeia? Can you think of more examples?

28. **The Accident:** Gus seems angry about the information

Dooley shares from the last entry in Theo's notebook. Why? Do you think he's justified in his feelings?

29. *Serenade:* Explain Dooley's reaction to the Minnesota Vikings' flip-flop. Why does this evidence seem important to him?

30. *Chocolate Chippers:* Gus' attitude toward Theo changes within this chapter. What causes the change?

31. *A Magic Button:* Make a prediction: What happened to the button?

32. *Lost Forever:* Notice a change in the ways Dooley regards Mrs. Hammond. Create a timeline for Dooley's feelings towards his teacher. Begin with his preconceived notions about her in chapter 3 and continue until this chapter when Dooley tells his dad, "Slade's brothers and Mrs. Hammond have been through a lot in the last few years. It would at least make them feel a little better if they knew that the accident didn't happen because of something stupid Slade did." (Keep this timeline so that you can add more to it at the end of the book.)

Think about it: Plot

- When considering the plot, imagine if the story were a mountain:
  - First you approach the mountain (INTRODUCTION). At this point, the characters and setting are introduced.
  - Next, the reader begins to climb the mountain (RISING TENSION). The characters begin to encounter conflicts.

- The readers eventually climb to the peak of the mountain (CLIMAX). Here the story builds in intensity and the characters fight their biggest problems.

- On the other side of the peak, the intensity begins to go down (FALLING ACTION). There will still be issues needing the characters' attention, but things begin to level off.

- Finally, the reader is on the other side of the mountain (RESOLUTION). The main issues should be resolved.

PART SEVEN: *(Chapters 33–38)*

*Creative Writing Prompt—Write an acrostic poem for the word: MOON

33. ***Rube Goldberg:*** Sketch out your own Rube Goldberg machine. Remember, it must complete a task.

34. ***Welcome to Sherwood Forest:*** Put yourself in Dooley's dance shoes. How is he feeling as his dad drives him to the dance? How about when he sees Nathan? Gus? Fiona? Simon?

35. ***Toil and Trouble:*** Gus' power as a Binoc (the ability to see things very far away, apparently even through walls) switches on during the dance. Who does Gus see? How does he describe them?

36. ***Call in the Cavalry:*** Dooley calls the Mulligan family for help as he battles the DuBois sisters. When you're in a difficult situation, who is the first person you call? What characteristics are essential for a person to be your "first call"?

37. Twilight Sings a Song: In Shakespeare's play Macbeth, we meet the Three Witches. They are prophetesses who tell the main character, a man named Macbeth, that he will be king. Eventually, they use Macbeth's ambition against him as they convince him to murder the man who might be crowned instead of him. Shakespeare's Three Witches are similar to the Graeae, three sisters from Greek mythology. These women are often portrayed as spinning, measuring and cutting the thread which determined a person's destiny and life span. It was said that the three sisters shared one eye and one tooth among them. Find connections between these sisters and the DuBois sisters.

38. Pumpkin: Everyone has a weakness, and cats are like Kryptonite for the DuBois sisters. What do you think is Dooley's main weakness?

Think about it: Characters Roles

- One the most important parts of any story is the characters. A reader can usually divide the characters into these main groups: The Protagonist (the main character, the hero), the Antagonist (the anti-hero, sometimes the villain), the Deuteragonist (the sidekick), Tertiary characters (semi-important characters who aren't essential to the story), Foil character (character who clashes with the Protagonist but isn't necessarily the villain). Assign the characters from Remember to these various roles. Does everyone fit? Research these additional role types—The Love Interest and The Confidant.

PART EIGHT: *(Chapters 39-40)*

*Creative Writing Prompt—Your memory is about to be erased. You have one minute to write down the ten things you most want to remember. What are they?

39. *How the Cracker Crumbles:* Design a logo for N.A.M.E.S. (North American Magical Enthusiasts Society)

40. *I'll Hold You in My Dreams:* Add this final encounter to your Dooley–Mrs. Hammond timeline. How does empathy (the ability to fully understand the feelings of another) play a part in their final scene?

Think about it: Resolution

- Look back at the description of a plot from PART 6. A resolution should tie up most loose ends, but it doesn't always have to be a happy ending. How would you rate the ending of Remember? Do you feel like story was resolved? What else do you want to know about the characters? Email the author at abbyrosserwrites@yahoo.com and let her know your thoughts!

ABOUT THE AUTHOR

Abby Rosser makes her home in Murfreesboro, Tennessee with her husband and four kids. She enjoys reading, watching movies, baking (and eating) desserts and being outside... but not all at the same time.

And she loves imagining stories (often when's she's doing most of the above).

Find out more about Abby at abbyrosser.com.

Also available from

WORDCRAFTS PRESS

The Awakening of Leeowen Blake
  by Mary Garner

Tears of Min Brock
  by J.E. Lowder

Stranger with a Black Case
  by Jennifer Odom

You've Got It, Baby!
  by Mike Carmichael

The Mirror Lies
  by Sandy Brownlee

www.WordCrafts.net

Made in the USA
Monee, IL
04 March 2020